Frommer's®
Honolulu, Waikiki & Oahu

12th Edition

By Jeanette Foster

WILEY

John Wiley & Sons, Inc.

Published by:
John Wiley & Sons, Inc.
111 River St.
Hoboken, NJ 07030-5774

ISBN 978-1-118-07465-7 (paper); ISBN 978-1-118-17768-6 (ebk); ISBN 978-1-118-17769-3 (ebk); ISBN 978-1-118-17770-9 (ebk)

Editor: Emil J. Ross
Production Editor: Faunette Johnston & Katie Robinson
Cartographer: Andrew Dolan
Photo Editor: Alden Gewirtz
Cover Photo Editor: Richard Fox
Design and Layout by Vertigo Design NYC
Graphics and Prepress by Wiley Indianapolis Composition Services
Front cover photo: Lanikai Beach at sunrise ©Pacific Stock / SuperStock, Inc.
Back cover photos: *Left:* Heliconia in the Lyon Arboretum ©Douglas Peebles Photography / Alamy Images. *Middle:* Hanauma Bay, Honolulu ©Marco Garcia. *Right:* Kaneohe Bay ©Douglas Peebles Photography / Alamy Images.

For information on our other products and services or to obtain technical support, please contact our Customer Care Department within the U.S. at 877/762-2974, outside the U.S. at 317/572-3993 or fax 317/572-4002.
Wiley also publishes its books in a variety of electronic formats. Some content that appears in print may not be available in electronic formats.
Manufactured in China

5 4 3 2 1

CONTENTS

4 WHERE TO STAY 85

5 WHERE TO EAT 122

6 OUTDOOR ACTIVITIES 154

7 EXPLORING OAHU 192

LIST OF MAPS

ABOUT THE AUTHOR

A resident of the Big Island, **Jeanette Foster** has skied the slopes of Mauna Kea—during a Fourth of July ski meet, no less—and gone scuba diving with manta rays off the Kona Coast. A prolific writer widely published in travel, sports, and adventure magazines, she's also the editor of *Zagat's Survey to Hawaii's Top Restaurants.* In addition to writing this guide, Jeanette is the author of *Frommer's Hawaii Day by Day, Frommer's Hawaii, Frommer's Maui, Frommer's Hawaii from $80 a Day, Frommer's Kauai, Frommer's Hawaii with Kids,* and *Frommer's Portable Big Island.*

ACKNOWLEDGMENTS

Much love and many heartfelt thanks to Priscilla Love for her excellent research on this book.
                                                                    —Jeanette Foster

HOW TO CONTACT US

In researching this book, we discovered many wonderful places—hotels, restaurants, shops, and more. We're sure you'll find others. Please tell us about them, so we can share the information with your fellow travelers in upcoming editions. If you were disappointed with a recommendation, we'd love to know that, too. Please write to:

Frommer's Honolulu, Waikiki & Oahu, 12th Edition
John Wiley & Sons, Inc. • 111 River St. • Hoboken, NJ 07030-5774
frommersfeedback@wiley.com

ADVISORY & DISCLAIMER

Travel information can change quickly and unexpectedly, and we strongly advise you to confirm important details locally before traveling, including information on visas, health and safety, traffic and transport, accommodations, shopping, and eating out. We also encourage you to stay alert while traveling and to remain aware of your surroundings. Avoid civil disturbances, and keep a close eye on cameras, purses, wallets, and other valuables.

While we have endeavored to ensure that the information contained within this guide is accurate and up-to-date at the time of publication, we make no representations or warranties with respect to the accuracy or completeness of the contents of this work and specifically disclaim all warranties, including without limitation warranties of fitness for a particular purpose. We accept no responsibility or liability for any inaccuracy or errors or omissions, or for any inconvenience, loss, damage, costs, or expenses of any nature whatsoever incurred or suffered by anyone as a result of any advice or information contained in this guide.

The inclusion of a company, organization, or website in this guide as a service provider and/or potential source of further information does not mean that we endorse them or the information they provide. Be aware that information provided through some websites may be unreliable and can change without notice. Neither the publisher nor author shall be liable for any damages arising herefrom.

FROMMER'S STAR RATINGS, ICONS & ABBREVIATIONS

Every hotel, restaurant, and attraction listing in this guide has been ranked for quality, value, service, amenities, and special features using a star-rating system. In country, state, and regional guides, we also rate towns and regions to help you narrow down your choices and budget your time accordingly. Hotels and restaurants are rated on a scale of zero (recommended) to three stars (exceptional). Attractions, shopping, nightlife, towns, and regions are rated according to the following scale: zero stars (recommended), one star (highly recommended), two stars (very highly recommended), and three stars (must-see).

In addition to the star-rating system, we also use seven feature icons that point you to the great deals, in-the-know advice, and unique experiences that separate travelers from tourists. Throughout the book, look for:

Special finds—those places only insiders know about

Fun facts—details that make travelers more informed and their trips more fun

Kids—best bets for kids and advice for the whole family

Special moments—those experiences that memories are made of

Overrated—places or experiences not worth your time or money

Insider tips—great ways to save time and money

Great values—where to get the best deals

The following abbreviations are used for credit cards:

AE	American Express	**DISC**	Discover	**V**	Visa
DC	Diners Club	**MC**	MasterCard		

TRAVEL RESOURCES AT FROMMERS.COM

Frommer's travel resources don't end with this guide. Frommer's website, **www.frommers.com**, has travel information on more than 4,000 destinations. We update features regularly, giving you access to the most current trip-planning information and the best airfare, lodging, and car-rental bargains. You can also listen to podcasts, connect with other Frommers.com members through our active-reader forums, share your travel photos, read blogs from guidebook editors and fellow travelers, and much more.

THE BEST OF OAHU

Everyone ventures to Oahu seeking a different experience. Some talk about wanting to find the "real" Hawaii, some are looking for heart-pounding adventure, some yearn for the relaxing and healing powers of the islands, and others are drawn by Hawaii's aloha spirit, in which kindness and friendliness prevail.

This book is designed to help you have the vacation of your dreams. For those too excited to page through from beginning to end, this chapter highlights the very best of what Honolulu and Oahu have to offer.

THE best OAHU EXPERIENCES

To have the absolute best experiences on Oahu, be prepared for a different culture, language, cuisine, and way of doing things. Slow down—you're on an island that operates on its own schedule. To really experience Oahu, we recommend the following:

o **Get Out on the Water:** You'll take home memories of an emerald island rising out of the cobalt sea with white wispy clouds set against an azure sky, or the Waikiki shoreline colored by the setting sun. There are many different

Kayaking through the Mokulua islands.

Snorkeling in Hanauma Bay's underwater park.

PREVIOUS PAGE: **Waikiki Beach at sunset.**

The Hawaiian Islands

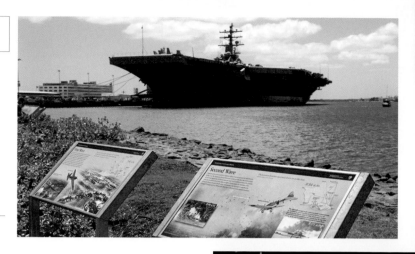

boats to choose from, ranging from tiny kayaks to 100-foot sightseeing vessels, even state-of-the-art boats guaranteed to prevent seasickness. See p. 165 for details on all kinds of cruises and watersports.

o **Plunge Under the Water:** Don mask, fins, and snorkel and dive into the magical world beneath the surface, where clouds of colorful tropical fish flit by, craggy old turtles lumber along, and tiny marine creatures hover over exotic corals. Can't swim? Take one of the many submarines or semisubmersibles. If you come to Hawaii and ignore the underwater world, you're missing half of what makes up this paradise. See p. 170.

TOP: **Pearl Harbor, with the USS *Missouri* in the background.** ABOVE RIGHT: **Men can do it too: traditional Hawaiian hula.**

o **Meet Local Folks:** If you go to Hawaii and see only people like the ones back home, you might as well stay home. Extend yourself, leave the resorts and tourist quarters, go out and learn about Hawaii and its people. Just smile and say "Howzit?" (which means "How's it going?")—and you'll usually make a new friend. Oahu is remarkably cosmopolitan; every ethnic group in the world seems to be here. It's fascinating to discover the varieties of food, culture, language, and customs.

o **Drive to the North Shore:** Just an hour's drive from Honolulu, the North Shore is another world: a pastoral, rural setting with magnificent beaches and a slower way of life. During the winter months, stop and watch the professionals surf the monster waves. See p. 162.

Oahu

5 mi
5 km

Kahuku Pt.

Kauai Channel

PACIFIC OCEAN

THE NORTH SHORE

Kaena Point State Park

Kaena Pt.

Dillingham Airport

Haleiwa

Waialua

Kahuku

Kamehameha

Pupukea-Paumalu Forest Reserve

Sunset Beach
Ehukai Beach
Pupukea
Waimea Beach Park

Kawela Bay

Kaena Point Game Mgmt. Area

Makua Valley Mil. Res.

Makua Keäau F.R.

Mokuleia Forest Reserve

Waianae Kai Forest Reserve

Lualualei Naval Res.

Schofield Barracks Mil. Res.

Kaala

Makaha
Makaha Beach Park
Lahilahi Pt.

Waianae

Maili

Nanakuli

Farrington Hwy.

LEEWARD OAHU (WAIANAE COAST)

Kapolei

Makakilo

Ko Olina Lagoons

Ewa Villages

Ewa Beach

Waipahu

Waipio

Mililani

Waipio Acres

Whitmore Village

Wahiawa Naval Res.

Wahiawa

Kamehameha

CENTRAL OAHU (EWA PLAIN)

Kamehameha

Malaekahana State Recreation Area
Mokuauia I.
Laie Pt.
Laie
Pounders Beach

Hauula

Sacred Falls State Park

Punaluu

Punaluu Bay

Kaliuwaa Bay

Kahana Valley State Park

Kahana Bay Beach Park

Ka'a'awa

Kualoa Regional Park
Kualoa Pt.

Waikane

Kahaluu

Kaneohe Bay M.C.B.

Moku Manu
Mokapu Pt.

Kaneohe Bay

Heeia

Kaneohe

Mokulua Is.
Lanikai Beach
Kailua Beach
Kailua

Kailua Bay

Bellows A.F. Sta.

Waimanalo Beach
Waimanalo

Makapuu Beach
Makapuu Pt.

Sandy Beach

Hawaii Kai

Hanauma Bay

Kaiwi Channel

THE WINDWARD COAST

EAST OAHU

Honolulu Watershed Forest Reserve

Ewa F.R.

Ewa Forest Reserve

Waiahole F.R.

Pacific Palisades

Pearl City

Aiea

Waimalu

Hickam A.F.B.

Honolulu Int'l Airport

HONOLULU

Ala Moana Beach
Waikiki Beach
Diamond Head

Mamala Bay

Nuuanu Pali

Pali Hwy.

Likelike Hwy.

Kalanianaole Hwy.

PACIFIC OCEAN

U.S. Naval Res.

Pearl Harbor

PACIFIC OCEAN

Kauai

Niihau

Oahu   Honolulu

Molokai   Maui

Lanai

Kahoolawe

Hawaii "The Big Island"

100 mi
100 km

5

o **Watch the Hula:** This is Hawaii, so you have to experience the hula. A hula performance is a popular way for visitors to get a taste of traditional Hawaiian culture. For a more genuine Hawaiian hula experience, catch the interactive hula *halau* performed Monday through Friday at 2pm at the Bishop Museum. See p. 196.

o **Experience a Turning Point in America's History:** The United States could no longer turn its back on World War II after December 7, 1941, the day that Japanese warplanes bombed Pearl Harbor. Standing on the deck of the USS *Arizona* Memorial, which straddles the eternal tomb for the 1,177 sailors and Marines trapped below deck when the battleship sank in 9 minutes, is a moment you'll never forget. See p. 205.

THE best BEACHES

o **Waikiki Beach:** This famous stretch of sand is the spot that originally put Hawaii on the tourist map. No beach anywhere is so widely known or so universally sought as this narrow, 1½-mile-long crescent of soft sand at the foot of a string of high-rise hotels. Home to the world's longest-running beach party, Waikiki attracts nearly five million visitors a year from every corner of the planet. In high season, it's packed towel-to-towel, but there's no denying the beauty of Waikiki. See p. 155.

o **Lanikai Beach:** Hidden and off the beaten tourist path, this beach on the windward side has a mile of powder-soft sand and water that's safe for swimming. It's the perfect isolated spot for a morning of swimming and relaxation. With the prevailing trade winds, it's also excellent for sailing and windsurfing. Sun-worshipers should arrive in the morning, as the shadow of the Koolau Mountains blocks the sun's rays in the afternoon. See p. 159.

Palms and sand on Lanikai Beach.

Quiet and romantic Malaekahana Beach.

o **Kailua Beach:** Imagine a 30-acre public park with a broad, grassy area with picnic tables, a public boat ramp, restrooms, a pavilion, a volleyball court, and food stands. Add a wide, sandy beach, great for diving, swimming, sailing, snorkeling, and board- and windsurfing, and you've got Kailua Beach, which is tops on the windward side of the island. On weekends, local families consider it *the* place to go. Weekdays, you practically have it all to yourself. See p. 160.

o **Kahana Bay Beach Park:** With salt-and-pepper sand, a crescent-shaped beach protected by ironwoods and *kamani* trees, and, as a backdrop, a lush junglelike valley interrupted only by jagged cliffs, you'd swear this beach was in Tahiti or Bora Bora. Kahana offers great swimming (even safe for children), good fishing, and perfect conditions for kayaking. Combine that with picnic areas, camping, and hiking trails, and you have one of the best beaches on the island. See p. 161.

o **Malaekahana Beach:** If you'd like to venture back to old Hawaii, before jet planes brought millions of people to Oahu and there were few footprints on the sand, then go north to the romantic wooded beach park at Malaekahana. This is a place to sit in quiet solitude or to beachcomb along the shore. There's good swimming most of the time, and good snorkeling when it's calm, but no lifeguard. Surprisingly, very few visitors come to Malaekahana—one of the best beaches on Oahu, it's a true find. See p. 163.

o **Sunset Beach:** Surfers around the world know this site, famous for its spectacular winter surf—the waves can be huge, thundering peaks reaching 15 to 20 feet. In the summer months, Sunset calms down and becomes a safe swimming beach. It's a great place to people-watch year-round, as you'll spot

Sunset Beach attracts all kinds of visitors.

everybody from wannabe *Baywatch* babes to King Kong surfers. See p. 163.

o **Waimea Bay:** Here is one of Oahu's most dramatic beaches. During much of the winter—October to April—huge waves come pounding in, creating strong rip currents. Even expert surfers think twice when confronted with 30-foot waves that crash on the shore with the force of a runaway locomotive. It's hard to believe that during the summer this same bay is glassy and calm—a great place for swimming, snorkeling, and diving. Oh, and by the way, despite what the Beach Boys croon in "Surfin' USA" (Why-a-*mee*-ah), it's pronounced Why-*may*-ah. See p. 163.

o **Pokai Bay:** If you dream of a powdered-sugar sand beach, a place you can swim, snorkel, and probably be the only one on the beach

A local boy flipping out on Pokai Bay.

(on weekdays), try this off-the-beaten-path shoreline. Surrounded by a reef, the waters inside are calm enough for children and offer excellent snorkeling. Come with aloha spirit and a respect for local customs—the residents here don't see too many visitors. See p. 165.

THE best SNORKELING & DIVING SITES

A different Hawaii greets anyone with a mask, snorkel, and fins. Under the sea, you'll find schools of brilliant tropical fish, slow-moving green sea turtles, darting game fish, slack-jawed moray eels, and prehistoric-looking coral. It's a kaleidoscope of color and wonder. For more on exploring Oahu's underwater world, see p. 168.

o **Hanauma Bay:** It can get very crowded, but—for clear, warm, calm waters, an abundance of fish that are so friendly they'll swim right up to your face mask, a beautiful setting, and easy access—there's no place like Hanauma Bay. Just wade in waist deep and look down to see more than 50 species of reef and inshore fish common to Hawaiian waters. Snorkelers hug the safe, shallow inner bay—it's really like swimming in an outdoor aquarium. Serious, experienced divers shoot "the slot," a passage through the reef, to gain access to Witch's Brew, a turbulent cove, and other outer-reef experiences. See p. 158.

A reef shark contemplates the wreck of the *Mahi*.

The lava grotto at Shark's Cove.

Snorkeling around Kapiolani's reef, off Waikiki Beach.

o **Wreck of the *Mahi*:** Oahu is a wonderful place to scuba dive, especially for those interested in wreck diving. One of the more famous wrecks in Hawaii is the *Mahi,* a 185-foot former minesweeper, which is easily accessible just south of Waianae. Abundant marine life makes it a great place to shoot photos—schools of lemon butterflyfish and *ta'ape* are so comfortable with divers and photographers that they practically pose. Eagle rays, green sea turtles, manta rays, and white-tipped sharks occasionally cruise by, and eels peek out from the wreck. See p. 168.

o **Kahuna Canyon:** One of the most magical summer dive spots is Kahuna Canyon. Walls rise from the ocean floor to create the illusion of an underwater Grand Canyon. Inside the canyon, crab, octopi, slipper, and spiny lobsters abound (be aware that taking them in the summer is illegal), and giant trevally, parrotfish, and unicorn tangs congregate. Outside, you're likely to see the occasional shark in the distance. See p. 168.

o **Shark's Cove:** Braver snorkelers might want to head to Shark's Cove, on the North Shore just off Kamehameha Highway, between Haleiwa and Pupukea. Sounds risky, we know, but we've never seen or heard of any sharks in this cove; and in summer, this big, lava-edged pool is one of Oahu's best snorkeling spots. Waves splash over the natural lava grotto and cascade like waterfalls into the pool full of tropical fish. Deep-sea caves to explore are to the right of the cove. See p. 162.

o **Kapiolani Park Beach:** The section known as Queen's Beach or Queen's Surf Beach in the center of this beach park, between the Natatorium and the Waikiki Aquarium, is great for snorkeling. That said, we prefer the reef in front of the Aquarium because it has easy access to the sandy shoreline and the waters are usually calm. Bonus: Since you're right next door to the Aquarium, if you see any flora or fauna and would like more information, you can pop inside. See p. 156.

THE best GOLF COURSES

Oahu is golf country, with 5 municipal, 9 military, and 20 private courses to choose from. The courses range from 9-hole public ones, perfect for beginners, to championship links that stump even the pros. See p. 182 for complete details.

o **Ko Olina Golf Club:** *Golf Digest* named this beautiful 6,867-yard, par-72 course one of "America's Top 75 Resort Courses" when it opened in 1992. The rolling fairways and elevated tees— and a few too many water features (always where you don't want them)—will definitely improve your game or humble your attitude. See p. 185.

o **Turtle Bay Resort:** Of the two courses to choose from here, we recommend the 18-hole **Arnold Palmer Course** (formerly the Links at Kuilima), designed by Arnold Palmer and Ed Seay. They never meant for golfers to get off too easy—this is a challenging course. The front 9 holes, with rolling terrain, only a few trees, and lots of wind, play like a course on the British Isles. The back 9 holes have narrower, tree-lined fairways and water. In addition to ocean views, the course circles

Volcanic walls loom over Makaha Resort Golf Club.

A beautiful and tricky water feature at Ko Olina Golf Club.

Punahoolapa Marsh, a protected wetland for endangered Hawaiian water-fowl. See p. 185.

o **Makaha Resort Golf Club:** Readers of *Honolulu* magazine named this challenging course Oahu's best. An hour's drive from downtown, this William Bell–designed course is in Makaha Valley on the island's leeward side. Incredibly beautiful, sheer, 1,500-foot volcanic walls tower over it, and swaying palm trees and bright bougainvillea surround it; an occasional peacock even struts across the fairways. "I was distracted by the beauty" is a great excuse for your score at day's end. See p. 186.

o **Olomana Golf Links:** This gorgeous course in Waimanalo is on the other side of the island from Waikiki and is popular with both local residents and visitors. The low-handicap golfer may not find this course difficult, but the striking views of the craggy Koolau mountain ridges are worth the greens fees alone. The par-72, 6,326-yard course starts off a bit hilly on the front 9, but flattens out by the back 9—which have their own special surprises, including tricky water hazards. See p. 183.

THE best WALKS

The weather on Oahu is usually sunny, with trade winds providing cooling breezes —perfect for a walk. Below are our favorites, from city to trail.

o **Diamond Head Crater:** Most everyone can make this moderate walk to the summit of Hawaii's most famous landmark. Kids love the top of the 760-foot volcanic cone, where they have 360-degree views of Oahu, up the leeward coast from Waikiki. The 1.4-mile round-trip takes about an hour. See p. 174.

o **Makiki–Manoa Cliffs Trails:** A 15-minute drive from downtown, this walk passes through a rainforest and along a ridgetop. The somewhat strenuous

Diamond Head rises above Honolulu and Waikiki Beach.

Paper dragons on sale in Chinatown.

Cooling off at Manoa Falls.

loop trail—it's more than 6 miles long, gains 1,260 feet in elevation, and takes about 3 hours to finish—is one you'll never forget: The nonstop views of the city and the shoreline are spectacular. See p. 176.

o **Manoa Falls Trail:** This easy .75-mile (one-way) hike is terrific for families; it takes less than an hour to reach idyllic Manoa Falls. The often-muddy trail follows Waihi Stream and meanders through the forest reserve past guava and mountain apple trees and wild ginger. The forest is moist and humid and inhabited by nothing more dangerous than giant bloodthirsty mosquitoes. See p. 177.

o **Chinatown:** Honolulu's Chinatown appeals to the senses: The pungent aroma of Vietnamese *pho* mingles with the sweet scent of burning incense; vendors and shoppers speak noisily in the open market; retired men tell stories over games of mah-jongg; and the constant buzz of traffic all contribute to the cacophony of sounds. No trip to Honolulu is complete without a visit to this exotic, historic district. See p. 210.

THE best VIEWS

o **Puu Ualakaa State Park:** Watching the sun set into the Pacific from a 1,048-foot hill named after a sweet potato is actually much more romantic than it sounds. *Puu Ualakaa* translates into "Rolling Sweet Potato Hill," which refers to how the early Hawaiians harvested the crop. Don't miss the sweeping panoramic views, which extend from Diamond Head across Waikiki and downtown Honolulu, over the airport and Pearl City, all the way to the Waianae range. Catch great photo ops during the day, romantic sunset views in the evening, and starry skies at night. See p. 204.

Honolulu lit up, as seen from Puu Ualakaa State Park.

o **Nuuanu Pali Lookout:** Oahu's best-looking side, the Windward Coast, can be seen in its full glory from the Nuuanu Pali Lookout, a gusty perch set amid jagged cliffs piercing the puffy white clouds that go racing by. A thousand feet below, the island is a carpet of green that runs to an azure Pacific dotted by tiny offshore islets. You'll feel like you're standing on the edge of the world. See p. 230.

Offerings at Puu O Mahuka Heiau.

o **Diamond Head Crater:** The view from atop this world-famous 720-foot-tall sleeping volcano is not to be missed. The 360-degree view from Koko Crater to Barbers Point and the Waianae mountains is worth the 560-foot hike. See p. 198.

o **Lanikai Beach:** This is one of the best places on Oahu to greet the sunrise. Watch the sky slowly move from pitch black to burnt orange as the sun begins to rise over the two tiny offshore islands of Mokulua. This is a five-senses experience: birds singing the sun up; a gentle breeze on your face; the taste of salt in the air; the smell of the ocean, the sand, and the fragrant flowers nearby; and the kaleidoscope of colors as another day dawns. See p. 230.

o **Puu O Mahuka Heiau:** Once the largest sacrificial temple on Oahu, Puu O Mahuka Heiau is now a state historic site. Located on a 300-foot bluff, the *heiau* encompasses some 5 acres. Hawaiians still come here to pray—you may see offerings such as *ti* leaves, flowers, and fruit. Don't disturb the offerings or walk on the stones—it's very disrespectful. The view from this bluff is awe-inspiring, from Waimea Bay all the way to Kaena Point. See p. 243.

THE best ADVENTURES FOR THRILL-SEEKERS

- o **Soar in Silence in a Glider:** Soaring in silence on gossamer-like wings, with a panoramic view of Oahu, is an unforgettable experience. Glider rides are available at Dillingham Air Field, in Mokuleia, on Oahu's North Shore. The glider is towed behind a plane; at the right altitude, the tow is dropped, and you (and the pilot) are left to soar in the thermal currents. See p. 188.

- o **Surf Waikiki in a Hawaiian Outrigger Canoe:** It's summertime and there's a South Pacific swell rolling into Waikiki from Tahiti; here's your chance to try surfing—in a Hawaiian outrigger canoe. Numerous beach concessions on Waikiki Beach offer the chance to paddle an outrigger canoe and surf back into Waikiki. You get a great view of the beach from offshore—and the thrill of actually catching a wave and gliding back into shore. See p. 155.

- o **Float on the Thermals on a Tandem Hang Glider:** See things from a bird's-eye view (literally) as you and an instructor float high above Oahu on a tandem hang glider. See p. 189.

- o **Leap into the Ocean:** Even though all the signs say DANGEROUS, STAY OFF THE ROCKS, a favorite pastime on Oahu is climbing the stone precipice at Waimea Beach Park and leaping into the ocean. This is for experienced swimmers in summer only, as the thundering winter waves drive everyone from the sea, except the professional surfers and the very, very stupid. See p. 163.

- o **Venture into the Deep:** It's Hawaii—you have to see what's under the waves. Try scuba diving; you can enjoy a "scuba experience" with absolutely no previous diving experience. Here's your opportunity to glide weightlessly through the ocean while you admire the multicolored marine creatures. See p. 168.

- o **Go Eye to Eye with a Shark:** You're 4 miles out from land, which is just a speck on the horizon, with hundreds of feet of open ocean. Suddenly from

Hanging out cliffside at Waimea Beach Park.

Gliding over Oahu.

A skimpy cage is all that separates man from shark on North Shore Shark Adventures.

out of the blue depths a shape emerges: the sleek, pale shadow of a 6-foot-long gray reef shark, followed quickly by a couple of 10-foot-long Galápagos sharks. Within a few heartbeats, you're surrounded by sharks on all sides. Do you panic? No, you are on North Shore Shark Adventures. See p. 169.

THE best PLACES TO DISCOVER THE REAL OAHU

Oahu isn't just any other beach destination. It has a wonderfully rich, ancient history and culture, and people who are worth getting to know. If you want to meet the "local" folks who live on Oahu, check out the following:

o **Watch the Ancient Hawaiian Sport of Outrigger Canoe Paddling:** From February to September, on weekday evenings and weekend days, hundreds of canoe paddlers gather at Ala Wai Canal and practice the Hawaiian sport of canoe paddling. Find a comfortable spot at Ala Wai Park, next to the canal, and watch this ancient sport come to life. See p. 191.

o **Attend a Hawaiian-Language Church Service:** Kawaiahao Church is the Westminster Abbey of Hawaii; the vestibule is lined with portraits of the Hawaiian monarchy, many of whom were coronated in this very building. The coral church is a perfect setting to experience an all-Hawaiian service, held every Sunday at 9am, complete with Hawaiian song. See p. 201.

o **Buy a Lei from Vendors in Chinatown:** A host of cultural sights and experiences are to be had in Honolulu's Chinatown. Wander through this several-square-block area, with its jumble of exotic shops offering herbs, Chinese groceries, and acupuncture services. Before you leave, be sure to check out the lei sellers on Maunakea Street (near N. Hotel St.), where Hawaii's finest leis go for as little as $3.50. See p. 210 for neighborhood walking tours and details on where to buy leis.

o **Observe the Fish Auction:** There is nothing else quite like the Honolulu Fish Auction. Fishermen bring their fresh catch in at 5am (sharp) Monday through Saturday, and the small group of buyers bids on all manner of fish. The auction lasts until all the fish are sold. It is well worth getting up early to enjoy this unique cultural experience. See p. 251.

Examining the goods at the Honolulu Fish Auction.

Ukeleles, among other things, can be found at the Aloha Flea Market.

Get a Bargain at the Aloha Flea Market: For $1 admission, it's an all-day show at the Aloha Stadium parking lot, where more than 1,000 vendors sell everything from junk to jewels. Go early for the best deals. Open Wednesdays and Saturdays 8am to 3pm and Sundays from 6:30am to 3pm.

THE best LUXURY HOTELS & RESORTS

Halekulani: Halekulani translates into "House Befitting Heaven," an apt description for this luxury resort spread over 5 acres of prime Waikiki beachfront property. When money is no object, this is the place to stay. The atmosphere of elegance envelops you as soon as you step into the lobby. Even if you don't stay here, drop by at sunset to sip on a mai tai at the gracious House Without a Key (see below) and listen to Sonny Kamehele sing Hawaiian songs as a graceful hula dancer sways to the music. See p. 92.

Embassy Suites Hotel–Waikiki Beach Walk: This ultraluxurious one- and two-bedroom-suite hotel chain (known for its complimentary, all-you-can-eat, cooked-to-order breakfast and evening manager's cocktail reception) has one of the most central locations in Waikiki and is loaded with amenities. When you pencil it out, it's actually a good "deal" for families. See p. 93.

Royal Hawaiian: Hidden in the jungle of concrete buildings that make up Waikiki is an oasis of verdant gardens and a shockingly pink building. The Royal Hawaiian hotel, affectionately called the "pink palace," is known around the world as a symbol of luxury. Since the first day it opened in 1927, the Royal has been the place to stay for celebrities, including Clark Gable, Shirley Temple, President Franklin Roosevelt, the Beatles, Kevin Costner, and others. Its location is one of the best on Waikiki Beach. See p. 95.

o **Moana Surfrider Hotel, A Westin Resort:** Step back in time to Old Hawaii at the grand Moana Surfrider Hotel, built in 1901. Entry is through the original colonial porte-cochere, past the highly polished wooden front porch with white wooden rocking chairs, and into the perfectly restored lobby, with its detailed millwork and intricate plaster detailing on the ceiling. Time seems to slow here, tropical flowers arranged in huge sprays are everywhere, and everyone seems to be smiling. At check-in, guests are greeted with a lei and a glass of fruit juice. This is a hotel not only with class but with historic charm. See p. 93.

The expansive pool at Waikiki's Halekulani resort.

o **Hilton Hawaiian Village Beach Resort & Spa:** This place is so big it even has its own post office. Some 3,000 rooms are spread over 20 acres with tropical gardens, thundering waterfalls, exotic wildlife, award-winning restaurants, nightly entertainment, two brand-new state-of-the-art spas, 100 different shops, children's programs, fabulous ocean activities, a secluded lagoon, three swimming pools, Hawaiian cultural activities, two minigolf courses, and Waikiki Beach. You could spend your entire vacation here and never leave the property. See p. 88.

o **Kahala Hotel & Resort:** Since 1964, when Conrad Hilton first opened this hotel as a place for rest and relaxation far from the crowds of Waikiki, the Kahala has always been rated one of Hawaii's premier hotels. A venerable who's who of celebrities have stayed at the hotel, including every president since Richard Nixon, a host of rock stars from the Rolling Stones to the Beach Boys, and a range of actors from John Wayne to Bette Midler. The Kahala is a completely up-to-date resort, with exotic Asian touches, but it retains the grace and elegance of a softer, gentler time in the islands. See p. 111.

o **J. W. Marriott Ihilani Resort & Spa at Ko Olina:** Located in the quiet of Oahu's west coast, 25 minutes west of Honolulu International Airport—and worlds away from the tourist scene of Waikiki—the Ihilani (which means "heavenly splendor") is the first hotel in the 640-acre Ko Olina Resort. It features a luxury spa and fitness center, plus championship tennis and golf. The plush rooms are spacious, with huge lanais and lagoon or ocean views from some 85% of the units. With luxury like this, who misses Waikiki? See p. 116.

o **Turtle Bay Resort:** After a $35-million renovation, this once sterling hotel is back. The resort is spectacular—an hour's drive from Waikiki, but eons away in its country feeling. Sitting on 808 acres, Turtle Bay is loaded with activities and 5 miles of shoreline with secluded white-sand coves. All the rooms have great views, but the separate beach cottages are positioned right on the ocean. (The views alone are worth the price.) The 42 bungalows have been renovated

The distinctly pink Royal Hawaiian hotel.

(hardwood floors, poster beds with feather comforters) and have their own check-in and private concierge. See p. 115.

THE best BARGAIN ACCOMMODATIONS

It is possible to stay on Oahu without having to take out a second mortgage. Here are some options.

- **The Breakers:** Full of old-fashioned Hawaiian aloha—and it's only steps from the sands of Waikiki—this two-story hotel has a friendly staff and a loyal following. Each of the tastefully decorated, large rooms comes with a lanai and a kitchenette, with prices starting at $130. See p. 97.

- **Royal Grove Hotel:** This small, family-owned hotel is a great bargain for frugal travelers. What you get here is old-fashioned aloha in cozy accommodations along the lines of Motel 6—basic and clean. And you can't do better for the price—this has to be *the* bargain of Waikiki. For $67 (about the same price a couple would pay to stay in a private room at the hostel in Waikiki), you get a room in the older Mauka Wing, with a double bed or two twins, plus a kitchenette with refrigerator and stove. See p. 109.

- **Ke Iki Beach Bungalows:** Snuggled on a large lot with its own 200-foot stretch of white-sand beach between two legendary North Shore surf spots (Waimea Bay and Banzai Pipeline), this collection of studio, one-, and two-bedroom cottages offers affordable family bungalows with complete kitchens. If you can live without being right on the ocean, the garden units start at $135. See p. 115.

THE best RESORT SPAS

o **Abhasa Waikiki Spa in the Royal Hawaiian:** This contemporary spa, spread out over 7,000 square feet, concentrates on natural, organic treatments in a soothing atmosphere, where the smell of eucalyptus wafts through the air. You can experience everything from the latest aromatherapy to thalassotherapy (soaking in a sweet-smelling hot bath) to shiatsu massages, but their specialty is a cold-laser, antiaging treatment that promises to give you a revitalized face in just 30 minutes. See p. 95.

o **Ihilani Spa at the J. W. Marriott Ihilani:** An oasis by the sea, this 35,000-square-foot modern, multistoried facility, filled with floor-to-ceiling windows overlooking lush tropical plants, is truly a spa in the literal sense of the word, meaning "health by water." It combines Hawaiian products with traditional therapies to produce some of the best water treatments in the state. You'll also find a fitness center, tennis courts, and aerobic and stretching classes. See p. 116.

o **Serenity Spa Hawaii:** This 5,000-square-foot spa has an extensive menu of treatments from Hawaiian *lomilomi* to hot lava rock to the very popular "Golden Touch" massage, which helps you get a glowing tan with applications of skin conditioners, tanning accelerators, and SPF sunscreen. See p. 94.

o **Spa Suites at the Kahala:** The Kahala Hotel & Resort (see above) has taken the concept of relaxation to a new level with former garden-view guest rooms converted to individual spas, each with a glass-enclosed shower, private changing area, infinity-edge deep soaking Jacuzzi tub, and personal relaxation area. No detail is overlooked, from the warm foot bath when you arrive to the refreshing tea served on your personal enclosed garden lanai after your treatment. See p. 112.

Ihilani Spa's Ho'onanea Suite, the ultimate in pampering.

An elegant spa suite at the Kahala Hotel & Resort.

o **SpaHalekulani:** Focusing on the healing traditions of the Pacific islands—Samoa, Tonga, and Tahiti, as well as Hawaii—this boutique oasis in Waikiki's most luxurious hotel, the Halekulani (see above), defines pampered comfort in a nurturing setting designed to relax even the most tense. From the time you step into the elegantly appointed, intimate spa to the last whiff of fragrant *maile,* their signature scent, this is truly a heavenly experience. Try something unique, like the Polynesian Nonu, a Samoan-inspired massage using stones and the nonu plant, or the Ton Ton Amma, a Japanese massage. See p. 92.

o **Turtle Bay Resort:** This Zen-like spa, positioned on the ground floor of Turtle Bay (see above) and facing the ocean, has six treatment rooms, a meditation waiting area, an outdoor workout space, and a complete fitness center and private elevator to rooms on the second floor that are reserved for guests getting spa treatments. For the ultimate in massages, book the oceanside cabana and listen to the gentle lull of the waves as they roll into the North Shore. See p. 115.

o **Waikiki Plantation Spa:** Located in the penthouse of the Outrigger Waikiki on the Beach hotel and overlooking the heart of Waikiki is this boutique spa with an "island-style" menu of treatments, from massages to facials to body wraps and polishes, all using the spa's own private label of lotions and oils. An express elevator zips you up to the 17th floor, where a lanai allows you to relax in total serenity. See p. 97.

THE best RESTAURANTS

o **Alan Wong's Restaurant:** One of Hawaii's premiere chefs, Alan Wong specializes in absolutely the best Pacific Rim cuisine. His restaurant is always packed, although the ambience is limited and it's located in a shopping mall in the suburbs—but for serious foodies this is heaven. Masterpieces at this shrine of Hawaii regional cuisine include warm California rolls made with salmon roe, wasabi, and Kona lobster instead of rice; luau *lumpia* (spring rolls) with butterfish and *kalua* (pit-roasted) pig; and ginger-crusted fresh *onaga* (snapper). *Opihi* (limpet) shooters and day-boat scallops in season are a must, while nori-wrapped tempura ahi is a perennial favorite. The menu changes daily, but the flavors never lose their sizzle. See p. 144.

o **Chef Mavro Restaurant:** Honolulu is abuzz over the wine pairings and elegant cuisine of George Mavrothalassitis, the culinary wizard from Provence who turned La Mer (at the Halekulani) and Seasons (at the Four Seasons Resort Wailea) into temples of fine dining. He brought his award-winning signature dishes with him and continues to prove his ingenuity with dazzling a la carte and prix-fixe menus. See p. 143.

o **Kaka'ako Kitchen:** If you're in the market for a quick and healthy breakfast, lunch, or dinner at budget prices, here's the place. It's not fancy; in fact, the trademark Styrofoam plates, warehouse ambience, and home-style cooking are the hallmarks of this local favorite in the Ward Centre. The menu, which changes every 3 to 4 months, includes seared ahi sandwiches with *tobiko* (flying-fish roe) aioli for lunch; and a signature charbroiled ahi steak, beef stew, five-spice *shoyu* chicken (similar to chicken teriyaki), the very popular meatloaf, and other multi-ethnic entrees for dinner. See p. 137.

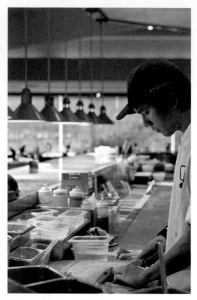

La Mer, with a view of Diamond Head in the distance.

The open kitchen at Roy's.

o **La Mer:** This is Hawaii's premier splurge restaurant, an oceanfront bastion of haute cuisine, a romantic, elegant, and expensive place where people dress up—not to be seen, but to match the ambience and food. It's an open-sided room with views of Diamond Head and the sound of trade winds rustling the nearby coconut fronds. Award-winning chef Yves Garnier melds classical French influences with island-fresh ingredients. See p. 123.

o **Morimoto Waikiki:** Masaharu Morimoto, star of the TV show *Iron Chef,* stars nightly at his signature restaurant for the newly opened Waikiki Edition hotel. The big 200-seat elegant dining room features the chef's signature cuisine, which blends traditional Japanese dishes with fresh Western ingredients—to wildly received applause. Dinner is the main attraction, where unforgettable dishes like hamachi tartare (raw hamachi fish) is served with an assortment of condiments like Morimoto's guacamole, a nori puree, rice crackers, sour cream, wasabi, and *yamamomo* (a Japanese peach). For the ultimate food-ie experience, order the Omakase menu (which translates to "in the chef's hands"): The chef will send out a multicourse tasting menu you'll remember as the highlight of your trip. Book in advance. See p. 126.

o **Ola at the Turtle Bay Resort:** Even if you're staying in Waikiki, plan a day at the beach on the North Shore and eat here for dinner. You won't regret it. First, the location—literally on the sandy beach next door to the Turtle Bay Resort. Second, the restaurant—an open-air beach pavilion. But the best part is . . . the food! The menu is filled with creative selections (like the ahi and lobster *poke* served with a wonton spoon) and some of the best food you'll have in Hawaii. See p. 151.

o **Olive Tree Cafe:** This temple of Greek and Mediterranean delights is the quintessential neighborhood magnet—casual, bustling, and consistently great. Owner Savas Mojarrad has a following of foodies, hipsters, artists, and all manner of loyalists who appreciate his integrity and generosity. Standards are always high, prices reasonable, the dishes fresh and homemade. Bring your own wine and sit down to fresh fish souvlaki, excellent marinated mussels, and sheep's cheese spanakopita. Mojarrad even makes the yogurt for his famous yogurt-mint-cucumber sauce, the souvlaki's ticket to immortality. Don't miss the chicken saffron, a Tuesday special. See p. 149.

o **The Pineapple Room:** Yes, it's in a department store, but it's Alan Wong, a culinary icon. The room features an open kitchen with a lava-rock wall and abundant natural light, but these are details—in this room, food is king. The dishes are terrific, particularly anything with ahi (for example, the ahi meatloaf). The menu changes regularly, but keep an eye out for the ginger scallion shrimp scampi, nori-wrapped tempura salmon, and superb gazpacho made of yellow and red Waimea tomatoes. See p. 133.

o **Roy's Restaurant:** Good food still reigns at this busy, noisy flagship Hawaii Kai dining room with the trademark open kitchen. Roy Yamaguchi's deft way with local ingredients, nostalgic ethnic preparations, and fresh fish makes his menu, which changes daily, a novel experience every time. Yamaguchi's special dinners with vintners are a Honolulu staple. See p. 149.

THE best SHOPPING

Products of Hawaii now merit their own festivals and trade shows throughout the year, and MADE IN HAWAII is a label to be touted. Here are a few places to score some finds.

o **Academy Shop:** The expansion of the Honolulu Academy of Arts made a good thing even better: The Academy's store now has a stunning selection of art books, stationery, jewelry, basketry, beadwork, ikats, saris, ethnic fabrics, fiber vessels, accessories, and contemporary gift items representing the art and craft traditions of the world. See p. 254.

o **Avanti Fashion:** Avanti aloha shirts and sportswear elevate tropical garb from high kitsch to high chic. Casual, comfortable, easily cared for, and light as a cloud, the authentic prints from the 1930s and '40s reproduced on silk look vintage but cost a fraction of collectibles' prices. The nostalgic treasures are available in retail stores statewide, but the best selection is in Waikiki. See p. 246.

Hawaiian fashion from Avanti.

- **Bailey's Antiques & Aloha Shirts:** Bailey's has one of the largest vintage aloha-shirt collections in Honolulu, with prices ranging from inexpensive to sky-high. Old Levi's jeans, mandarin jackets, vintage vases, household items, shawls, purses, and an eye-popping assortment of bark-cloth fabrics (the real thing, not repros) are among the mementos in this monumental collection. See p. 246.

- **Contemporary Museum Gift Shop:** This gets our vote as the most beautiful setting for a gift shop, and its contents are a bonus: extraordinary art-related books, avant-garde jewelry, cards and stationery, home accessories, and gift items made by artists from Hawaii and across the country. Only the best is sold here. See p. 254.

- **Honolulu Chocolate Co.:** Life's greatest pleasures are dispensed here with abandon: expensive gourmet chocolates made in Honolulu, Italian and Hawaiian biscotti, boulder-size chocolate "turtles," truffles, chocolate-covered coffee beans, and jumbo apricots in white and dark chocolate, to name a few. See p. 249.

- **Mana Hawaii:** Experience authentic Hawaiian culture in the heart of Waikiki at this mega-culture shop, the brainchild of five successful Native Hawaiian partners who combined their talents into one. You'll find everything from Hawaiian books to Hawaiian-made gifts, clothing, jewelry, and art, even hula implements and ukuleles, plus healing Hawaiian lotions and oils. See p. 254.

- **Native Books & Beautiful Things:** Hawaii is the content and context in this shop of books, crafts, and gift items made by island artists and crafters. The musical instruments, calabashes, jewelry, leis, books, fabrics, clothing, home accessories, jams and jellies are all high quality and made in-state—a celebration of Hawaiiana. See p. 254.

- **Silver Moon Emporium:** Owner Lucie Talbot-Holu has a gift for discovering fashion treasures. Exquisite clothing and handbags, reasonably priced footwear, hats, jewelry, scarves, and a full gamut of other treasures pepper this attractive boutique. See p. 260.

- **Zuke's Magic & Jokes:** You don't have to be Harry Potter to enter here, but you may feel like him. Amateur and professional magicians stream into this magic store, open only on Saturday, to get the latest "tricks" and learn the art of illusion. See p. 255.

THE best SPOTS FOR SUNSET COCKTAILS

- **Sunset Lanai:** The *Hau* tree shaded Robert Louis Stevenson as he wrote poems to Princess Kaiulani. Today it frames the ocean view from the Sunset Lanai, next to the Hau Tree Lanai restaurant in the New Otani Kaimana Beach Hotel. Sunset Lanai is the favorite watering hole of Diamond Head–area beachgoers who love Sans Souci Beach, the ocean view, the mai tais and sashimi platters, and the live music during weekend sunset hours. See p. 107.

- **House Without a Key:** Oahu's quintessential sunset oasis in the Halekulani hotel claims several unbeatable elements: It's outdoors on the ocean, with a view of Diamond Head; it offers great hula and steel guitar music; and

Relaxing under the *Hau* tree at Sunset Lanai.

it serves one of the best mai tais on the island. You know it's special when even jaded Honoluluans declare it their favorite spot for send-offs, reunions, and gorgeous sunsets. See p. 263.

o **Mai Tai Bar:** Perched a few feet from the sand, this open-air bar at the Royal Hawaiian hotel boasts sweeping views of the South Shore and Waianae Mountains and one of the most pleasing views of Waikiki Beach. Surfers and paddlers ride the waves while the light turns golden and crowns Diamond Head with a halo. Sip a mighty mai tai while entertainers Carmen and Keith Haugen serenade you on stage. See p. 263.

A cocktail poured with flair at Duke's.

o **Duke's Canoe Club:** It's crowded at sunset, but who can resist listening to the top Hawaiian musicians in this upbeat atmosphere a few feet from the sands of Waikiki? Come in from the beach or from the street (the club is part of the Outrigger Waikiki Hotel)—it's always a party at Duke's. Entertainment here is tops, and it reaches a crescendo at sunset. See p. 266.

o **Jameson's by the Sea:** The mai tais here are dubbed the best in Surf City, and the view, although not perfect, doesn't hurt either. Across the street from the harbor, this open-air roadside oasis is a happy stop for North Shore wave watchers and sunset-savvy sightseers. See p. 151.

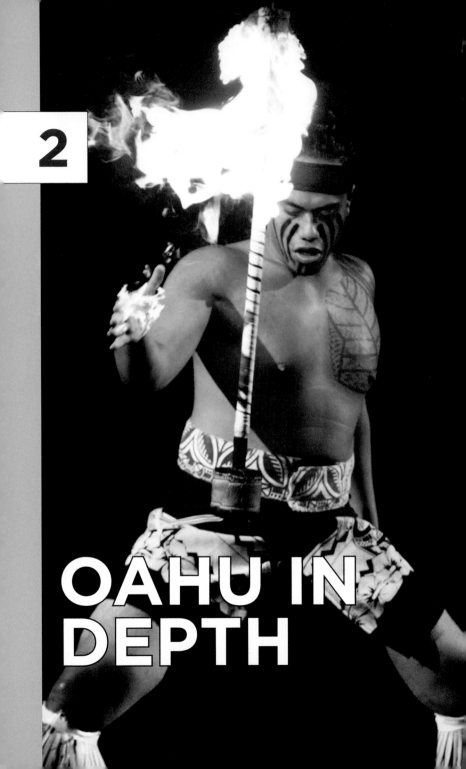

2

OAHU IN DEPTH

Oahu's main city, the fast-paced urban Honolulu, is not only the state capital but offers Hawaii's hottest nightlife, its best shopping, and diverse restaurants. Next door is the world famous vacation playground, Waikiki, complete with every imaginable visitor amenity. But the island's North Shore and the windward side present a different face: miles of white-sand beaches and a slower, country way of life.

Centuries of the indigenous Hawaiian culture have given the people of the islands the "spirit of aloha," a warm, welcoming attitude that invites visitors to come and share this exotic paradise. Mother Nature has carved out verdant valleys, hung brilliant rainbows in the sky, and trimmed the islands with sandy beaches in a spectrum of colors, from white to black to even green and red.

Visitors are drawn to this island not only for its incredible beauty, but also for its opportunities for adventure: swimming in a sea of rainbow-colored fish, hiking into a rainforest, or watching whales leap out of the ocean as you tee off on one of the country's top golf courses. Others come to rest and relax in a land where the pace of life moves at a slower rate and the sun's rays soothe and allow both body and mind to regenerate and recharge.

Venturing to the island of Oahu is not your run-of-the-mill vacation; rather it's an experience in the senses that will remain with you, locked into your memory, long after your tan fades. Years later, a sweet smell, the warmth of the sun on your body, or the sound of the wind through the trees will take you back to the time you spent in the Hawaiian Islands.

THE ISLAND OF OAHU TODAY
A Cultural Renaissance

A conch shell sounds, a young man in a bright feather cape chants, torchlight flickers at sunset on Waikiki Beach, and hula dancers begin telling their graceful centuries-old stories. It's a cultural scene out of the past, come to life once again—for Hawaii is enjoying a renaissance of hula, chant, and other aspects of its ancient culture.

The biggest, longest, and most elaborate celebrations of Hawaiian culture are the Aloha Festivals, which encompass more than 500 cultural events from August to October. "Our goal is to teach and share our culture," says Gloriann Akau, an island manager of the statewide Aloha Festivals. "In 1946, after the war, Hawaiians needed an identity. We were lost and needed to regroup. When we started to celebrate our culture, we began to feel proud. We have a wonderful culture that had been buried for a number of years. This brought it out again. Self-esteem is more important than making a lot of money."

FACING PAGE: **Dancing with flames at the World Fire-Knife Championships.**

In 1985, native Hawaiian educator, author, and *kupuna* (respected elder) George Kanahele started integrating Hawaiian values into hotels in the 50th state. "You have the responsibility to preserve and enhance the Hawaiian culture, not because it's going to make money for you, but because it's the right thing to do," Kanahele told the Hawaii Hotel Association. "Ultimately, the only thing unique about Hawaii is its Hawaiianess. Hawaiianess is our competitive edge."

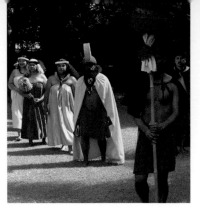
The Royal Court at an Aloha Festival.

From general managers to maids, resort employees went through hours of Hawaiian cultural training. They held focus groups to discuss the meaning of aloha—the Hawaiian concept of unconditional love—and applied it to their work and their lives. Now many hotels have joined the movement and instituted Hawaiian cultural programs. No longer content with teaching hula as a joke, resorts now employ a real *kumu hula* (hula teacher) to instruct visitors and have a *kupuna* (elder) take guests on treks to visit *heiau* (temples) and ancient petroglyph sites.

As a result, the Hawaiian culture is among the top respected resources in the state. The visitor industry wants tourists to have a "true" experience of Hawaii's culture, especially in Waikiki, where the majority of visitors land.

The Question of Sovereignty

The Hawaiian cultural renaissance has also made its way into politics. Many *kanaka maoli* (native people) are demanding restoration of rights taken away more than a century ago when the U.S. overthrew the Hawaiian monarchy. Their demands were not lost on President Bill Clinton, who was picketed at a Democratic political fundraiser at Waikiki Beach in July 1993. Four months later, Clinton signed a document stating that the U.S. Congress "apologizes to Native Hawaiians on behalf of the people of the United States for the overthrow of the Kingdom of Hawaii on January 17, 1893, with the participation of agents and citizens of the United States, and deprivation of the rights of Native Hawaiians to self-determination."

But even neonationalists aren't convinced that complete self-determination is possible. Each of the 30 identifiable sovereignty organizations (and more than 100 splinter groups) has a different stated goal, ranging from total independence to nation-within-a-nation status, similar to that of Native Indians. In 1993, the state legislature created a Hawaiian Sovereignty Advisory Commission to "determine the will of the native Hawaiian people." The commission planned to pose the sovereignty question in a referendum open to anyone over 18 with Hawaiian blood, no matter where they live. The question still remains unanswered.

LOOKING BACK: OAHU & HAWAII'S HISTORY

Paddling outrigger canoes, the first ancestors of today's Hawaiians followed the stars and birds across the ocean to Hawaii, which they called "the land of raging fire." Those first settlers were part of the great Polynesian migration that settled the vast triangle of islands stretching between New Zealand, Easter Island, and Hawaii. No one is sure exactly when they came to Hawaii from Tahiti and the Marquesas Islands, some 2,500 miles to the south, but a bone fishhook found at the southernmost tip of the Big Island has been carbon-dated from A.D. 700. Chants claim that the Mookini Heiau (a temple made from stones), also on the Big Island, was built in A.D. 480.

An entire Hawaiian culture arose from these settlers, with each island becoming a separate kingdom. Across each kingdom, though, some things were consistent: The *alii* (high-ranking chiefs) created a caste system and established taboos—and anyone that broke those taboos could be sacrificed. Plus sailors became farmers and fishermen, and the inhabitants built temples, fish ponds, and aqueducts to irrigate taro plantations.

The "Fatal Catastrophe"

No ancient Hawaiian ever imagined a *haole* (a white person; literally, one with "no breath") would ever appear on one of these islands. But then one day in 1778, just such a person sailed into Waimea Bay on Kauai, where he was welcomed as the god Lono.

The man was 50-year-old Captain James Cook, already famous in Britain for "discovering" much of the South Pacific. Now on his third great voyage of exploration, Cook had set sail from Tahiti northward across uncharted waters to find the mythical Northwest Passage that was said to link the Pacific and Atlantic oceans. On his way, Cook stumbled upon the Hawaiian Islands quite by chance. He named them the Sandwich Islands, for the Earl of Sandwich, first lord of the admiralty, who had bankrolled the expedition.

Overnight, stone-age Hawaii entered the age of iron. Nails were traded for fresh water, pigs, and the affections of Hawaiian women. The sailors brought syphilis, measles, and other diseases to which the Hawaiians had no natural immunity, thereby unwittingly wreaking havoc on the native population.

After his unsuccessful attempt to find the Northwest Passage, Cook returned to Kealakekua Bay on the Big Island, where a fight broke out over an alleged theft, and the great navigator was killed by a blow to the head. After this "fatal catastrophe," the British survivors sailed home.

But Hawaii was now on the sea charts, and traders on the fur route between Canada and China anchored in Hawaii to get fresh water. More trade—and more disastrous liaisons—ensued.

Two more sea captains left indelible marks on the islands. The first was American John Kendrick, who in 1791 filled his ship with sandalwood and sailed to China. By 1825, Hawaii's sandalwood forests were gone, enabling invasive plants to take charge. The second captain was Englishman George Vancouver, who in 1793 left cows and sheep, which spread out to the high-tide lines. King Kamehameha I sent for cowboys from Mexico and

Captain James Cook, Hawaii's first *haole*.

Spain to round up the wild livestock, thus beginning the islands' *paniolo* (cowboy) tradition.

The tightly woven Hawaiian society began to unravel after the death in 1819 of King Kamehameha I, who had used guns seized from a British ship to unite the islands under his rule. One of his successors, Queen Kaahumanu, abolished the old taboos of the *alii* and opened the door for religion of another form.

Staying to Do Well

In April 1820, missionaries bent on converting the "pagans" arrived from New England. The missionaries clothed the natives, banned them from dancing the hula, and nearly dismantled their ancient culture. They tried to keep the whalers and sailors out of the bawdy houses, where a flood of whiskey quenched fleet-size thirsts and the virtue of native women was never safe. They taught reading and writing, created the 12-letter Hawaiian alphabet, started a printing press, and began recording the islands' history, which until then was only an oral account in memorized chants.

Children of the missionaries became the islands' business leaders and politicians. They married Hawaiians and stayed on in the islands, causing one wag to remark that the missionaries "came to do good and stayed to do well." In 1848, King Kamehameha III proclaimed the Great Mahele (division), which enabled commoners and eventually foreigners to own crown land. In two generations, more than 80% of all private land was in *haole* (foreign) hands. Sugar planters imported waves of immigrants (Chinese starting in 1852, Japanese in 1885, and Portuguese in 1878) to work the fields as contract laborers.

King David Kalakaua was elected to the throne in 1874. This popular "Merrie Monarch" built Iolani Palace in Honolulu in 1882, threw extravagant parties, and lifted the prohibitions on the hula and other native arts. For this, he was much loved. He also gave Pearl Harbor to the United States; it became the westernmost bastion of the U.S. Navy. In 1891, King Kalakaua visited chilly San Francisco, caught a cold, and died in the royal suite of the Sheraton Palace. His sister, Queen Liliuokalani, assumed the throne.

A Sad Farewell

On January 17, 1893, a group of American sugar planters and missionary descendants, with the support of U.S. Marines, imprisoned Queen Liliuokalani in her own palace, in Honolulu, where she later penned the sorrowful lyric "Aloha Oe," Hawaii's song of farewell. The monarchy was dead.

A new republic was then established, controlled by Sanford Dole, a powerful sugar-cane planter. In 1898, through annexation, Hawaii became an American territory ruled by Dole. His fellow sugar-cane planters, known as the Big Five, controlled banking, shipping, hardware, and every other facet of economic life on the islands.

Oahu's central Ewa Plain soon filled with row crops. The Dole family planted pineapple on its vast acreage. Planters imported more contract

Handsome Iolani Palace, built by King Kalakaua.

IS EVERYONE hawaiian IN HAWAII?

The plantations brought so many different people to Hawaii that the state is now a rainbow of ethnic groups: Living here are Caucasians, African Americans, American Indians, Eskimos, Japanese, Chinese, Filipinos, Koreans, Tahitians, Vietnamese, Native Hawaiians, Samoans, Tongans, and other Asian and Pacific Islanders. Add to that a few Canadians, Dutch, English, French, Germans, Irish, Italians, Portuguese, Scottish, Puerto Ricans, and Spaniards.

In combination, it's a remarkable potpourri. Many people retain an element of the traditions of their homeland. Some Japanese Americans in Hawaii, generations removed from the homeland, are more traditional than the Japanese of Tokyo. And the same is true of many Chinese, Koreans, Filipinos, and others, making Hawaii a kind of living museum of various Asian and Pacific cultures.

laborers from Puerto Rico (1900), Korea (1903), and the Philippines (1907–31). Most of the new immigrants stayed on to establish families and become a part of the islands. Meanwhile, the native Hawaiians became a landless minority.

For nearly a century on Hawaii, sugar was king, generously subsidized by the U.S. government. The sugar planters dominated the territory's economy, shaped its social fabric, and kept the islands in a colonial plantation era with bosses and field hands. But the workers eventually went on strike for higher wages and improved working conditions, and the planters found themselves unable to compete with cheap third-world labor costs.

The Tourists Arrive

Tourism proper began in the 1860s on the neighbor islands: Kilauea volcano (located on the Big Island of Hawaii) was one of the world's prime attractions for adventure travelers. In 1865, a grass Volcano House was built on the rim of Halemaumau Crater to shelter visitors; it was Hawaii's first tourist hotel. But tourism really got off the ground with the demise of the plantation era.

In 1901, W. C. Peacock built the elegant Beaux Arts Moana Hotel on Waikiki Beach, and W. C. Weedon convinced Honolulu businessmen to bankroll his plan to advertise Hawaii in San Francisco. Armed with a stereopticon and tinted photos of Waikiki, Weedon sailed off in 1902 for 6 months of lecture

PIDGIN: 'EH FO' real, BRAH

If you venture beyond the tourist areas, you might hear another local tongue: pidgin English, a conglomeration of slang and words from the Hawaiian language. "Broke da mouth" (tastes really good) is a favorite pidgin phrase and one you might hear; "'Eh fo' real, brah" means "It's true, brother." You could be invited to hear an elder "talk story" (relating myths and memories). But because pidgin is really the province of the locals, your visit to Hawaii is likely to pass without your hearing much of it at all.

DO YOU HAVE TO speak HAWAIIAN IN HAWAII?

Almost everyone here speaks English. But many folks in Hawaii now speak Hawaiian as well. All visitors will hear the words *aloha* and *mahalo* (thank you). If you've just arrived, you're a *malihini*. Someone who's been here a long time is a *kamaaina*. When you finish a job or your meal, you are *pau* (finished). On Friday it's *pau hana*, work finished. You eat *pupu* (Hawaii's version of hors d'oeuvres) when you go *pau hana*.

The Hawaiian alphabet, created by the New England missionaries, has only 12 letters: the five regular vowels (*a, e, i, o,* and *u*) and seven consonants (*h, k, l, m, n, p,* and *w*). The vowels are pronounced in the Roman fashion: that is, *ah, ay, ee, oh,* and *oo* (as in "too")—not *ay, ee, eye, oh,* and *you,* as in English. For example, *huhu* is pronounced *who-who.* Most vowels are sounded separately, though some are pronounced together, as in Kalakaua: Kah-lah-*cow*-ah.

Below are some basic Hawaiian words that you'll often hear in Hawaii and see throughout this book. For a more complete list of Hawaiian words, go to www.wehewehe.org or http://hawaiiandictionary.hisurf.com.

alii Hawaiian royalty
aloha greeting or farewell
halau school
hale house or building
heiau Hawaiian temple or place of worship
kahuna priest or expert
kamaaina old-timer
kapa tapa, bark cloth
kapu taboo, forbidden
keiki child
kupuna respected elder

lanai porch or veranda
lomilomi massage
mahalo thank you
makai a direction, toward the sea
mana spirit power
mauka a direction, toward the mountains
muumuu loose-fitting gown or dress
ono delicious
pali cliff
paniolo Hawaiian cowboy(s)
wiki quick

tours to introduce "those remarkable people and the beautiful lands of Hawaii." He drew packed houses. A tourism promotion bureau was formed in 1903, and about 2,000 visitors came to Hawaii that year.

The steamship was Hawaii's tourism lifeline. It took 4½ days to sail from San Francisco to Honolulu. Streamers, leis, and pomp welcomed each Matson liner at downtown's Aloha Tower. Well-heeled visitors brought trunks, servants, and Rolls-Royces, and stayed for months. Hawaiians amused visitors with personal tours, floral parades, and shows spotlighting that naughty dance, the hula.

Beginning in 1935 and running for the next 40 years, Webley Edwards's weekly live radio show, "Hawaii Calls," planted the sounds of Waikiki—surf, sliding steel guitar, sweet Hawaiian harmonies, drumbeats—in the hearts of millions of listeners in the United States, Australia, and Canada.

By 1936, visitors could fly to Honolulu from San Francisco on the *Hawaii Clipper,* a seven-passenger Pan American Martin M-130 flying boat, for $360 one-way. The flight took 21 hours, 33 minutes. Modern tourism was born, with five flying boats providing daily service. The 1941 visitor count was a brisk 31,846 through December 6.

32

World War II & Its Aftermath

On December 7, 1941, Japanese Zero fighter planes came out of the rising sun to bomb American warships based at Pearl Harbor. This was the "day of infamy" that plunged the United States into World War II.

The attack brought immediate changes to the islands. Martial law was declared, stripping the Big Five cartel of its absolute power in a single day. Japanese Americans and German Americans were interned. Hawaii was "blacked out" at night, Waikiki Beach was strung with barbed wire, and Aloha Tower was painted in camouflage. Only young men bound for the Pacific came to Hawaii during the war years. Many came back to graves in a cemetery called Punchbowl.

The postwar years saw the beginnings of Hawaii's faux culture. Harry Yee invented the Blue Hawaii cocktail and dropped in a tiny Japanese parasol. Vic Bergeron created the mai tai, a drink made of rum and fresh lime juice, and opened Trader Vic's, America's first themed restaurant that featured the art, decor, and food of Polynesia. Arthur Godfrey picked up a ukulele and began singing *hapa-haole* tunes on early TV shows. In 1955, Henry J. Kaiser built the Hilton Hawaiian Village, and the 11-story high-rise Princess Kaiulani Hotel opened on a site where the real princess once played. Hawaii greeted 109,000 visitors that year.

Statehood

In 1959, Hawaii became the 50th state of the United States. That year also saw the arrival of the first jet airliners, which brought 250,000 tourists to the state. The personal touch that had defined aloha gave way to the sheer force of numbers. Waikiki's room count nearly doubled in 2 years, from 16,000 units in 1969 to 31,000 in 1971, and kept increasing until city fathers finally clamped down on growth. By 1980, annual arrivals had reached four million.

The Japanese attack on Pearl Harbor.

In the early 1980s, the Japanese began traveling overseas in record numbers, and they brought lots of yen to spend. Their effect on sales in Hawaii was phenomenal: European boutiques opened branches in Honolulu, and duty-free shopping became the main supporter of Honolulu International Airport. Japanese investors competed for the chance to own or build part of Hawaii. Hotels sold so fast and at such unbelievable prices that heads began to spin with dollar signs.

In 1986, Hawaii's visitor count passed five million. Two years later, it went over six million. Expensive fantasy megaresorts bloomed on the neighbor islands like giant artificial flowers, swelling the luxury market with ever-swankier accommodations.

The visitor count was at a record 6.7 million in 1990 when the bubble burst in early 1991 with the Gulf War and worldwide recessions. In 1992, Hurricane Iniki devastated Kauai. Airfare wars sent Americans to Mexico and the Caribbean. Overbuilt with luxury hotels, Hawaii slashed its room rates, giving middle-class consumers access to high-end digs at affordable prices—a trend that continues as Hawaii struggles to stay atop the tourism heap.

Hawaii was finally back to record-breaking visitor counts (6.9 million) in 2000. Then September 11, 2001, sent a blow to Hawaii—tourism dropped abruptly, sending Hawaii's economy into a tailspin. But people eventually started traveling again, and in 2003, visitor arrivals were up to 6.3 million. By 2005, Hawaii's economy was recovering, the number of visitors to the state shot up to 6.75 million, business was booming in construction, and real-estate sales were higher than ever.

Just 3 years later, the economic pendulum swung the opposite way. Real estate in Hawaii, as on the mainland, dropped in value and sales plummeted. Although a record number of visitors, some nine million, had come to Hawaii in 2007, the economic downturn in 2008 saw the closure of Aloha Airlines (which had served Hawaii for 61 years before closing) and ATA Airlines, as well as the shutting down of all operations (both cattle ranch and visitor accommodations) of Molokai Ranch, the island's largest employer and landowner.

Today, Waikiki and the rest of the state has recovered remarkably well in the dire straights of the world wide economy. The visitor industry is on the upswing, while agriculture and military spending (two of Hawaii's other key industries) also are up.

ART & ARCHITECTURE

Yes, you can still see re-created thatched-roof huts from ancient Hawaii. However, they won't be on the street but in Honolulu's Bishop Museum (p. 196) or at the Polynesian Cultural Center (p. 235). You also can get a great feel of what life was like in the 19th century for the American missionaries who ventured to this "heathen" land by visiting the Mission Houses Museum (p. 203). Turn of the 20th century architecture can still be observed in downtown Honolulu.

The art scene in Honolulu is more vibrant than ever, especially with the Hawaii State Art Museum (housed in the original Royal Hawaiian Hotel, built in 1872, during the time of King Kamehameha V; p. 199), filled with works created by artists living in Hawaii; the Honolulu Academy of Arts (p. 199), the state's only general fine arts museum, with an excellent collection of Asian arts; and the Contemporary Museum (p. 197), three acres of sculptured gardens and displays of contemporary art in the museum.

HONOLULU, WAIKIKI & OAHU IN POP CULTURE

In addition to the books discussed below, those planning an extended trip to Hawaii should check out *Frommer's Honolulu & Oahu Day by Day, Frommer's Kauai, Frommer's Maui, Frommer's Maui Day by Day, Frommer's Hawaii with Kids,* and *Frommer's Hawaii 2012.*

Books

FICTION

The first book people think about is James A. Michener's *Hawaii* (1974). This epic novel manages to put the island's history into chronological order, but remember, it is still fiction, and very sanitized fiction, too. For a more contemporary look at life in Hawaii today, one of the best novels is *Shark Dialogues,* by Kiana Davenport (1995). The novel tells the story of Pono, the larger-than-life matriarch, and her four daughters of mixed races. Davenport skillfully weaves legends and myths of Hawaii into the "real life" reality that Pono and her family face in the complex Hawaii of today.

Lois-Ann Yamanaka uses a very "local" voice and stark depictions of life in the islands in her fabulous novels *Wild Meat and the Bully Burgers* (1996), *Blu's Hanging* (1997), and *Heads by Harry* (1999).

NONFICTION

Mark Twain's writing on Hawaii in the 1860s offers a wonderful introduction to Hawaii's history. His travelogues have been collected in *Mark Twain in Hawaii: Roughing It in the Sandwich Islands* (1990). A great depiction of the Hawaii of 1889 is *Travels in Hawaii,* by Robert Louis Stevenson (1973).

For contemporary voices on Hawaii's unique culture, one of the best books to get is *Voices of Wisdom: Hawaiian Elders Speak,* by M. J. Harden (1999). Some 24 different *kahuna* (experts) in their fields were interviewed about their talent, skill, or artistic practice. These living treasures talk about how Hawaiians of yesteryear viewed nature, spirituality and healing, preservation and history, dance and music, arts and crafts, canoes, and the next generation.

Native Planters in Old Hawaii: Their Life, Lore, and Environment (2004) was originally published in 1972 but is still one of the most important ethnographic works on traditional Hawaiian culture, portraying the lives of the common folk and their relationship with the land before the arrival of Westerners. The revised edition, with a great index that allows you to find anything, is an excellent resource for anyone interested in Hawaii.

Honolulu Stories: Two Centuries of Writing, edited by Gavan Daws and

Robert Louis Stevenson (right), seated with King Kalakaua.

Bennett Hymer (2008), is a fascinating 1,000-plus-page book filled with the writings of various authors over the past 200 years. More than 350 selections—ranging from short stories, excerpts from novels, and scenes from plays, musicals, and operas to poems, songs, Hawaiian chants, cartoons, slams, and even stand-up comedy routines—are contained in this must-read for anyone interested in Hawaii. The authors range from Hawaiian kings and queens to Hawaiian chefs and commoners, including some well-known writers (translated from seven different languages)—all telling their own stories about Honolulu.

Flora & Fauna

Because Hawaii is so lush with nature and blessed with plants, animals, and reef fish seen nowhere else on the planet, a few reference books can help you identify what you're looking at and make your trip more interesting. In the botanical world, Angela Kay Kepler's *Hawaiian Heritage Plants* (1998) is the standard for plant reference. In a series of essays, Kepler weaves culture, history, geography, botany, and even spirituality into her vivid descriptions of plants. You'll never look at plants the same way. There are great color photos and drawings to help you sort through the myriad species. Another great resource is *Tropicals,* by Gordon Courtright (1988), which is filled with color photos identifying everything from hibiscus and heliconia to trees and palms.

The other necessary reference to have in Hawaii is one that identifies the colorful reef fish you will see snorkeling. The best of the bunch is John E. Randall's *Shore Fishes of Hawaii* (1998). Two other books on reef-fish identification, with easy-to-use spiral bindings, are *Hawaiian Reef Fish: The Identification Book,* by Casey Mahaney (1993), and *Hawaiian Reef Fish,* by Astrid Witte and Casey Mahaney (1998).

To learn everything you need to identify Hawaii's unique birds, try H. Douglas Pratt's *A Pocket Guide to Hawaii's Birds* (1996).

History

There are many great books on Hawaii's history; best to start at the beginning with the formation of the Hawaiian Islands, vividly described in David E. Eyre's *By Wind, By Wave: An Introduction to Hawaii's Natural History* (2000). In addition to chronicling the natural history of Hawaii, Eyre describes the complex interrelationships among the plants, animals, ocean, and people. He points out that Hawaii has become the "extinction capital of the world," but rather than dwelling on that fact, he urges readers to do something about it and carefully spells out how.

For a history of "precontact" Hawaii (before Westerners arrived), David Malo's *Hawaiian Antiquities* (1976) is the preeminent source. Malo was born around 1793 and wrote about the Hawaiian lifestyle at that time, as well as the beliefs and religion of his people. It's an excellent reference book, but not a fast read. For more readable books on old Hawaii, try *Stories of Old Hawaii,* by Roy Kakulu Alameida (1997), on myths and legends; *Hawaiian Folk Tales,* by Thomas G. Thrum (1998); and *The Legends and Myths of Hawaii,* by His Hawaiian Majesty King David Kalakaua (1992).

The best story of the 1893 overthrow of the Hawaiian monarchy is told by Queen Liliuokalani, in her book *Hawaii's Story by Hawaii's Queen Liliuokalani* (1990). When it was written in 1898, it was an international plea for justice for her people, but it is a poignant read even today. It's also a must-read for people interested in current events and the recent rally for sovereignty in the 50th state. Two contemporary books on the question of Hawaii's sovereignty are Tom Coffman's *Nation Within: The Story of America's Annexation of the Nation of Hawaii* (1998) and Thurston Twigg-Smith's *Hawaiian Sovereignty: Do the Facts Matter?* (2000), which explores the opposite view. Twigg-Smith, former publisher of the statewide newspaper *The Honolulu Advertiser,* is the grandson of Lorrin A. Thurston, one of the architects of the 1893 overthrow of the monarchy. His so-called "politically incorrect" views present a different look on this hotly debated topic.

An insightful look at history and its effect on the Hawaiian culture is *Waikiki, A History of Forgetting and Remembering,* by Andrea Feeser (2006). A beautiful art book (designed by Gaye Chan), this is not your typical coffee-table book, but a different look at the cultural and environmental history of Waikiki. Using historical texts, photos, government documents, and interviews, this book lays out the story of how Waikiki went from a self-sufficient agricultural area to a tourism mecca, detailing the price that was paid along the way.

Television

HAWAII FIVE-0 *Hawaii Five-0* premiered on Monday, September 20, 2010, 42 years to the date from the premiere of the original hit show in 1968. Filmed on the island of Oahu and featuring scenes from Waikiki and Honolulu, it, like the original, follows a state police task force set up to fight crime. The original series ran from 1968 to 1980; it is yet to be determined whether the remake can live up to the original's long life.

LOST This original series, filmed all over the island of Oahu, aired on ABC between 2004 and 2010, and revolved around the lives of the survivors of the crash of a commercial passenger jet flying between Sydney and Los Angeles, on a mysterious tropical island somewhere in the South Pacific Ocean.

MAGNUM, P.I. From 1980 to 1988, this drama, broadcast on CBS, and filmed on Oahu, told the story of Thomas Magnum (Tom Selleck), a private investigator living in Honolulu.

Film

Our favorite movies filmed on Oahu that don't necessarily depict Oahu are:

JURASSIC PARK Filmed on the islands of Kauai and Oahu, Steven Spielberg's 1993 megahit, which was billed as "an adventure 65 million years in the making," is the story of dinosaurs on the loose at the site of the world's only dinosaur farm and theme park, where creatures from the past are produced using harvested DNA.

THE KARATE KID, PART II In one of those instances where the sequel is actually better than the original, this 1986 movie takes our hero Daniel LaRusso (Ralph Macchio) and his mentor, Mr. Miyagi (Pat Morita), to Miyagi's homeland, Okinawa, to visit his dying father and confront his old rival. An entire Okinawan village was re-created on Oahu's Windward Coast.

The survivors of *Lost* lost in Oahu's rain forest.

THE LOST WORLD: JURASSIC PARK In Steven Spielberg's 1997 follow-up to *Jurassic Park,* dinosaurs have been bred and then escaped following the abandonment of the project in the first installment. The sequel features much more Hawaiian scenery than the original.

PIRATES OF THE CARIBBEAN: ON STRANGER TIDES The 2011 American adventure fantasy film, and the fourth film in the "Pirates of the Caribbean" series (following *Pirates of the Caribbean: At World's End*), was filmed on Oahu (and Kauai). In the film, Captain Jack Sparrow (Johnny Depp) is joined by his former lover Angelica (Penélope Cruz) in his search for the Fountain of Youth, confronting the infamous, real-life, legendary pirate Blackbeard (Ian McShane) along the way.

Our favorite films made in Hawaii and about Hawaii are:

BLUE CRUSH The 2002 surfer film, filmed on Oahu's North Shore, was directed by John Stockwell and stars Kate Bosworth, Michelle Rodriguez, Sanoe Lake, and Mika Boorem. In it, a beautiful surf girl is distracted by a hunky football player while she is trying to prepare for a big surfing competition.

BLUE HAWAII Chad Gates (Elvis Presley), upon discharge from the Army, returns to Hawaii to enjoy life with his buddies and girlfriend, against the wishes of his parents, who want him to work for the family business. Elvis Presley, Joan Blackman, and Angela Lansbury make this 1961 film a classic, with great music and beautiful Hawaiian scenery from the early 1960s.

50 FIRST DATES This 2004 romantic comedy stars Drew Barrymore and Adam Sandler in a story about a young woman (Barrymore) who has lost her short-term memory in a car accident and who now relives each day as if it were October 13. She follows the same routine every day, until she meets Henry Roth (Sandler), who falls in love with her and seeks a way to forge a long-term relationship.

FORGETTING SARAH MARSHALL This underrated 2008 romantic comedy—about a composer who vacations in Hawaii to escape a depressing breakup, only to encounter his ex and her new boyfriend at his hotel—was shot on Oahu, at the Turtle Bay Resort. Directed by Nicholas Stoller, it stars Jason Segel, Kristen Bell, Mila Kunis, and Russell Brand.

FROM HERE TO ETERNITY Fred Zinnemann's 1953 multiple-Oscar winner, set in pre–World War II Hawaii, tells the story of several army soldiers stationed on Oahu on the eve of Pearl Harbor. The film won Best Picture, Best Supporting Actor (Frank Sinatra), Best Supporting Actress (Donna Reed), and five other awards.

HAWAII George Roy Hill's 1966 adaptation of the James Michener novel features amazing island scenery and stars Julie Andrews, Max von Sydow, and Richard Harris. It is a great introduction to the early history of Hawaii.

MOLOKAI: THE STORY OF FATHER DAMIEN This 1999 film follows the life of Belgian priest Damien de Veuster from 1872, the year before his arrival in Kalaupapa, through his years ministering to the patients with Hansen's disease at Kalaupapa, until his death at the Molokai settlement in 1889.

PEARL HARBOR Michael Bay's 2001 film depicts the time before, during, and after the December 7, 1941, Japanese attack (with the best re-creation of the Pearl Harbor attack ever put on film), while simultaneously telling the story of two best friends and the woman they both love.

PICTURE BRIDE Japanese director Kayo Hatta presents this 1995 film about a Japanese woman who travels to Hawaii to marry a man that she has never met, but has only seen through photos and letters. She soon discovers that he is twice her age and that much turmoil awaits her in her new home. Beautifully filmed on the North Shore of Oahu.

TORA! TORA! TORA! This 1970 film tells the story of the Japanese attack on Pearl Harbor as seen from both American and Japanese perspectives.

The ukulele is instrumental to Hawaiian music.

Music

Hawaiian music ranges from traditional ancient chants and hula, to slack-key guitar, to contemporary rock, to a new genre, Jawaiian, a cross of reggae, Jamaican, and Hawaiian. To listen to Hawaiian music, check out Hawaiian 105 (www.hawaiian105.com). Below are our picks for Hawaiian music.

- o **Best of the Gabby Band,** by Gabby Pahinui (traditional Hawaiian)
- o **Gently Weeps,** by Jake Shimabukuro (contemporary Hawaiian)
- o **Hapa,** by Hapa (contemporary Hawaiian)
- o **Hawaiian Blossom,** by Raiatea Helm (traditional Hawaiian)
- o **Hawaiian Tradition,** by Amy Hanaiali'i Gilliom (traditional Hawaiian)
- o **Honolulu City Lights,** by Keola & Kapono Beamer (contemporary Hawaiian)
- o **Legends of Hawaiian Slack Key Guitar,** by various artists (a collection of slack-key guitar music and a 2007 Grammy winner)
- o **Masters of Hawaiian Slack Key, Vol. 1,** by various artists (a collection of slack-key guitar music and a 2006 Grammy winner)
- o **Na Leo Hawaii,** by the Master Chanters of Hawaii (chanting)
- o **Na Pua O Hawaii,** by Makaha Sons (contemporary Hawaiian)
- o **Wonderful World,** by Israel Kamakawiwo'ole (contemporary Hawaiian)

EATING & DRINKING IN OAHU
Hawaii Regional Cuisine

Hawaii regional cuisine (HRC) was established in the mid-1980s in a culinary revolution that catapulted Hawaii into the global epicurean arena. The international training, creative vigor, fresh ingredients, and cross-cultural menus of the 12 HRC chefs who originally championed the cuisine have made the islands a dining destination applauded nationwide. (In a tip of the toque to island tradition, *ahi*—a word ubiquitous in Hawaii—has replaced *tuna* on many chic New York menus.)

HRC today is even more popular. Peter Merriman, a founding member of HRC and a recipient of the James Beard Award for Best Chef: Northwest/ Hawaii (along with George Mavrothalassitis of Chef Mavro Restaurant; p. 143), describes the current trend in Hawaii as a refinement, a tweaking upward, of everything from fine dining to down-home local cooking. This means sesame- or nori-crusted fresh catch on plate-lunch menus, and *huli-huli* (Hawaiian rotisserie) chicken at five-diamond eateries, paired with Beaujolais and leeks and gourmet long rice.

At the same time, HRC, the style of cooking that put Hawaii on the international culinary map, has become watered down, a buzzword: "A lot of restaurants are paying lip service," says Merriman. As it is with things au courant, it is easy to make a claim but another thing to live up to it. As Merriman points out, HRC was never solely about technique; it is equally about ingredients and the chef's creativity and integrity. "We continue to get local inspiration," says Merriman. "We've never restricted ourselves." If there is a fabulous French or Thai dish, chefs like Merriman will prepare it with local ingredients and add a creative edge that makes it distinctively Hawaii regional.

Here's a sampling of what you can expect to find on a Hawaii regional menu: seared Hawaiian fish with *lilikoi* (passion fruit) shrimp butter; taro-crab cakes; Pahoa corn cakes; Molokai sweet-potato or breadfruit vichyssoise; Ka'u orange sauce and Kahua Ranch lamb; fern shoots from Waipio Valley; Maui onion soup and Hawaiian bouillabaisse, with fresh snapper, Kona crab, and fresh aquacultured shrimp; blackened ahi summer rolls; herb-crusted *onaga* (snapper); and gourmet Waimanalo greens, picked that day. You may also encounter locally made cheeses, squash and taro risottos, Polynesian *imu*-baked foods (in an underground oven), and guava-smoked meats. If there's pasta or risotto or rack of lamb on the menu, it could be nori (red algae) linguine with *opihi* (limpet) sauce, or risotto with local seafood served in taro cups, or rack of lamb in cabernet and *hoisin* sauce (fermented soybean, garlic, and spices). Watch for *ponzu* sauce, too; it's lemony and zesty, much more flavorful than the soy sauce it resembles.

Plate Lunches & More

At the other end of the spectrum is the vast and endearing world of "local food." By that we mean plate lunches and poke, shave ice and *saimin,* bento lunches and *manapua*—cultural hybrids all.

Reflecting a polyglot population of many styles and ethnicities, Hawaii's idiosyncratic dining scene is eminently inclusive. Consider surfer chic: Barefoot in the sand, in a swimsuit, you chow down on a **plate lunch** ordered from a lunch wagon, consisting of fried mahimahi, "two scoops rice," macaroni salad, and a few leaves of green, typically julienned cabbage. (Generally, teriyaki beef and *shoyu* chicken are options.) Heavy gravy is often the condiment of choice, accompanied by a soft drink in a paper cup or straight out of the can. Like **saimin**—the local version of noodles in broth topped with scrambled eggs, green onions, and sometimes pork—the plate lunch is Hawaii's version of high camp.

But it was only a matter of time before the humble plate lunch became a culinary icon in Hawaii. These days, even the most chichi restaurant has a version of this modest island symbol (not at plate-lunch prices, of course), while vendors selling the real thing—carb-driven meals served from wagons—have lines that never end.

A traditional plate lunch, on the beach of course.

Because this is Hawaii, at least a few licks of poi—cooked, pounded taro (the traditional Hawaiian staple crop)—are a must. Other **native foods** include those from before and after Western contact, such as *laulau* (pork, chicken, or fish steamed in *ti* leaves), *kalua* pork (pork cooked in a Polynesian underground oven known here as an imu), *lomi* salmon (salted salmon with tomatoes and green onions), squid *luau* (cooked in coconut milk and taro tops), *poke* (cubed raw fish seasoned with onions and seaweed and the occasional sprinkling of roasted *kukui* nuts), *haupia* (creamy coconut pudding), and *kulolo* (steamed pudding of coconut, brown sugar, and taro).

Bento, another popular quick meal available throughout Hawaii, is a compact, boxed assortment of picnic fare usually consisting of neatly arranged sections of rice, pickled vegetables, and fried chicken, beef, or pork. Increasingly, however, the bento is becoming more health conscious, as in macrobiotic or vegetarian brown-rice bentos. A derivative of the modest lunch box for Japanese immigrants who once labored in the sugar and pineapple fields, bentos are dispensed everywhere, from department stores to corner delis and supermarkets.

Also from the plantations come **manapua,** a bready, doughy sphere filled with tasty fillings of sweetened pork or sweet beans. In the old days, the Chinese "manapua man" would make his rounds with bamboo containers balanced on a rod over his shoulders. Today you'll find white or whole-wheat manapua containing chicken, vegetables, curry, and other savory fillings.

The daintier Chinese delicacy **dim sum** is made of translucent wrappers filled with fresh seafood, pork hash, and vegetables, served for breakfast and lunch in Chinatown restaurants. The Hong Kong–style dumplings are ordered fresh and hot from bamboo steamers rolled on carts from table to table. Much like hailing a taxi in Manhattan, you have to be quick and loud for dim sum.

For dessert or a snack, particularly on Oahu's North Shore, the prevailing choice is **shave ice,** the Island version of a snow cone. Particularly on hot, humid days, long lines of shave-ice lovers gather for heaps of finely shaved ice topped with sweet tropical syrups. (The sweet-sour *li hing mui* flavor is a current favorite.) The fast-melting mounds, which require prompt, efficient consumption, are quite the local summer ritual for sweet tooths. Aficionados order shave ice with ice cream and sweetened adzuki beans plopped in the middle.

Ahi, *Ono* & *Opakapaka*: A Hawaiian Seafood Primer

The seafood in Hawaii has been described as the best in the world. And why not? Without a doubt, the islands' surrounding waters, including the waters of the remote northwestern Hawaiian Islands, and a growing aquaculture industry contribute to the high quality of the seafood here.

The reputable restaurants in Hawaii buy fresh fish daily at predawn auctions or from local fishermen. Some chefs even catch their ingredients themselves.

"Still wiggling" and "just off the hook" are the ultimate terms for freshness in Hawaii.

Although some menus include the Western description for the fresh fish used, most often the local nomenclature is listed, turning dinner into a confusing, quasiforeign experience for the uninitiated. To help familiarize you with the menu language of Hawaii, here's a basic glossary of Island fish:

Ahi Yellowfin or big-eye tuna, important for its use in sashimi and poke at sushi bars and in Hawaii regional cuisine.

Aku Skipjack tuna, heavily used by local families in home cooking and poke.

Ehu Red snapper, delicate and sumptuous, yet lesser known than opakapaka.

Hapuupuu Grouper, a sea bass whose use is expanding.

Hebi Spearfish, mildly flavored, and frequently featured as the "catch of the day" in upscale restaurants.

Kajiki Pacific blue marlin, also called *au,* with a firm flesh and high fat content that make it a plausible substitute for tuna.

Kumu Goatfish, a luxury item on Chinese and upscale menus, served *en papillote* or steamed whole, Oriental style, with scallions, ginger, and garlic.

Mahimahi Dolphin fish (the game fish, not the mammal) or dorado, a classic sweet, white-fleshed fish requiring vigilance among purists because it's often disguised as fresh when it's actually "fresh-frozen"—a big difference.

Monchong Bigscale or sickle pomfret, an exotic, tasty fish, scarce but gaining a higher profile on Hawaiian Island menus.

Nairagi Striped marlin, also called *au,* good as sashimi and in poke, and often substituted for ahi in raw-fish products.

Onaga Ruby snapper, a luxury fish, versatile, moist, and flaky.

Ono Wahoo, firmer and drier than the snappers, often served grilled and in sandwiches.

Opah Moonfish, rich and fatty, and versatile—cooked, raw, smoked, and broiled.

Opakapaka Pink snapper, light, flaky, and luxurious, suited for sashimi, poaching, sautéing, and baking; the best-known upscale fish.

Papio Jack trevally, light, firm, and flavorful, and favored in Island cookery.

Shutome Broadbill swordfish, of beeflike texture and rich flavor.

Tombo Albacore tuna, with a high fat content, suitable for grilling.

Uhu Parrotfish, most often encountered steamed, Chinese style.

Uku Gray snapper of clear, pale-pink flesh, delicately flavored and moist.

Ulua Large jack trevally, firm-fleshed and versatile.

WHEN TO GO

Most visitors don't come to Hawaii when the weather's best in the islands; rather, they come when it's at its worst everywhere else. Thus, the **high season**—when prices are up and resorts are often booked to capacity—is generally from mid-December through March or mid-April. The last 2 weeks of December, in particular, are the prime time for travel to Hawaii. If you're planning a holiday trip, make your reservations as early as possible, expect crowds, and prepare to pay top dollar for accommodations, car rentals, and airfare.

The **off-season,** when the best rates are available and the islands are less crowded, is spring (mid-Apr to mid-June) and fall (Sept to mid-Dec)—a paradox because these are the best seasons to be in Hawaii, in terms of reliably great weather. If you're looking to save money, or if you just want to avoid the crowds, this is the time to visit. Hotel rates and airfares tend to be significantly lower, and good packages are often available.

Note: If you plan to come to Hawaii between the last week in April and early May, be sure you book your accommodations, interisland air reservations, and car rentals in advance. In Japan, the last week of April is called **Golden Week** because three Japanese holidays take place one after the other. Waikiki is especially busy with Japanese tourists during this time, but the neighboring islands also see dramatic increases.

Due to the large number of families traveling in **summer** (June–Aug), you won't get the fantastic bargains of spring and fall. However, you'll still do much better on packages, airfare, and accommodations than you will in the winter months.

Climate

Because Hawaii lies at the edge of the tropical zone, it technically has only two seasons, both of them warm. There's a dry season that corresponds to **summer** (Apr–Oct) and a rainy season in **winter** (Nov–Mar). It rains every day somewhere in the islands any time of the year, but the rainy season sometimes brings enough gray weather to spoil your tanning opportunities. Fortunately, it seldom rains in one spot for more than 3 days straight.

The **year-round temperature** doesn't vary much. At the beach, the average daytime high in summer is 85°F (29°C), while the average daytime high in winter is 78°F (26°C); nighttime lows are usually about 10°F cooler. But how warm it is on any given day really depends on *where* you are on the island.

Each island has a leeward side (the side sheltered from the wind) and a windward side (the side that gets the wind's full force). The **leeward** sides (the west and south) are usually hot and dry, while the **windward** sides (east and north) are generally cooler and moist. When you want arid, sunbaked, desertlike

Waikiki's Average Temperature & Number of Rainy Days

MONTH	HIGH (°F/°C)	LOW (°F/°C)	WATER TEMP. (°F/°C)	RAINY DAYS
JAN	80/27	70/21	75/24	10
FEB	80/27	66/19	74/23	9
MAR	81/27	66/19	74/23	9
APR	82/28	69/21	75/24	9
MAY	84/29	70/21	76/24	7
JUNE	86/30	72/22	77/25	6
JULY	87/31	73/23	78/26	7
AUG	88/31	74/23	79/26	6
SEPT	88/31	74/23	80/27	7
OCT	86/30	72/22	79/26	9
NOV	84/29	70/21	77/25	9
DEC	81/27	67/19	76/24	10

weather, go leeward. When you want lush, wet, junglelike weather, go windward.

Sun All the Time

Your best bets for total year-round sun are **Waikiki Beach** and the **Ko Olina** (southwest) coast of Oahu.

Hawaii is also full of **microclimates,** thanks to its interior valleys, coastal plains, and mountain peaks. So if the weather doesn't suit you, just go to the other side of the island—or head into the hills.

On rare occasions, the weather can be disastrous, as when Hurricane Iniki crushed Kauai in September 1992 with 225 mph winds. Tsunamis have swept Hilo and the south shore of Oahu. But those are extreme exceptions. Mostly, one day follows another here in glorious, sunny procession, each quite like the other.

Holidays

When Hawaii observes holidays (especially those over a long weekend), travel between the islands increases, interisland airline seats are fully booked, rental cars are at a premium, and hotels and restaurants are busier.

Federal, state, and county government offices are closed on all federal holidays.

State and county offices are also closed on local holidays, including Prince Kuhio Day (Mar 26), honoring the birthday of Hawaii's first delegate to the U.S. Congress; King Kamehameha Day (June 11), a statewide holiday commemorating Kamehameha the Great, who united the islands and ruled from 1795 to 1819; and Admissions Day (third Fri in Aug), which honors the admittance of Hawaii as the 50th state on August 21, 1959.

Other special days celebrated in Hawaii by many people but which involve no closing of federal, state, and county offices are the Chinese New Year (which can fall in Jan or Feb; in 2012, it's Jan 23 and the year of the Dragon; in 2013, it's Feb 10 and the year of the Snake), Girls' Day (Mar 3), Buddha's Birthday (Apr 8), Father Damien's Day (Apr 15), Boys' Day (May 5), Samoan Flag Day (in Aug), Aloha Festivals (Sept–Oct), and Pearl Harbor Day (Dec 7).

Oahu Calendar of Events

Please note that, as with any schedule of upcoming events, the following information is subject to change; always confirm the details before you plan your trip around an event.

For an exhaustive list of events beyond those listed here, check http://events. frommers.com, where you'll find a searchable, up-to-the-minute roster of what's happening in cities all over the world.

JANUARY

Volcom Pipeline Pro, Banzai Pipeline, North Shore. Competition is judged on the best wave selection and maneuvers on the wave. Call ℂ **760/722-7777** (www. surftransworld.net). January or February.

Sony Open, Waialae Country Club. A $1.2-million PGA golf event featuring the top men in golf. Call ℂ **808/792-9300.** Early to mid-January.

Pacific Islands Arts Festival at Thomas Square, across from Honolulu Academy of Arts, Honolulu. More than 100 artists and handicraft artisans, entertainment, food, and demonstrations fill the day. Admission is free.

Call ☏ **808/696-6717.** Mid-January.

Narcissus Festival, Honolulu. Taking place around the Chinese New Year, this cultural festival includes a queen pageant, cooking demonstrations, and a cultural fair. Call ☏ **808/533-3181.**

Sand Castle Building Contest, Kailua Beach Park. Students from the University of Hawaii School of Architecture compete against professional architects to see who can build the best, most unusual, and most outrageous sand sculpture. Call ☏ **808/956-7225.**

Punahou School Carnival, Punahou School, Honolulu. This event has everything you can imagine in a school carnival, from high-speed rides to homemade jellies. All proceeds go to scholarship funds for Hawaii's most prestigious high school. Call ☏ **808/944-5753.** Early to mid-February.

Buffalo's Big Board Classic, Makaha Beach. This contest involves traditional Hawaiian surfing, long boarding, and canoe-surfing. Call ☏ **808/951-7877.** Depending on surf conditions, it can be held in February or March.

St. Patrick's Day Parade, Waikiki (Fort DeRussy to Kapiolani Park). Bagpipers, bands, clowns, and marching groups parade through the heart of Waikiki, with lots of Irish-style celebrating all day. Call ☏ **808/536-4138** (O'Toole's Pub). March 17.

Prince Kuhio Day Celebrations. On this state holiday, various festivals throughout Hawaii celebrate the birth of Jonah Kuhio Kalanianaole, who was born on March 26, 1871, and elected to Congress in 1902. Call ☏ **808/240-6369.** March 26.

Easter Sunrise Service, National Memorial Cemetery of the Pacific, Punchbowl Crater, Honolulu. For a century, people have gathered at this famous cemetery for Easter sunrise services. Call ☏ **808/532-3720.** April 8, 2012.

Outrigger Canoe Season. From May to September, canoe paddlers across the state participate in outrigger canoe races nearly every weekend. Call ☏ **808/383-7798,** or go to **www.y2kanu.com** for this year's schedule of events.

Lei Day Celebrations, various locations. May Day is Lei Day in Hawaii, celebrated with lei-making contests, pageantry, arts and crafts. Call ☏ **808/768-3041** or go to **www.honolulu.gov/ parks/programs/leiday** for Oahu events. May 1.

World Fire-Knife Dance Championships & Samoa Festival, Polynesian Cultural Center, Laie. Junior and adult fire-knife dancers from around the world converge on the center for one of the most amazing performances you'll ever see. Authentic Samoan food and cultural festivities round out the fun. Call ☏ **808/293-3333** or go to **www.polynesian culturalcenter.com.** Mid-May.

Lantern Floating Hawaii, Magic Island at Ala Moana Beach Park, Honolulu. The Shinnyoen Temple's ceremonial floating of some 700 lanterns takes place at sunset, representing an appeal for peace and harmony. Hula and music follow the ceremony. Call ☏ **808/942-1848** or go to **www.lanternfloating hawaii.com.** Memorial Day weekend.

Memorial Day, National Memorial Cemetery of the Pacific, Punchbowl Crater, Honolulu. The armed forces hold a ceremony recognizing those who died for their country, beginning at 9am. Call ☏ **808/532-3720.** Last Monday in May.

Daylight Saving Time

Since 1966, most of the United States has observed daylight saving time from the first Sunday in April to the last Sunday in October. In 2007, these dates changed, and now daylight saving time lasts from 2am on the second Sunday in March to 2am on the first Sunday in November. **Note that Hawaii does *not* observe** **daylight saving time.** So when daylight saving time is in effect in most of the U.S., Hawaii is 3 hours behind the West Coast and 6 hours behind the East Coast. When the U.S. reverts to standard time in November, Hawaii is 2 hours behind the West Coast and 5 hours behind the East Coast.

JUNE

King Kamehameha Celebration. This state holiday (officially June 11, but celebrated on weekend closest to June 11) features a massive floral parade, *hoolaulea* (party), and much more. Call ✆ **808/586-0333** or go to **www.kamehameha daycelebration.org**. Most events in 2012 will be held June 9 to 10.

King Kamehameha Hula Competition, Neal Blaisdell Center, Honolulu. This is one of the top hula competitions in the world, with dancers from as far away as Japan. It's held the third weekend in June. Call ✆ **808/586-0333** or go to **www.hulacomp.com**. Mid- to late June.

JULY

Fourth of July Fireworks, Desiderio and Sills Field, Schofield Barracks. A free daylong celebration, with entertainment, food, and games, ends with a spectacular fireworks show. Call ✆ **808/655-0110.** July 4.

Molokai to Oahu Paddleboard Race, starts on Molokai and finishes on Oahu. Some 70 participants, from an international field, journey to Molokai to compete in this 32-mile race, considered to be the world championship of long-distance paddleboard racing. The race begins at Kepuhi Beach on Molokai at 7am and finishes at Maunaloa Bay on Oahu around 12:30pm. Call ✆ **808/638-8208.** Mid-to late July.

Ukulele Festival, Kapiolani Park Bandstand, Waikiki. This free concert features a ukulele orchestra of some 600 students, ages 4 to 92. Hawaii's top musicians all pitch in. Call ✆ **808/732-3739** or go to **www.roysakuma.net**. Late July.

Queen Liliuokalani Keiki Hula Competition, Neal Blaisdell Center, Honolulu. More than 500 *keiki* (children) representing 22 *halau* (hula schools) from the islands compete in this dance fest. The event is broadcast a week later on KITV-TV. Call ✆ **808/521-6905.** Late July.

Hawaii State Farm Fair, Bishop Museum, Honolulu. The annual state fair is a great one: It features displays of Hawaii agricultural products (including orchids), educational and cultural exhibits, entertainment, and local-style food. Call ✆ **808/847-3511** or go to **www.bishopmuseum. org**. Late July or early August.

Transpac Yacht Race. This international yacht race is held during July in odd-numbered years only (2013, 2015, and so on). Sailors from the United States, Japan, Australia, New Zealand, Europe, and Hawaii race from Long Beach to Honolulu. They then participate in a series of races around the state. Call ✆ **808/944-9666** or go to **www. transpacrace.com**.

AUGUST

Duke's OceanFest Hoolaulea, Waikiki. Nine days of water-oriented competitions and festivities celebrate the life of Duke Kahanamoku. Events include the Hawaii Paddleboard Championship, the Pro Surf Longboard Contest, the International Tandem Surfing Championship, the Corona Extra Duke Volleyball Classic, a Surf Polo Tournament, and a Hawaiian luau (the luau is $60 at the door). Call ☎ **808/545-4880** or go to **www.dukefoundation. org**. Mid-August.

Admissions Day. Hawaii became the 50th state on August 21, 1959. On the third Friday in August, the state takes a holiday (all state-related facilities are closed).

Hawaiian Slack-Key Guitar Festival Gabby Style, Queen Kapiolani Park Bandstand, Waikiki. The best of Hawaii's folk music—slack-key guitar— performed by the best musicians in Hawaii. It takes place from noon to 6pm and is absolutely free. Call ☎ **808/226-2697** or go to **www. slackkeyfestival.com**. Third Sunday in August.

SEPTEMBER
Aloha Festivals, various locations. Parades and other events celebrate Hawaiian culture and friendliness through-out the state. Call ☎ **808/589-1771** or go to **www.alohafestivals.com**.

OCTOBER
Hana Hoohiwahiwa O Kaiulani, Sheraton Princess Kaiulani, Waikiki. This hotel commemo-rates the birthday of its namesake, Princess Victoria Kaiulani, with a week of special activities: complimentary hula les-sons, lei-making, ukulele lessons, and more. The crowning touch is the Princess Kaiulani Keiki Hula Festival, which showcases performances by more than 200 *keiki* from *halau* on the island of Oahu. Admission is free. Call ☎ **808/922-5811.** Late October.

Hawaii International Film Festival, various locations throughout the state. This cinema festival with a cross-cultural spin features filmmakers from Asia, the Pacific Islands, and the United States. Call ☎ **808/550-8457** or go to **www.hiff.org**. First 2 weeks in November.

NOVEMBER
Triple Crown of Surfing, North Shore. The world's top professional surfers compete in events for more than $1 million in prize money. Go to **www. triplecrownofsurfing. com**. Held between mid-November and mid-De-cember, whenever condi-tions are best.

DECEMBER
Festival of Lights, Honolulu Hale, Honolulu. The mayor throws the switch to light up the 40-foot-tall Norfolk pine and other trees in front of Honolulu Hale. Call ☎ **808/768-4385** or go to **www.hawaii forvisitors.com**. Early December.

Honolulu Marathon, Honolulu. This is one of the largest marathons in the world, with more than 30,000 competitors. Call ☎ **808/734-7200** or go to **www.honolulu marathon.org**. Second Sunday in December.

Sheraton Hawaii Bowl, Aloha Stadium, Honolulu. A Pac 10 team plays a Big 12 team in this na-tionally televised col-legiate football classic. Call ☎ **808/483-2500.** Christmas Eve day.

THE LAY OF THE LAND

The first Hawaiian islands were born of violent volcanic eruptions that took place deep beneath the ocean's surface about 70 million years ago—more than 200 million years after the major continental land masses had been formed. As soon as the islands emerged, Mother Nature's fury began to carve beauty from bar-ren rock. Untiring volcanoes spewed forth rivers of fire that cooled into stone. Severe tropical storms, some with hurricane-force winds, battered and blasted the cooling lava rock into a series of shapes. Ferocious earthquakes flattened, shattered, and reshaped the islands into precipitous valleys, jagged cliffs, and recumbent flatlands. Monstrous surf and gigantic tidal waves rearranged and polished the lands above and below the reaches of the tide.

It took millions of years for nature to shape the familiar form of Diamond Head on Oahu, Maui's majestic peak of Haleakala, the waterfalls of Molokai's northern side, the reefs of Hulopoe Bay on Lanai, and the lush rainforests of the Big Island. The result is an island chain like no other—a tropical dreamscape of a landscape rich in flora and fauna, surrounded by a vibrant underwater world.

The Flora of the Islands

Hawaii is filled with sweet-smelling flowers, lush vegetation, and exotic plant life. Here's a brief rundown.

AFRICAN TULIP TREES Even from afar, you can see the flaming red flowers on these large trees, which can grow to be more than 50 feet tall. The buds hold water, and Hawaiian children use the flowers as water pistols.

ANGEL'S TRUMPETS These small trees can grow up to 20 feet tall, with an abundance of large (up to 10-in. diameter) pendants—white or pink flowers that resemble, well, trumpets. The Hawaiians call them *nana-honua,* which means "earth gazing." The flowers, which bloom continually from early spring to late fall, have a musky scent. ***Warning:*** All parts of the plant are poisonous and contain a strong narcotic.

ANTHURIUMS Anthuriums originally came from the tropical Americas and the Caribbean islands. More than 550 species exist, but the most popular are the heart-shaped red, orange, pink, white, and purple flowers with tail-like spathes. Look for the heart-shaped green leaves in shaded areas. These exotic plants have no scent but will last several weeks as cut flowers.

BANYAN TREES Among the world's largest trees, banyans have branches that grow out and away from the trunk, forming descending roots that grow down to the ground to feed and form additional trunks, making the tree very stable during tropical storms.

BIRDS-OF-PARADISE These natives of Africa have become something of a trademark of Hawaii. They're easily recognizable by the orange and blue flowers nestled in gray-green bracts, looking somewhat like birds in flight.

BOUGAINVILLEA Originally from Brazil, these vines feature colorful, tissue-thin bracts, ranging in color from majestic purple to fiery orange, that hide tiny white flowers.

BREADFRUIT TREES A large tree—more than 60 feet tall—with broad, sculpted, dark-green leaves, the famous breadfruit produces a round, head-size green fruit that's a staple in the diets of all Polynesians. When roasted or baked, the whitish-yellow meat tastes somewhat like a sweet potato.

BROMELIADS There are more than 1,400 species of bromeliads, of which the pineapple plant is the best known. "Bromes," as they're affectionately called, are generally spiky plants ranging in size from a few inches to several feet in diameter. They're popular not only for their unusual foliage, but also for their strange and wonderful flowers. Used widely in landscaping and interior decoration, especially in resort areas, bromeliads are found on every island.

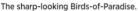
The sharp-looking Birds-of-Paradise.

Hibiscus in bloom.

COFFEE Hawaii is the only state that produces coffee commercially. Coffee is an evergreen shrub with shiny, waxy, dark-green pointed leaves. The flower is a small, fragrant white blossom that develops into half-inch berries that turn bright red when ripe. Oahu's North Shore has a thriving coffee plantation.

GINGER White and yellow ginger flowers are perhaps the most fragrant in Hawaii. Usually found in clumps growing 4 to 7 feet tall in areas blessed by rain, these sweet-smelling, 3-inch-wide flowers are composed of three dainty petal-like stamens and three long, thin petals. Ginger was introduced to Hawaii in the 19th century from the Indonesia-Malaysia area. Look for white and yellow ginger from late spring to fall. If you see ginger on the side of the road, stop and pick a few blossoms—your car will be filled with a divine fragrance the rest of the day.

Other members of the ginger family frequently seen in Hawaii include red, shell, and torch ginger. Red ginger consists of tall green stalks with foot-long red "flower heads." The red "petals" are actually bracts, which protect the 1-inch-long white flowers. Red ginger, which does not share the heavenly smell of white ginger, lasts a week or longer when cut. Look for red ginger from spring through late fall. Shell ginger, which originated in India and Burma, thrives in cool, wet mountain forests. These plants, with their pearly white, clamshell-like blossoms, bloom from spring to fall.

Perhaps the most exotic ginger is the red or pink torch ginger. Cultivated in Malaysia as seasoning, torch ginger rises directly out of the ground. The flower stalks, which are about 5 to 8 inches in length, resemble the fire of a lighted torch. This is one of the few types of ginger that can bloom year-round.

HELICONIA Some 80 species of the colorful heliconia family came to Hawaii from the Caribbean and Central and South America. The bright yellow, red, green, and orange bracts overlap and appear to unfold like origami birds.

2

OAHU IN DEPTH

The Lay of the Land

The most obvious heliconia to spot is the lobster claw, which resembles a string of boiled crustacean pincers. Another prolific heliconia is the parrot's beak: Growing to about hip height, it's composed of bright-orange flower bracts with black tips. Look for parrot's beaks in spring and summer.

HIBISCUS The 4- to 6-inch hibiscus flowers bloom year-round and come in a range of colors, from lily white to lipstick red. The flowers resemble crepe paper, with stamens and pistils protruding spirelike from the center. Hibiscus hedges can grow up to 15 feet tall. The yellow hibiscus is Hawaii's official state flower.

JACARANDA Beginning around March and sometimes lasting until early May, these huge lacy-leaved trees metamorphose into large clusters of spectacular lavender-blue sprays. The bell-shaped flowers drop quickly, leaving a majestic purple carpet beneath the tree.

MACADAMIA A transplant from Australia, macadamia nuts have become a commercial crop in recent decades in Hawaii, especially on the Big Island and Maui. The large trees—up to 60 feet tall—bear a hard-shelled nut encased in a leathery husk, which splits open and dries when the nut is ripe.

MONKEYPOD TREES The monkeypod is one of Hawaii's most majestic trees; it grows more than 80 feet tall and 100 feet across. Seen near older homes and in parks, the leaves of the monkeypod drop in February and March. Its wood is a favorite of woodworking artisans.

NIGHT-BLOOMING CEREUS Look along rock walls for this spectacular night-blooming flower. Originally from Central America, the vinelike member of the cactus family has green scalloped edges and produces foot-long white flowers that open as darkness falls and wither as the sun rises. The plant also bears an edible red fruit.

ORCHIDS To many minds, nothing says Hawaii more than orchids. The most widely grown variety—and the major source of flowers for leis and garnish for tropical libations—is the vanda orchid. The vandas used in Hawaii's commercial flower industry are generally lavender or white, but they grow in a rainbow of colors, shapes, and sizes. The orchids used for corsages are the large, delicate cattleya; the ones used in floral arrangements—you'll probably see them in your hotel lobby—are usually dendrobiums.

PANDANUS Called *hala* by Hawaiians, pandanus is native to Polynesia. Thanks to its thick trunk, stiltlike supporting roots, and crown of long, swordlike leaves, the hala tree is easy to recognize. In what is quickly becoming a dying art, Hawaiians weave the *lau* (leaves) of the hala into hats, baskets, mats, bags, and the like.

PLUMERIA Also known as frangipani, this sweet-smelling, five-petal flower, found in clusters on trees, is the most popular choice of lei makers. The Singapore plumeria has five creamy-white petals, with a touch of yellow in the center. Another popular variety, *ruba*—with flowers from soft pink to flaming red—is also used in leis. When picking plumeria, be careful of the sap from the flower—it's poisonous and can stain clothes.

PROTEA Originally from South Africa, this unusual oversize shrub comes in more than 40 different varieties. The flowers of one species resemble pincushions; those of another look like a bouquet of feathers. Once dried, proteas will last for years.

SILVERSWORD This very uncommon and unusual plant is seen only on the Big Island and in the Haleakala Crater on Maui. The rare relative of the sunflower family blooms between July and September. The silversword in bloom is a fountain of red-petaled, daisylike flowers that turn silver soon after blooming.

TARO Around pools, near streams, and in neatly planted fields, you'll see these green heart-shaped leaves, whose dense roots are a Polynesian staple. The ancient Hawaiians pounded the roots into poi. Originally from Sri Lanka, taro not only is a food crop, but is also grown for ornamental reasons.

The Fauna of the Islands

When the first Polynesians arrived in Hawaii between A.D. 400 and 800, scientists say they found some 67 varieties of endemic Hawaiian birds, a third of which are now believed to be extinct. They did not find any reptiles, amphibians, mosquitoes, lice, fleas, or even a cockroach.

There were only two endemic mammals: the hoary bat and the monk seal. The **hoary bat** must have accidentally blown to Hawaii at some point, from either North or South America. It can still be seen during its early evening forays, especially around the Kilauea Crater on the Big Island.

The **Hawaiian monk seal,** a relative of warm-water seals found in the Caribbean and the Mediterranean, was nearly slaughtered into extinction for its skin and oil during the 19th century. These seals have recently experienced a minor population explosion; sometimes they even turn up at various beaches throughout the state. They're protected under federal law by the Marine Mammals Protection Act. If you're fortunate enough to see a monk seal, just look; don't disturb one of Hawaii's living treasures.

The first Polynesians brought a few animals from home: dogs, pigs, and chickens (all were for eating), as well as rats (stowaways). All four species are still found in the Hawaiian wild today.

BIRDS

More species of native birds have become extinct in Hawaii in the last 200 years than anywhere else on the planet. Of 67 native species, 23 are extinct and 30 are endangered. Even the Hawaiian crow, the **alala,** is threatened.

The **ae'o,** or Hawaiian stilt—a 16-inch-long bird with a black head, black coat, white underside, and long pink legs—can be found in protected wetlands.

Hawaii's state bird is the **nene.** It's being brought back from the brink of extinction through strenuous protection laws and captive breeding. A relative of the Canada goose, the nene stands about 2 feet high and has a black head and yellow cheeks. The approximately 500 nene in existence can be seen in only three places: on Maui at Haleakala National Park, and on the Big Island at Mauna Kea State Recreation Area bird sanctuary and on the slopes of Mauna Kea.

A newborn nene chick.

The Hawaiian short-eared owl, the **pueo,** which grows to between 12 and 17 inches, can be seen at dawn and dusk on Kauai, Maui, and the Big Island. According to legend, spotting a pueo is a good omen.

SEA LIFE

Approximately 680 species of fish are known to inhabit the waters

> ### 💬 Leapin' Lizards!
>
> **Geckos** are harmless, soft-skinned, insect-eating lizards that come equipped with suction pads on their feet, enabling them to climb walls and windows to reach tasty insects such as mosquitoes and cockroaches. You'll see them on windows outside a lighted room at night or hear their cheerful chirp.

around the Hawaiian Islands. Of those, approximately 450 species stay close to the reef and inshore areas.

CORAL The reefs surrounding Hawaii are made up of various coral and algae. The living coral grows through sunlight that feeds a specialized algae, which, in turn, allows the development of the coral's calcareous skeleton. The reef, which takes thousands of years to develop, attracts and supports fish and crustaceans, which use it for food and habitat. Mother Nature can batter the reef with a strong storm, but humans have proven far more destructive.

The corals most frequently seen in Hawaii are hard, rocklike formations named for their familiar shapes: antler, cauliflower, finger, plate, and razor coral. Some coral appears soft, such as tube coral; it can be found in the ceilings of caves. Black coral, which resembles winter-bare trees or shrubs, is found at depths of more than 100 feet.

REEF FISH Of the approximately 450 types of reef fish here, about 27% are native to Hawaii and are found nowhere else in the world. During the millions of years it took for the islands to sprout up from the sea, ocean currents—mainly from Southeast Asia—carried thousands of marine animals and plants to Hawaii's reef; of those, approximately 100 species adapted and thrived. You're likely to spot one or more of the following fish while underwater.

Angelfish can be distinguished by the spine, located low on the gill plate. These fish are very shy; several species live in colonies close to coral.

Blennies are small, elongated fish, ranging from 2 to 10 inches long, with the majority in the 3- to 4-inch range. Blennies are so small that they can live in tide pools; you might have a hard time spotting one.

Butterflyfish, among the most colorful of the reef fish, are usually seen in pairs (scientists believe they mate for life) and appear to spend most of their day feeding. There are 22 species of butterflyfish, of which three (bluestripe, lemon or milletseed, and multiband or pebbled butterflyfish) are endemic. Most butterflyfish have a dark band through the eye and a spot near the tail resembling an eye, meant to confuse their predators (moray eels love to lunch on them).

Moray and **conger eels** are the most common eels seen in Hawaii. Morays are usually docile except when provoked or when there's food around. Unfortunately, some morays have been fed by divers and now associate divers with food; thus, they can become aggressive. But most morays like to keep to themselves. While morays may look menacing, conger eels look downright happy, with big lips and pectoral fins (situated so that they look like big ears) that give them the appearance of a perpetually smiling

Butterflyfish on parade.

Sea turtles are some of Hanauma Bay's denizens.

face. Conger eels have crushing teeth so they can feed on crustaceans; because they're sloppy eaters, they usually live with shrimp and crabs that feed off the crumbs they leave.

Parrotfish, one of the largest and most colorful of the reef fish, can grow up to 40 inches long. They're easy to spot—their front teeth are fused together, protruding like buck teeth that allow them to feed by scraping algae from rocks and coral. The rocks and coral pass through the parrotfish's system, resulting in fine sand. In fact, most of the white sand found in Hawaii is parrotfish waste; one large parrotfish can produce a ton of sand a year. Native parrotfish species include yellowbar, regal, and spectacled.

Scorpion fish are what scientists call "ambush predators": They hide under camouflaged exteriors and ambush their prey. Several kinds sport a venomous dorsal spine. These fish don't have a gas bladder, so when they stop swimming, they sink—that's why you usually find them "resting" on ledges and on the ocean bottom. They're not aggressive, but be very careful where you put your hands and feet in the water so as to avoid those venomous spines.

Surgeonfish, sometimes called *tang,* get their name from the scalpel-like spines located on each side of the body near the base of the tail. Several surgeonfish, such as the brightly colored yellow tang, are boldly colored; others are adorned in more conservative shades of gray, brown, or black. The only endemic surgeonfish—and the most abundant in Hawaiian waters—is the convict tang, a pale white fish with vertical black stripes (similar to a convict's uniform).

Wrasses are a very diverse family of fish, ranging in length from 2 to 15 inches. Wrasses can change gender from female to male. Some have brilliant coloration that changes as they age. Several types of wrasse are endemic to Hawaii: Hawaiian cleaner, shortnose, belted, and gray (or old woman).

GAME FISH Hawaii is known around the globe as *the* place for big-game fish—marlin, swordfish, and tuna. Six kinds of **billfish** are found in the offshore waters around the islands: Pacific blue marlin, black marlin, sailfish,

A humpback whale showing off.

broadbill swordfish, striped marlin, and shortbill spearfish. Hawaii billfish range in size from the 20-pound shortbill spearfish and striped marlin to the 1,805-pound Pacific blue marlin, the largest marlin ever caught with rod and reel in the world.

Tuna ranges in size from small (1 lb. or less) mackerel tuna used as bait (Hawaiians call them *oioi*) to 250-pound yellowfin ahi tuna. Other local species of tuna are big-eye, albacore, kawakawa, and skipjack.

Other types of fish, also excellent for eating, include **mahimahi** (also known as dolphin fish or dorado), in the 20- to 70-pound range; **rainbow runner,** from 15 to 30 pounds; and **wahoo,** from 15 to 80 pounds. Shoreline fishermen are always on the lookout for **trevally** (the state record for a giant trevally is 191 lb.), **bonefish, ladyfish, threadfin, leatherfish,** and **goatfish.** Bottom fishermen pursue a range of **snapper**—red, pink, gray, and others—as well as **sea bass** (the state record is a whopping 563 lb.) and **amberjack** (which weigh up to 100 lb.).

WHALES **Humpback whales** are popular visitors who come to Hawaii to mate and calve every year, beginning in November and staying until spring—April or so—when they return to Alaska. On every island, you can take winter whale-watching cruises that will let you observe these magnificent leviathans up close. You can also spot them from shore—humpbacks grow to up to 45 feet long, so when one breaches (jumps out of the water), you can see it for miles.

Humpbacks are among the biggest whales found in Hawaiian waters, but other whales—such as **pilot, sperm, false killer, melon-headed, pygmy killer,** and **beaked**—can be seen year-round, especially in the calm waters off the Big Island's Kona Coast.

SHARKS Yes, there *are* sharks in Hawaii, but you more than likely won't see one unless you're specifically looking. About 40 different species of sharks inhabit the waters surrounding Hawaii, ranging from the totally harmless

whale shark (at 60 ft., the world's largest fish), which has no teeth and is so docile that it frequently lets divers ride on its back, to the not-so-docile, extremely uncommon **great white shark.** The most common sharks seen in Hawaii are **white-tip** or **gray reef sharks** (about 5 ft. long) and **black-tip reef sharks** (about 6 ft. long).

Hawaii's Ecosystem Problems

Officials at Hawaii Volcanoes National Park on the Big Island saw a potential problem a few decades ago with people taking a few rocks home with them as "souvenirs." To prevent this problem from escalating, the park rangers created a legend that the fiery volcano goddess, Pele, would punish these souvenir-seekers with bad luck. There used to be a display case in the park's visitor center filled with letters from people who had taken rocks from the volcano, relating stories of all the bad luck that followed. Most begged Pele's forgiveness and instructed the rangers to please return the rock to the exact location that was its original home.

Unfortunately, Hawaii's other ecosystem problems can't be handled as easily.

MARINE LIFE Hawaii's beautiful and abundant marine life has attracted so many visitors that they threaten to overwhelm it. A great example of this is Oahu's **Hanauma Bay.** Crowds flock to this marine preserve, which features calm, protected swimming and snorkeling areas loaded with tropical reef fish. Its popularity has forced government officials to limit admissions and charge an entrance fee. Commercial tour operators have also been restricted.

Hawaii's **reefs** have faced increasing impact over the years as well. Runoff of soil and chemicals from construction, agriculture, and erosion can blanket and choke a reef, which needs sunlight to survive. Human contact with the reef can also upset the ecosystem. Coral, the basis of the reef system, is very fragile; snorkelers and divers grabbing onto it can break off pieces that took decades to form. Feeding the fish can also upset the balance of the ecosystem (not to mention upsetting the digestive systems of the fish). In areas where they're fed, the normally shy reef fish become more aggressive, surrounding divers and demanding food.

FLORA The rainforests are among Hawaii's most fragile environments. Any intrusion—from hikers carrying seeds on their shoes to the rooting of wild boars—can upset the delicate balance of these complete ecosystems. In recent years, development has moved closer and closer to the rainforests.

FAUNA The biggest impact on the fauna in Hawaii is the decimation of native birds by feral animals, which have destroyed the bird's habitats, and by mongooses that have eaten the birds' eggs and young. Government officials are vigilant about snakes because of the potential damage they can do to the remaining bird life.

A recent pest introduced to Hawaii is the coqui frog. That loud noise you hear after dark, especially on the eastern side of the Big Island and various parts of Maui, including the Kapalua Resort area and on the windward side of the island, is the cry of the male coqui frog looking for a mate. A native of Puerto Rico, where the frogs are kept in check by snakes, the coqui frog came to Hawaii in some plant material, found no natural enemies, and has spread across the Big Island and Maui. A chorus of several hundred coqui frogs is deafening (it's been measured at 163 decibels, or the noise level of a jet engine from 100 ft.). In some places, like Akaka Falls, on the Big Island, there are so many frogs that they are now chirping during daylight hours.

RESPONSIBLE TRAVEL

If there is one place on the planet that seems ideally suited for ecotourism and sustainable travel, it's Hawaii, a place people visit because of the ecology—the ocean, the beach, the mountains, and overall beauty of the place. It seems only natural that the maintenance of its environment would be a concern, both to the people who live there and the visitors who come to enjoy all its ecosystem has to offer.

In fact, Hawaii has a long history of environmental stewardship. The ancient Hawaiians not only knew about sustainability, but also practiced it in their daily lives. They had to! When the ancient Hawaiians occupied the islands they did not have the luxury of "importing" goods from anywhere else. They had the land under their feet and the ocean to gain subsistence from, and those resources had to last not only for their own lifetime, but also for the lifetimes of generations to come. So these ancient people lived in harmony with the land and sea, and had a complex social structure that managed resources and forbid the taking of various resources during certain times of the year, to allow those resources to replenish themselves.

Now fast forward to the 21st century. Today we, the current stewards of the islands of Hawaii, are just beginning to appreciate just how wise and advanced the ancient Hawaiians were. In some ways, the state of Hawaii is a pioneer when it comes to the various ways it protects and saves its natural resources. (For example, Hawaii is second only to California in the number of marine reserves in the National System of Marine Protected Areas.) And yet in other ways, modern Hawaii still falls short of the ancient Hawaiians, whose unique system sustained, without imports, the entire population.

Ongoing Environmental Initiatives

The State of Hawaii has several excellent stewardship programs to preserve the ocean environment and its resources, such as Marine Life Conservation Districts (an ocean version of parks), Fishery Management Areas (where what you can take from the ocean is restricted), Fishery Replenishment Areas, and Estuarine Reserves. On land, there are corresponding programs to protect the environment from the Soil and Water Conservation District to Watershed Reserves.

In the visitor industry, the majority of hotels have adopted green practices, not only to save the environment, but also to save them money. Nearly every hotel in the state will have a card in your room asking you to really consider if you need a new towel or if you can hang it up and use it one more day. Various statewide organization have numerous programs recognizing hotels which are helping the environment, such as the Green Business Awards Program, which recently recognized the **Hyatt Regency Waikiki** for its Environmental Management System in 1,229 rooms, which installed 6,000 LED bulbs and fixtures throughout the hotel, re-lamping every guest room with CFL bulbs, creating a 1,428,325 kWh reduction in electricity use as well as a 4.5 million gallon reduction in water usage. Over the past 5 years, the Hyatt estimates a 20% reduction in their electricity, gas, and water usage.

Also recognized were the **J. W. Marriott Ihilani at Ko Olina** and the **Kahala Hotel and Resort.** The J. W. Marriott Ihilani has implemented green measures such as lighting retrofits and recycling, keeping 62 tons out of the landfill. The Kahala Hotel & Resort put the property's air-conditioning systems on an energy management program and installed ceiling fans in all guestrooms, which can be used as an alternative for A/C. The property also uses deep water wells to cool the refrigeration systems, saving them 380,000 kWh of electricity and 4.5 million gallons of water annually. Their CFL-bulb retrofit in all guestrooms resulted in an estimated reduction of 180,000 kWh per year. With the installation of high-efficiency water aerators and fixtures, the Kahala Hotel has estimated a 40% to 50% reduction in water usage.

Every island has recycling centers (varying from collection of recyclable bottles only to places that take everything); for a list of recycling centers close to where you will be staying, visit the website of the **Hawaii State Department of Health** (http://hi5deposit.com/redcenters.html).

Restaurants across the state are using more local products and produce than ever. Many proudly tell you that all of their products were grown, grazed, or caught within 100 miles of their restaurant. You can support this effort by asking the restaurant which items on its menu are grown or raised on the island, then ordering those (Kona coffee instead of coffee from Central America; local fish instead of imported seafood, and so on).

Below are some more helpful hints for travelers to Hawaii; keep these in mind during your adventure to the islands, so that your ecological footprint on Hawaii will be minimal.

WHAT VISITORS CAN DO IN & AROUND THE OCEAN

1. Do not touch anything in the ocean. In fact, unless you are standing on the sandy bottom where the waves roll into shore, try not to walk or stand on the ocean floor. The no-touch rule of thumb is not only for your protection—there are plenty of stinging, stabbing things out there that could turn your vacation into a nightmare—but also for the protection of the marine environment. Coral is composed of living things, which take years to grow, and a careless brush of your hand or foot could destroy them. Fragile habitats for marine critters can be damaged forever by your heavy foot.

2. Do not feed the fish, or any other marine creature. They have their own food and diet, and they can be irreparably harmed by your good intentions if you feed them "people food" or, even worse, some "fish food" you have purchased.

3. Leave the ocean and beach area clearer than you found it. If you see trash in the ocean (plastic bags, bottles, and so on) remove it. You may save the life of a fish, turtle, marine mammal, or even a seabird by removing that trash, which kills hundreds of marine inhabitants every year. The same thing is true of the beach: Pick up trash, even if it's not yours.

4. The beach is not an ashtray. Do not use the sand for your cigarette butts. How would you like someone using your living room carpet as his ashtray?

5. Look at, but don't approach, turtles or Hawaiian monk seals resting on the shoreline. The good news is that the number of turtles and Hawaiian monk

seals on the main Hawaiian Islands is increasing. But while visitors may not know it, both are protected by law. You must stay 100 feet away from them. So take photos, but do not attempt to get close to the resting sea creatures. (And no, they are not dead or injured, just lounging.)

6. If you plan to go fishing, practice catch and release. Let the fish live another day. Ask your charter boat captain if they practice catch and release; if they say no, book with someone else.

7. If you are environmentally conscious, we do not recommend that you rent jet skies, which have a significant environmental impact.

WHAT VISITORS CAN DO ON LAND

1. Don't litter. (This includes throwing a cigarette butt out of your car.)

2. Before you go hiking, in addition to the safety tips outlined on p. 287, scrub your hiking shoes (especially the soles) to get rid of seeds and soil.

3. When hiking, carry a garbage bag so you can carry out everything you carried in, including your litter. (And if you see other garbage on the trail, carry it out, too.)

4. Stay on the trail. Wandering off a trail is not only dangerous to you (you can get lost, fall off overgrown cliffs, or get injured by stepping into a hidden hole), but you could possibly carry invasive species into our native forests.

5. Do not pick flowers or plants along your hike. Just leave the environment the way you found it.

TRANSPORTATION CONCERNS

Most visitors coming to Hawaii seem to think "convertible" when they think of renting a car, or they think "SUV" for off-road adventures. If you're thinking "hybrid," you'll have to check your budget, because hybrids from car-rental agencies are not only hard to find, but extremely expensive in Hawaii. Car-rental agencies do have a variety of cars to rent, though, and you can make a point of selecting the car that gets the best gas mileage. Also, ask for a white car, as it will use less energy to air-condition than a dark-colored car.

QUESTIONS TO ponder

One of the toughest questions in Hawaii is "What is the carrying capacity of the islands?" How much can be built before Hawaii becomes overbuilt, or unable to support the increased infrastructure and increased population? How many people can Hawaii hold, and how many visitors, before the beaches are too crowded, the lifestyle is corrupted, and the islands have more concrete than open green spaces?

Along those same lines, the people of Hawaii are constantly debating cultural issues versus social issues. For example, current laws regarding ancient burial sites can stop, reroute, or delay construction projects ranging from building roads to shopping centers. How much do we protect and preserve versus how much do we allow new infrastructure or buildings to be built to meet modern wants and needs?

Volunteering on Vacation

If you are looking for a different type of experience during your next vacation to Hawaii, you might want to consider becoming a volunteer and leaving the islands a little nicer than when you arrived. People interested in volunteering at beach and ocean cleanups can contact the **University of Hawaii Sea Grant College Program** (✆ **808/397-2651**, ext. 256) or **Hawaii Wildlife Fund** (www.wildhawaii.org). For eco-volunteering on land, contact **Malama Hawaii** (http://malamahawaii.org/blog/category/volunteer), a statewide organization dedicated to *malama* (taking care) of the culture and environment of Hawaii. At this site you will find a range of opportunities on various islands, such as weeding gardens and potting plants in botanical gardens, restoring taro patches, cleaning up mountain streams, bird watching, and even hanging out at Waikiki Beach helping with a reef project.

Hawaiian Culture

One of Hawaii's most cherished resources is the Hawaiian culture. After years of being ignored, the Hawaiian culture is flourishing more than ever today. Part of the Hawaii school system are the Hawaiian emersion schools, where all children (not just Hawaiians) can attend schools from kindergarten through college taught in the Hawaiian language. And cultural events in Hawaii are very popular.

If you want to support Hawaiian culture, plan to attend such cultural events as Hawaiian music and dance performances (see the Calendar of Events, p. 44).

Search out locally owned establishments (look for our recommendations in this book). Attempt to buy souvenirs made in Hawaii by local residents (we have recommendations in the shopping chapter).

If you visit a cultural site, like an ancient *heiau* (temple), the protocol calls for reverence. Be as respectful as you would at a cathedral or church. Never climb or sit on rock walls at a *heiau*. Never take anything from a *heiau,* even rocks, and never pick flowers there. You may see offerings of flowers or fruit—do not disturb them.

HOW TO FIT IN LIKE A LOCAL

Most visitors to Hawaii want to fit in and be respectful of the local residents. The best way to do that is to be friendly and practice the same common courtesy that you do in your own neighborhood. If you smile and are polite to local residents, chances are they will smile back at you. There are a few things you might want to think about:

1. Be super polite when driving. People in Hawaii do not use their car horn as a comment on other people's driving. Most Hawaii residents use their car horn only as a greeting to a friend.

2. Another driving comment—you may be on vacation, but not everyone here is, so check your rearview mirror. If you are impeding traffic by driving slow, pull off the road. If you want to watch the sunset, pull off the road. If you have a long line of cars behind you, pull off the road.

3. Dress respectfully. Just because it's Hawaii and warm does not mean that it is acceptable to wear your swimwear into a restaurant. A good rule of thumb is to ask yourself: Would I wear this outfit to a restaurant or retail store at home?

4. Remember Hawaii is part of the United States, and is, in fact, a state. A good way to alienate local residents is to say something like "I'm from the States." Or "Back in the States, we do it this way."

SPECIAL-INTEREST TRIPS & GUIDED TOURS

If all you want is a fabulous beach and a perfectly mixed mai tai, then Hawaii has what you're looking for. But the islands' wealth of natural wonders is equally hard to resist; the year-round tropical climate and spectacular scenery tend to inspire almost everyone to get outside and explore.

If you don't have your own snorkel gear or other watersports equipment, or if you just don't feel like packing it, don't fret: Everything you'll need is available for rent in the islands. We discuss all kinds of places to rent or buy gear in the chapters that follow.

Setting Out on Your Own Versus Using an Outfitter

There are two ways to go: Plan all the details before you leave and either rent gear or schlep your stuff 2,500 miles across the Pacific, or go with an outfitter or a guide and let someone else worry about the details.

In Hawaii, it's often preferable to go with a local guide who is familiar with the conditions at both sea level and summit peaks, knows the land and its flora and fauna in detail, and has all the gear you'll need. It's also good to go with a guide if time is an issue or if you have specialized interests. If you really want to see native birds, for instance, an experienced guide will take you directly to the best areas for sightings. And many forests and valleys in the interior of the islands are either on private property or in wilderness preserves accessible only on guided tours. The downside? If you go with a guide, plan on spending at least $100 a day per person. We've recommended the best local outfitters and tour-guide operators in chapter 7.

But if you have the time, already own the gear, and love doing the research and planning, try exploring on your own. Chapter 7 discusses the best spots to set out on your own, from the top offshore snorkel and dive spots to great daylong hikes, as well as the federal, state, and county agencies that can help you with hikes on public property; we also list references for spotting birds, plants, and sea life. We recommend that you always use the resources available to inquire about weather, trail, or surf conditions; water availability; and other conditions before you take off on your adventure.

For hikers, a great alternative to hiring a private guide is taking a guided hike offered by the **Nature Conservancy of Hawaii,** 923 Nu'uanu Ave., Honolulu, HI 96817 (© **808/537-4508**); or the **Hawaii Chapter of the Sierra Club** (www.hi.sierraclub.org/oahu). Both organizations offer guided hikes in preserves and special areas during the year, as well as day- to weeklong work trips to restore habitats and trails and to root out invasive plants. It might not sound like a dream vacation to everyone, but it's a chance to see the "real" Hawaii—including wilderness areas that are ordinarily off-limits.

All Nature Conservancy hikes and work trips are free (donations are appreciated). However, you must reserve a spot for yourself, and a deposit is required for guided hikes to ensure that you'll show up; your deposit is refunded once you do. The hikes are generally twice a month on Oahu.

The Sierra Club offers weekly hikes on Oahu. They are led by certified Sierra Club volunteers and are classified as easy, moderate, or strenuous. These half- or all-day affairs cost $1 for Sierra Club members and $5 for nonmembers (bring exact change). For a copy of the club newsletter, which lists all outings and trail-repair work, visit the Sierra Club website.

Local ecotourism opportunities are also discussed in this chapter (p. 67). For more information, contact the **Hawaii Ecotourism Association** (© **877/300-7058;** www.hawaiiecotourism.org).

Using Activities Desks to Book Your Island Fun

If you're unsure of which activity or which outfitter or guide is the right one for you and your family, you might want to consider booking through a discount activities center or activities desk. Not only will they save you money, but good activities centers should also be able to help you find, say, the snorkel cruise that's right for you, or the luau that's most suitable for both you *and* the kids.

Remember, however, that it's in the activities agent's best interest to sign you up with outfitters from which they earn the most commission. Some agents have no qualms about booking you into any activity if it means an extra buck for them. If an agent tries to push a particular outfitter or activity too hard, be skeptical. Conversely, they'll try to steer you away from outfitters who don't offer big commissions. For example, Trilogy, the company that offers Maui's most popular snorkel cruises to Lanai (and the only one with rights to land at Lanai's Hulopoe Beach), offers only minimum commissions to agents and does not allow agents to offer any discounts at all. As a result, most activities desks will automatically try to steer you away from Trilogy.

Another word of warning: Stay away from activities centers that offer discounts as fronts for timeshare sales presentations. Using a free or discounted snorkel cruise or luau tickets as bait, they'll suck you into a 90-minute presentation—and try to get you to buy into a Hawaii timeshare in the process. Because their business is timeshares, not activities, they won't be as interested, or as knowledgeable, about which activities might be right for you.

Finally, you can reserve activities yourself and save the commission by booking via the Internet. Most outfitters offer 10% to 25% off their prices if you book online.

Outdoor Activities A to Z

Here's a brief rundown of the many outdoor activities available in Hawaii. For our recommendations on the best places to go, the best shops for renting equipment, and the best outfitters to use, see chapter 7.

BIRDING Many of Hawaii's tropical birds are found nowhere else on earth. There are curved-bill honeycreepers, black-winged red birds, and the rare o'o, whose yellow feathers Hawaiians once plucked to make royal capes. When you go birding, take along *A Field Guide to the Birds of Hawaii and the Tropical Pacific,* by H. Douglas Pratt, Phillip L. Bruner, and Delwyn G. Berett (1987).

BOATING Almost every type of nautical experience is available in the islands, from old-fashioned Polynesian outrigger canoes to America's Cup racing sloops to submarines. You'll find details on all these seafaring experiences in the section on "Watersports," p. 165.

No matter which type of vessel you choose, be sure to see the Hawaiian Islands from offshore if you can afford it. It's easy to combine multiple activities into one cruise: Lots of snorkel boats double as sightseeing cruises and, in winter, whale-watching cruises. The main harbor for visitor activities is Kewalo Basin, in Honolulu.

BODYBOARDING (BOOGIE BOARDING) & BODYSURFING Bodysurfing—riding the waves without a board, becoming one with the rolling water—is a way of life in Hawaii. Some bodysurfers just rely on hands to ride the waves; others use hand boards (flat, paddlelike gloves). For additional maneuverability, try a boogie board or bodyboard (also known as belly boards or *paipo* boards). These 3-foot-long boards support the upper part of your body and are very maneuverable in the water. Both bodysurfing and bodyboarding require a pair of open-heeled swim fins to help propel you through the water. The equipment is inexpensive and easy to carry, and both sports can be practiced in the small, gentle waves. See p. 165 for details on where to rent boards and where to go.

CAMPING Hawaii's year-round balmy climate makes camping a breeze. However, tropical campers should always be ready for rain, especially in Hawaii's wet winter season, but even in the dry summer season as well. And remember to bring a good mosquito repellent. If you're heading to the top of Hawaii's volcanoes, you'll need a down mummy bag. If you plan to camp on the beach, bring a mosquito net and a rain poncho. Always be prepared to deal with contaminated water (purify it by boiling, filtering, or by using iodine tablets) and the tropical sun (protect yourself with sunscreen, a hat, and a long-sleeved shirt). Also be sure to check out the "Health" section (p. 287) for hiking and camping tips.

There are many established campgrounds at beach parks, including Malaekahana Beach. For more details on getting regulations and camping information for any of Hawaii's national or state parks, see p. 173.

Hawaiian Trail and Mountain Club, P.O. Box 2238, Honolulu, HI 96804, offers an information packet on hiking and camping throughout the islands. Send $2 and a legal-size, self-addressed, stamped envelope for information. Another good source is the *Hiking/Camping Information Packet,* available from **Hawaii Geographic Maps and Books,** 49 S. Hotel St., Honolulu, HI 96813 (✆ **800/538-3950** or 808/538-3952; hawaii geographicsociety@gmail. com), for $7. The Society prefers that people contact them via email. The **University of Hawaii Press,** 2840 Kolowalu St., Honolulu, HI 96822 (✆ **808/956-8255;** www.uhpress.hawaii.edu), has an excellent selection of hiking, backpacking, and

---

📎 **Travel Tip**

When planning sunset activities, be aware that Hawaii, like other places close to the equator, has a very short (5–10 min.) twilight period after the sun sets. After that, it's dark. If you hike out to watch the sunset, be sure you can make it back quickly, or else take a flashlight.

bird-watching guides, especially *The Hiker's Guide to the Hawaiian Islands,* by Stuart M. Ball, Jr. (2000).

GOLF Nowhere else on earth can you tee off to whale spouts, putt under rainbows, and play around a live volcano. Hawaii has some of the world's top-rated golf courses. But be forewarned: Each course features hellish natural hazards, such as razor-sharp lava, gusty trade winds, an occasional wild pig, and the tropical heat. And greens fees tend to be very expensive. Still, golfers flock here from around the world and love every minute of it. See p. 182 for coverage of the resort courses worth splurging on (with details, where applicable, on money-saving twilight rates), as well as the best budget and municipal courses. Also see p. 11, "The Best Golf Courses."

A few tips on golfing in Hawaii: There's generally wind—10 to 30 mph is not unusual between 10am and 2pm—so you may have to play two to three clubs up or down to compensate. Bring extra balls: The rough is thick, water hazards are everywhere, and the wind wreaks havoc with your game. On the greens, your putt will *always* break toward the ocean. Hit deeper and more aggressively in the sand because the type of sand used on most Hawaii courses is firmer and more compact than on mainland courses (lighter sand would blow away in the constant wind). And bring a camera—you'll kick yourself if you don't capture those spectacular views.

HIKING Hiking in Hawaii is a breathtaking experience. The islands have hundreds of miles of trails, many of which reward you with a hidden beach, a private waterfall, an Eden-like valley, or simply an unforgettable view. However, rock climbers are out of luck: Most of Hawaii's volcanic cliffs are too steep and brittle to scale.

Hawaiian Trail and Mountain Club (www.htmclub.org), offers information and links on hiking and camping in Hawaii; **Hawaii Geographic Maps and Books,** 49 S. Hotel St., Honolulu, HI 96813 (© 800/538-3950 or 808/538-3952; hawaiigeographicsociety@gmail.com), offers the *Hiking/Camping Information Packet* for $7. (The Society prefers that people contact them via email.) Also note that the **Hawaii State Department of Land and Natural Resources, Forestry, and Wildlife,** 1151 Punchbowl St., No. 325, Honolulu, HI 96809 (© 808/587-0166; www.hawaiitrails. org), will send you free topographic trail maps or you can download maps from their website.

The **Nature Conservancy of Hawaii,** 923 Nu'uanu Ave., Honolulu, HI 96817 (© 808/537-4508 on Oahu, 808/572-7849 on Maui, or 808/856-7658 on Molokai; www.nature.org/hawaii); or the **Hawaii Chapter of the Sierra Club,** both offer guided hikes in preserves and special areas during the year.

A couple of terrific books on hiking are *The Hiker's Guide to the Hawaiian Islands* and *The Hiker's Guide to Oahu,* both by Stuart M. Ball, Jr. (2000).

Before you set out on the trail, see "Health" on p. 287 for tips on hiking safety.

HORSEBACK RIDING One of the best ways to see Hawaii is on horseback; riding opportunities are offered for just about every age and level of experience. Be sure to bring a pair of jeans and closed-toe shoes to wear on your ride.

KAYAKING Hawaii is one of the world's most popular destinations for ocean kayaking. Beginners can paddle across a tropical lagoon to two uninhabited islets off Lanikai Beach on Oahu, while more experienced kayakers can take on open ocean. See "Watersports," on p. 165 for local outfitters and tour guides.

SCUBA DIVING Some people come to the islands solely to take the plunge into the tropical Pacific and explore the underwater world. Hawaii is one of the world's top ten dive destinations, according to *Scuba Diving* magazine. Here you can see the great variety of tropical marine life (more than 100 endemic species found nowhere else on the planet), explore sea caves, and swim with sea turtles and monk seals in clear, tropical water. If you're not certified, try to take classes before you come to Hawaii so you don't waste time learning and can dive right in.

If you dive, **go early in the morning.** Trade winds often rough up the seas in the afternoon, so most operators schedule early-morning dives that end at noon. To organize a dive on your own, order *The Oahu Snorkelers and Shore Divers Guide,* by Francisco B. de Carvalho (2003).

Tip: It's usually worth the extra bucks to go with a good dive operator. See p. 168; we've listed the operators that'll give you the most for your money.

STAND-UP PADDLING A new sport in Hawaii, stand-up paddling consists of, well, standing on an oversized surfboard and using a long handed paddle to propel yourself over the water. There are numerous places to both practice this sport as well as take lessons, especially in Waikiki, on the North Shore, and on the windward side at Kailua.

SNORKELING Snorkeling is one of Hawaii's main attractions, and almost anyone can do it. All you need is a mask, a snorkel, fins, and some basic swimming skills. In many places, all you have to do is wade into the water and look down at the magical underwater world.

If you've never snorkeled before, most resorts and excursion boats offer snorkeling equipment and lessons. You don't really need lessons, however; it's plenty easy to figure out for yourself, especially once you're at the beach, where everybody around you will be doing it. If you don't have your own gear, you can rent it from one of dozens of dive shops and activities booths.

While everyone heads for Oahu's Hanauma Bay—the perfect spot for first-timers—other favorite snorkel spots abound all over the island. See "Watersports" on p. 165.

Some snorkeling tips: Always snorkel with a buddy. Look up every once in a while to see where you are and if there's any boat traffic. Don't touch anything; not only can you damage coral, but camouflaged fish and shells with poisonous spines may also surprise you. Always check with a dive shop, lifeguards, or others on the beach about the area in which you plan to snorkel and ask if there are any dangerous conditions you should know about.

SPORTFISHING You can also try for spearfish, swordfish, various tuna, mahimahi (dorado), rainbow runners, wahoo, barracuda, trevallies, bonefish, and such bottom fish as snappers and groupers—and the biggest catch of them all, marlin. Visiting anglers currently need no license.

Charter fishing boats range widely both in size (from small 24-foot open skiffs to luxurious 50-foot-plus yachts) and in price (from about $100

2

Special-Interest Trips & Guided Tours

OAHU IN DEPTH

per person to "share" a boat with other anglers for a half-day, to $900 a day to book an entire luxury sportfishing yacht on an exclusive basis). Shop around. Prices vary according to the boat, the crowd, and the captain. Also, many boat captains tag and release marlin or keep the fish for themselves (sorry, that's Hawaii style). If you want to eat your mahimahi for dinner or have your marlin mounted, tell the captain before you go.

Money-saving tip: Try contacting the charter-boat captain directly and bargaining. Many charter captains pay a 20% to 30% commission to charter-booking agencies and may be willing to give you a discount if you book directly.

SURFING The ancient Hawaiian practice of *hee nalu* (wave sliding) is probably the sport most people picture when they think of Hawaii. Believe it or not, you, too, can do some wave sliding—just sign up at any one of the numerous surfing schools (p. 171). On world-famous Waikiki Beach, just head over to one of the surf stands that line the sand; these guys say they can get anybody up and standing on a board. If you're already a big kahuna in surfing, see p. 171 for the best deals on rental equipment and the best places to hang ten.

TENNIS Tennis is a popular sport in the islands. See p. 189 for details on free municipal courts as well as the best deals on private courts. The etiquette at the free county courts is to play only 45 minutes if someone is waiting.

WHALE-WATCHING Every winter, pods of Pacific humpback whales make the 3,000-mile swim from the chilly waters of Alaska to bask in Hawaii's summery shallows, fluking, spy hopping, spouting, breaching, and having an all-around swell time. About 1,500 to 3,000 humpback whales appear in Hawaiian waters each year.

Humpbacks are one of the world's oldest, most impressive inhabitants. Adults grow to be about 45 feet long and weigh a hefty 40 tons. Humpbacks are officially an endangered species; in 1992, the waters around Maui, Molokai, and Lanai were designated a Humpback Whale National Marine Sanctuary. Despite the world's newfound ecological awareness, humpbacks and their habitats and food resources are still under threat from whalers and pollution.

The season's first whale is usually spotted in November, but the best time to see humpback whales in Hawaii is **between January and April.** Just look out to sea. You'll also find a variety of whale-watching cruises, which will bring you up close and personal with the mammoth mammals; see p. 172 for more details.

Not So Close! They Hardly Know You

In the excitement of seeing a whale or a school of dolphins, don't forget that they're protected under the **Marine Mammals Protection Act.** You must stay at least 300 feet (the length of a football field) away from all whales, dolphins, and other marine mammals. This applies to swimmers, kayakers, and windsurfers. And, yes, visitors have been prosecuted for swimming with dolphins! If you have any questions, call the **National Marine Fisheries Service** (*C* 808/541-2727) or the **Hawaiian Islands Humpback Whale National Marine Sanctuary** (*C* 800/831-4888).

Money-saving tip: Book a snorkeling cruise during the winter whale-watching months. The captain of the boat will often take you through the best local whale-watching areas on the way, and you'll get two activities for the price of one. It's well worth the money.

WINDSURFING Hawaii is a top windsurfing destination. World-class windsurfers head to the wind and the waves offshore. Others, especially beginners, set their sails for Oahu's Kailua Bay, where gentle onshore breezes make learning this sport a snap.

Guided Tours

If your time is limited, you might want to consider a guided island tour. These tours are informative, can give you a good overview of Honolulu or Oahu in a limited amount of time, and are surprisingly entertaining.

E Noa Tours, 1141 Waimanu St., Ste. 105, Honolulu (© **800/824-8804** or 808/591-2561; www.enoa.com), offers a range of tours, from island loops to explorations of historic Honolulu. These narrated tours are on air-conditioned, 27-passenger minibuses. The Majestic Grand Circle Island tour ($80 for adults, $67 for children 6–11, $59 for children under 6), stops at Diamond Head Crater, Hanauma Bay, Byodo-In Temple, Sunset Beach, Waimea Valley (admission included), and various beach sites along the way. Other tours go to the Pearl Harbor/USS *Arizona* Memorial and the Polynesian Cultural Center.

Waikiki Trolley Tours ★, 1141 Waimanu St., Ste. 105, Honolulu (© **800/824-8804** or 808/596-2199; www.waikikitrolley.com), offers three fun tours of sightseeing, entertainment, dining, and shopping. These tours are a great way to get the lay of the land. You can get on and off the trolley as needed (trolleys come along every 2–20 min.). An all-day pass (8:30am–11:35pm) is $30 for adults, $20 for seniors, and $14 for children (4–11); a 4-day pass is $52 for adults, $31 for seniors, and $20 for children. For the same price, you can experience the 2-hour narrated Ocean Coastline tour of the southeast side of Oahu, an easy way to see the stunning views.

Polynesian Adventure Tours, 1049 Kikowaena Place, Honolulu (© **800/622-3011** or 808/833-3000; www.polyad.com), offers several excursions. The all-day island tour starts at $71 for adults, $42 for children under 12; the half-day scenic shore tour is $30 for adults, $23 for children 3 to 11; the half-day USS *Arizona* Memorial Excursion is $32 for adults and $22 for children 3 to 11.

For those who'd prefer a self-guided driving tour, **TourTalk-Oahu** (© **877/585-7499;** www.tourtalkhawaii.com) offers a complete package of 78-minute narrated compact discs, driving instructions, and a 72-page booklet containing color maps, photos, cultural and historical information, and Hawaii facts for $25.

WALKING TOURS

The **Mission Houses Museum,** 553 S. King St., at Kawaiahao Street (© **808/531-0481;** www.missionhouses.org; TheBus no. 2), offers a guided tour of the Visitors' Center, frame House and Printing Office, Tuesday to Saturday at 11am, 1pm, and 2:45pm. Admission is $10 adults, $8 seniors, and $6 children age 6 and up, age 5 and under free.

The **Hawaii Geographic Society** (© **800/538-3950;** hawaiigeographic society@gmail.com) presents numerous interesting and unusual tours, such as "A

A Bird's-Eye View

To understand why Oahu was the island of kings, see it from the air. **Island Seaplane Service** ★★ (📞 808/836-6273; www.islandseaplane.com) operates flights departing from a floating dock in the protected waters of Keehi Lagoon (parallel to Honolulu International Airport's runway) in either a six-passenger DeHavilland Beaver or a four-passenger Cessna 206. There's nothing quite like feeling the slap of the waves as the plane skims across the water and then effortlessly lifts into the air.

Your tour will give you aerial views of Waikiki Beach, Diamond Head Crater, Kahala's luxury estates, and the sparkling waters of Hanauma and Kaneohe bays. The half-hour tour ($135) ends here, while the 1-hour tour ($250) continues on to Chinaman's Hat, the Polynesian Cultural Center, and the rolling surf of the North Shore. The flight returns across the island, flying over Hawaii's historic wartime sites: Schofield Barracks and the USS *Arizona* and *Missouri* memorials in Pearl Harbor.

Taking off with the Island Seaplane Service.

Temple Tour," which includes Chinese, Japanese, Christian, and Jewish houses of worship; an archaeology tour in and around downtown Honolulu; and others. Each is guided by an expert from the Hawaii Geographic Society and must have a minimum of three people; the cost is $15 per person. The society's brochure, *Historic Downtown Honolulu Walking Tour,* is a fascinating self-guided tour of the 200-year-old city center. If you'd like a copy, contact **Hawaii Geographic Maps and Books,** 49 S. Hotel St. (P.O. Box 1698), Honolulu, HI 96808, or at hawaiigeographicsociety@gmail.com.

For self-guided walking tours of Honolulu, see p. 210.

ECOTOURS

Oahu isn't just high-rises in Waikiki or urban sprawl in Honolulu; it also has extinct craters, hidden waterfalls, lush rainforests, forgotten coastlines, and rainbow-filled valleys. To experience the other side of Oahu, contact **Oahu Nature Tours** (📞 808/924-2473; www.oahunaturetours.com). It offers seven different eco-tours, starting at $27 per person, and provides everything: expert guides

2

OAHU IN DEPTH

Special-Interest Trips & Guided Tours

67

Rolling Through Waikiki on a Segway

One of our favorite ways to tour Waikiki is on a Segway Personal Transporter, the silly looking two-wheeled machine that resembles a push lawn mower (big wheels and a long upright handle). Amazingly enough, within just a few minutes you get the hang of this contraption, which works through a series of high-tech stabilization mechanisms that read the motion of your body to turn or go forward or backward (it's propelled forward through twisting the hand throttle). And it's fun—think back to the first time you rode your bicycle and the incredible freedom of zipping along without walking. **Glide Ride Tours and Rentals,** at the Aloha Tower, 1 Aloha Tower Dr. (*© **808/941-3151;** www. segwayofhawaii.com), will instruct you on the Segway (they make sure that you are fully competent before you leave their training area), then take you on an introductory tour (you must be 16 years of age or over and weigh more than 80 pounds). The tours range from a 30-minute introductory tour for $49 per person to a 2½- to 3-hour tour of Waikiki, Kapiolani Park, and Diamond Head, for $130 per person.

(geologists, historians, archaeologists), round-trip transportation, entrance fees, bottled water, and use of day packs, binoculars, flashlights, and rain gear.

For more information on responsible and sustainable travel, see p. 56.

SPECIALTY TOURS

Below are a couple of little-known, off-the beaten path tours.

Hawaii Coffee Company ★★, 1555 Kalani St. (*© **808/847-3600;** www.hicoffeeco.com), has an excellent "behind the scenes" tour of their LION and Royal Kona Coffee facility as well as their Hawaiian Island Tea Company. You will be met in the retail/cafe area of their facility and taken through the 55,000-square-foot plant on a step-by-step tour of how Hawaii's oldest and largest coffee company processes and roasts their dozens of different brands and types of coffee. Allow 30 to 45 minutes for the tour, plus extra time to try the various coffees in the cafe. This is one of the best places on the island to stock up on a few bags of coffee or boxes of teas. Not only are the prices competitive, but, in November and December, exclusive specialty Christmas coffee can be purchased at this location. Free tours are given Monday through Thursday, 10 times a day (call for current tour times and reservations). The E Noa Trolley no. 10 also stops here.

For those looking for a really different look at Honolulu and the island, **Oahu Ghost Tours** (*© **877/597-7325;** www.oahughosttours.com) offers a look at the island's supernatural history. Originally started by Glen Grant (1947–2003), who dedicated his life to exploring stories and sightings of the paranormal, the company has continued his investigations of ghosts, unusual sightings, and the unexplainable. The tours range from **Honolulu City Haunts,** a 2-mile walking tour of places where supernatural events still occur today ($34 adults and $29 children 11 and younger), to **Sacred Spirits Tour,** a 5-hour walking tour of the most sacred Native Hawaiian spots on Oahu ($56 adults and $43 children 11 and younger), to **Orbs of O'ahu,** a driving tour that circles the island, stopping at some of the "most haunted" locations ($54 adults and $43 children 11 and younger).

For information on self-guided special-interest trips, see p. 60.

3

SUGGESTED OAHU ITINERARIES

F irst and foremost, yes, it's possible to have a fabulous vacation in Hawaii and not have to take out a second mortgage. The next most common question readers ask is: "What should I do in Hawaii?"

Our response: How much time do you have, and what do you like to do?

The purpose of this chapter is to give you expert advice on the best things to see and do, and how to do them in an orderly fashion so you're not driving madly from one end of the island to the other.

Here's the best advice we can give you: **Do not plan to see more than one island per week.** This isn't the Caribbean, where islands are so close to each other that you can island-hop. With the exception of the ferry between Maui and Lanai, getting from one island to another is an all-day affair that consists of: packing and checking out of your hotel, driving to the airport (most island airports are a 30- to 60-minute drive from resort areas), dropping off your rental car, checking in (and standing in long lines) 90 minutes before your scheduled flight, flying from one island to the next, waiting for your luggage (sometimes the wait for the luggage is just as long or longer than your interisland flight), getting yet another rental car, driving 30 to 60 minutes to your hotel, checking in, and so on. Don't waste a day of your vacation seeing our interisland air terminals.

Also, **don't max out your days.** You're in Hawaii—which means you should allow some time to do nothing but relax. Ease into your vacation. Due to jet lag, you'll probably be tired your first day, and hitting the pillow at 8 or 9pm might sound good. Don't be surprised if you wake up your first morning in Hawaii before the sun comes up. Your internal clock might still be set 2 to 6 hours earlier than Hawaii's.

Finally, think of your first trip to Hawaii as a "scouting" trip. Hawaii is too beautiful, too sensual, too enticing to see just once in a lifetime. You'll be back. You don't need to see and do everything on this trip. In fact, if you fall in love with something in the itinerary below, go back again.

One last thing—you'll need a car to get around the islands, so remember to plan for that expense, and with recent cut backs in the rental fleet, book your car as soon as you book your airline. Oahu has an adequate public transportation service, TheBus, but it's set up for Hawaiian residents, not tourists carrying coolers, towels, toys, and other things to the beach (all carry ons must fit under the bus seat). So plan to rent a car, but also to get out of it as much as possible. Hawaii is not a place to see from your car window. You have to get out to smell the sweet perfume of plumeria, to feel the warm rain on your face, to hear the sound of the wind through a bamboo forest, and to plunge into the gentle waters of the Pacific.

THE ISLAND OF OAHU IN BRIEF
Honolulu

Hawaii's largest city looks like any other big metropolitan center with tall buildings. In fact, some cynics refer to it as "Los Angeles West." But within Honolulu's

PREVIOUS PAGE: **Diamond Head Crater as seen from above.**

Mainlanders sometimes find the directions given by locals a bit confusing. Seldom will you hear east, west, north, and south; instead, islanders refer to directions as either **makai** (ma-*kae*), meaning toward the sea, or **mauka** (*mow*-kah), toward the mountains. In Honolulu, people use **Diamond Head** as a direction meaning to the east (in the direction of the world-famous crater called Diamond Head), and **Ewa** as a direction meaning to the west (toward the town called Ewa, on the other side of Pearl Harbor).

So, if you ask a local for directions, this is what you're likely to hear: "Drive 2 blocks *makai* (toward the sea), then turn Diamond Head (east) at the stoplight. Go 1 block and turn *mauka* (toward the mountains). It's on the Ewa (western) side of the street."

boundaries, you'll find rainforests, deep canyons, valleys and waterfalls, a nearly mile-high mountain range, coral reefs, and gold-sand beaches. The city proper—where most of Oahu's residents live—is approximately 12 miles wide and 26 miles long, running east to west, roughly between Diamond Head and Pearl Harbor. Within the city are seven hills laced by seven streams that run to Mamala Bay.

Surrounding the central area is a plethora of neighborhoods, ranging from the quiet suburbs of **Hawaii Kai** to *kamaaina* (old-timer) neighborhoods such as **Manoa.** These areas are generally quieter and more residential than Waikiki, but they're still within minutes of beaches, shopping, and all the activities Oahu has to offer.

WAIKIKI Some say that Waikiki is past its prime—that everybody goes to Maui now. If it has fallen out of favor, you couldn't prove it by us. Waikiki is the very incarnation of Yogi Berra's comment about Toots Shor's famous New York restaurant: "Nobody goes there anymore. It's too crowded."

When King Kalakaua played in Waikiki, it was "a hamlet of plain cottages . . . its excitements caused by the activity of insect tribes and the occasional fall of a coconut." The Merrie Monarch, who gave his name to Waikiki's main street, would love the scene today. Some five million tourists visit Oahu every year, and 9 out of 10 of them stay in Waikiki. This urban beach is where all the action is; it's backed by 175 high-rise hotels with more than 33,000 guest rooms and hundreds of bars and restaurants, all in a 1½-square-mile beach zone. Waikiki means honeymooners and sun seekers, bikinis and bare buns, a round-the-clock beach party every day of the year—and it's all because of a thin crescent of sand that was shipped over from Molokai. Staying in Waikiki puts you in the heart of it all, but also be aware that this is an on-the-go place with traffic noise 24 hours a day and its share of crime—and it's almost always crowded.

ALA MOANA A great beach as well as a famous shopping mall, Ala Moana is the retail and transportation heart of Honolulu, a place where you can both shop and suntan in one afternoon. All bus routes lead to the open-air **Ala Moana Shopping Center,** across the street from **Ala Moana Beach Park.** This 50-acre, 200-shop behemoth attracts 56 million customers a year. (People fly up from Tahiti just to buy their Christmas gifts here.) Every European designer from Armani to Vuitton is represented in Honolulu's answer to Beverly Hills's Rodeo Drive. For our purposes, the neighborhood called "Ala Moana" extends along Ala Moana Boulevard from Waikiki in the direction of Diamond Head to downtown Honolulu in the Ewa direction (west) and includes the **Ward Centre** and **Ward Warehouse complexes** as well as **Restaurant Row.**

DOWNTOWN A tiny cluster of high-rises west of Waikiki, downtown Honolulu is the financial, business, and governmental center of Hawaii. On the waterfront stands the iconic 1926 Aloha Tower, now the centerpiece of a harbor-front shopping and restaurant complex known as the **Aloha Tower Marketplace.** The entire history of Honolulu can be seen in just a few short blocks: Street vendors sell papayas from trucks in skyscraper-lined concrete canyons; joggers and BMWs rush by Iolani Palace, where descendants of the original missionaries (with help from the U.S. Marines) overthrew Hawaii's last queen and stole her kingdom; burly bus drivers sport fragrant white ginger flowers on their dashboards; Methodist churches look like Asian temples; and businessmen wear aloha shirts to billion-dollar meetings.

On the edge of downtown is the **Chinatown Historic District,** the oldest Chinatown in America. This is still one of Honolulu's liveliest neighborhoods, a nonstop pageant of people, sights, sounds, smells, and tastes—not all Chinese, now that Southeast Asians, including many Vietnamese, share the old storefronts. Go on a Saturday morning, when everyone shops here for fresh goods such as ginger root, fern fronds, and hogs' heads.

Among the historic buildings and Pan-Pacific corporate headquarters are a few hotels, mainly geared toward business travelers. Most visitors prefer the sun and excitement of Waikiki or choose a quieter neighborhood outside the city.

MANOA VALLEY First inhabited by white settlers, the Manoa Valley, above Waikiki, still has vintage *kamaaina* homes, one of Hawaii's premier botanical gardens in the Lyon Arboretum, the ever-gushing Manoa Falls, and the 320-acre campus of the University of Hawaii, where 50,000 students hit the books when they're not on the beach.

KAHALA Except for the estates of world-class millionaires and the luxurious Kahala Hotel & Resort (home of Hoku's, an outstanding beachfront restaurant), there's not much out to the east of downtown that's of interest to visitors.

East Oahu

Beyond Kahala lies East Honolulu and such suburban bedroom communities as Aina Haina, Niu Valley, and Hawaii Kai, among others, all linked by the Kalanianaole Highway and loaded with homes, condos, fast-food joints, and shopping malls. It looks like Southern California on a good day. A few reasons to come here: to have dinner at **Roy's,** the original and still-outstanding Hawaii regional cuisine restaurant, in Hawaii Kai; to snorkel at **Hanauma Bay** or watch daredevil surfers at **Sandy Beach;** or just to enjoy the natural splendor of the lovely coastline, which might include a hike to **Makapuu Lighthouse.**

The Windward Coast

The windward side is the opposite side of the island from Waikiki. On this coast, trade winds blow cooling breezes over gorgeous beaches; rain squalls inspire lush, tropical vegetation; and miles of subdivisions dot the landscape. Bed-and-breakfasts, ranging from oceanfront estates to tiny cottages on quiet residential streets, are everywhere. Vacations here are spent enjoying ocean activities and exploring the surrounding areas. Waikiki is just a quick 15-minute drive away.

KAILUA The biggest little beach town in Hawaii, Kailua sits at the foot of the sheer green Koolau Mountains, on a great bay with two of Hawaii's best beaches. The town itself is a funky low-rise cluster of timeworn shops and homes. Kailua has become the B&B capital of Hawaii; it's an affordable alternative to Waikiki, with rooms and vacation rentals from $60 a day and up. With the prevailing trade winds whipping up a cooling breeze, Kailua attracts windsurfers from around the world.

KANEOHE After you clear the trafficky maze of town, Oahu returns to its more natural state. Helter-skelter suburbia sprawls around the edges of Kaneohe, one of the most scenic bays in the Pacific. A handful of B&Bs dot its edge. This beautiful bay beckons you to get out on the water; you can depart from Heeia Boat Harbor on snorkel or fishing charters and visit Ahu o Laka, the sandbar that appears and disappears in the middle of the bay. From here, you'll have a panoramic view of the Koolau Range.

KUALOA/LAIE The upper northeast shore is one of Oahu's most sacred places, an early Hawaiian landing spot where kings dipped their sails, cliffs hold ancient burial sites, and ghosts still march in the night. Sheer cliffs stab the reef-fringed seacoast, while old fishponds are tucked along the two-lane coast road that winds past empty gold-sand beaches around beautiful Kahana Bay. Thousands "explore" the South Pacific at the **Polynesian Cultural Center,** in Laie, a Mormon settlement with its own Tabernacle Choir of sweet Samoan harmony.

The North Shore

Here's the Hawaii of Hollywood—giant waves, surfers galore, tropical jungles, waterfalls, and mysterious Hawaiian temples. If you're looking for a quieter vacation, closer to nature, and filled with swimming, snorkeling, diving, surfing, or just plain hanging out on some of the world's most beautiful beaches, the North Shore is your spot. The artsy little beach town of **Haleiwa** and the surrounding shoreline seem a world away from Waikiki. The North Shore boasts good restaurants, shopping, and cultural activities—but here they come with the quiet of country living. Bed-and-breakfasts are the most common accommodations, but there's one first-class hotel and some vacation rentals as well. *Be forewarned:* It's a long trip—nearly an hour's drive—to Honolulu and Waikiki, and it's about twice as rainy on the North Shore as in Honolulu.

Central Oahu: The Ewa Plain

Flanked by the Koolau and Waianae mountain ranges, the hot, sun-baked Ewa Plain runs up and down the center of Oahu. Once covered with sandalwood forests (hacked down for the China trade) and later the sugar-cane and pineapple backbone of Hawaii, Ewa today sports a new crop: suburban houses stretching to the sea. But let your eye wander west to the Waianae Range and Mount Kaala (at 4,020 feet the highest summit on Oahu); up there in the misty rainforest, native birds thrive in the hummocky bog. In 1914, the U.S. Army pitched a tent camp on the plain; author James Jones would later call **Schofield Barracks** "the most beautiful army post in the world." Hollywood filmed Jones's *From Here to Eternity* here.

Leeward Oahu: The Waianae Coast

The west coast of Oahu is a hot and dry place of dramatic beauty: white-sand beaches bordering the deep blue ocean, steep verdant green cliffs, and miles of Mother Nature's wildness. Except for the luxurious **J. W. Marriott Ihilani Resort and Spa at Ko Olina, Roy's Ko Olina Restaurant** (a sister of Roy's in Hawaii Kai), and the **Makaha Golf Course,** you'll find virtually no tourist services out here. The funky west coast villages of Nanakuli, Waianae, and Makaha are the last stands of native Hawaiians. This side of Oahu is seldom visited, except by surfers bound for **Yokohama Bay** and those coming to see needle-nose **Kaena Point** (the island's westernmost outpost), which has a coastal wilderness park.

OAHU IN 1 WEEK

The island of Oahu is so stunning that the *alii,* the kings of Hawaii, made it the capital of the island nation. You can see all of Oahu's highlights in 1 week, presuming that you're staying in Waikiki; if you're in another location, be sure to factor in travel time. In this itinerary, I've included the all-star things to do and see on this island: Waikiki Beach, Waikiki Aquarium, Pearl Harbor Memorial, Polynesian Cultural Center, Hanauma Bay, Sea Life Park, Bishop Museum, historic downtown Honolulu, Kailua Bay, shopping, art galleries, and a few surprises.

DAY 1: Waikiki Beach ★★

Lather up with sunscreen, put on your sunglasses and a hat, and plop down on the most famous beach in the world. If you have kids in tow, or if an hour in Hawaii's intense sun is all you can handle, consider checking out Hawaii's water world by dropping by the **Waikiki Aquarium** (p. 207), or take the children to the **Honolulu Zoo** (p. 200). For insight into Waikiki's past, take the **Waikiki Historic Trail,** a 2-mile trail marked with bronzed surf boards (p. 208). Try to see the sunset on your first day—just sit anywhere on Waikiki Beach; if you'd like a liquid libation, all the hotels on the beach can accommodate you—and then get an early dinner.

DAY 2: Pearl Harbor ★★★

Most likely you'll be awake early, so take advantage of it: Drive or take a tour bus to the **USS *Arizona* Memorial at Pearl Harbor** (p. 205). Entry is free. The best time to go is early in the morning; by the afternoon, the lines are 2 hours long. Next, stop by the **USS *Missouri* Memorial** (p. 206), the **USS *Bowfin* Submarine Museum and Park** (p. 206), and the **Pacific Aviation Museum Pearl Harbor** (p. 203). On your way back, either head for the beach at **Ala Moana Beach Park** (p. 155) or embark on a shopping spree across the street at the **Ala Moana Shopping Center** (p. 255). Plan a dinner in Honolulu or surrounding areas.

DAY 3: The Polynesian Cultural Center ★★★

You might want to sleep late today. Around or after noon, head for the **Polynesian Cultural Center,** in Laie (p. 235). Allow at least 2 hours (if not the entire afternoon) to tour this mini-glimpse of the Pacific, where you'll walk through various "villages" filled with interactive activities, entertainment, and cultural events. Continue driving down the coast road to the small town

Oversized fish and an undersized visitor at Waikiki's Aquarium.

of **Kailua,** and eat dinner at **Lucy's Grill 'n Bar** (p. 150) to avoid heavy traffic over the Pali back to Waikiki.

DAY 4: Hanauma Bay & Sea Life Park ★★

If it's not Tuesday (when the park is closed), head out in the morning for spectacular snorkeling at **Hanauma Bay** (p. 156). You could spend the entire day here, but remember that Hawaii's sun is intense, and you don't want sunburn to ruin your vacation. After a couple of hours, wander down the coast to **Sea Life Park**

The guns of the USS *Missouri.*

(p. 232). If you have kids, this is a must-stop. Otherwise, you can continue "beach-hopping" along the coastline with stops at **Sandy Beach, Makapuu Point and Makapuu Beach Park,** and **Waimanalo Beach,** before turning back to take the Pali Highway. Be sure to stop at the **Pali Lookout** (p. 230) on your way back to Waikiki.

DAY 5: Honolulu ★

Head to downtown Honolulu for a historic hike around the old town, and try to visit: **Iolani Palace** (p. 200), **Kawaiahao Church** (p. 201), and the **Mission Houses Museum** (p. 203). For a bird's-eye view of where you've been and the whole of Honolulu, go to the top of **Aloha Tower,** at Aloha Tower Marketplace. Stop for lunch either at the Aloha Tower Marketplace or at one of the nearby restaurants. Spend the afternoon at the **Bishop Museum** (p. 196) to immerse yourself in Hawaiian culture. Plan dinner outside of Waikiki.

DAY 6: Kailua Beach Park ★

On your last full day on Oahu, travel over the Pali Highway to the Windward side of the island, to spend a day at **Kailua Beach Park.** This is the perfect beach for relaxing or snorkeling or trying something different such as kayaking or windsurfing. You can spend the entire day here, take an afternoon hike at **Hoomaluhia Botanical Gardens** (p. 234), or venture to another beach park such as **Kahana Bay** or **Malaekahana Bay State Recreation Area.**

Quaint Kawaiahao Church.

DAY 7: Waikiki

What you do today depends on how much time you have on your last day here—and how much energy. You might just hang out in **Waikiki** and perhaps take a surfing lesson, ride a surfing canoe, or venture underwater in an **Atlantis Submarine** (p. 170). For the energetic, get up early and climb **Diamond Head** (p. 198). Art lovers should definitely check out the **Honolulu Academy of Arts** (p. 199); the **Contemporary Museum** (p. 197), where you should have lunch; and the **Hawaii State Art Museum** (p. 199). Shoppers can head to Waikiki for the **Ala Moana Shopping Center,** the **DFS Galleria,** and the **Royal Hawaiian Shopping Center;** bargain hunters should make the 45-minute drive out to the **Waikele Premium Outlets.** On your way to the airport, stop on **Maunakea Street in Chinatown** and buy a lei from one of the numerous lei makers (p. 253) to take back as a sweet-smelling memory of your trip.

OAHU IN 2 WEEKS

Two weeks really gives you time to discover Oahu. After you check out the highlights mentioned above, visit historic Chinatown, relax on the beaches of the North Shore, take fabulous hikes, explore the waters surrounding the island, browse the art galleries and museums, go shopping, relax in spas, or take time to find unique experiences on the island.

DAY 8: Chinatown ★★

See a different side of Hawaii by walking the streets of Honolulu's **Chinatown.** Take the walking tour we recommend on p. 210. Plan to at least have lunch in this exotic part of Oahu (p. 72).

DAY 9: The North Shore ★★★

Get up early, drive across Oahu, and have breakfast at **Cafe Haleiwa** (p. 152) with the surfers. Wander across the street to the **Paradise Found Cafe** (p. 153) to pick up a picnic lunch, then head out to the beach.

A sunset cruise on the *Navatek I* catamaran.

Depending on what you want to do and what the weather is like, here are some choices for a day at the beach: In the summer, when the waves are flat, **Waimea Beach Park** is great for swimming, snorkeling, and bodysurfing, in the winter, watch surfers take on huge 30-foot waves. If you want to go snorkeling or diving, **Pupukea Beach Park** is excellent. On your way home, return to Haleiwa and stop at the **shrimp trucks** (p. 150) for a cheap and delicious meal.

DAY 10: Manoa & Diamond Head ★★

Spend the day hiking, either into the **rainforest** (see **Manoa Falls Hike** on p. 177) or up to the top of an **old volcano** (see **Diamond Head Hike** on p. 174). Serious hikers might check out the **Makiki-Manoa** series of trails (p. 176). Of course, after all that exercise, you might want to plan a massage in the afternoon at one of **Hawaii's best spas** (p. 20). You'll deserve it.

DAY 11: On the Water ★★

See Hawaii from a different angle—get out on the water for a day. Even if you think you get seasick, take the lunch cruise on *Navatek I.* It's designed with stabilizers to guarantee that you won't get green around the gills. You can enjoy a great lunch and Hawaiian music as you cruise off Waikiki

Heading below decks on Atlantis Submarines.

The American drawings collection at the Honolulu Academy of Arts.

(p. 166). Or plunge underwater with **Atlantis Submarines** (p. 170), where you can view below the ocean blue without getting wet. Plan to eat a fish dinner in Waikiki that night (p. 71).

DAY 12: Honolulu's Art ★★

Start the day at the **Contemporary Museum** (p. 197) and plan to stay for lunch at the **Cafe** (p. 144). From there, travel into Honolulu to the **Hawaii State Art Museum** (p. 199) and then on to the **Honolulu Academy of Arts** (p. 199). After a day of art, take in a show in Honolulu (p. 70).

DAY 13: Shopping ★★

With more than 1,000 stores in Oahu, where's a shopper to begin?! Check out our suggestions for all kinds of shopping (p. 244), ranging from **aloha wear** to **great souvenirs** to the **best discount shopping** spots on the island. You might want to take in a luau on your last night in Hawaii (p. 270).

DAY 14: Spas ★★

Before you board your plane for hours of discomfort, plan for a few hours at a **spa.** Oahu has several world-class spas sprinkled throughout the island. Check out our favorites on p. 20.

OAHU'S CULTURE & HISTORY

Spend a week seeing the old Hawaii, from the sacred and cultural sites where priests once healed people and where members of royalty were born, to the historic sites of the missionaries, the old plantations, and World War II. The highlights include Waikiki, Pearl Harbor, downtown Honolulu, Chinatown, Central Oahu—all a vivid reminder of the past.

DAY 1: Waikiki Beach ★★

To get an overview of Waikiki's past, start off with the 2-mile **Waikiki Historic Trail** (p. 208), marked by a 6-foot-tall surfboard explaining the history of today's favorite resort area. Next, hop on a Segway Personal Transporter with **Glide Ride Tours and Rentals** (p. 68). After a lesson to make sure you are competent, head off for a tour of Waikiki, Kapiolani Park, and Diamond Head. At sunset, wander along the sand at Waikiki Beach and listen to the Hawaiian music coming from every hotel. Plan dinner at either **Hula Grill** (p. 130) or **Duke's** (p. 129).

DAY 2: Pearl Harbor ★★★

Unfortunately, no trip to Honolulu would be complete without a visit to the **USS *Arizona* Memorial at Pearl Harbor** (p. 205), where 1,177 U.S. sailors died in a bombing attack by the Japanese on December 7, 1941. Get there early, preferably by the 7:30am opening—otherwise face long lines (waits up to 2 hr.). After spending a couple of hours here, go next door to the **USS *Bowfin* Submarine Museum and Park** (p. 206), one of just 15 World War II submarines still in existence. If you're ready for more, wander down to the **USS *Missouri* Memorial** (p. 206), where the Japanese signed the surrender agreement on September 2, 1945, ending World War II. Definitely take the tour to get the full impact of this historic vessel. Finish with the **Pacific Aviation Museum Pearl Harbor** (p. 203), where you can sit behind the controls of a simulated plane that flew in World War II. To get a feel for that fateful day in 1941 that propelled the U.S. into the war, sign up for the unforgettable **Island Seaplane Service**'s tour of the entire island (p. 67). Finish the day by wandering through the **(Punchbowl) National Cemetery of the Pacific** (p. 203) to see the true cost of any war. For an evening activity to cheer you up, try a stand-up comedian (p. 269) or a show in Waikiki (p. 269).

DAY 3: Honolulu ★★

If you really want to "understand" Hawaii, take the 45-minute tour of the **Iolani Palace** (p. 200), where you'll see how Hawaiian royalty lived. When sugar planters and descendants of missionaries overthrew the Kingdom of Hawaii on January 17, 1893, Hawaii's last queen, Liliuokalani, was put under house arrest and this palace also became a jail. Next, wander down the street to the crowning achievement of the missionaries, **Kawaiahao Church** (p. 201), which holds its Sunday service in Hawaiian at 9am. To learn more about the missionaries who traveled from New England to

Oahu from above, as seen by the Island Seaplane Service.

A surfboard marking the Waikiki Historic Trail.

Hawaii (via Cape Horn) to spread the gospel, stop by the **Mission Houses Museum** (p. 203). Make one last call at the **Royal Mausoleum,** the final resting place of both royalty and missionaries, and then relax over dinner at **Hau Tree Lanai** (p. 129), which offers ocean views.

DAY 4: The Bishop Museum & Polynesian Cultural Center ★★

While the **Hawaii Maritime Center** has been shuttered due to economic conditions, it may be open in the near future; call ahead to check. If it is open, plan to be there at 9am, to spend at least an hour wandering through this fascinating reproduction of Hawaii's history, from the ancient journey of Polynesians to the days of the four-masted schooners to today. Next, head out of Honolulu, stopping by Hawaii's premier cultural and historical museum, the **Bishop Museum** (p. 196), where you could spend days. Limit this visit to a couple of hours before heading out to the North Shore via Haleiwa town. Grab a terrific burger or sandwich at **Kua Aina** (p. 137), or sit down for lunch at **Cafe Haleiwa** (p. 152), and then head over to the **Polynesian Cultural Center.** Try to get there as close to the noon opening time as possible to avoid crowds. Allow at least 2 hours to tour this 42-acre lagoon park (and more time if you have kids). It's pricey to get in (tickets start at $50), so stay as long as you like. At sunset, drive back toward Haleiwa and watch the sun set behind the mountains at the Hawaiian sacred temple, **Puu O Mahuka.** Plan to enjoy a leisurely dinner at **Haleiwa Joe's** (p. 151).

DAY 5: The Plantations ★

Take the hour-long tour of **Hawaii's Plantation Village** (p. 238), a restored 50-acre settlement that depicts what life was like on the plantations of 1852 to 1947. The chief mode of transportation at that time was the railroad. You can experience the Old Oahu Railway trains at the **Hawaiian Railway** (p. 238). And to see what a plantation looks like today, stop by the **Dole Pineapple Plantation** (p. 237). Take the afternoon off and go to the beach.

DAY 6: Chinatown ★★

Spend the day seeing a different side of Hawaii by walking the streets of Honolulu's **Chinatown;** take the walking tour we recommend on p. 210. Plan to have lunch in this exotic part of Oahu; try **Little Village Noodle House** (p. 141).

DAY 7: Shopping ★

Culture hounds will be mesmerized by the **Contemporary Museum Gift Shop** (p. 254), the **Honolulu Academy of Arts' Shop** (p. 254), and the **Royal Hawaiian Shopping Center's**

An antique narrow-gauge Hawaiian Railway traincar.

Little Hawaiian Craft Shop (p. 254). Artists and collectors could spend an entire day at **Native Books & Beautiful Things** (p. 254), **Nohea Gallery** (p. 255), and **Bishop Museum's Shop Pacifica** (p. 255). So many things to buy and so little time. At least pick up a book, so you can start planning your next trip to Hawaii.

OAHU FOR FAMILIES

If you have enough trouble getting your kids out of the house in the morning, dragging them thousands of miles away may seem like an insurmountable challenge. But family travel can be immensely rewarding, giving you new ways of seeing the world through smaller pairs of eyes. The following itinerary gives you the nuts and bolts you need to plan an affordable, safe, and fun family vacation on Oahu.

DAY 1: Waikiki Beach ★★

Lather everybody up in sunscreen, take sunglasses and a hat, and plop down on a beach the kids will love—Waikiki. If they get tired of playing in the surf, you might consider a catamaran ride or an outrigger canoe ride (p. 165). After an hour or so on the beach, take the kids to see the marine critters at the **Waikiki Aquarium** (p. 207) or stop by the **Honolulu Zoo** (p. 200). They'll drop off to sleep early.

DAY 2: An Island Drive ★★

Most likely, you'll still be on mainland time today—take advantage of it and get up early for a drive around the island. Head out for **Sea Life Park,** which opens at 10:30am, and spend a couple of hours on the shows, exhibits, and interactive activities. Grab lunch in Kailua at **Zippy's** (p. 142), and head up the coast to the **Polynesian Cultural Center** (p. 235), in Laie. Plan at least 2 to 3 hours (or as long as the kids will last) here. On the way home, stop at one of the **shrimp trucks in Haleiwa** (p. 150) and have a picnic dinner.

A "Hawaiian zebra" at the Honolulu Zoo.

The safest way to observe a volcano, from the Bishop Museum.

The physics of bubbles at the Hawaii Children's Discovery Center.

DAY 3: Pearl Harbor & Diamond Head ★★

Don't miss the **USS *Arizona* Memorial** at Pearl Harbor (p. 205). Arrive before the 7:30am opening, or lines will be lengthy. After a few hours here, head next door to the **USS *Bowfin* Submarine Museum and Park** (p. 206), one of just 15 World War II submarines still in existence. If energy levels hold out, hit the **USS *Missouri* Memorial** (p. 206), where the Japanese signed the surrender agreement on September 2, 1945, that ended World War II. Finish Pearl Harbor by seeing the **Pacific Aviation Museum Pearl Harbor** (p. 203), where the kids can sit behind the controls of a simulated plane that flew in World War II. Depending on how tired the kids are at this point, you can head to the beach or hike up to the top of **Diamond Head** (p. 198) to see the sunset view.

DAY 4: Hanauma Bay & the Bishop Museum ★★

If it's not Tuesday (when the park is closed for maintenance), head out for **Hanauma Bay** (p. 156) to snorkel in the clear, warm water. After lunch take the kids to the **Bishop Museum** (p. 196), where they can explore the interior of a volcano and climb to the top to get a bird's-eye view of an erupting caldera, watch a hula, see the skeleton of a whale, and check out war weapons the Hawaiians used.

DAY 5: Chinatown ★★

If it's open (**Note:** It was closed due to insufficient funds at press time), the kids won't want to leave the **Hawaii Maritime Museum,** where they can follow the ancient journey of Polynesian voyagers all the way to the nostalgic days of the SS *Lurline,* which once brought tourists from San Francisco. After a few hours, wander over to **Chinatown** (p. 72) for lunch; the kids will be enthralled with the exotic foodstuffs at the outdoor markets.

DAY 6: Wet 'n' Wild Water Park ★

Take the kids to **Wet 'n' Wild** (p. 241). They'll love this 29-acre water park; in fact, plan to spend the entire day here. Highlights include a football field–sized wave pool, a 65-foot-high free-fall slide, a water-toboggan bullet slide, inner-tube slides, a body-flume slide, rivers, and a zillion other things that will entertain them for hours. You'll also find restaurants here, along with a few food carts, shops, and Hawaiian performances. Bring plenty of sunscreen.

DAY 7: The Children's Discovery Center ★★

In case of rain, take the kids to **Hawaii Children's Discovery Center,** 111 Ohe St. (© **808/524-5437;** www.discoverycenterhawaii.org), perfect for ages 2 to 13. This 37,000-square-foot place of color, motion, and activities will entertain them for hours, with hands-on exhibits and interactive stations. Meanwhile, Mom and Dad can get some rest.

OAHU FOR ADVENTURE LOVERS

If you're looking for a vacation filled with adventure, Oahu provides plenty of opportunities, from gliding over the rolling surf to plunging under the sea to diving out of a plane, even coming eye to eye with sharks. You can make your entire vacation as thrilling and as heart-pounding as you desire, or you can experience just a couple days of spicy escapades. Below is an itinerary that you can pick and choose from, or—as we say in Hawaii—you can "go for broke."

DAY 1: Waikiki Beach ★★

At **Waikiki Beach** (p. 155), learn to surf, ride in a Hawaiian surfing canoe, or snorkel. Ease into your vacation and go to bed early, so you'll be raring to go the next day.

DAY 2: Under the Water ★★

Take your pick: Sign up for **scuba diving** (p. 168); dive down in the Atlantis **Submarine** (p. 170), which takes you below the water's surface in the comfort of a high-tech submarine; or get out on the water in a boat. Even if you've gotten seasick in the past, ***Navatek I*** (p. 166) guarantees a smooth ride.

DAY 3: Manoa, Diamond Head & Hanauma Bay ★★

Spend the day hiking, either into the rainforest (see Manoa Falls Hike on p. 177) or up to the top of an **old volcano** (see **Diamond Head Hike** on p. 174). Serious hikers might check out the **Makiki-Manoa** series of trails (p. 176). In the afternoon (except Tues, when the park is closed), get a mask, snorkel, and fins at **Snorkel Bob's** (p. 165) and go to **Hanauma Bay** (p. 156).

DAY 4: In the Air ★★

Soar through the air on gossamer-like wings via a **glider ride** (p.188); get a bird's-eye view from a **hang glider** (p. 189); or, for the truly adventurous, leap from a plane in a **sky-diving** venture (p. 189). If these sound a bit *too*

A glider silently soaring over Oahu's mountains.

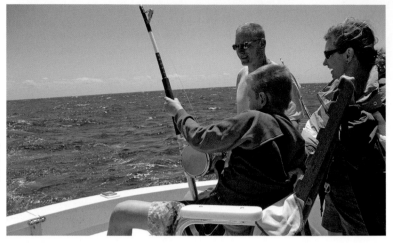

Sportfishing for mahimahi out of Kewalo Basin.

adventurous, take to the air in the **Island Seaplane Service**'s unforgettable tour of the entire island (p. 67). Plan to spend the rest of the day at one of Hawaii's beaches along the **North Shore** (p. 162).

DAY 5: On the Water ★★

Serious fishermen from around the globe dream of catching a "grander"—a Pacific Blue Marlin weighing a thousand pounds or more. You might try your luck by booking a **sportfishing boat** at Kewalo Basin (p. 170). Or spend the day in the water with **spinner dolphins**—with **Wild Side Tours** (p. 167), you can get up close and personal with these protected marine mammals.

DAY 6: The North Shore & Waikiki Aquarium ★★

The truly adventurous will actually pay money to come face to face with a shark. Of course, a 6-foot x 6-foot x 10-foot aluminum cage separates the two of you. (You're the one in the cage, as the shark—or sharks!—swim around you.) Call **North Shore Shark Adventures** (p. 169) for this unforgettable experience. If you'd like a little more protection, head over to the **Waikiki Aquarium** (p. 207) and view some sharks through protective glass.

DAY 7: Spas ★★

After a week of adventures, plan a few hours at a spa. Oahu has several world-class spas sprinkled throughout the island. Check out our favorites in on p. 20.

4

WHERE TO STAY

T hough the island of Oahu is not the biggest in the Hawaiian chain, it offers the widest variety of accommodations. Should you stay in near-palatial surroundings where kings, heads of state, billionaires, and rock stars have spent the night, or in a quaint bed-and-breakfast on the North Shore where the rolling surf lulls you to sleep? Should you choose the bright lights and action of Waikiki or the quiet comforts of Kahala? Oahu has the perfect place for everyone.

The major **high season** is mid-December to March. At this time of year, rooms are always booked and rates are at the top end. Secondary high season is June to September, when rates are expensive, but bookings are somewhat easier. The **low season,** with fewer tourists, cheaper rates, and possible "deals" on rooms is April to June and September to mid-December.

Be sure to factor in Oahu's 17.5% tax, and don't forget about parking charges —which average around $25 a day in Waikiki.

WAIKIKI

Some five million tourists visit Oahu every year, and 9 out of 10 of them choose accommodations in Waikiki, a 500-acre beachfront neighborhood of Honolulu. Here's where you'll find all the action—from fast food to fine dining, nightlife including everything from the sweet sounds of Hawaiian melodies to spicy dance music, shopping from bargains to brand names, and every ocean activity you can imagine. Staying here puts you in the heart of it all, but be aware that Waikiki is an on-the-go city with crowds, traffic, noise, and its fair share of crime.

Waikiki, Ewa End

All the hotels listed below are located in the area bordered by the ocean to Ala Wai Boulevard, and between Ala Wai Terrace, in the Ewa Beach direction (or western side of Waikiki), and Olohana Street and Fort DeRussy Park, in the Diamond Head direction (or eastern side of Waikiki).

VERY EXPENSIVE

Hawaii Prince Hotel Waikiki ★★ For a vacation with a view (and the feel of a palace), stay in this striking $150-million modern structure—actually, twin 33-story high-tech towers. The high-ceilinged lobby is a mass of pink Italian marble with English slate accents; a grand piano sits in the midst of the raised seating area, where high tea is served every afternoon. A glass-encased elevator with views of Honolulu whisks you up to your room. All bedrooms, which are larger than the average Waikiki hotel room, face the Ala Wai Yacht Harbor, with floor-to-ceiling sliding-glass windows that let you enjoy the view (sorry, no lanais);

PREVIOUS PAGE: **The confectionary pink Royal Hawaiian Hotel.**

the higher the floor, the higher the price.

Following Japanese standards, the level of service is impeccable; no detail is ignored, and no request is too small. The outdoor pool is one of the few saltwater pools in Waikiki, with no chemi-

Lounging on a Lanai

Don't go asking for a balcony in Oahu; you won't find one. Instead, islanders call them lanais. If you're into balcony lounging, be sure to request a lanai with an ocean view.

cals or chlorine added. The location is perfect for shopping—Ala Moana Center is a 10-minute walk away—and Waikiki's beaches are just a 5-minute walk away (both are also accessible via the hotel's shuttle bus). Culinary options include two great restaurants, one with award-winning Japanese cuisine and one with Euro-Asian buffets (Prince Court, p. 127), plus a lobby cafe coffee bar in the morning and a wine bar in the afternoon.

100 Holomoana St. (just across Ala Wai Canal Bridge, on the ocean side of Ala Moana Blvd.), Honolulu, HI 96815. www.princeresortshawaii.com. © **800/321-OAHU** [6428] or 808/956-1111. Fax 808/946-0811. 521 units. $390–$520 double; from $610 suite. Extra person $60. Children 17 and under stay free in parent's room. AE, DC, DISC, MC, V. Valet parking $21, self-parking $15. Bus: 19 or 20. **Amenities:** 2 restaurants; outdoor bar; babysitting; concierge; executive-level rooms; 27-hole golf club a 40-min. shuttle ride away in Ewa Beach; small but newly renovated fitness room; Jacuzzi; outdoor pool; room service; small day spa. *In room:* A/C, TV, fridge, hair dryer, Wi-Fi ($12/day).

Trump International Hotel Waikiki Beach Walk ★★★ Overlooking the Fort DeRussy Park—and from the upper floors, the beach of Waikiki—this 38-story, 464-unit high-rise proudly bears the name of the U.S.'s most famous real estate developer, Donald Trump. The luxury hotel, made up of condominium units, has only one caveat: It's not on the beach. But it is across the street from the beach (well, across the street and behind another large condominium hotel). However, Trump offers a "beach attaché," sort of a beach butler to help carry your beach toys (or you can get a complimentary beach bag with cooler, drinks, towels, and reading material) from the hotel to the beach. They also offer a beach desk on the beach for renting lounge chairs, umbrellas, and so on. They will even take your order and deliver lunch, if you ask.

An exquisite spa, two restaurants (including **BLT Steak**), and excellent concierge service make this property one of Waikiki's most luxurious accommodations. Just a few notes: There is a very small "plunge" pool on the property (families with kids, take note—this is not a pool for them). Although absolutely beautiful and luxurious, the property does not "feel" like Hawaii, but more like a luxury hotel in New York. If you are looking for a taste of the islands, this may not be your place.

Smoking vs. Nonsmoking in Your Hotel

Hawaii is a nonsmoking state, with strict antismoking laws in public areas. Most hotels, resorts, condos, and vacation rentals have a no-smoking policy in their rooms, and the majority of bed-and-breakfast units forbid smoking in the rooms. Be sure to check the policy of your accommodations before you book. If you want a room you can smoke in, be sure to request it.

4

WHERE TO STAY

Waikiki

Ala Moana Hotel **1**	The Equus **2**
Aqua Bamboo and Spa **35**	Hale Koa Hotel **8**
Aqua Island Colony Hotel **22**	Halekulani **19**
Aqua Waikiki Wave **27**	Hawaii Prince Hotel Waikiki **3**
Aston at the Waikiki Banyan **38**	Hilton Hawaiian Village Beach Resort & Spa **6**
Aston Waikiki Beach Hotel **40**	Hilton Waikiki Beach **37**
Aston Waikiki Joy **12**	Holiday Inn Waikiki Beachcomber **28**
Best Western Aqua Coconut Plaza **10**	Holiday Surf **23**
The Breakers **13**	Hotel Renew **41**
Diamond Head Bed & Breakfast **44**	Hyatt Regency Waikiki **33**
DoubleTree by Hilton Alana Waikiki Hotel **7**	Ilikai Hotel **4**
Embassy Suites Hotel Waikiki Beach Walk **15**	Ilima Hotel **24**

223 Saratoga Rd. (at Kalia Rd.), Waikiki, HI 96815. www.trumpwaikikihotel.com. ☎ **877/683-7401** or 808/683-7401. Fax 808/683-7788. 464 units. $329–$379 studio; $449–$729 1-bed-room. AE, DC, DISC, MC, V. Valet parking $28. Bus: 19 or 20. **Amenities:** 2 restaurants; lounge; babysitting; concierge; fitness center; outdoor "plunge" pool; room service; spa. *In room:* A/C, TV, hair dryer, complimentary high-speed Internet access, kitchen.

EXPENSIVE

Hilton Hawaiian Village Beach Resort & Spa ★★ ☺ Sprawling over 20 acres on a gorgeous stretch of Waikiki Beach, Waikiki's biggest resort is a minicity unto itself, so big it even has its own post office. You'll find tropical gardens dotted with exotic birds, award-winning restaurants, 100 different shops, a secluded lagoon, and two minigolf courses. This is a great place to stay with the kids: The

Ala Wai Golf Course

Ala Wai Blvd.

Leahi Ave.
Paki Ave.

Nohonani St.
Nahua St.
Walina St.
Kanekapolei St.
Kaiulani Ave.

Seaside Ave.

Cleghorn St.

Pualani Wy.

22   23   24   25   26   34

27

International Market Place

28

Kalakaua Ave.

30   31

29

Waikiki Beach

Kaiulani Ave.
Pr. Edward St.
Koa Ave.

35   36   37   38

32   33

Liliuokalani Ave.
Kealohilani Ave.
Ohua
Paoakalani

Kuhio Ave.
Cartwright Rd.
42
Lemon Rd.
43
41

39

40

Kuhio Beach Park

Kapahulu Ave.

Honolulu Zoo

Monsarrat Ave.

Kalakaua Ave.

Kapiolani Park

Gray's Beach

Bay

Queen's Surf Beach

Waikiki Aquarium

To Diamond Head

Natatorium

44

Kai Aloha Apartment Hotel **14**
Moana Surfrider, A Westin Resort **31**
New Otani Kaimana Beach Hotel **44**
Ocean Resort Hotel Waikiki **42**
Ohana Waikiki Malia **11**
Ohana Waikiki West **26**
Outrigger Reef on the Beach **18**
Outrigger Waikiki Shore **17**
Outrigger Waikiki on the Beach **30**
Patrick Winston's Waikiki Condos **25**
Queen Kapiolani Hotel **43**
Ramada Plaza Waikiki **5**

Royal Grove Hotel **36**
Royal Hawaiian **29**
Sheraton Princess Kaiulani Hotel **32**
Sheraton Waikiki **21**
Trump International Hotel Waikiki Beach Walk **16**
Waikiki Beach Marriott Resort & Spa **39**
Waikiki Parc **20**
Waikiki Sand Villa **34**
Wyndham Vacation Resorts Royal Garden at Waikiki **9**

children's program, one of Waikiki's best, offers a wide range of educational and fun activities, and at three of the resort's restaurants, kids ages 4 to 11 eat free. In 2007, the property underwent a "Village Rejuvenation," with a total revamp of the Duke Kahanamoku Lagoon.

Rooms, which range from simply lovely to ultradeluxe, are housed in five towers, each with its own restaurants and shopping. This division reduces the chaotic, impersonal feeling you can get from a resort this size. Still, this is the place for a lively, activity-packed vacation; those seeking a more intimate experience might want to look elsewhere. All rooms are large and beautifully furnished; if you can afford it, we highly recommend the ones in the Alii Tower, located right on the ocean. Guests in these 348 amenity-laden rooms and suites get the royal treatment, including in-room registration, an exclusive health club and pool, and the full attention of a multilingual staff.

The superluxe **Mandara Spa** ★★ also features a state-of-the-art fitness center. And—not that you should plan to do business on your vacation—there is a 24-hour hotel business center on property for those who must stay in touch. The latest addition to the village was the recently opened $6-million **Ocean Crystal Chapel,** Waikiki's only free-standing resort wedding chapel.

2005 Kalia Rd. (at Ala Moana Blvd.), Honolulu, HI 96815. www.hiltonhawaiianvillage.com. 🕾 **800/HILTONS** [445-8667] or 808/949-4321. Fax 808/951-5458. 2,860 units. $209–$339 double; suites from $345. Extra person $50. Children 18 and under stay free in parent's room. AE, DC, DISC, MC, V. Valet parking $30, self-parking $24. Bus: 19 or 20. **Amenities:** 12 restaurants (including Bali Steak and Seafood, p. 126); 5 bars; babysitting; children's program; concierge; concierge-level rooms; fitness center (fee); 6 outdoor pools; room service; spa; watersports equipment rentals. *In room:* A/C, TV, fridge, hair dryer, high-speed Internet ($17/day).

MODERATE

DoubleTree by Hilton Alana Waikiki Hotel ★ This boutique hotel operated by the Hilton Hawaiian Village is a welcome oasis of beauty, comfort, and service. It's an intimate choice, offering the amenities of a much larger, more luxurious hotel at affordable prices. In 2010, the guest rooms underwent a nearly $3-million renovation with new carpet, wallpaper, curtains, refinished and reupholstered furniture, 25-inch TVs, and "Sweet Dream" pillow beds. Some rooms may be small but make good use of the space and offer all the amenities you'd expect from a more expensive hotel. Wireless Internet access is available throughout the hotel, and hard-wired DSL service is on four floors. Many guests are business travelers who expect top-drawer service—and the Alana Waikiki delivers. The staff is attentive to detail and willing to go to great lengths to make you happy. Waikiki Beach is a 10-minute walk away, and the convention center is about a 7-minute walk.

1956 Ala Moana Blvd. (on the Ewa side, near Kalakaua Ave.), Honolulu, HI 96815. www.double tree.com. 🕾 **800/222-TREE** [8733] or 808/941-7275. Fax 808/949-0996. 317 units. $139–$209 double; from $239 suite. Extra person $40. Children under 18 stay free in parent's room. AE, DC, DISC, MC, V. Valet parking $27. Bus: 19 or 20. **Amenities:** Bar; concierge; poolside fitness center; outdoor heated pool; room service. *In room:* A/C, TV, fridge, hair dryer, high-speed Internet ($10/day).

Ilikai Hotel You can't beat the location of the Ilikai Hotel—sitting at the entrance to Waikiki, it overlooks the Ala Wai Harbor and is within walking distance to numerous restaurants and shops. It features a rooftop pool with cabanas, reflecting pool in the lobby/courtyard, spa, second-floor pool, and cafe in the porte-cochere. Public areas display the spectacular ocean view, and rooms overlook the ocean and mountains. Recently the Aqua Hotels and Resorts has taken over the management here and is offering deals for seniors, and family packages. Check the website for online deals, which can make this property very appealing economy-wise.

1777 Ala Moana Blvd. (at Hobron Lane), Honolulu, HI 96815. www.ilikaihotel.com. 🕾 **800/367-8434** or 808/949-3811. Fax 808/947-0892. 343 units. $159–$454 double. AE, DC, DISC, MC, V. Valet parking $22. Bus: 19 or 20. **Amenities:** Restaurant; bar; concierge; concierge-level rooms; fitness room; Jacuzzi; pool; room service. *In room:* A/C, TV, hair dryer; free high-speed Internet; kitchen (in some units).

Wyndham Vacation Resorts Royal Garden at Waikiki 🎁 This quiet, boutique hotel, tucked away on a tree-lined side street, is now being turned into a time share by Wyndham Hotels. It's located in a "quiet" area of Waikiki, and though the hotel is smaller, they offer more personal service than some of the big ones. Plus it has a tropical garden area with pool, good sized rooms, and a moderate price for Waikiki. With the new ownership the rates have been lowered, but keep in mind that the beach is a few blocks away (about a 10–15 min. walk, but worth it at these prices), and it is a time share, so you may be approached with a sales pitch.

440 Olohana St. (btw. Kuhio Ave. and Ala Wai Blvd.), Honolulu, HI 96815. www.royalgardens. com. ☎ **800/989-0971** or 808/943-0202. Fax 808/946-8777. 210 units. $116–$124 studios; from $161–$174 1-bedroom suites. Extra person $30. Children under 12 stay free in parent's room. AE, DC, DISC, MC, V. Valet parking only $14. Bus: 19 or 20. **Amenities:** Lounge; 2 Jacuzzis; 2 freshwater outdoor pools (1 w/cascading waterfall); 2 saunas; laundry rooms. *In room:* A/C, fridge, microwave, hair dryer, Internet access ($10/day), kitchenette, TV, washer/dryer (some rooms).

INEXPENSIVE

The Equus Formerly the Hawaii Polo Inn but now under the management of Aqua Hotels and Resorts, this small boutique hotel was renovated and upgraded a few years ago. The very comfortable inn is within walking distance of the Ala Moana Shopping Center, Waikiki Beach, and the Hawaii Convention Center. All but one of the modest-sized rooms are shower-only, and studio suites are proportionally small but have microwaves and hot plates. *Warning:* Ala Moana Boulevard is very noisy; ask for a room in the back or bring earplugs. Also, the neighborhood can be a little dicey after dark.

1696 Ala Moana Blvd. (btw. Hobron Lane and Ala Wai Canal), Honolulu, HI 96815. www.equus hotel.com. ☎ **866/406-2782** or 808/949-0061. Fax 808/949-4906. 68 units. $84–$204 double; from $164 suite; from $85 studio with kitchenette in Aqua Waikiki Marina next door. Extra person $25. Children 18 and under stay free in parent's room. AE, DISC, MC, V. Parking $20. Bus: 19 or 20. **Amenities:** Tiny outdoor wading pool. *In room:* A/C, TV, fridge, hair dryer, Internet (free), microwave.

Ramada Plaza Waikiki Just 2 blocks from the beach, 2 blocks from Ala Moana Shopping Center, and a 7-minute walk from the convention center, this former Holiday Inn has a great location and offers the Ramada chain's usual amenities for prices that are quite reasonable for Waikiki. All rooms, which have a modern look, are equipped with either a king-size bed or two doubles. The property sits back from the street, so noise is minimal. Staff is unbelievably friendly.

1830 Ala Moana Blvd. (btw. Hobron Lane and Kalia Rd.), Honolulu, HI 96815. www.ramada plazawaikiki.com. ☎ **888/992-4545** or 808/955-1111. Fax 808/947-1799. 199 units. $96–$144 double; from $232 suite. Children 19 and under stay free in parent's room. AE, DC, DISC, MC, V. Parking $15. Bus: 19 or 20. **Amenities:** Restaurant; small fitness room; outdoor pool; room service. *In room:* A/C, TV, fridge, hair dryer, Wi-Fi (free).

Mid-Waikiki, Makai

All the hotels listed below are between the ocean and Kalakaua Avenue, and between Fort DeRussy in the Ewa (west) direction and Kaiulani Street in the Diamond Head (east) direction.

A ROOM FOR everyone

Among the largest hotel chains in Waikiki, Outrigger and Ohana hotels offer excellent accommodations across the board. The **Outrigger properties** are more resort-oriented, with amenities like concierge service, children's programs, and a variety of restaurants and shops. You'll be comfortable at any of its outposts: **Outrigger Waikiki on the Beach** (p. 97), **Outrigger Reef on the Beach** (p. 94), and **Outrigger Waikiki Shore Resort Condo** (p. 96).

There are plenty of packages available for these properties. Ask about other deals, like a fifth night free, discount rates for seniors over 50, family plans (children 17 and under stay free in parent's room using existing bedding), even romance and honeymoon packages. To inquire about current offerings and make reservations at any of the Outrigger properties throughout the islands, contact **Outrigger Hotels & Resorts** (www.outrigger.com; ✆ **800/ OUTRIGGER** or 808/942-7722).

The Ohana Hotels offer clean, dependable, moderately priced, and well-appointed rooms in central locations. The chain's price structure is based entirely on location, room size, and amenities. Check the website, where "best available rates" start at $79 (a true bargain in Waikiki!). Ohana also offers other deals, including air and car-rental packages; for information, contact **Ohana Hotels & Resorts** (www. ohanahotels.com; ✆ **800/462-6262**).

VERY EXPENSIVE

Halekulani ★★★ ☺ Here's the ultimate heavenly Hawaii vacation. Halekulani translates as "house befitting heaven"—an apt description of this luxury resort spread over 5 acres of prime Waikiki beachfront. Its five buildings are connected by open courtyards and lush, tropical gardens. Upon arrival, you're immediately greeted and escorted to your room, where registration is handled in comfort and privacy. About 90% of the rooms face the ocean, and they're big (averaging 620 sq. ft.), each with a separate sitting area and a large, furnished lanai. Each bathroom features a deep soaking tub, a separate glassed-in shower, and a marble basin. Recent renovations to this luxury property include total refurbishment of the rooms, new entertainment centers with DVD players, a bedside control panel, wireless Internet service, and a new spa.

Other perks include complimentary tickets to any or all of the following: Iolani Palace, the Bishop Museum, the Contemporary Museum and the Honolulu Academy of Arts, and the Honolulu Symphony. A great children's program is offered during holidays. The hotel's restaurants (including La Mer, p. 123; and Orchids, p. 126) are outstanding, and the **House Without a Key** ★★ (p. 263) is surely one of the world's most romantic spots for sunset cocktails, light meals, and entertainment. You can't find a better location on Waikiki Beach or a more luxurious hotel.

2199 Kalia Rd. (at the ocean end of Lewers St.), Honolulu, HI 96815. www.halekulani.com. ✆ **800/367-2343** or 808/923-2311. Fax 808/926-8004. 455 units. $490–$680; from $960 suite. Extra person $125. 1 child under 17 stays free in parent's room using existing bedding; additional rollaway bed $40. Maximum 3 people per room. AE, DC, MC, V. Parking $22. Bus: 19 or 20. **Amenities:** 3 superb restaurants (including La Mer and Orchids); 2 bars (including Lewers Lounge, p. 268); babysitting; bike rentals; children's program in summer and at Christmas; 24-hr.

concierge; fitness center; gorgeous outdoor pool; room service; spa; watersports equipment rentals. *In room:* A/C, TV/DVD, hair dryer, minibar, Wi-Fi (free).

EXPENSIVE

Embassy Suites Waikiki Beach Walk ★★★ ☺ This ultraluxurious outpost of the hotel chain, known for its complimentary, all-you-can-eat, "cooked to order" breakfast and evening manager's cocktail reception, has one of the best central locations in Waikiki: It lies amid the shops and restaurants of the newly opened **beach walk** (p. 98), just across the street from the beach. The one- and two-bedroom suites feature top-of-the-line furniture, Hawaiian decor (such as bronze hula lamps), plush mattresses, high-quality linen, granite bathroom counters, CD/MP3 players, and views from every window (some are ocean-view). The amenities here are numerous; each suite features a separate living room, flat-panel LCD TV, minifridge, wet bar, microwave, coffeemaker, and lots of entertainment electronics to keep the teenagers happy. The two-towered property is connected via a huge lobby area (with sun deck, swimming pool, waterfall, and covered terrace where those yummy breakfasts are served). At first glance the prices may seem high, but when you add in the included breakfast, evening reception, and amenities, it pencils out to quite a deal for families.

201 Beachwalk St., Honolulu, HI 96815 www.waikikibeach.embassysuites.com. ℂ**800/EMBASSY** [362-2779] or 808/921-2345. Fax 808/921-2343. 421 suites. $242–$349 1-bedroom; $442–$600 2-bedroom. Extra person (over 2 people) in 1-bedroom $60. AE, DC, DISC, MC, V. Parking $25. Bus: 19 or 20. **Amenities:** Complimentary "cooked to order" breakfast and cocktail party daily; nearby restaurants and bars; bike rentals; children's program in summer and at Christmas; 24-hr. concierge; 24-hour fitness center; outdoor pool and whirlpool spa; room service (lunch and dinner); watersports equipment rentals. *In room:* A/C, TV/DVD, CD/MP3 player, small fridge, hair dryer, microwave, Wi-Fi (free), free local calls.

Moana Surfrider, A Westin Resort ★★ ☺ This wonderful property was Waikiki's first hotel—it dates from 1901 and is listed on the National Register of Historic Places. The rooms have the usual comfy Westin amenities: Heavenly Beds, flat-screen TVs, and the Westin Kids Club child-care program. Plus, there is a spa on property, which fills most of the second floor. It's hard to get a bad room here—most bedrooms have ocean views and all come with bedside controls, luxury amenities, and comfy plush bathrobes. Our pick is the Banyan Wing, where the historic rooms are modern replicas of the hotel's first rooms. They are small and don't have lanais, but they're all reminiscent of Hawaii circa the turn of the century, when steam-ship travel with big trunks was the only way to see the islands. Back then, the Moana was considered an innovation in the travel industry: Each guest room featured a private bathroom and a telephone—an unheard-of luxury in the early 20th century. And yesteryear lives on at this grand hotel: The female employees wear traditional Victorian-era muumuu, and the aloha spirit that pervades this classy and charming hotel is infectious.

One of the best reasons to stay here is the hotel's prime stretch of beach, with a lifeguard, beach chairs, towels, and any other service you desire. The **Beach Bar** and a poolside snack bar are located in an oceanfront courtyard centering on a 100-year-old banyan tree, where live music is featured in the evenings.

2365 Kalakaua Ave. (ocean side of the street, across from Kaiulani St.), Honolulu, HI 96815. www. moana-surfrider.com or www.starwoodhotelshawaii.com. ℂ**800/325-3535** or 808/922-3111. Fax 808/923-0308. 793 units. $245–$380 double; from $1,050 suite. Plus resort fee $21/day.

B&B Etiquette

In Hawaii, it is traditional and customary to remove your shoes before entering anyone's home. The same is true for most bed-and-breakfast facilities. Most hosts post signs or will politely ask you to remove your shoes before entering the B&B. Not only does this keep the place clean, but you'll also be amazed at how relaxing it is to walk around barefoot. If this custom is unpleasant to you, a B&B may not be for you.

If you've never stayed at a B&B before, here are a few other hints: Generally the hosts live on the property, and their part of the house is off-limits to guests (you do not have the "run of the house"). Most likely there will be a common area that you can use. Don't expect daily maid service. Your host may tidy up, but will not do complete maid service. Also don't expect amenities like little bottles of shampoo and conditioner—this is a B&B, not a resort. Remember you are sharing your accommodations with other guests, so be considerate when you come in late at night.

Extra person and rollaway bed $90. Children under 18 stay free in parent's room using existing bedding. AE, DC, DISC, MC, V. Valet parking $33; self-parking at sister property $26. Bus: 19 or 20. **Amenities:** 3 restaurants; bar; babysitting; children's program; concierge; nearby fitness room (about a 2-min. walk down the beach at the Sheraton Waikiki); outdoor pool; room service; watersports equipment rentals. *In room:* A/C, TV, fridge, hair dryer, high-speed Internet access ($14–$19 per day).

Outrigger Reef on the Beach ★ ☺ The same value and quality that we've come to expect in every Outrigger hotel are definitely in evidence here, only multiplied by a factor of ten. Even the standard rooms in this 16-story oceanfront hotel are large and comfortable. The prime beachfront location and loads of facilities (including the wonderful **Serenity Spa Hawaii ★★★,** p. 20) help make this one of the chain's most attractive properties. Even if you aren't staying here, wander through the renovated lobby, filled with rare and historic Hawaiian artifacts (like a century-old canoe made of koa wood). The guest rooms all have huge closets, plenty of amenities, and spacious lanais; the price is entirely dependent on the view. Roomy bathrooms feature granite vanity tops, ceramic floor tiles, and lighted makeup mirrors. Just added: free high-speed Internet connection (most hotels charge from $11 a day) and free local phone calls. If money is no object, book the Deluxe Oceanfront units, which feature oversize Jacuzzi bathtubs with ocean views of Waikiki Beach. The on-site **Shorebird Beach Broiler** is an immensely popular oceanside spot offering buffet breakfasts and broil-your-own dinners. Another on-property restaurant is **Kani Ka Pila Grille,** which features nightly performances by legendary Hawaiian musicians.

2169 Kalia Rd., Honolulu, HI 96815. www.outrigger.com. **☏ 800/OUTRIGGER** [688-7444] or 808/923-3111. Fax 800/622-4852. 525 units. $209–$382 double; from $499 suite. Ask about package deals, like 5th night free or discount rates for seniors over 50. Extra person $50. Children 17 and under stay free in parent's room using existing bedding. AE, DC, DISC, MC, V. Valet-only parking $25. Bus: 19 or 20. **Amenities:** 3 restaurants (including Hula Grill Waikiki, p. 130; and Duke's Waikiki, p. 129); 3 bars; showroom w/nightly entertainment; babysitting; concierge; concierge-level rooms; fitness center; Jacuzzi; giant outdoor pool; room service; new Waikiki Plantation Spa; watersports equipment rentals. *In room:* A/C, TV, fridge, hair dryer, high-speed Internet access (free), kitchenette (in some units), free calls to Hawaii and U.S. mainland.

Royal Hawaiian ★★ This flamingo-pink oasis, hidden away among blooming gardens within the concrete jungle of Waikiki, is the height of luxury. Built by Matson steamship lines, the Spanish-Moorish "Pink Palace" opened in 1927 on the same spot where Queen Kaahumanu had her summer palace—on one of the best stretches of Waikiki Beach.

Pass through the lush garden with a spectacular banyan tree, then step into the black terrazzo-marble lobby, which features hand-woven pink carpets and giant floral arrangements. Historic touches include Hawaiian craft displays (quilts, leis, weaving) by local artists every Monday, Wednesday, and Friday, and a new guest activity program with ukulele lessons, lei making, *lauhala* weaving, hula classes, historic tours, and evening "talk story" sessions featuring Hawaiian legends. We were won over by the Historic Wing's rooms, which contain carved wooden doors, four-poster canopy beds, flowered wallpaper, and period furniture. If you prefer the newer rooms, the latest decor is more Tommy Bahama, with a tropical palm tree motif.

One of Waikiki's best spas, **Abhasa** ★★ (ⓒ 808/922-8200; www. abhasa.com), is located on-site. This large contemporary spa concentrates on natural, organic treatments in a soothing atmosphere (the smell of eucalyptus wafts through the air) with everything from the latest aromatherapy thalassotherapy (soaking in a sweet-smelling hot bath of salt water) to shiatsu massages. Its specialty is a cold-laser, anti-aging treatment that promises to give you a refreshed, revitalized face in just 30 minutes.

In the culinary department, the Surf Lanai has replaced the Surf Room as the properties' oceanfront eatery featuring American cuisine (hamburgers), along with another beachfront restaurant, Azure, with Hawaii Regional Cuisine. The Royal Hawaiian luau is done in grand style on Monday nights. And the hotel's **Mai Tai Bar** ★★ is one of the most popular places in Waikiki for its namesake drink, which supposedly originated here.

2259 Kalakaua Ave. (at Royal Hawaiian Ave., on the ocean side of the Royal Hawaiian Shopping Center), Honolulu, HI 96815. www.royal-hawaiian.com or www.starwoodhotelshawaii.com. ⓒ **800/325-3535** or 808/923-7311. Fax 808/924-7098. 527 units. $285–$350 double; from $610 suite. Plus Resort Fee $21/day. Extra person $125. Ask about special packages. AE, DC, DISC, MC, V. Valet parking $33; self-parking at Sheraton Waikiki $25. Bus: 19 or 20. **Amenities:** 2 restaurants; landmark bar; babysitting; bike rentals; excellent year-round children's program; multilingual concierge desk; preferential tee times at various golf courses; excellent nearby fitness room (next door at the Sheraton Waikiki); good-size outdoor pool; room service; full-service spa (Abhasa); watersports equipment rentals. *In room:* A/C, TV, fridge, hair dryer, high-speed Internet access ($15/day).

Sheraton Waikiki ★ ☺ Occupying two 30-story towers, this is by far the biggest of Waikiki's four beachfront Sheratons. The lobby is immense and filled with shops, travel desks, and people, including loads of conventioneers. If you're not comfortable with crowds, book elsewhere. However, size has its advantages: The Sheraton has everything from a fabulous kids' program (boogie boarding, kite flying, nightly movies) to historical walks and cooking demonstrations for Mom and Dad. Plus, you can "play and charge" (back to your room tab) at Waikiki's other Sheraton hotels.

In 2011, the Sheraton also added The Link @ Sheraton (complimentary Wi-Fi and computers in the lobby for the guest's use) and partnered up with Core Fitness to create Core Fitness by Sheraton, featuring a fully equipped gym and complimentary aerobics classes.

After 39 years of operation, the Sheraton Waikiki also closed its 30th-floor restaurant, the Hanohano Room, and converted it into a Premiere Club Lounge. The $1-million conversion from restaurant to Executive- or Conceriege-level lounge included the addition of The Club, which offers Club Guest Room members such upgrades and amenities as a continental breakfast, evening appetizers and cocktails, a media wall, free Wi-Fi and computer stations (including a printer), and concierge service. Club-level rooms will be priced at a $75 premium over rack rates and will be located on the 22nd and 30th floors (with access to the Premiere Club Lounge). The rooms will have extra amenities such as robes, slippers, and extra toiletries.

That said, it's hard to get a bad room here. A whopping 1,200 units have some sort of ocean view, and 650 rooms overlook Diamond Head. Accommodations are spacious, with big lanais for taking it all in. The Sheraton has a minimalist design, and amenities include its trademark Sweet Sleeper bed, big LCD flat-screen TVs, and high-speed Internet ($14–$25/day). For the budget-conscious, the Sheraton Manor Hotel occupies a separate adjacent wing and offers all the services and beachfront of the main hotel. The views aren't the best, and the rooms are small and modestly appointed (no lanais), but the price is hard to beat.

2255 Kalakaua Ave. (at Royal Hawaiian Ave., on the ocean side of the Royal Hawaiian Shopping Center and west of the Royal Hawaiian), Honolulu, HI 96815. www.sheraton.com or www.starwoodhotelshawaii.com. ℂ **800/325-3535** or 808/922-4422. Fax 808/923-8785. 1,852 units. $225–$329 double; from $405 suite. Plus Resort Fee $21/day. Extra person $90. Children under 18 stay free in parent's room. AE, DC, DISC, MC, V. Valet parking $33; self-parking $25. Bus: 19 or 20. **Amenities:** 4 restaurants; 3 bars; nightclub; babysitting; bike rentals; children's program; concierge; access to Makaha Golf Club's golf and tennis facilities (about 1 hr. away); fitness center; 2 large outdoor pools, including one of the biggest and sunniest along the Waikiki beachfront; room service; watersports equipment rentals. *In room:* A/C, TV, fridge, hair dryer, high-speed Internet access ($14–$25 per day), kitchenette, minibar.

Outrigger Waikiki Shore ★★ As soon as you arrive, you'll see why everyone wants to stay here: the location (right on Waikiki beach, close to restaurants and shopping) and the view (a spectacular panoramic vista of the entire shoreline from Diamond Head to Honolulu). The apartments—which are privately owned and decorated and then rented through Outrigger—range in size from studios to two-bedrooms. Each has a fully equipped kitchen, big lanai, spacious sitting area, washer/dryer, and fabulous views. Full-time residents also live in this complex, so it tends to be quiet and security is tight—entry to the units is through a locked gate and keyed elevators. Because this establishment is part of the Outrigger chain, guests have full access to the Outrigger Reef (right next door), including its pool, exercise room, and business center. Daily maid service, a few on-site shops, and plenty of assistance from the front desk give this condominium stay all the benefits of hotel service with the roominess of your own apartment. As you might expect, reservations are hard to get; book *way* in advance.

2161 Kalia Rd. (on the ocean at Saratoga Rd., across the street from Ft. DeRussy), Honolulu, HI 96815. www.outrigger.com. ℂ **800/OUTRIGGER** [688-7444]. Fax 800/622-4852. 168 units. $175–$279 studio double; $205–$379 1-bedroom apt. (sleeps up to 4); $345–$395 2-bedroom apt. (up to 6). Extra person $50. Ask about Outrigger package deals such as free car rental or bed-and-breakfast deals. AE, DC, DISC, MC, V. Valet parking $30 (at the Reef next door). Bus: 19 or 20. **Amenities:** Outdoor pool; access to all the facilities at the Outrigger Reef next door (including 3 restaurants, 3 bars, babysitting, children's program, concierge, fitness room,

Jacuzzi). *In room:* A/C, TV/VCR, fridge, hair dryer, kitchen, washer/dryer, complimentary high speed Internet access.

MODERATE

The Breakers ★ 🌀 Just a 2-minute walk from numerous restaurants, shopping, and Waikiki Beach, The Breakers is about old-fashioned Hawaiian aloha, comfortable frugal accommodations, and family-friendly prices. This two-story 1950s hotel has an accommodating staff and a loyal following. Its six buildings are set around a pool and a tropical garden blooming with brilliant red and yellow hibiscus; wooden jalousies and shoji doors further the tropical ambience. Each of the tastefully decorated, slightly oversize rooms comes with a lanai, kitchenette, and shower-only bathroom. Every Wednesday and Friday, you're invited (as a paying guest) to a formal Japanese tea ceremony from 10am to noon at the Urasenke Tea House next door.

250 Beach Walk (btw. Kalakaua Ave. and Kalia Rd.), Honolulu, HI 96815. www.breakers-hawaii. com. 📞 **800/426-0494** or 808/923-3181. Fax 808/923-7174. 64 units (all with shower only). $130–$150 double; $185 garden studio double. Each additional person $20. AE, DC, MC, V. Limited free parking (just 7 stalls); additional parking across the street $16/day. Bus: 19 or 20. **Amenities:** Restaurant (poolside bar Mon–Fri, grill Fri lunch only); outdoor pool. *In room:* A/C, TV, fridge, hair dryer (on request), kitchenette.

Outrigger Waikiki on the Beach ★ ☺ Not only do you get the value and quality of the Outrigger chain at Outrigger Waikiki on the Beach (including spacious rooms and plenty of amenities), you also get a terrific Waikiki Beach location and prices much lower than this property's neighbors (Moana Surfrider; p. 93). The price is entirely dependent on the view. The just-added free high-speed Internet access (most hotels charge at least $10–$11 a day) and free local phone calls make this hotel one of the chain's most attractive properties. And don't miss the **Hula Grill Waikiki** (p. 130).

2335 Kalakaua Ave. (btw. the Royal Hawaiian Shopping Center and the Moana Surfrider), Honolulu, HI 96815. www.outrigger.com. 📞 **800/OUTRIGGER** [688-7444] or 808/923-0711. Fax 800/622-4852. 525 units. $189–$389 double; from $299 suite. Ask about package deals, such as 3rd night free or discount rates for seniors over 50. Extra person $50. Children 17 and under stay free in parent's room using existing bedding. AE, DC, DISC, MC, V. Valet-only parking $30. Bus: 19 or 20. **Amenities:** 3 restaurants (including Hula Grill Waikiki, p. 130; and Duke's Waikiki, p. 129); 3 bars; showroom w/nightly entertainment; babysitting; year-round children's program; concierge; concierge-level rooms; fitness center; new Waikiki Plantation Spa; Jacuzzi; giant outdoor pool; room service; watersports equipment rentals. *In room:* A/C, TV, fridge, hair dryer, high-speed Internet access (free), kitchenette (in some units), free calls to Hawaii and U.S. mainland.

Waikiki Parc ★★ This hotel is a great Waikiki secret, designed for the 20s-to-30s crowds. The "hidden" property offers lots of bonuses: terrifically located, just 100 yards from the beach, it's managed and run by the ultraluxury Halekulani hotel (but comes at a more reasonable price). The compact, beautifully appointed rooms have a contemporary, Hawaiian-Zen decor. Rooms are more spacious, with wired Internet access (the thick concrete walls, plus the density of Waikiki buildings, make wireless reception practically impossible); lanais with ocean, mountain, or city views; and adjustable floor-to-ceiling shutters for those who want to sleep in. The Parc features the same level of service that has made the Halekulani famous and offers an excellent restaurant, **Nobu Waikiki,** known for its famous chef and cutting-edge Japanese cuisine.

WAIKIKI beach WALK

If you haven't been to Waikiki in a few years, you'll be pleasantly surprised at the Waikiki Beach Walk. One of Waikiki's biggest projects in decades, the total renovation of an 8-acre area bound by Saratoga Road, Kalakaua Avenue, Lewers Street, and Kalia Road makes the area much more welcoming and visitor friendly than the crowded, narrow streets of just a few years ago. The project, by Outrigger Hotels & Resorts, cost some $460 million.

Phase One, completed in 2007, reconfigured the formerly very congested area (lots of delivery trucks double-parked, crammed sidewalks, and no vegetation) into an oasis of broad sidewalks, tropical foliage, water features, open space, and new, totally renovated hotels. Eleven hotels were razed, upgraded, or changed to suites or condos. Five hotels and one timeshare condominium remain. The bad news for budget travelers is that more-affordable near-oceanfront hotels, neighborhood eateries, and small independent shops have been replaced by luxury properties with 90,000 square feet of swank shops and trendy restaurants to match, all linked through pedestrian bridges and connecting walkways.

Other changes to the hotels in this area include:

- The former 480-room Ohana Reef Towers is now a 193-condominium unit timeshare, operated by Outrigger and renamed **Wyndham Waikiki Beach Walk.**

- The Ohana Edgewater and Ohana Coral Seas were razed and replaced by **Waikiki Beach Walk,** a 90,000-square-foot retail/entertainment complex with 40 retail shops, four major restaurants, four smaller food and beverage spots, and an open pedestrian plaza.

- The former Ohana Waikiki Village and the Ohana Waikiki Tower hotels, which had a total of 881 rooms, were demolished and an **Embassy Suites Waikiki Beach Walk,** with a total of 421 suites, was built to replace them.

- The **Outrigger Reef on the Beach** totally refurbished its rooms.

- The **Ohana Islander Waikiki,** on the corner of Kalakaua Avenue and Lewers Street, renovated its 280 units.

2233 Helumoa Rd. (at Lewers St.), Honolulu, HI 96815. www.waikikiparc.com. ☏ **800/422-0450** or 808/921-7272. Fax 808/923-1336. 297 units. $180–$251 double. Extra person $65. Children 17 and under stay free in parent's room. Ask about room and package deals that start at just $269 a night. AE, DC, MC, V. Valet parking $35; or self-parking $20. Bus: 19 or 20. **Amenities:** 2 restaurants; weekly wine reception; babysitting; concierge; fitness center; 8th-floor pool deck; room service. In room: A/C, TV, fridge, hair dryer, high-speed Internet access ($10/day).

INEXPENSIVE

Kai Aloha Apartment Hotel ⚑ If you are on a tight budget and want to experience the Waikiki of 40 years past, stay here. This small apartment hotel just a block from the beach is reminiscent of the low-key hotels that used to line the blocks of Waikiki in the good old days. It offers one-bedroom apartments and studios, all furnished in modest rattan and colorful island prints. Each of the one-bedroom units has a bedroom with either a queen-size bed or two twins, a living room with a couch and two additional twins (Hawaiian houses of 40 years ago all had extra guest beds, called *punee*, in the living room), a full kitchen, a dining table, and even voicemail. Rooms are large enough to accommodate a roll-away bed for a fifth person. Glass jalousies take advantage of the cooling trade winds, and there's air-conditioning for very hot days. Studios have two twin beds, kitchenettes, balconies, Plexiglas roofs in the bathroom (the forerunner of the skylight), and screen doors for ventilation. The units aren't exactly designer showrooms, but they do offer a homey, comfortable feel and daily maid service. Plus, you're sure to forgive the lack of aesthetics when you're presented with the bill. A large deck on the second floor is a great place to sip early-morning coffee or watch the sun sink into the Pacific.

235 Saratoga Rd. (across from Fort DeRussy and Waikiki post office, btw. Kalakaua Ave. and Kalia Rd.), Honolulu, HI 96815. www.kaialohahotel.com. (℃) **808/923-6723.** Fax 808/922 7592. 18 units. $85–$90 studio double; $100 1-bedroom double. Extra person $20. 2-night minimum. AE, MC, V. Parking at separate pay lot across the street for $16. Bus: 19 or 20. *In room:* A/C, TV, fridge, kitchenette, and complimentary computer with Internet access available in the office for guests during office hours.

A HOTEL FOR MILITARY PERSONNEL

Hale Koa Hotel ★★ 🏄 We wish we could stay here—but we're not allowed. This is a very exclusive hotel, for active-duty and retired military, reservists, National Guard, and their immediate families only. It's first-class, right on Waikiki Beach, with the grassy lawns of Fort DeRussy on the other side. The price structure, which depends on military rank (lower ranks get cheaper rates), is 50% to 75% less than what comparable Waikiki hotels charge. The hotel sits on 66 landscaped acres with picnic tables and barbecue grills. The only drawback is that it's usually booked; some guests reserve up to a year in advance.

2055 Kalia Rd. (across from Fort DeRussy, btw. Dewey Way and Saratoga Rd.), Honolulu, HI 96815. www.halekoa.com. (℃) **800/367-6027** or 808/955-0555. Fax 800/HALE-FAX [425-3329]. 817 units. Lower ranked enlisted personal rates $91–$222 double, depending on room views; higher rank $113–$289. Extra person $15. AE, DC, DISC, MC, V. Parking $7. Bus: 19 or 20. **Amenities:** 4 restaurants and bars (occasional dinner shows); babysitting; concierge desk; fitness room; Jacuzzi; 2 outdoor pools; room service; sauna; 4 lit tennis courts; racquetball and beach volleyball courts. *In room:* A/C, TV, hair dryer, high speed Internet access ($10/day).

Mid-Waikiki, Mauka

These mid-Waikiki hotels, on the mountain side of Kalakaua Avenue, are a little farther away from the beach than those listed above. They're all between Kalakaua Avenue and Ala Wai Boulevard, and between Kalaimoku Street in the Ewa direction and Kaiulani Street in the Diamond Head direction.

EXPENSIVE

Ilima Hotel ★ ☺ One of Hawaii's small, well-located condo-style hotels, the 17-story, pale-pink Ilima (named for the native orange flower used in royal leis) was once a moderately priced property, but has raised its rates recently, making this property on the pricey side. Rooms are huge; the location is great (near the International Market Place and the Royal Hawaiian Shopping Center, and 2 blocks from Waikiki Beach). A tasteful koa-wood lobby lined with works by Hawaiian artists greets you upon arrival. Perks include free local phone calls and a full kitchen in every unit; in addition, all the couches fold out into beds, making this a particularly good deal for families. (Kids will appreciate the Nintendo games in each room.) The one-bedroom units now have Jacuzzi tubs. The three sun decks, dry sauna, and truly nice people staffing the front desk help you enjoy your vacation. The only caveat: no ocean views.

445 Nohonani St. (near Ala Wai Blvd.), Honolulu, HI 96815. www.hotelwaikiki.com. © **800/801-9366** or 808/923-1877. Fax 808/924-2617. 99 units. $178–$258 double; $230–$280 1-bedroom (rate for 4); $300–$350 2-bedroom (rate for 4, sleeps up to 6); $560–$600 3-bedroom (rate for 6, sleeps up to 8). Extra person $10. Discounts available for seniors and business travelers. AE, DC, DISC, MC, V. Limited free on-site parking, $18 across the street. Bus: 19 or 20. **Amenities:** Exercise room; outdoor pool w/sauna. *In room:* A/C, TV, fridge, hair dryer, high-speed Internet access (free) in deluxe rooms (floors 10–16), kitchen.

MODERATE

Aqua Waikiki Wave ★ 👙 It is hard to believe that from the wreck of the old Coral Reef hotel, this sleek, modern oasis has emerged. The result of $7.6 million in renovations is a clean, hip decor with bright white walls, offset by the burnt orange fabric on the bed headboard that extends up to the ceiling. Potted plants and live orchids freshen up the rooms and flat-screen TVs and free Wi-Fi or high-speed Internet access bring them into the 21st century. About a 10-minute walk from the beach and next door to the International Market Place, rooms at the Wave either have two queen-size beds or a king (with very sleepable mattresses). The decades-old bathrooms have new plumbing, modern fixtures, and resurfaced tiles and tubs.

2299 Kuhio Ave (at Duke's Lane), Honolulu, HI 96817. www.aquaresorts.com. © **866/406-2782** or 808/922-1262. Fax 808/922-5048. 247 units. $128–$150 double; from $172 suite. Extra person $20. AE, DISC, MC, V. Parking $20. Bus: 19 or 20. **Amenities:** 2 restaurants; babysitting; fitness room; outdoor pool; spa. *In room:* A/C, TV/DVD, fridge, hair dryer, free Wi-Fi, free local calls.

Aston Waikiki Joy Tucked away down a narrow path on a side street, this boutique hotel offers outstanding personal service and a Jacuzzi in every room. The Italian marble–accented open-air lobby and the tropical veranda set the scene for the beautifully decorated guest rooms, each with a marble entry, tropical-island decor, and a lanai wide enough for you to sit and enjoy the views. Another plus: All the rooms are soundproof. The suites are even more luxurious: either a king-size bed or two doubles, a fridge, a microwave, a coffeemaker, and a wet bar. Executive suites come with two double beds and a kitchen with microwave and full fridge, and the executive king suites add a separate living room and bedroom. However, a few downsides do exist: The 1960s hotel has had some renovations (new carpet in the rooms, new paint), but it still is older. Plus the rack rates (even with a complimentary continental breakfast) are on the high side (check the Internet for deals), especially since the pool is extremely small and the property is located about a 10- to 15-minute walk to the beach. And although there's a sandwich/coffee shop onsite, the food's nothing to brag about. *Tip:* Check the website under "e-specials"; as we went to press the best rate for rooms started from $99.

320 Lewers St. (btw. Kuhio and Kalakaua aves.), Honolulu, HI 96815. www.astonhotels.com. © **877/997-6667** or 808/923-2300. Fax 808/924-4010. 94 units. $107–$168 double; $131–$187 double club suite; $180–$257 junior suite with kitchen (sleeps up to 4); $215–$307 1-bedroom executive suite with kitchen (up to 4). Rates include continental breakfast. Extra person $30 for certain rooms. Check the website for special deals and packages. AE, DC, DISC, MC, V. Valet-only parking $19. Bus: 19 or 20. **Amenities:** Restaurant; bar (karaoke); concierge; minuscule outdoor

pool w/dry sauna. *In room:* A/C, TV, fridge, hair dryer, Internet access ($10/day), kitchenette (full kitchen in suites).

Best Western Coconut Waikiki Built in 1962, this small, boutique hotel was totally renovated in 2008 into a comfortable inn with modern decor and amenities (such as free high-speed Internet and flat-screen TVs in every room). Formerly known as the Coconut Plaza, it's been managed by a host of companies; its current owner, Best Western, has made it a very affordable and welcoming place to stay. One of the main reasons to stay here is the price (which includes a continental breakfast) and its location—only a 10-minute walk to the beach and near a bus stop for those without a car. Rooms are comfy and spacious enough for a couple (if you have kids, get a second room). Staff is very friendly and helpful in pointing out things to do and places to eat. It is not on the water, but ask for a room with a mountain view and you'll be just as awe-inspired.

450 Lewers St. (at Ala Wai Blvd.), Honolulu, HI 96815. www.bestwesternhawaii.com/hotels/best-western-coconut-waikiki-hotel. *©* **808/923-8828.** Fax 808/923-3473. 80 units. $130–$180 double; from $450 suite. Rates include continental breakfast. Extra person $40. AE, DC, MC, V. Valet parking $22. Bus: 19 or 20. **Amenities:** Free high-speed Internet access in lobby; tiny outdoor pool w/sun deck. *In room:* A/C, TV, fridge, hair dryer, high-speed Internet access (free), kitchenette.

Holiday Inn Waikiki Beachcomber One of the pluses to this property is the great location—a block from Waikiki Beach, across the street from the up-scale Royal Hawaiian Shopping Center, and next door to bargain shopping at the International Market Place. The rooms feature Berber carpets, contemporary furniture, voicemail, and shower-only bathrooms. Sadly, the passing of Don Ho in 2007 meant the closing of his show, but another awe-inspiring show is in residence here: *The Magic of Polynesia,* with illusionist John Hirokana.

2300 Kalakaua Ave. (at Duke's Lane), Honolulu, HI 96815. www.waikikibeachcomberresort.com. *©* **800/462-6262** or 808/922-4646. Fax 808/926-9973. 492 units (all with shower only). $139–$214 double; from $405 suite. Extra person from $30. Check the website for special AAA and senior rates. AE, DC, DISC, MC, V. Parking $18. Bus: 19 or 20. **Amenities:** Poolside coffee shop; outdoor pool; free Wi-Fi in lobby. *In room:* A/C, TV, fridge, hair dryer, high-speed Internet access (free), complimentary local and mainland phone calls and newspaper delivery.

Ohana Waikiki Malia ☺ This large hotel—part of the cluster of Ohana Hotels on Kuhio Avenue and its surrounding blocks—just went through a $6.6-million dollar renovation of rooms and public spaces in 2010. It offers huge rooms with lanais and either a king-size bed or twins. Recently added are the one-bedroom suites with kitchenettes, great for families. Like those at most Ohana Hotels, the windows have black-out curtains, which not only keep the blaring morning sun out, but also help with the noise from busy Kuhio Avenue. Because a pool isn't on the premises, guests are welcome to use the one at the Ohana Waikiki Surf West across the street. But why bother? One of the most famous beaches in the world is just 3 blocks away. Wheelchair-accessible rooms outfitted with wide doorways and special grips in the bathroom are available.

2211 Kuhio Ave. (btw. Royal Hawaiian Ave. and Lewers St.), Honolulu, HI 96815. www.ohanahotels.com. *©* **800/462-6262** or 808/923-7621. Fax 800/622-4852 or 808/921-4804. 327 units. $105–$135 double; $125–$145 1-bedroom suite with kitchenette (up to 4 guests). Check the website for specials, discounts (seniors and AAA), and packages. Extra person $30. AE, DC, DISC, MC, V.

Parking $20. Bus: 19 or 20. **Amenities:** Restaurant (24-hr. coffee shop); access to amenities at other Ohana properties (childcare, dining, and more). *In room:* A/C, TV, free high-speed Internet access, fridge, hair dryer, kitchenette (some units).

Patrick Winston's Waikiki Condos 🎁 Looking for a condo priced to fit a tight budget, with a hefty dose of old-fashioned aloha? Try Patrick Winston's rentals, located on a quiet side street. When this five-story condominium hotel was built in 1981, Winston bought one unit; he has since acquired 24 more, spent hundreds of thousands of dollars on refurbishment, and put his spacious suites on the market at frugal prices. Staying here is like having a personal concierge; Winston has lots of terrific tips on where to eat, where to shop, and how to get the most for your money, and he can book any activity you want.

Three types of units are available: standard/budget rooms, one-bedroom suites, and ground-floor junior business suites. All have sofa beds, separate bedrooms, lanais with breakfast tables and chairs, ceiling fans, full kitchens, and showers in the bathrooms; most have washers and dryers. All are individually decorated. Eight units are "standard budget," which means the carpet has not been replaced or the walls need repainting, but they're otherwise a terrific deal. Waikiki Beach is just a 10- to 15-minute walk away, shopping is a half-block away, and restaurants are within a 5- to 10-minute walk. ***Note:*** This area of Waikiki is a little scary at night—it's not totally safe for a single woman to be wandering about here by herself. Also be aware there is no maid service (you are the maid) and that a one-time cleaning fee increases your total bill by $100.

Hawaiian King Building, 417 Nohonani St., Ste. 409 (btw. Kuhio Ave. and Ala Wai Blvd.), Honolulu, HI 96815. www.winstonswaikikicondos.com. ✆ **800/545-1948** or 808/924-3332. Fax 808/922-3894. 10 units (all with shower only). $125–$145 1-bedroom; $145–$165 business suite; $165–$185 1-bedroom with den. Cleaning fee $75–$100. Extra person $10. 7-night minimum. Ask for the Frommer's readers' discount. AE, DC, DISC, MC, V. Limited parking $14. Bus: 19 or 20. **Amenities:** Bar; babysitting; small outdoor pool surrounded by a tropical courtyard. *In room:* A/C, TV, fridge, hair dryer, kitchen, washer/dryer (in most units).

Sheraton Princess Kaiulani Hotel ★ This hotel is prized for its moderate rates (for a Sheraton). Portraits of the hotel's eponym, Princess Kaiulani, heir to the throne, who died in 1899 at the age of 24, fill the large open-air lobby. The regal, youthful face looks out on the site that was once her royal estate. A huge swimming pool sits behind a row of restaurants and shops facing Kalakaua Avenue. The lobby connects the three buildings of the Princess Kaiulani: the 11-story original hotel that opened in 1955, the 11-story Kaiulani Wing, and the 29-story Ainahau Tower—the latter two opened in 1960. The rooms, which are perfectly fine if unremarkable, have double-insulated doors with added soundproofing. (We wish every hotel in noisy Waikiki had this feature. You can't hear the blaring sirens or the sound of garbage cans being emptied at 3am.) The hotel's dinner and cocktail show, "Creation—A Polynesian Odyssey," is a fun, but touristy, musical-theater excursion through the South Pacific.

120 Kaiulani Ave. (at Kalakaua Ave., across the street from the Sheraton Moana Surfrider), Honolulu, HI 96815. www.sheraton.com. ✆ **800/325-3535** or 808/922-5811. Fax 808/923-9912. 1,150 units. $99–$155 double; from $850 studio suite. Plus resort fee $21/day (covers Internet access and self-parking). Extra person $60; children 17 and under stay free in parent's room. Inquire about package deals and Starwood Preferred Guest deals. AE, DC, MC, V. Bus: 19 or 20. **Amenities:** 2 restaurants; bar; concierge; fitness room and good children's program across the street

at Sheraton Waikiki; outdoor pool; room service; spa at Royal Hawaiian. *In room:* A/C, TV, fridge, hair dryer, high-speed Internet access.

INEXPENSIVE

Aqua Island Colony Hotel This off-the-beaten-track property combines the advantages of a condominium with the amenities of a hotel. All of the units have private lanais and daily maid service and can sleep up to four. Studios have kitchenettes, and the one-bedrooms—which can sleep up to four—have full kitchens. The views are spectacular: jagged mountains and lush valleys, Diamond Head, or the sparkling Pacific Ocean. The only drawback is the minuscule bathrooms: Ours was so small that the door didn't clear the toilet. The tub/shower combo was also cramped—you might need to shower with your elbows close to your side to avoid hitting the walls. Access via car (usually tricky on Waikiki's one-way streets) is very convenient from Ala Wai Boulevard.

445 Seaside Ave. (at Ala Wai Blvd.), Honolulu, HI 96815. www.aquaresorts.com. ☎ **866/406-2782** or 808/923-2345. Fax 808/921-7105. 160 units. $79–$139 double; $109–$129 studio with kitchenette; $149–$229 1-bedroom with kitchen (sleeps 4). Check for Internet specials. AE, DC, DISC, MC, V. Parking $18. Bus: 19 or 20. **Amenities:** Jacuzzi; outdoor pool; sauna. *In room:* A/C, TV, high-speed Internet access ($11/day), fridge, hair dryer, full kitchen or kitchenette (some units).

Holiday Surf 🐟 Three blocks, or about a 10- to 15-minute walk, from Waikiki Beach lies this 1960s apartment hotel, run since 1964 by the Chun family. Overlooking the Ala Wai Canal, the six-story building can be noisy, but air-conditioning drowns out the street noise and the location is within walking distance of Waikiki attractions, dining, and shopping. The 315-square-foot studios are composed of an immaculately clean bedroom/living room combo, with a bed on one side and a full kitchen across the room. The one-bedroom units are larger and have separate bedrooms (great for families). Some of the rooms have been upgraded, thus the range in prices.

2303 Ala Wai Blvd. (corner of Nohonani St.), Honolulu, HI 96815. www.holidaysurfhotel.com. ☎ **808/923-8488.** Fax 808/923-1475. 34 units. $77–$90 studio double; $88–$103 1-bedroom double. Extra person $20. AE, MC, V. Parking $13. Bus: 19 or 20. **Amenities:** Spa. *In room:* A/C, TV/ VCR/DVD, fridge, Internet access ($12/day), kitchen.

Ohana Waikiki West On the upside, this chain hotel has lots of guest services and facilities, which include a lounge, room service, and lots of shops (even a pharmacy). All of the rooms have refrigerators and shower-only bathrooms; some have kitchenettes. The downside is Waikiki Beach is a 10-minute walk from the hotel and it is located on a very noisy part of Kuhio Avenue. If you are enamored with the budget price and figure a good pair of ear plugs will do the trick, go ahead and book. But if you are a light sleeper, we'd suggest picking another property.

2330 Kuhio Ave. (btw. Nahua and Walina sts.), Honolulu, HI 96815. www.ohanahotels.com. ☎ **800/462-6262** or 808/922-5022. Fax 800/622-4852 or 808/924-6414. 661 units. $85–$105 double; $109–$125 double with kitchenette. Check website for promotions and discounts (seniors and AAA). Extra person $30. AE, DC, DISC, MC, V. Parking $20. Bus: 19 or 20. **Amenities:** 2 restaurants (a branch of Chili's and a bakery/deli); 2 bars (1 poolside, 1 country & western); outdoor pool; room service (Chili's). *In room:* A/C, TV, free high-speed Internet access, fridge, hair dryer, kitchenette (some units).

Waikiki, Diamond Head End

You'll find all these hotels between Ala Wai Boulevard and the ocean, and between Kaiulani Street (1 block east of the International Marketplace) and Diamond Head itself.

VERY EXPENSIVE

Hyatt Regency Waikiki ★ This is one of Waikiki's biggest hotels, a $100-million project sporting two 40-story towers and covering nearly an entire city block, just across the street from the Diamond Head end of Waikiki Beach. Some may love the location, but others will find this behemoth too big and impersonal—you can get lost just trying to find the registration desk (which by the way, is not located on the ground level but on the second floor).

The guest rooms are spacious and luxuriously furnished. But, please—when most rooms go for at least $319, why does the hotel have to charge you an extra couple of bucks for coffee to be used in the "free coffeemaker" in your room? (Not only that, but if you want to empty your minibar to use it as a fridge, the cost is $12!) The deluxe ocean-view rooms overlooking Waikiki Beach are fabulous, but can be noisy (traffic on the avenue is constant). You can upgrade to the Regency Club floors, where the rooms are nicer (and the coffee is free); you'll also be entitled to an expedited check-in and entry to a private rooftop sun deck and Jacuzzi and the Regency Club, which has concierge service all day and serves complimentary continental breakfast and afternoon *pupu* (Hawaii-style appetizers).

The 10,000-square-foot, two-story luxury spa offers all the massage services, body treatments, and facials you can imagine.

2424 Kalakaua Ave. (at Kaiulani St., across the street from the beach), Honolulu, HI 96815. www.waikiki.hyatt.com. **℃ 800/492-8804** or 808/923-1234. Fax 808/926-3415. 1,230 units. $319–$444 double; $469–$569 Regency Club double; from $844 suite. Extra person $75 ($125 Regency Club). Children under 18 stay free in parent's room using existing bedding. Check website for special packages. AE, DISC, MC, V. Valet parking $29; self-parking $25. Bus: 19 or 20. **Amenities:** 4 restaurants (including Ciao Mein, p. 128); elegant poolside bar; babysitting; children's program (Fri–Sat evening in winter, daily in summer); concierge; concierge-level rooms; fitness room; Jacuzzi; outdoor pool w/view of Waikiki; room service; spa. *In room:* A/C, TV, fridge, hair dryer, high-speed Internet access ($10/day).

EXPENSIVE

Hilton Waikiki Beach Not to be confused with the Hilton Hawaiian Village, at the other end of Waikiki and located on the beach, this property is located several long blocks from the beach and a few blocks from the zoo. In 2007, Hilton took over this 37-floor hotel, and spent $50 million in renovations to make the former moderate Radisson hotel into a high-tech, 21st-century luxury hotel. However, the rack rates are high. This hotel is a 5-minute walk to the beach—but at these rates you could stay *on* the beach (see "Outrigger Waikiki on the Beach," p. 97)! If you can find a good rate on the Internet for this hotel, then go for it; otherwise, you can get a much better deal elsewhere. Each of the sleek, modern rooms has high-speed Internet ($11/day) and a flat-screen 42-inch high-def plasma TV with multimedia monitor for a laptop computer, game station console, video/camera, or MP3 player. The contemporary rooms feature Hilton's comfy beds, and the bathrooms feature marble, natural stone, and top-end amenities. All rooms are the same; the floor and the view determine the price. (***Tip:*** From the 18th floor and up, the mountain views overlooking the Ala Wai Canal are spectacular and not as pricey as the oceanview rooms.) Hilton has added a 24-hour eatery, **MAC 24-7** (p. 129), which comes in handy if you arrive late at night.

2500 Kuhio Ave. (at Liliuokalani Ave.), Honolulu, HI 96815. www.waikikiprincekuhio.hilton.com. ✆ **800/HILTONS** [445-8667] or 808/922-0811. Fax 808/921-5507. 601 units. $189–$249 double; from $369 suite for 4. Extra person $40. AE, DC, DISC, MC, V. Valet-only parking $25. Bus: 19 or 20. **Amenities:** Restaurant; bar; concierge; concierge-level rooms; small fitness room; Jacuzzi; outdoor pool; room service. *In room:* A/C, TV, fridge, hair dryer, high-speed Internet access ($10/day).

Waikiki Beach Marriott Resort & Spa This 1,310-room hotel has a lot to offer, including a terrific location just across the street from Waikiki Beach, great restaurants (including renowned Maui chef D. K. Kodama's **Sansei Seafood Restaurant & Sushi Bar,** p. 130, and **d.k Steakhouse,** p. 128), a terrific spa, and lots of nightly entertainment. The 5¼-acre property has two towers (one 33 stories, the other 25 stories) and a list of amenities to keep you happy, from an espresso bar to an array of shops. The newly done rooms feature comfortable island-style decor, marble flooring, and granite counters in the bathroom.

Despite that, rates here have been creeping up every year since the resort opened in 2002 with moderate prices. With rack rates beginning at $209 (and topping off at $370), we feel you can do better elsewhere in Waikiki. *Tip:* You may be able to get rooms for half price by checking the Internet for specials.

Even if you don't stay here, spa aficionados won't want to miss the **Spa Olakino & Salon ★**. Conceived and managed by Paul Brown, a well-known hair stylist with numerous salons in Hawaii, this boutique spa offers a unique experience: The spa looks directly onto Waikiki Beach (well, actually Kuhio Beach, at the far end of Waikiki). The "menu" of treatments is one of the most enchanting we've seen. We recommend the Na La'au, which starts with a Hawaiian lomilomi massage (using traditional native Hawaiian plants such as kukui nut oil), then goes on to a noni-plant-and-ti-leaf body wrap, and concludes with a trip to a private steam room and shower.

2552 Kalakaua Ave. (entrance on Ohua Ave.), Honolulu, HI 96815. www.marriottwaikiki.com. ✆ **800/367-5370** or 808/922-6611. Fax 808/921-5255. 1,310 units. $209–$370 double; from $500 suite. Extra person $50. Children under 18 stay free in parent's room using existing bedding. AE, DC, DISC, MC, V. Valet parking $33; self-parking $28. Bus: 19 or 20. **Amenities:** 5 restaurants (including Sansei Seafood Restaurant & Sushi Bar, p. 130, and d.k Steakhouse, p. 128); 2 bars; babysitting; concierge; fitness room; Jacuzzi; outdoor pool w/view of Waikiki; room service; elegant spa.; 24-hr. Doctors On Call medical service. *In room:* A/C, TV, hair dryer, Wi-Fi ($16/day).

Nickel-and-Dime Charges at High-Priced Hotels

Several upscale resorts in Hawaii have begun a practice that we find distasteful and dishonest: charging a so-called "resort fee." This daily fee (generally in the $20-per-day range) is added on to your bill for such "complimentary" items as a daily newspaper, local phone calls, and use of the fitness facilities—amenities that the resort has been happily providing free to its guests for years. In most cases you do not have an option to decline the resort fee—in other words, this is a sneaky way to increase the nightly rate without telling you.

MODERATE

Aston at the Waikiki Banyan ☺ The one-bedrooms here combine the homey comforts of a condo apartment with the amenities of a hotel. You'll get daily maid service, bellhop service, the assistance of the front desk, and access to an enormous sixth-floor recreation deck with a panoramic mountain view, complete with sauna, barbecue areas, snack bar, and children's play area—a great boon for families (kids 12 and under get a toy when you check in), plus there's a children's library with games and terrific Hawaiian books. The open-air lobby has some impressive lacquer artwork, hand-carved and painted in Hong Kong. All bedrooms have a fully equipped full-size kitchen, a breakfast bar that opens to a comfortably furnished living room (with sofa bed), and a separate bedroom with two double beds or a king-size bed. The one we stayed in had an old-fashioned air conditioner in the wall, but it did the job. Each apartment opens onto a fairly good-size lanai with chairs, a small table, and a partial ocean view, with some buildings blocking the way. *Tip:* For apartments starting at $130, check the website under "hot deals."

201 Ohua Ave. (on mountain side, at Kuhio Ave.), Honolulu, HI 96815. www.astonhotels.com. ✆ **866/77-HAWAII** (774-2924) or 808/922-0555. Fax 808/922-0906. 307 units. $140–$232 for up to 5. Check website for special rates and package deals. AE, DC, DISC, MC, V. Self-parking $10. Bus: 19 or 20. **Amenities:** Barbecue; children's playground; huge outdoor pool; free tennis courts; 2 whirlpools. *In room:* A/C, TV, fridge, hair dryer, high-speed Internet access ($10/day), kitchen.

Aston Waikiki Beach Hotel The location of this hotel, directly across the street from the beach, couldn't be better, especially when coupled with the hotel's unique "Breakfast on the Beach"—you get a free breakfast, which you can pack up in an insulated carrying bag and walk across the street to eat. Several food stations offer everything from burritos (veggie, ham, or cheese), pastries, fruit, and cereals to a Japanese breakfast of miso, rice, and fish. There are also a couple of great restaurants, **Tiki's Grill & Bar** and **Wolfgang Puck Express,** on property. That's the good news; the bad news is the rooms are small—averaging 225 to 266 square feet (though 85% of them have ocean views). If you need more space, this may not be the hotel for you. *Tip:* For the best rate, check the website under "e-specials," or choose one of their package deals.

2570 Kalakaua Ave. (at Paoakalani St.), Honolulu, HI 96815. www.astonhotels.com. ✆ **866/77-HAWAII** [774-2924] or 808/922-2511. Fax 808/923-3656. 717 units. $149–$257 double; from $253 suite. Extra person $45. Check website for special rates and package deals. AE, DC, DISC, MC, V. Valet parking $27. Bus: 19 or 20. **Amenities:** 2 restaurants (including Tiki's Grill & Bar, p. 131); bar; outdoor pool. *In room:* A/C, TV, fridge, hair dryer, high-speed Internet access ($10/day).

Aqua Bamboo and Spa ★ ⚐ Formerly a very neglected budget hotel just a block from Waikiki Beach, Bamboo has been transformed into a contemporary "condotel" (a condominium/hotel) with an Asian flair. The rooms are stylish and functional, with modern furniture, marble bathrooms, and kitchenettes or kitchens. The location is good, too—it's within walking distance to numerous restaurants, shopping, and the Honolulu Zoo, and just 10 minutes to the beach. Because it's small, the staff gives guests personalized attention. As at all the Aqua Resort properties, there's a complimentary continental breakfast every morning—but unlike other Aquas, this hotel has its own spa on property. When booking, be sure to "reserve" a parking space, because the parking lot has a limited number.

2425 Kuhio Ave. (at Kaiulani Ave.), Honolulu, HI 96815. www.aquaresorts.com. © **866/406-2782** or 808/922-7777. Fax 808/922-9473. 90 units. $114–$145 double; $129–$154 studio double; from $263 1-bedroom; from $454 luxury 2-bedroom suite. AE, DISC, MC, V. Valet parking $22. Bus: 19 or 20. **Amenities:** Complimentary continental breakfast; concierge; fitness center; Jacuzzi; outdoor pool; sauna; spa. *In room:* A/C, TV, fridge, hair dryer, high-speed Internet access (free), kitchenette or kitchen.

Diamond Head Bed & Breakfast ★ 🎁

Hostess Joanne Trotter offers a quiet, relaxing place to stay on the far side of Kapiolani Park, away from the hustle and bustle of Waikiki. Staying here is like venturing back 50 years to a time when *kamaaina* (native-born) families built huge houses with airy rooms opening onto big lanais and tropical gardens. The house is filled with family heirlooms and Joanne's artwork. One of the two rooms features the beyond-king-size carved koa bed that once belonged to Princess Ruth, a member of Hawaii's royal family. You'll feel like royalty sleeping in it.

3240 Noela Dr. (at Paki Ave.), off Diamond Head Rd.), Honolulu, HI 96815. www.diamondheadbnb. com. ©/fax **808/923-3360.** 3 units. $130–$145 double. Rates include full breakfast. Extra person $20. 2-night minimum. No credit cards. Free parking. Bus: 2. *In room:* TV, fridge, hair dryer.

Hotel Renew ★★ 🎁

After millions in renovations, the renewed Hotel Renew offers an oasis of tranquility, excellent taste, and high-tech electronic equipment in a sea of schlocky aging Waikiki hotels. Located a block and a half from the beach, the hotel ushers guests to a seated area for check-in while their luggage is whisked to their rooms. The new rooms are designed with a clean decor, with black and white walls, discreet lighting, and the slight aroma of scented candles in the air. But it's the electronics that won us over: a 50-inch high-def flat-screen TV in some rooms, complimentary high-speed Internet access, a host of 500-plus movies, even an iPod docking station. A daily continental breakfast is included, and when you depart, you'll receive a fresh flower lei to remember your sweet time here.

129 Paoakalani Ave (at Lemon Rd.), Honolulu, HI 96815. www.hotelrenew.com. © **888/485-7639** or 808/687-7700. Fax 808/687-7701. 70 units. $156–$225 double. Extra person $40. AE, DISC, MC, V. Parking $22. Bus: 19 or 20. **Amenities:** Cafe and lounge; complimentary continental breakfast; concierge; spa. *In room:* A/C, TV/DVD, CD player, fridge, hair dryer, high-speed Internet access (free).

New Otani Kaimana Beach Hotel ★ 🎁

This is one of Waikiki's best-kept secrets: a boutique hotel nestled right on a lovely stretch of beach at the foot of Diamond Head, with Kapiolani Park just across the street. Robert Louis Stevenson's description of Sans Souci, the beach fronting the hotel, still holds true: "If anyone desires lovely scenery, pure air, clear sea water, good food, and heavenly sunsets, I recommend him cordially to the Sans Souci." The Waikiki-side guest rooms are teeny-tiny, barely with room for two, but tastefully decorated in pale pastels; they open onto lanais with ocean and park views. A good budget buy is the park-view studio with kitchen, which you can stock with provisions from the on-site Mini-Mart, open until 11pm.

Because the hotel overlooks Kapiolani Park, guests have easy access to activities such as golf, tennis, jogging, and bicycling; kayaking and snorkeling are available at the beach. The hotel also arranges for visitors to climb to the top of Diamond Head. The airy lobby opens onto the alfresco **Hau Tree**

Lanai restaurant (p. 129) and features music nightly. The beachfront **Sunset Lanai Lounge** ★ is great for cocktails and has live Hawaiian music at lunch on Friday.

2863 Kalakaua Ave. (ocean side of the street just Diamond Head of the Waikiki Aquarium, across from Kapiolani Park), Honolulu, HI 96815. www.kaimana.com. ℂ **800/356-8264** or 808/923-1555. Fax 808/922-9404. 124 units. $149–$414 double; from $165 studio; from $245 junior suite; from $210 regular suite. Extra person $50. Children 12 and under stay free in parent's room using existing bedding. Check website for special packages. AE, DC, DISC, MC, V. Valet parking $18. Bus: 2 or 14. **Amenities:** 2 restaurants (including the Hau Tree Lanai, p. 129); beachfront bar; babysitting; concierge; fitness room; room service; watersports equipment rentals. *In room:* A/C, TV, free high-speed Internet, fridge, hair dryer, kitchenette (in some units), minibar (on request).

INEXPENSIVE

Ocean Resort Hotel Waikiki This large dual-tower hotel on a relatively quiet street is just a short walk from the Honolulu Zoo, Kapiolani Park, and the Waikiki Aquarium, and just 2 minutes from the beach. The property has a bright, clean look. The Diamond Tower houses the budget rooms; at 325 square feet, they boast new carpet, bedspreads, drapes, and other interior redesigns. These rooms have showers only; tub/shower combos are available in the more expensive Pali Tower rooms. All rooms in both towers have refrigerators, and the rooms with kitchenettes have two-burner hot plates and cooking utensils; those from the ninth floor up also have small lanais. Only studios and suites have coffeemakers, so if you want one, ask for it when you reserve. The on-site restaurant offers steak and seafood.

175 Paoakalani Ave. (near Kuhio Ave.), Honolulu, HI 96815. www.oceanresort.com. ℂ **800/367-2317** or 808/922-3861. Fax 808/924-1982. 450 units. $85–$132 double; $105–$150 studio with kitchenette, suites from $211. Senior and AAA specials start at $77. AE, DC, DISC, MC, V. Parking $15 valet only. Bus: 19 or 20. **Amenities:** Restaurant; bar; babysitting; 2 outdoor pools; currency exchange desk. *In room:* A/C, TV, high speed Internet access ($11/day), fridge, hair dryer, kitchenette (studios).

Queen Kapiolani Hotel This budget property, managed by Aqua Resorts, is named for Queen Kapiolani (1834–99), the wife of Hawaii's last king, David Kalakaua (1836–91), and the theme here harks back to the days of the Hawaiian monarchs. The 19th-century flavor includes 10-foot chandeliers in the main dining room and a full-size portrait of the queen in the lobby. The hotel just underwent renovations in 2010; however, the budget rooms remain quite small. For just a few bucks more, get the superior room. Not only is it double in size, but its shoreline views are vastly improved. The property's location is great—across the street from Kapiolani Park, a block to the beach, and within walking distance of the Honolulu Zoo, the Waikiki Aquarium, and the activities of Waikiki, including the municipal tennis courts. For even more savings, book through the website.

150 Kapahulu Ave. (at Lemon Rd., across from Kapiolani Park), Honolulu, HI 96815. www.queenkapiolani.com. ℂ **800/533-2317** or 808/922-1941. Fax 808/922-1982. 315 units. $99–$159 double; $139 studio with kitchenette; $179–$199 1-bedroom suite with kitchenette (sleeps up to 4). Check for Internet specials, which start at $80. Extra person $40. Children 18 and under stay free in parent's room. AE, DC, DISC, MC, V. Parking $12 self only. Bus: 19 or 20. **Amenities:** Restaurant; bar; babysitting; concierge; large outdoor pool; municipal tennis courts nearby. *In room:* A/C, TV, high speed Internet access ($10/day), fridge, hair dryer, some kitchenettes.

Royal Grove Hotel ★ 🔥 This is a great bargain for frugal travelers. You can't miss the Royal Grove—it's bright pink. Among Waikiki's canyons of corporate-owned high-rises, it's also a rarity in another way: The Royal Grove is a small, family-owned hotel. What you get here is old-fashioned aloha in cozy accommodations along the lines of Motel 6—basic and clean. For years Frommer's readers have written in about the aloha spirit of the Fong family; they love the potluck dinners and get-togethers the Fongs have organized so their guests can get to know one another. And you can't do better for the price—this has to be *the* bargain of Waikiki. For $55 (about the same price a couple would pay to stay in a private room at the hostel in Waikiki), you get a clean room in the older Mauka Wing, with two twin beds, plus a kitchenette with refrigerator and stove. We suggest that you spend a few dollars more and go for an air-conditioned room ($64) to help drown out the street noise. Even the most expensive unit, a one-bedroom suite with three beds and kitchenette for $80, is half the price of similar accommodations elsewhere. At these rates, you won't mind that maid service is only twice a week.

The hotel is built around a courtyard pool, and the beach is just a 3-minute walk away. All of Waikiki's attractions are within walking distance. *Tip:* If you book 7 nights or more from April to November, you'll get a discount on the already low rates.

151 Uluniu Ave. (btw. Prince Edward and Kuhio aves.), Honolulu, HI 96815. www.royalgrovehotel. com. ☎ **808/923-7691.** Fax 808/922-7508. 85 units. $55–$60 double (no A/C); $67–$90 standard double; $90–$100 standard 1-bedroom. Extra person $10. Children 5 and under stay free in parent's room. AE, DC, DISC, MC, V. Nearby parking $10. Bus: 19 or 20. **Amenities:** Pool. *In room:* A/C (in most rooms), TV, fridge, kitchen.

Waikiki Sand Villa ☺ Frugal travelers, take note: This very affordable hotel is located on the quieter side of Waikiki, across the street from the Ala Wai Canal. The 10-story tower has medium-size rooms, most with a double bed plus a single bed (convenient for families) and a lanai with great views of the green mountains. The adjacent three-story building features studio apartments with kitchenettes (fridge, stove, and microwave). For guests arriving early or catching a late flight, there's a hospitality room (complete with shower) for late checkout, and a luggage-storage area.

2375 Ala Wai Blvd. (entrance on Kanekapolei Ave.), Honolulu, HI 96815. www.waikikisandvilla hotel.com. ☎ **800/247-1903** or 808/922-4744. Fax 808/926-7587. 214 units. $100–$125 double; from $135 studio with kitchenette; from $250 suite. Rates include continental breakfast served poolside every morning. Extra person $28. Children under 17 stay free in parent's room using existing bedding. Internet specials start as low as $69. AE, DC, DISC, MC, V. Valet-only parking $16. Bus: 19 or 20. **Amenities:** 70-ft. outdoor pool w/adjoining whirlpool spa. *In room:* A/C, TV w/Nintendo, fridge (in some units), high-speed Internet access (free), kitchenette (in some units), microwave (in some units).

HONOLULU BEYOND WAIKIKI

The city of Honolulu extends far beyond the tourist zones of Waikiki. It encompasses a fairly large area, and most of Oahu's population calls it home. Downtown Honolulu is relatively small, occupying only a handful of blocks. The financial, government, and corporate headquarters of businesses are found here. Other neighborhoods range from the quiet suburbs of Hawaii Kai to the *kamaaina* neighborhoods such as Manoa. With the exception of the heart of downtown, these neighborhoods are generally quieter than Waikiki, more residential, yet within minutes of beaches, shopping, and all the activities Oahu has to offer.

Ala Moana

Ala Moana Hotel After a multimillion-dollar transformation, this former 1,152-room hotel (on 36 floors) has been converted to a hotel-condominium (sometimes called a condotel). The units are individually owned, though most are put onto the rental market for guests. Renovations include redone suites and a new pool, sun deck, and fitness center/spa. The Outrigger/Ohana Resort manages the hotel, which means it runs as smoothly as their brand properties. The main advantage of staying here is the proximity to Waikiki, the downtown financial and business district, the new convention center, and Hawaii's largest mall, Ala Moana Shopping Center. The rooms vary in price according to size: The cheaper rooms are small but come with two double beds and all the amenities you'll need to make your stay comfortable. The views of Waikiki and Honolulu from the upper floors are spectacular. *Tip:* Book on the website and save—rooms start at $129 ($100 off the rack rate).

410 Atkinson Dr. (at Kona St., next to Ala Moana Center), Honolulu, HI 96814. www.alamoana hotel.com. ℂ **800/367-6025** or 808/955-4811. Fax 808/944-6839. 1,152 units. $109–$169 double; from $259 suite. Extra person $40. Children under 18 stay free in parent's room. AE, DC, DISC, MC, V. Valet parking $20; self-parking $15. Bus: 19 or 20. **Amenities:** 2 restaurants; 2 bars (including Rumours Nightclub, p. 265, plus a Polynesian show); concierge; small fitness room; large outdoor pool; limited room service. *In room:* A/C, TV, fridge, hair dryer, high-speed Internet access (free).

Pagoda Hotel This is where local residents from neighbor islands stay when they come to Honolulu. Close to shopping and downtown (but *not* close to the beach), the Pagoda has been serving Hawaii's island community for decades. This modest hotel has very plain, motel-like rooms: clean and utilitarian with no extra frills. Ask for a mountain-view room to avoid the street noise. There's easy access to Waikiki via TheBus—the nearest stop is just half a block away. Studios and one- and two-bedroom units have kitchenettes. *Tip:* Check the website for room/rental-car package deals.

1525 Rycroft St. (btw. Keeaumoku and Kaheka sts.), Honolulu, HI 96814. www.pagodahotel.com. ℂ **800/367-6060** or 808/923-4511. Fax 808/955-5067. 361 units. From $88 double hotel room; from $110 studio with kitchenette; from $95 1-bedroom double; from $153 2-bedroom double (sleeps up to 5); lowest rates Sun–Thurs. Extra person $35. Free cribs available. AE, DC, DISC, MC, V. Parking $9. Bus: 5 or 6. **Amenities:** Restaurant; bar; babysitting; 2 outdoor pools. *In room:* A/C, TV, fridge, hair dryer, high-speed Internet access ($10/day), kitchenette (in some units).

Downtown

Aston at the Executive Centre Hotel ★ Located in the heart of downtown, this is the perfect hotel for the business traveler, close to the business and financial center of Honolulu and with a staff that is quick to assist in any way. Vacationers, on the other hand, won't like the long walk to the beach. The hotel occupies the top 10 floors of a 40-story, multi-use, glass-walled tower. Every room is a spacious suite, with three phones, a whirlpool bathtub, and unobstructed views of the city, the mountains, and Honolulu Harbor. Executive suites add a full kitchen, washer/dryer, and VCR. All guests awaken to a local newspaper outside their doors. Local phone calls are free. The only downside is that units are privately owned, so quality is inconsistent—some are fantastic, but some need work.

1088 Bishop St. (at S. Hotel St.), Honolulu, HI 96813. www.astonhotels.com. © **866/77-HAWAII** [774-2924] or 808/539-3000. Fax 808/523-1088. 114 suites. $260–$282 suite; $312–$332 1-bedroom. Rates include continental breakfast. Extra person $25. Children under 17 stay free in parent's room. AE, DC, DISC, MC, V. Parking $24. Bus: 1, 2, 3, 9, or 12. **Amenities:** Restaurant; concierge; fitness center w/free weights and aerobic equipment; outdoor pool. *In room:* A/C, TV, fridge, hair dryer, free high-speed Internet, kitchenette, washer/dryer (some rooms), in-room jet spa.

Near Honolulu International Airport

If you have a late-night flight, a long layover between flights, a delayed flight, or a long period of time between your noon checkout and your flight, consider the services of the hotel choices near the airport: **Best Western—The Plaza Hotel,** 3253 N. Nimitz Hwy., Honolulu (www.bestwestern.com; © **800/800-4683** or 808/836-0661), where rooms go from $109 to $169 (now charging $10 per day for parking); and the **Ohana Honolulu Airport Hotel,** 3401 Nimitz Hwy. (www.ohanahotels.com; © **800/462-6262** or 808/836-0661), with rooms from $99 (up to superior rooms with breakfast for $205). Both offer free airport shuttle service. These are certainly not where you should spend your Hawaiian vacation, but are good overnight resting places.

Manoa

Manoa Valley Inn ✋ Listed on the National Register of Historic Places, this historic 1915 Gothic bed-and-breakfast offers a very different Honolulu vacation. Completely off the tourist trail, it's an oasis of peace and tranquility, nestled on a quiet residential street near the University of Hawaii. It offers a charming venture into the past, with rooms filled with antiques, old-fashioned rose wallpaper, and king-size koa-wood beds. The two top-floor rooms share a full bathroom; the others have private bathrooms. It's about a 20-minute drive to Waikiki Beach, so this is not a good fit for people wanting easy beach access. But if you seek a journey into Hawaii's past, along with a stay in a charming bed-and-breakfast, you'll love it here.

2001 Vancouver Dr. (at University Ave.), Honolulu, HI 96822. www.manoavalleyinn.com. © **808/947-6019.** Fax 808/946-6168. 7 units, 2 with shared bathroom. $89–$115 double with shared bathroom; $120–$149 double with private bathroom (shower only). Rates include continental breakfast. MC, V. Free parking. Bus: 4 or 6. Children 8 and older preferred. *In room:* A/C (in some units), TV (in some units), free Wi-Fi (some rooms).

Kahala

Kahala Hotel & Resort ★★★ ☺ In one of Oahu's most prestigious residential areas, the Kahala offers the peace and serenity of a neighbor-island vacation, but with the conveniences of Waikiki just a 10-minute drive away. The decor of the rooms resembles the stylish interiors of most of the multimillion-dollar homes in the surrounding Kahala area, and features custom-designed wall-to-wall carpeting, tropical ceiling fans, retro Island artwork, and two- or four-poster beds with comfy Stearns & Foster pillow-top mattresses made up with Egyptian-cotton linens. The plantation decor is augmented with state-of-the-art technology, including high-speed wireless Internet, 40-inch flat-screen TVs, iPod or MP3 player hookups, and cordless phones.

The lush grounds include an 800-foot crescent-shaped beach and a 26,000-square-foot lagoon (home to two bottle-nosed dolphins, sea turtles, and tropical fish). Other extras that make this property outstanding: Hawaiian cultural programs, shuttle service to Waikiki and major shopping centers, free scuba lessons in the pool, daily dolphin-education talks by a trainer from Sea Life Park, and a great year-round children's program. A must-do indulgence is the fabulous spa, which features treatments in former guest rooms redesigned for individualized massages, body scrubs, rubs, wraps, and other pampering therapies.

5000 Kahala Ave. (next to the Waialae Country Club), Honolulu, HI 96816. www.kahalaresort. com. © **800/367-2525** or 808/739-8888. Fax 808/739-8800. 343 units. $425–$1,025 double; from $1,700 suite. Extra person $175. Children 17 and under stay free in parent's room. Check the website's "Specials & Packages" for discounts. AE, DC, DISC, MC, V. Parking $25. **Amenities:** 5 restaurants (including Hoku's, p. 148); 4 bars (including Veranda, p. 268); babysitting; complimentary use of bikes; year-round children's program; concierge; nearby golf course; great fitness center w/steam rooms, Jacuzzis, and dry sauna; large outdoor pool; room service; tennis courts; watersports equipment rentals. *In room:* A/C, TV, hair dryer, minibar, Wi-Fi ($15/day).

Hawaii Kai

Aloha B&B ★ Perched on a hillside in the residential community of Hawaii Kai is this very affordable B&B, complete with swimming pool, panoramic ocean views, and continental breakfast on the outdoor lanai. Two bedrooms (one with king-size bed, one with twins) share a bathroom and a half (no waiting for the toilet!); the other room has a private bathroom. Hostess Phyllis Young has lots of beach toys and equipment (including coolers and chairs) she will loan you for the day. She'll even do a load of laundry for you for $6. There's no smoking anywhere on the property, which is just a 10-minute drive to snorkeling in Hanauma Bay and about a 15-minute drive to Waikiki and downtown Honolulu.

909 Kahauloa Place, Honolulu, HI 96825. www.home.roadrunner.com/~alohaphyllis. © **808/395-6694.** Fax 808/396-2020. 3 units with shared bathrooms. $85–$100 double. Rates include continental breakfast. 3-night minimum. Credit cards through Paypal. Free parking. Bus: 22 (stops at the bottom of a steep, uphill climb). **Amenities:** Swimming pool. *In room:* TV, Wi-Fi (free).

J&B's Haven Brits Joan and Barbara Webb have had a successful bed-and-breakfast on Oahu since 1982. Barbara, who has lived in Hawaii since 1970, and her mother Joan, who moved to Hawaii in 1981, are both knowledgeable about Oahu's attractions and love introducing guests to the Hawaii they love. Their beautiful house in Hawaii Kai is just 15-minute car ride to Waikiki. It's close to Hanauma Bay, Sandy Beach, and Sea Life Park, and is within easy reach of three shopping centers with excellent restaurants. The house features two rooms: the large master bedroom, with private bathroom, king-size bed, minifridge, and microwave; and a smaller room with private bathroom, queen-size bed, small fridge, and microwave. *Note:* This is a smoke-free house. Two very friendly dogs live inside, so if you're allergic to canine housemates, you might look elsewhere.

Kahena St. (at Ainapo St., off Hawaii Kai Dr.), Hawaii Kai. Reservations: P.O. Box 25907, Honolulu, HI 96825. www.home.roadrunner.com/~jnbshaven. © **808/396-9462.** 2 units. $80–$95 double. Rates include expanded continental breakfast. 3-night minimum. No credit cards. Free parking. Bus: 1. *In room:* A/C (room with king-size bed), TV, fridge, microwave.

THE WINDWARD COAST

The windward, or eastern, side of the island is where the trade winds blow, rain squalls support lush, tropical vegetation, and subdivisions dot the landscape. The communities of Kailua and Kaneohe dominate here. Bed-and-breakfasts (ranging from oceanfront estates to tiny cottages on quiet residential streets) abound. This is the place for "island" experiences—but you're still within a 30-minute drive to Waikiki.

Kailua & Kaneohe

Pat O'Malley, of **Pat's Kailua Beach Properties,** 204 S. Kalaheo Ave., Kailua, HI 96734 (www.patskailua.com; ℂ **808/261-1653** or 808/262-4128; fax 808/261-0893), books a wide range of houses and cottages on or near Kailua Beach. Rates start at $100 a day for a studio cottage near the beach and go up to $600 per day for a multimillion-dollar oceanfront home with room to sleep eight. All units are fully furnished, with everything from cooking utensils to telephone and TV, even washer/dryers.

Alii Bluffs Windward Bed & Breakfast Located on a quiet residential street just 15 minutes from the beach, this traditional B&B is filled with antiques and collectibles, as well as the owners' original art. The guest wing has two rooms, one with a double bed and adjacent bathroom, the other with two extra-long twins and a bathroom across the hall. The yard blooms with tropical plants, and the view of Kaneohe Bay from the pool area is breathtaking. Lots of extras make this B&B stand out from the crowd: daily maid service, a large breakfast served on the poolside lanai, afternoon tea, and sewing kits in the bathroom—they'll even lend you anything you need for the beach.

46–251 Ikiiki St. (off Kamehameha Hwy.), Kaneohe, HI 96744. www.hawaiiscene.com/aliibluffs. ℂ **800/235-1151** or 808/235-1124. Fax 808/235-1124. 2 units. $70–$80 double. Rates include continental breakfast. 3-night minimum. MC, V. Free parking. Bus: 55 or 65. Children must be 16 or older. **Amenities:** Outdoor pool. *In room:* Hair dryer, no phone.

Lanikai Bed & Breakfast ★ 🏠 This old-time bed-and-breakfast, a *kamaaina* home that reflects the Hawaii of yesteryear, is now into its second generation of owners. The 1,000-square-foot upstairs apartment, which easily accommodates four, is decorated in Old Hawaii bungalow style. There's a king-size bed in one bedroom, twin beds in the other bedroom, a large living/dining room, a big bathroom, a kitchenette, and all the modern conveniences (such as DVD players), plus oversize windows to let you enjoy the wonderful views. Or you can follow the ginger- and ti-lined path to a 540-square-foot honeymooner's delight, a quaint studio with a huge patio outside and queen-size bed and sitting area with DVD/VCR combo, cordless phone, answering machine, and recently remodeled full-size kitchen. The units are stocked with breakfast fixings (bagels, juice, fruit, coffee, tea) and all the beach equipment you'll need (towels, mats, chairs, coolers, water jugs). If the B&B is booked, the website lists other accommodations around Lanikai-Kailua.

277 Mokulua Dr. (btw. Onekea and Aala Dr. in Lanikai), Kailua, HI 96734. www.lanikaibeach rentals.com/vacationrentalsoahu.htm. ℂ **808/261-7895** or 808/261-1059. 2 units. $160 studio double; $175 apt. double or $250 for 3 or 4. Cleaning fee $50–$75. Rates include breakfast items in fridge. 5-night minimum. MC, V. Free parking. Bus: 52, 55, or 56. **Amenities:** Washer/dryer; gas grill. *In room:* TV/DVD, fridge, hair dryer, high-speed Internet access (free), kitchenette or kitchen.

Paradise Bay Resort ☺ Formerly Schrader's Windward Country Inn, this resort changed ownership in 2010. Since the purchase, the new owners have been doing a full remodel of the property: All of the rooms and cottages have new plumbing and wiring, hardwood and slate floors, and new furniture. There are plans to add a spa in the future. The property is nestled in a tranquil, tropical setting on Kaneohe Bay, only a 40-minute drive from Waikiki. The complex is made up of cottage-style motels and a collection of older homes, as well as a picnic area with barbecue grills. The cottages contain either a kitchenette with refrigerator and microwave or a full kitchen. Prices are based on the views: Depending how much you're willing to pay, you can look out over a Kahuluu fishpond, the Koolau Mountains, or Kaneohe Bay. Watersports are available at an additional cost; don't miss the complimentary 2-hour boat cruise with snorkeling and kayaking. Evening activities include a dinner and Hawaiian music night and mojito party night with free *pupu*. **Tip:** When booking, ask for a unit with a lanai; that way you'll end up with at least a partial view of the bay.

47–039 Lihikai Dr. (off Kamehameha Hwy.), Kaneohe, HI 96744. www.paradisebayresorthawaii. com. ☏ **800/735-5071** or 808/239-5711. Fax 808/239-6658. 44 units. $145–$350 1-bedroom double; $195–$350 2-bedroom for 4; $450–$525 3-bedroom for 6; $595–$695 4-bedroom for 8; $695–$795 5-bedroom for 10. Rates include continental breakfast. Extra person $50. 3-night minimum. AE, DC, DISC, MC, V. Free parking. Bus: 52, 55, or 56. **Amenities:** Outdoor pool; watersports equipment rentals. *In room:* TV, free Wi-Fi, fridge, kitchenette.

Sheffield House ☺ If you have kids or someone with disabilities needing a room, here's your place. Unlike many other B&Bs, Sheffield House, in the suburbs of Kailua, welcomes children. The owners, Paul Sheffield and his wife, Rachel, have three kids, so such things as a portable baby bed are no problem. There are two units, a one-bedroom and a guest room (which is shower-only and fully wheelchair-accessible), each with a private entry (through elaborately landscaped tropical gardens) and a full kitchen. The two spaces can be combined and rented as a two-bedroom/two-bathroom suite.

131 Kuulei Rd. (at Kalaheo Dr.), Kailua, HI 96734. www.hawaiisheffieldhouse.com. ☏/fax **808/262-0721.** 2 units. $105–$125 double guest room; $130–$155 apt. for 4; $235–$280 2-bedroom for 6. Extra person $20. Cleaning fee $45. Off-season discounts may apply. Rates include 1st day's continental breakfast. 4-night minimum. MC, V. Free parking. Bus: 56 or 57. *In room:* TV, fridge, kitchen.

THE NORTH SHORE

The North Shore is the Hawaii of Hollywood: giant waves, surfers galore, tropical jungles, waterfalls, and mysterious Hawaiian temples. If you're looking for a quieter vacation, closer to nature, filled with swimming, snorkeling, diving, surfing, or just plain hanging out on some of the world's most beautiful beaches, the North Shore is for you. It boasts good restaurants, shopping, and cultural activities, along with the quiet of country living. The North Shore doesn't have many accommodations or an abundance of tourist facilities—some say that is its charm. Bed-and-breakfasts are the most common options, but there are some deluxe facilities to consider. **Be forewarned:** The ocean is rough here in winter, and it's nearly an hour's drive from the North Shore to Honolulu and Waikiki.

    Team Real Estate, 66-250 Kamehameha Hwy., Ste. D-103, Haleiwa, HI 96712 (www.teamrealestate.com; ☏ **800/982-8602** or 808/637-3507; fax

808/637-8881), manages vacation rentals on the North Shore. Its units range from $65-a-night condos to $120 one-bedroom apartments to $835-per-night 11-bedroom oceanfront luxury homes. A minimum stay of 1 week is required for some properties, but shorter stays are available as well.

Ke Iki Beach Bungalows This collection of studio, one-, and two-bedroom cottages is located on a beautiful beach. Snuggled on a large lot with its own 200-foot stretch of white sand between two legendary surf spots (Waimea Bay and Banzai Pipeline), the units are affordable if compact: very small bedrooms with a small kitchen (with all the necessary essentials) and living room. But, hey, with the ocean just outside, how much time are you going to spend inside? (If you can live without being right on the ocean, the garden units are also a great deal.) The winter waves are too rough for most swimmers, but there's a large lava reef nearby with tide pools to explore and, on the other side, Shark's Cove, a relatively protected snorkeling area. Nearby are tennis courts and a jogging path. All units have full kitchens and their own barbecue areas.

59–579 Ke Iki Rd. (off Kamehameha Hwy.), Haleiwa, HI 96712. www.keikibeach.com. © **866/638-8229** or 808/638-8229. Fax 808/637-6100. 11 units. $150 double garden-view studio; $155 double garden-view 1-bedroom; $185–$215 double beachfront 1-bedroom; $155–$185 double garden-view 2-bedroom; $210–$230 double beachfront 2-bedroom. Cleaning fee $55–$100 per week or per visit (if less than a week). Extra person stays free. AE, MC, V. Free parking. Bus: 52. **Amenities:** Complimentary watersports equipment and bikes. *In room:* TV, CD player, fridge, kitchen, wireless Internet access.

Santa's by the Sea ★ 🏠 This certainly must be where Santa Claus comes to vacation: St. Nick knows a bargain when he sees it. The location, price, and style make this a must-stay if you plan to visit the North Shore. It's one of the few North Shore B&Bs right on the beach—and not just any beach, but the famous Banzai Pipeline. You can go from your bed to the sand in less than 30 seconds to watch the sun rise over the Pacific. Hosts Gary and Cyndie offer an impeccable one-bedroom unit with finely crafted woodwork, bay windows, and a collection of unique Santa figurines and one-of-a-kind Christmas items. It may sound tacky, but somehow it gives the apartment a country charm. Honeymooners, take note: Privacy abounds here. The unit has its own entrance, a living room with VCR and stereo, a bathroom with shower only, and a full kitchen with everything a cook could need. There's also a barbecue area. Fruit, cereal, bread, coffee, tea, and juice are provided on the first morning, to get you started.

Ke Waena Rd. (off Kamehameha Hwy.), Haleiwa, HI 96712. Reservations c/o Hawaii's Best Bed & Breakfasts, 571 Pauku St., Kailua, HI 96734. www.santasbythesea.com. © **800/262-9912** or 808/263-3100. Fax 808/62-5030. 1 unit (shower only). $225 double. Rates include breakfast items in fridge. Extra person $15. Prefer 3-night minimum. No credit cards. Free parking. Bus: 52 or 55. **Amenities:** Washer/dryer; ocean-side gazebo. *In room:* A/C (in bedroom), TV/VCR, fridge, hair dryer, computer with Internet access (free), kitchen.

Turtle Bay Resort ★★★ Get out of urban Waikiki and enjoy the countryside of Oahu's north shore from Turtle Bay's spectacular location on the beach. The resort is an hour's drive north of Honolulu, but it feels eons away. It's very private, relaxed, and the property is top drawer. Turtle Bay has tons of activities across 808 acres and 5 miles of shoreline with secluded white-sand coves. It's located on Kalaeokaunu Point ("point of the altar"), where ancient Hawaiians once built a small altar to the fish gods. (The altar's remains are now at the Bishop Museum.)

Although the resort is 4 decades old, management continues to upgrade the property and the hotel and grounds look fresh and new. Once you step into the lobby, with floor-to-ceiling windows framing the dramatic ocean view, you'll know you are in Hawaii. All rooms have ocean views and balconies and now feature marble floors and countertops in the bathroom, as well as comfy bedding. If you can afford it, book the separate beach cottages: Positioned right on the ocean (the views alone are worth the price), the 42 bungalows boast hardwood floors, four-poster beds with feather comforters, and butler service, even their own private check-in and concierge.

The new soothing **Spa Luana** offers six treatment rooms, a meditation waiting area, and an outdoor workout area, plus a complete fitness center and a private elevator to the spa's reserved rooms on the second floor. The signature restaurant, **21 Degrees North** (p. 151), is so good that people drive from all over the island to eat there.

57–091 Kamehameha Hwy. (Hwy. 83), Kahuku, HI 96731. www.turtlebayresort.com. ☎ **800/203-3650** or 808/293-6000. Fax 808/293-9147. 443 units. $229–$300 double; from $470 cottage; from $332 suite; from $616 villa. Extra person $50. Children 17 and under stay free in parent's room. Daily $25 resort fee for self-parking, Internet access, and more. Check website for special packages. AE, DC, DISC, MC, V. Bus: 52 or 55. **Amenities:** 4 restaurants (including 21 Degrees North, p. 151; and Ola, p. 151); 2 bars (live entertainment Fri–Sat at the Bay Club Lounge, plus a poolside bar); babysitting; concierge; 36 holes of golf; 2 Jacuzzis; 2 outdoor heated pools (w/80-ft. water slide); room service; spa w/fitness center; 10 Plexipave tennis courts; watersports equipment rentals; stable w/horseback riding. *In room:* A/C, TV, fridge, hair dryer, high-speed Internet access (included in resort fee).

LEEWARD OAHU: THE WAIANAE COAST

This area is a new frontier for Oahu visitors. Currently, there is only one exquisite resort in this beach-lined rural section of Oahu, but more are planned. Here's a chance to escape, far, far away from the hustle and bustle of Waikiki. This is the sunny side of the island, with little rain and lots of sandy beaches. People who love to play golf, enjoy the ocean, and participate in cultural activities will have plenty to do. However, outside the Ko Olina Resort area, there is little in the way of fine dining or interesting shopping.

J. W. Marriott Ihilani Resort & Spa at Ko Olina ★★★ ☺ When the 640-acre Ko Olina Resort community opened, some 17 miles and 30 minutes west of Honolulu Airport (and worlds away from the tourist scene of Waikiki), critics wondered who would want to stay so far from the city. Lots of people, it turns out. Ihilani ("heavenly splendor") is nestled in a quiet location between the Pacific Ocean and the first of four man-made beach lagoons. Featuring a luxury spa and fitness center, plus tennis and one of Hawaii's premier golf courses, it's a haven of relaxation and well-being. The spa alone is reason enough to come here: Treatments include thalassotherapy, Swiss showers, Vichy showers, Roman pools, and various kinds of massages. You can even have a fitness-and-relaxation program custom-designed.

It's hard to get a bad room in the 15-story building—some 85% of the units enjoy lagoon or ocean views. Accommodations are luxuriously appointed and spacious (680 sq. ft.), and come with huge lanais outfitted with very comfortable, cushioned teak furniture. A state-of-the-art comfort-control-system panel operates the ceiling fans, air-conditioning, and lights. Luxurious marble bathrooms have deep soaking tubs, separate glass-enclosed showers, and many amenities. Other extras include a daily newspaper, transportation to Waikiki and Ala Moana Shopping Center, a 3-mile coastal fitness trail, and a stretch of four white-sand beaches for ocean activities. The championship 18-hole Ko Olina Golf Course was designed by Ted Robinson.

The Ihilani's children's program puts all others to shame, offering year-round outdoor adventures and indoor learning activities for toddlers and teens alike. Other amenities for the kids include a Computer Learning Center, a 125-gallon fish tank, and an evening lounge for teen-themed parties.

92-1001 Olani St., Kapolei, HI 96707. www.ihilani.com. ℰ **800/626-4446** or 808/679-0079. Fax 808/679-0080. 387 units. $309–$795 double; from $665 suite. Extra person $50. Children under 17 (maximum 2) stay free in parent's room using existing bedding. Ask about Paradise Plus package rates, which include a free car rental or daily breakfast for 2 starting at $369. AE, DC, DISC, MC, V. Parking $29. No bus service. **Amenities:** 3 restaurants; 2 bars (w/nightly entertainment poolside); babysitting; excellent children's program; concierge; championship 18-hole Ko Olina Golf Course; 2 outdoor pools; room service; world-class spa; tennis club w/pro shop; watersports equipment rentals. *In room:* A/C, TV, hair dryer, minibar, complimentary newspaper delivery, Wi-Fi ($13/day).

OAHU'S CAMPGROUNDS & WILDERNESS CABINS

If you plan to camp, you must bring your own gear or buy it here—no one on Oahu rents out gear. If you bring your own equipment, remember that you can't transport fuel (even in a canister) on the plane. If your camping stove requires butane fuel, just leave it at home; butane is very difficult to find in Hawaii.

The best places to camp on Oahu are listed below (for locations, see the "Camping on Oahu" map on p. 119). TheBus's Circle Island route can get you to or near all these sites, but remember: On TheBus, you're allowed only one bag, which has to fit under the seat. If you have more gear, you're going to have to drive or take a cab.

Note: Reservations for all state parks on the island of Oahu cannot be made more than 30 days in advance. To make a reservation, go on line to **www.hawaiistateparks.org/camping/fees.cfm**, and click "Online Reservations." Camping fees are $18 per night per site for 6 people (each site holds 10 people); an additional fee of $3 will be applied to each extra person over six people. Payment can be made with a credit card.

Honolulu

SAND ISLAND STATE RECREATION AREA ★

Believe it or not, there is a campground in Honolulu. It's just south of Honolulu Harbor at a waterfront park. Don't be put off by the heavy industrial area you have to drive through to reach this 102-acre park with grassy lawns, ironwood trees, and sandy beaches. Campers have great views—better than those of some of the guests in the $400-a-night rooms in Waikiki—of the entire Honolulu coastline all the way to Waikiki. In addition to the scenery, the most popular activity here is shoreline fishing, especially along the western shore of Sand Island. Swimming is an option, but watch out for the rocks along the shoreline bottom; the water quality is occasionally questionable too. The park is also a good base camp for visiting Honolulu attractions; it's just 15 minutes from Waikiki or Pearl Harbor.

Only tent camping is allowed in this park, and only on Friday, Saturday, and Sunday nights. You'll find picnic tables (some under small covered shelters), restrooms with cold showers only, and potable water. You'll need a permit; the fee is $18 per campsite per night. Applications are accepted no earlier than 30 days in advance and can be purchased online at **www.hawaiistateparks.org/camping/fees.cfm**, or by writing to the **Department of Land and Natural Resources,** State Parks Division, P.O. Box 621, Honolulu, HI 96809 (© **808/587-0300**). Permits are given for a maximum of 5 days in every 30-day period (and because you can only stay on weekends, 5 consecutive days aren't possible). The gates close at 6:45pm in the fall and winter (from the weekend after Labor Day until Mar 31) and 7:45pm in the spring and summer (Apr 1 until the Fri after Labor Day). The gates do not open until 7am the next morning; cars cannot enter or leave during that period. TheBus 19 stops at Nimitz Highway and Puuhale Road; it's just over a mile to walk to the park entrance.

Central Oahu

KEAIWA HEIAU STATE RECREATION AREA ★

At the southern end of central Oahu, above Halawa Heights, this 385-acre wooded park offers a cool mountain retreat with hiking trails and picnic facilities. This area, in the foothills of the Koolaus, is filled with eucalyptus, ironwood, and Norfolk pines. The remains of the *Heiau Ho'ola* (Temple of Treating the Sick) are on the grounds, and specimens of Hawaiian medicinal plants are on display. An excellent 5-mile hiking trail, the **Aiea loop,** offers magnificent views of Pearl Harbor and the mountains. There's tent camping only; campers have the choice of flat, open grassy areas or slightly sloping areas with shade trees. Facilities include picnic tables, restrooms with cold showers, outdoor grills, a dishwashing area, a covered pavilion, drinking water, and a public phone. Supplies are available in Aiea, 2 miles away.

You'll need a permit, which costs $18 per campsite per night; applications are accepted no earlier than 30 days in advance. Online at **www.hawaiistateparks.org/parks/oahu/keaiwa.cfm** or write to the **Department of Land and Natural Resources** (see "Sand Island State Recreation Area," above, for address and telephone number). Permits are limited to a 5-day stay in every 30-day period. Camping is permitted Friday through Tuesday nights. The gates close at 6:45pm in the fall and winter (from the weekend after Labor Day until Mar 31) and 7:45pm in the spring and summer (Apr 1 until the Fri after Labor Day). The gates do not open until 7am the next morning; cars cannot enter or leave during that period.

The Windward Coast

HOOMALUHIA BOTANICAL GARDENS ★

This relatively unknown windward-side camping area, outside Kaneohe, is a real find. *Hoomaluhia* means "peace and tranquillity," an apt description for the 400-acre botanical garden. It's hard to believe you're just a half-hour from downtown Honolulu, considering the rare plants all around and the craggy cliffs in the background. The

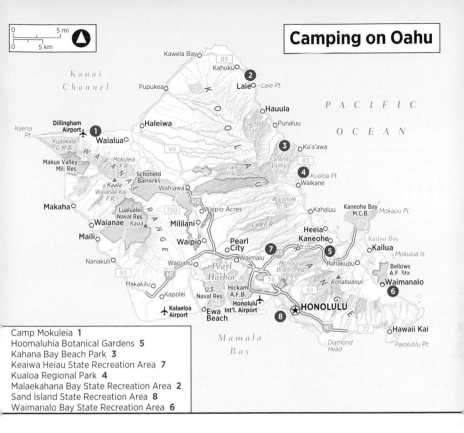

Camp Mokuleia **1**
Hoomaluhia Botanical Gardens **5**
Kahana Bay Beach Park **3**
Keaiwa Heiau State Recreation Area **7**
Kualoa Regional Park **4**
Malaekahana Bay State Recreation Area **2**
Sand Island State Recreation Area **8**
Waimanalo Bay State Recreation Area **6**

gardens are laid out with areas devoted to the plants specific to tropical America, native Hawaii, Polynesia, India, Sri Lanka, and Africa. A 32-acre lake sits in the middle of the scenic park (no swimming or boating allowed, though), and there are numerous **hiking trails.** The Visitors Center can suggest a host of activities, ranging from guided walks to demonstrations of ancient Hawaiian plant use. The facilities for this tent-camp area include restrooms, cold showers, dishwashing stations, picnic tables, grills, and water. A public phone is available at the Visitors Center, and shopping and gas are available in Kaneohe, 1 mile away.

Permits are free, but that may be changing. You have to get here on a Friday no later than 3pm, as the office is not open on weekends. Stays are limited to Friday, Saturday, and Sunday nights only. You must apply in person, and at this time permits can only be obtained at the gardens. For inquiries and reservations, contact **Hoomaluhia Botanical Gardens,** 45-680 Luluku Rd. (at Kamehameha Hwy.), Kaneohe, HI 96744 (www.hawaiistateparks.org/parks/oahu/keaiwa.cfm; © **808/233-7323**). The gate is locked at 4pm and doesn't open again until 9am the next morning. TheBus no. 55 (Circle Island) stops 4 miles from the park entrance.

KUALOA REGIONAL PARK ★★

This park has a spectacular setting on a peninsula on Kaneohe Bay. The gold-sand beach is excellent for snorkeling, and fishing can be rewarding (p. 160).

Two campgrounds are available: Campground A—in a wooded area with a sandy beach and palm, ironwood, kamani, and monkeypod trees—is mainly used for groups, but has a few sites for families, except during the summer, when the Department of Parks and Recreation conducts a children's camping program here. Campground B is on the main beach; it has fewer shade trees, but a great view of Mokolii Island. Facilities at both sites include restrooms, showers, picnic tables, drinking fountains, and a public phone. Campground A also has sinks for dishwashing, a volleyball court, and a kitchen building. Gas and groceries are available in Kaaawa, 2½ miles away. Gate hours are 7am to 8pm; if you're not back by then, you're locked out for the night.

Permits are free but limited to 3 to 5 days (no camping in the "A" section Mon–Thurs; no camping in the "B" section on Thursday). Contact the **Honolulu Department of Parks and Recreation,** 650 S. King St., Honolulu, HI 96713 (www.honolulu.gov/parks/parkuse.htm; © **808/768-3440**). You must apply for a camping permit in person at any satellite City Hall. Kualoa Regional Park is in the 49 to 600 area of Kamehameha Highway, across from Mokolii Island. Take TheBus no. 55.

KAHANA BAY BEACH PARK ★★

Under Tahiti-like cliffs, with a beautiful, gold-sand crescent beach framed by pine-needle casuarina trees, Kahana Bay Beach Park is a place of serene beauty. You can swim, bodysurf, fish, hike, picnic, or just sit and listen to the trade winds whistle through the beach pines.

Both tent and vehicle camping are allowed at this oceanside oasis. Facilities include restrooms, picnic tables, drinking water, public phones, and a boat-launching ramp. Note that the restrooms are at the north end of the beach, far away from the camping area, and there are no showers. You'll need a permit; the fee is $18 per campsite per night. There's a 5-night limit, and no camping at all on Wednesday or Thursday nights. You can get a permit from the **Department of Land and Natural Resources,** State Parks Division, P.O. Box 621, Honolulu, HI 96809 (www.hawaiistateparks.org/camping/fees.cfm; © **808/587-0300**).

Kahana Bay Beach Park is in the 52 to 222 block of Kamehameha Highway (Hwy. 83) in Kahana. You can also get there via TheBus no. 55.

WAIMANALO BAY STATE RECREATION AREA ★

Just outside the town of Waimanalo is one of the most beautiful beachfront camping grounds on Oahu: Steep verdant cliffs in the background, a view of Rabbit Island off shore, and miles of white-sand beach complete the picture of Waimanalo Bay State Recreation Area. This campground is close to Sea Life Park and relatively close to Hanauma Bay, Makapuu, and Sandy Beach.

Ocean activities abound: great swimming offshore, good surfing for beginners, and plentiful fishing grounds. There is tent camping only at the 12 sites, which ensures plenty of privacy. The campsites (in numbered slots) are all in the open grassy lawn between the ironwood trees and the shoreline. Each campsite has its own picnic table, barbecue grill, and garbage can. Other facilities in the area include a central restroom with showers, water fountains, and a dishwashing sink. A public telephone is by the caretaker's house.

Permits are free but limited to 5 nights (no camping on Wed or Thurs nights). Contact the **Honolulu Department of Parks and Recreation,** 650 S. King St., Honolulu, HI 96713 (www.honolulu.gov/parks/camping.htm; © **808/523-4525**), for information and permits. Permits are not issued until 2 weeks before your camping dates.

TheBus no. 57 stops on Kalanianaole Highway (Hwy. 72), about a mile's walking distance to the park entrance.

The North Shore

MALAEKAHANA BAY STATE RECREATION AREA ★★★

This beautiful camping site has a mile-long gold-sand beach, with two areas for tent camping. Facilities include picnic tables, restrooms, showers, sinks, drinking water, and a phone. Stays are limited to 5 nights (no camping on Wed or Thurs nights). Camping fees are $18 per campsite per night; permits can be obtained at any state parks office, including the **Department of Land and Natural Resources,** State Parks Division, P.O. Box 621, Honolulu, HI 96809 (www.hawaiistateparks.org/camping/fees.cfm; ℭ **808/587-0300**). The park gate is closed between 6:45pm and 7am; vehicles cannot enter or exit during those hours. Groceries and gas are available in Laie and Kahuku, less than a mile away.

The recreation area is on Kamehameha Highway (Hwy. 83) between Laie and Kahuku. You can take TheBus no. 55.

CAMP MOKULEIA ★★

A quiet, isolated beach on Oahu's North Shore, 4 miles from Kaena Point, is the centerpiece of this 9-acre campground. Camping is available on the beach or in a grassy, wooded area. Activities include swimming, surfing, shore fishing, and beachcombing. Facilities include tent camping, cabins, and lodge accommodations. The tent-camping site has portable chemical toilets, a water spigot, and outdoor showers; there are no picnic tables or barbecue grills, so come prepared. The cabins sleep up to 22 people in bunk beds. The cabins are $238 per night for the 14-bed cabin and $344 per night for the 22-bed cabin. Rooms at the lodge (must have a group of 15 for meal service) are $95 for a shared bathroom and $95 to $105 for a private bathroom. "Home cooked" meals can be had for $9 to $10. Tent camping is $15 per person, per night. Many groups use the camp, but there's a real sense of privacy. Parking is $3 per day. Reservations are required; contact **Camp Mokuleia,** 68-729 Farrington Hwy., Waialua, HI 96791 (www.visitcampmokuleia.com; ℭ **808/637-6241**).

Camp Mokuleia is on Farrington Highway, west of Haleiwa.

WHERE TO EAT

5

Y ou won't go hungry on Oahu. The full range of choices here includes glamorous chef-owned restaurants, neighborhood cafes, fast-food joints, ethnic spots, and shopping-mall food courts and eateries.

The culinary scene seems to change each year, and the current trends in Hawaii center on emphasizing organic and locally grown produce (with some restaurants actually naming the farms that grew the lettuce); small plates, sample tastings, and even bite-size desserts; interesting and unusual specialty sandwiches on a variety of breads (from spelt to wraps); and exotic salt (in a range of colors and flavors). Hawaii regional cuisine (HRC; p. 39) and Pacific regional cuisine still reign supreme in Hawaii, as well as Pan-Asian and Mediterranean.

Whatever you have a hankering for, you'll find it on Oahu. Our advice is to be adventurous, try new and different cuisines, and sample foods you've never heard of. It's moments like these that create great memories.

The recommendations below are organized by location, beginning with Waikiki, proceeding to neighborhoods west and east of Waikiki, and ending with the Windward Coast and the North Shore.

WAIKIKI
Very Expensive

La Mer ★★★ FRENCH This is *the* splurge restaurant of Hawaii, an ocean-front bastion of haute cuisine, where two of the state's finest chefs (George Mavrothalassitis and Philippe Padovani, each with his own eponymous restaurant now) quietly redefined Hawaiian fine dining. La Mer is romantic, elegant, and expensive; dress up not to be seen, but to match the ambience and food. It's the only AAA Five Diamond restaurant in the state, with a second-floor, open-sided room with views of Diamond Head and the sound of trade winds rustling the nearby coconut fronds. Michelin Award–winning chef Yves Garnier melds

---

Hey, No Smoking in Hawaii

Well, not totally no smoking, but Hawaii has one of the toughest laws against smoking in the U.S. It's against the law to smoke in public buildings, including airports, shopping malls, grocery stores, retail shops, buses, movie theaters, banks, convention facilities, and all government buildings and facilities. There is no smoking in restaurants, bars, and nightclubs. Most bed-and-breakfasts prohibit smoking indoors; more and more hotels and resorts are becoming nonsmoking, even in public areas. Also, there is no smoking within 20 feet of a doorway, window, or ventilation intake (no hanging around outside a bar to smoke, you must go 20 ft. away). Even some beaches have no-smoking policies (and on those that allow smoking, you face stiff fines for littering cigarette butts). In Hawaii, breathing fresh clean air is "in" and smoking is "out."

FACING PAGE: **A panko-crusted ahi roll at Sansei Seafood Restaurant & Sushi Bar.**

Arancino **8**	Eggs 'n Things **7**	Morimoto **2**	Sarento's Top of the I **3**
Bali Steak & Seafood **4**	Hula Grill Waikiki **11**	Orchids **9**	Singha Thai Cuisine **5**
Cha Cha Cha **10**	Hy's Steak House **13**	Prince Court **1**	Tiki's Grill & Bar **15**
Ciao Mein **12**	Keo's in Waikiki **6**	Sansei Seafood	
d.k Steakhouse **14**	La Mer **9**	Restaurant & Sushi	
Duke's Waikiki **11**	MAC 24-7 **1**	Bar **14**	

classical French influences with fresh Island ingredients. Winners include the signature crispy-skin filet of onaga with truffle jus, tomato confit, and fresh basil; and the delightful local fish baked in a rosemary-salt crust. The wine list, desserts, and service—formal without being stiff—complete the dining experience.

At the Halekulani, 2199 Kalia Rd. ✆ **808/923-2311.** www.halekulani.com. Reservations recommended. Jackets or long-sleeved shirts required for men. Prix-fixe menus $90 for 2 courses, $120 for 3 courses, $135 for 4 courses; $180 for "Ultimate" dinner with vintage Madeira. AE, DC, MC, V. Daily 6–10pm.

Michel's ★★ FRENCH/HAWAII REGIONAL This dining room, on the sand at Sans Souci Beach, has windows that open to the ocean air. One side looks

0   1/4 mi
0   1/4 km

Ala Wai Golf Course

Ala Wai Blvd.

Seaside Ave.
Nohonani St.
Nahua St.
Walina St.
Kanekapolei St.
Kailuani Ave.
Kaiulani Ave.
Cleghorn St.
Ave.
Ave.
Pualani Wy.
Leahi Ave.
Paki Ave.

13

Pr. Edward St.
Liliuokalani Ave.
Kealohilani Ave.
Ohua
Paoakalani
Kuhio Ave.
Kapahulu Ave.

International Market Place

Koa Ave.

Cartwright Rd.

Honolulu Zoo

Kalakaua Ave.

12

11

Lemon Rd.

Kuhio Beach Park

14

15

Waikiki Beach

Monsarrat Ave.

Kapiolani Park

Gray's Beach

Kalakaua Ave.

Queen's Surf Beach

M a m a l a   B a y

Waikiki Aquarium

To Diamond Head

Natatorium

toward the sunset, with torches on the breakwater, and a hula moon above the palm fronds; the Waikiki skyline is visible on the other. If that wasn't enough to lure you in, they also have live music nightly (beginning at 6:30pm). All tables have ocean views, and dining here is less stiff and more welcoming than in by-gone years. Jackets are no longer required for men, but collared shirts and long pants are preferred. Chef Hardy Kintscher has added his touch to the classics (onion soup, steak tartare, chateaubriand, bouillabaisse) and prepares fresh sea-food, vegetarian creations, and rack of lamb with restraint and creativity.

At the Colony Surf Hotel, 2895 Kalakaua Ave. ✆ **808/923-6552.** www.michelshawaii.com. Reservations recommended. Collared shirts and long pants preferred for men; no shorts or beachwear permitted. Main courses $42–$65. AE, DC, MC, V. Daily 5:30–9pm; Sun brunch 10am–1pm (1st Sun of each month only).

Morimoto ★★★ JAPANESE Masaharu Morimoto, the star of the TV show *Iron Chef,* stars nightly at his just-opened signature restaurant. The big, elegant dining room features the Morimoto's signature cuisine, which blends traditional Japanese dishes with fresh Western ingredients, to wildly received applause.

Dinner is the main attraction, where unforgettable dishes like hamachi tartare are served with an assortment of condiments, including Moromoto's guacamole, a nori puree, rice crackers, sour cream, wasbi, and *yamamomo* (a Japanese peach). For the ultimate foodie experience, order the *omakase* ("in the chef's hands") menu, an elaborate and decadent multicourse tasting menu. Morimoto also serves a traditional Japanese breakfast (as well as Western breakfast options—don't miss the banana macadamia nut pancakes), and has a range of options for lunch, from sandwiches and entrees to offerings from the sushi bar. You can even eat on the lanai.

At the Waikiki Edition hotel, 1775 Ala Moana Blvd (at Hobron Ln). ✆ **808/943-5900.** www.morimotowaikiki.com. Reservations recommended for dinner. Breakfast entrees $7–$29; lunch entrees $18–$85; dinner entrees $18–$110; *omakase* menu $110. AE, DC, MC, V. Daily 6:30–10am, 11am–2:30pm, and 5:30–10pm (Fri–Sat 5:30–11pm).

Expensive

Bali Steak & Seafood ★★ CONTINENTAL/PACIFIC RIM This is another memorable oceanfront dining room—pale and full of light, with a white grand piano at the entrance and sweeping views of the ocean. (Ask for a table by the window.) The menu merges island cooking styles and ingredients, as in the signature roasted mahimahi with Hamakua tomato vinaigrette, Kahuku corn, and Thai basil. Or try the wonderful surf and turf—Kona lobster and filet mignon, both with a mustard aioli sauce and a side of pureed potatoes; or the popular Bali seafood medley, which combines butter-and-Thai-basil-seared island fish, scallops, shrimp, and lobster, served with Yukon potato puree and curry sauce. Save room for their mouthwatering desserts.

At the Hilton Hawaiian Village, 2005 Kalia Rd. ✆ **808/949-4321,** ext. 43. www.hiltonhawaiianvillage.com/dining. Reservations recommended. Main courses $26–$48. AE, DC, DISC, MC, V. Tue–Sat 5–9pm.

Hy's Steak House STEAKHOUSE This steakhouse is as good as it gets. Think dark, clubby, lots of leather, good Scotch, and filet mignon. This is a great choice for steak lovers with hefty pocketbooks or for those who have tired of Hawaii regional cuisine. Hy's has demonstrated admirable staying power in the cult of low fat, still scoring high among carnivores while offering ample alternatives, such as a grilled vegetable platter and excellent salads prepared tableside (the spinach and Caesar are textbook-perfect). "The Only" is its classic best, a kiawe-grilled New York strip steak served with a secret signature sauce. Garlic lovers swear by the "Garlic Steak Diane," a richly endowed rib eye with sliced mushrooms.

2440 Kuhio Ave. ✆ **808/922-5555.** www.hyshawaii.com. Reservations recommended. Main courses $27–$63 or market price. AE, DC, DISC, MC, V. Mon–Fri 6–10pm; Sat–Sun 5:30–10pm.

Orchids ★★ SEAFOOD Orchids highlights fresh local produce and seafood with elegant presentations in a fantasy setting with consummate service. Blinding white linens and a view of Diamond Head from the open oceanfront dining room will start you off with a smile. (The parade of oiled bodies traversing the seawall is part of the entertainment.) At lunch, seafood curry, though pricey, is a winner, as are the tagine of roasted vegetables and the Nicoise salad with seared tuna. The Hawaii-centric lunch special is an excellent way to sample this fare, $34 for three courses. For dinner, onaga is steamed with ginger, Chinese parsley, shiitake mushrooms, and soy sauce, then drizzled with hot sesame oil—delightful. Delicate Moi is seared and served with shaved fennel, pearl onions and olives and a Ka'u orange vinaigrette, another pleaser with Mediterranean undertones. Lamb, chicken, and beef entrees are offered as well, and the desserts, especially the chocolate hazelnut dacquoise and the Halekulani signature coconut cake, are extraordinary. **Sunday brunch ★★★**, with its outstanding selection of dishes, is one of the best in Hawaii.

At the Halekulani, 2199 Kalia Rd. ☏ **808/923-2311.** www.halekulani.com. Reservations recommended. Dinner main courses $26–$60; 4-course prix-fixe dinner $65; Sun brunch $57 adults, $29 children 5–12. AE, DC, MC, V. Mon–Sat 7:30–11am, 11:30am–2pm, and 6–10pm; Sun 9:30am–2:30pm and 6–10pm.

Prince Court ★ HAWAII REGIONAL   Floor-to-ceiling windows, sunny views of the harbor, and top-notch buffets are Prince Court's attractions, especially at lunch, when locals and visitors line up for the international spread. Chef Khamtan Tanhchaleun keeps the menu fresh and the dining room busy. The harbor view is particularly pleasing at sunset or on Friday nights when fireworks light up the sky. Wednesdays and Thursdays, diners can sample everything from island seafood to Hawaii regional specialties (such as melt-in-your-mouth ahi carpaccio) and excellent grilled and roasted meats at the buffet. Desserts, too, are legendary, especially the custard-drenched bread pudding and the macadamia nut pie.

At the Hawaii Prince Hotel Waikiki, 100 Holomoana St. ☏ **808/944-4494.** Reservations recommended. Dinner prix fixe and buffet $37–$57 (no a la carte for dinner), breakfast buffet $21, weekend brunch $37, luncheon buffet $26, seafood dinner buffet $46. AE, DC, MC, V. Daily 6–10:30am; Mon–Sat 11am–2pm; Sun brunch 10am–1pm; Mon–Thurs 6–9:30pm; Fri–Sun 5:30–9:30pm.

Sarento's Top of the I ★ ITALIAN   The ride up in the glass elevator at this special-occasion Italian restaurant is an event in itself, and diners rave about the romantic view of the city—but Sarento's is not all show. The stellar chopped "Gabriella" salad; the pan-roasted opakapaka with lump crab meat, cremini mushrooms, and lemon butter; and the fennel-crusted ahi tuna with grilled

5

WHERE TO EAT

Waikiki

127

vegetable ratatouille prove that Sarento's means business. The pasta selections include lobster ravioli and the simple (and divine) rigatoni alla vodka. Veal lovers come for the osso buco with saffron risotto. Dishes can be buttery, so leave your inhibitions at the door.

In the Renaissance Ilikai Waikiki, 1777 Ala Moana Blvd. ☏ **808/955-5559.** www.tristar restaurants.com. Reservations recommended. Main courses $20–$39. AE, DC, DISC, MC, V. Sun–Thurs 5:30–9pm; Fri–Sat 5:30–9:30pm.

Moderate

Arancino ITALIAN When jaded Honolulu residents venture into Waikiki for dinner, it had better be good. And Arancino is. The cheerful cafe with Monet-yellow walls and tile floors has respectable pastas, wonderful pizzas, fabulous red-pepper salsa and rock-salt focaccia, we-try-harder service, and reasonable prices. The risotto changes daily, and you should not miss the Gorgonzola-asparagus pizza if it's on the menu. Expect a line on the sidewalk to get in, but it's worth the wait.

255 Beach Walk (second location at Waikiki Marriott Beach, 2552 Kalakaua Ave.). ☏ **808/923-5557.** www.arancino.com. Main courses $12–$35. AE, DC, DISC, MC, V. Daily 11:30am–2:30pm and 5–10pm.

Ciao Mein ITALIAN/CHINESE Risotto with chopsticks, fried rice with a fork—such is the cross-cultural way of Ciao Mein, which is 15 years old and still going strong. The large, pleasant dining room, efficient service, surprisingly good Chinese food, and award-winning menu have made this a haven for noodle lovers. The honey-walnut shrimp, with snap peas and honey-glazed nuts, and the angel-hair pasta with spicy ginger-garlic shrimp, are big hits, and Ciao Mein's tiramisu packs a creamy, ambrosial kick. The antipasto is Italian, and the seafood fun (as in chow fun) lasagna is a form of Ciao Mein's "collision cuisine"—a mix of Chinese and Italian. Choose from six different pastas and six sauces.

In the Hyatt Regency Waikiki, 2424 Kalakaua Ave. ☏ **808/923-2426.** Reservations recommended. Main courses $21–$40, prix fixe $47–$78. AE, DC, DISC, MC, V. Daily 6–10pm.

d.k Steakhouse ★ STEAKHOUSE Attention carnivores: This steakhouse opened in 2004 to rave reviews, giving the national steakhouse chains and the top local steakhouses a run for their money. Locally known chef D. K. Kodama (of Sansei Seafood Restaurant & Sushi Bar, p. 130; and Vino Italian Tapas & Wine Bar, p. 141) and Hawaii's top sommelier Chuck Furuya have created the ultimate steakhouse for the 21st century at very reasonable prices (especially for Waikiki). Purists will love the prime grade and dry-aged (in-house for 10 days) New York strip and filet mignon, served unadorned or topped with either three-peppercorn sauce au poivre, blue crab and béarnaise sauce, shiitake mushroom demiglace, or D. K.'s own sesame seed–miso sauce. The ultimate treat is the 22-ounce, bone-in rib eye (dry-aged for 15 days): Every bite has a melt-in-your-mouth richness that steak fans will remember forever. We recommend booking a table outside on the lanai and coming early to watch the sun set over Waikiki Beach. The decor is romantic, with dim lighting, intimate wooden booths, and tiny bar lights. Steak alternatives include a fresh catch, lamb chops, and broiled herbed chicken.

Waikiki Beach Marriott Resort, 2552 Kalakaua Ave., 3rd floor. ☏ **808/931-6280.** www. dksteakhouse.com. Reservations recommended. Main courses $18–$65. AE, DISC, MC, V. Daily 5:30–10pm.

EATING IN WAIKIKI 24-7

If your flight to Honolulu arrives late and you're starving, your knight in shining armor in Waikiki is **MAC 24-7** (which stands for Modern American Cooking, 24 hours a day, 7 days a week), at the **Hilton Waikiki Prince Kuhio Hotel,** 2500 Kuhio Ave. (at Liliuokalani Ave.; ℂ **808/921-5564**). All day, every day, the kitchen offers everything from breakfast, lunch, and dinner to snacks and desserts, and the bar pours drinks all day, except between 4 and 6am. It's not just for late-night dining (although it comes in handy, as Waikiki eateries shut down by 10–11pm); it's also a great place to get picnic lunches during the day.

The cuisine is coffee shop/diner "comfort" food, reasonably priced for Waikiki ($4–$28, with most entrees in the $15–$28 range), and plenty of it. Portions can feed two and, in some cases, three people. Our pick for best meal of the day is breakfast, where the six-pack of buttery cinnamon rolls ($6) will feed three and the yummy wild blueberry pancakes ($15) are supersized (three pancakes, each one 14 in. in diameter), plenty for two hungry people. Another must-try from the menu: the delicious meatloaf with garlic mashed potatoes and mushroom gravy ($18). The view from the floor-to-ceiling windows is of the landscaped gardens in the lobby. The decor is sophisticated but sparse with splashes of bright color, and the waitstaff is friendly and helpful.

Duke's Waikiki ★ 🍴 STEAKHOUSE/SEAFOOD Hip, busy, and on the ocean—this is what dining in Waikiki should be. There's hardly a time when the open-air dining room isn't filled with good Hawaiian music. Duke's is popular among singles, but don't dismiss it as a pickup bar—its ambience is stellar. Named after fabled surfer Duke Kahanamoku, the casual, upbeat hotspot buzzes with diners and Hawaiian-music lovers throughout the day. The lunch and **Barefoot Bar** menus include pizza, sandwiches, burgers, salads, and appetizers such as mac-nut and crab wontons and the ever-popular grilled chicken quesadillas. Dinner fare is steak and seafood, with decent marks for the fresh catch, prepared in your choice of five styles. Live entertainment is featured nightly from 4pm to midnight, with no cover. Be prepared to fight the crowds if you come at sunset.

In the Outrigger Waikiki on the Beach, 2335 Kalakaua Ave. ℂ **808/922-2268.** www.hulapie.com. Reservations recommended for dinner. Main courses $19–$32, breakfast buffet $15. AE, DC, DISC, MC, V. Daily 7am–midnight.

Hau Tree Lanai ★ PACIFIC RIM Informal and delightful, this Honolulu institution scores higher on ambience than on food. The outdoor setting and earnest menu make it a popular informal dining spot; an ancient hau tree provides shade and charm for diners. A diverse parade of beachgoers at Sans Souci Beach (called "Dig Me Beach" for its eye-candy sunbathers) round out the scenery. Breakfast here is a must: Choices include salmon Florentine, served with a fresh-baked scone; poi pancakes; Belgian waffles; eggs Benedict; and the Hawaiian platter of miniature poi pancakes, eggs, and a medley of island sausages. Lunchtime offerings include an assortment of burgers, sandwiches, salads, and fresh-fish and pasta specialties. Dinner selections are more ambitious and less reliable: fresh *opah* (moonfish), red snapper, opakapaka, ahi, lamb, beef, pork, and chef's specials, in preparations ranging from grilled to stuffed and over-the-top rich.

At the New Otani Kaimana Beach Hotel, 2863 Kalakaua Ave. 🕐 **808/921-7066.** www.kaimana. com/dining.htm. Reservations recommended. Breakfast $10–$16, lunch $12–$17, dinner $25–$39. AE, DC, DISC, MC, V. Mon–Sat 7–10:45am, 11:45am–2pm, and 5:30–9pm; Sun 7–10:45am and 5:30–9pm. Late lunch in the open-air bar daily 2–4pm.

Hula Grill Waikiki ★★ 🍴 HAWAII REGIONAL This is the best place for breakfast in Waikiki: Not only does it have a terrific view of all of Waikiki (clear to Diamond Head), but the food is fabulous and a great value. Breakfast is a generous selection of pancakes (banana, mac-nut, pineapple, even coconut) and eggs (from crab cake eggs Benedict to a ham, bacon, and Portuguese sausage omelet with cheddar). Then come back for a romantic dinner—the restaurant is decorated in a 1930s Hawaii waterfront home theme, with such touches as an ohia log bar, hula doll collection, slate flooring, and lauhala pine–soffited ceilings. Signature dinner entrees at the beachside bistro include Hawaiian ceviche, fire-grilled *ono* (wahoo), oven-roasted sesame opah, and a nightly collection of specials.

In the Outrigger Waikiki on the Beach, 2335 Kalakaua Ave. 🕐 **808/923-HULA** [923-4852]. www. hulagrillwaikiki.com. Reservations recommended for dinner. Breakfast $6–$14, main courses $17–$33. AE, DC, MC, V. Daily 6:30–10:45am, 4:30–6pm (happy hour with light menu), and 4:45–10pm.

Keo's in Waikiki ★ THAI Fresh spices, spirited dishes, and a familiar crop of Thai delights: Keo's has a splashy tropical ambience and a menu that both islanders and visitors love. Owner Keo Sananikone grows his own herbs, fruits, and vegetables without pesticides on his North Shore farm. Satay shrimp; basil-infused eggplant with tofu; "evil jungle prince" (shrimp, chicken, or vegetables in a basil-coconut-chili sauce); Thai garlic shrimp with mushrooms; pad Thai noodles; and the ever-delectable panang, green, and yellow curries are among his abiding delights.

2028 Kuhio Ave. 🕐 **808/951-9355.** www.keosthaicuisine.com. Reservations recommended. Main courses $15–$20, prix fixe $30–$45. AE, DC, DISC, MC, V. Daily 4-10:30pm

Sansei Seafood Restaurant & Sushi Bar ★★ SUSHI/PACIFIC RIM Perpetual award-winner D. K. Kodama, who built Kapalua's Sansei into one of Maui's most popular eateries, has become a local legend with his exuberant brand of sushi and fusion cooking. Although some of the flavors (sweet Thai chili sauce with cilantro, for example) may be too fussy for sushi purists, choices abound on the extensive menu, including the award-winning trademark Asian rock shrimp

---

Tasty Tours for the Hungry Traveler

See Honolulu—one restaurant at a time. Former Honolulu newspaper food critic and chef Matthew Gray has put together **"Hawaii Food Tours"** to show you a side of Hawaii that you might not discover on your own. He offers three different types of tours, all with transportation from your Waikiki hotel in an air-conditioned van and all with running commentary on Hawaii's history, culture, and archi-tecture. Our favorite was the "Hole-in-the-Wall Tour," a lunch tour from 9:15am to 2:30pm for $99 per person, where you visit at least four different **ethnic** restaurants (Vietnamese, Indian, local food, and dessert). Matthew has already preordered the best dishes from their menus. For information and booking, call 🕐 **808/926-FOOD** (926-3663), or go to **www.hawaiifoodtours.com.**

cake; the Sansei Special sushi roll (crab, cilantro, cucumber, and avocado with a sweet chili sauce); seared foie gras nigiri sushi (duck liver lightly seared over sushi rice, accompanied by caramelized onion and ripe mango); and the wonderful mango crab salad hand roll (with mango, blue crab, greens, and peanuts all wrapped in soybean paper with a sweet Thai chili vinaigrette). More traditional selections range from very fresh yellowtail sushi to Japanese miso eggplant.

At the Waikiki Beach Marriott Resort, 2552 Kalakaua Ave., 3rd floor. ℭ **808/931-6286.** www. sanseihawaii.com. Reservations recommended. Sushi $6–$20, main courses $16–$40. AE, DISC, MC, V. Sat–Wed 5:30–10pm; Thurs–Fri 5:30pm–1am.

Singha Thai Cuisine THAI The Royal Thai dancers arch their graceful fingers nightly in classical Thai dance on the small center stage, but you may be too busy tucking into your blackened ahi summer rolls to notice. That use of local organic ingredients, and the imaginative combination dinners, are among the special touches of this Thai-Hawaiian fusion restaurant. The complete combo dinners, which serve two to five, cover many tastes and are an ideal way for the uninitiated to sample the elements of Hawaii regional and Thai cuisine that have had an influence on the chef. Highlights of the diverse menu, which extensively utilizes fresh fish (mahimahi, ono, ahi, opakapaka, onaga, and uku) in traditional Thai preparations—unusual for a Thai restaurant—might include local fresh catch with Thai chili and black-bean sauce; red, green, yellow, and vegetarian curries; and spicy lemongrass soup with shrimp. The entertainment and indoor-outdoor dining add to this first-class experience.

1910 Ala Moana Blvd. (at the Ala Moana end of Waikiki). ℭ **808/941-2898.** www.singhathai. com. Reservations recommended. Main courses $17–$34; complete dinners $35. AE, DC, DISC, MC, V. Daily 4–11pm.

Tiki's Grill & Bar PACIFIC RIM This casual eatery, decorated in palm wood flooring with fish nets hanging from the ceiling and lava-rock walls, is located on the second floor of the Aston Waikiki Beach Hotel overlooking Waikiki Beach—so you'll want to grab an outside table on the lanai before sunset. A 30-foot volcano is the showpiece in the bar (where you can snack on *pupu,* or appetizers). In November 2010, Chef Ron Nasuti, formerly executive chef for Roy's Hawaii Kai, took over the reins in the kitchen. Since then, he's moved the menu from American to more decidedly Pacific Rim. Tiki's signature dish, king salmon glazed with lemongrass beurre blanc, remains, but the grilled opah has a new fresh Kamuela tomato, cilantro, and chili sauce. The desserts are all bite-size, too—at $2 each, they're not only easy on the calories, but also on the wallet. Live Hawaiian music is featured nightly in the bar.

In the Aston Waikiki Beach Hotel, 2570 Kalakaua Ave. (at Paoakalani St.). ℭ **808/923-TIKI** [923-8454]. www.tikisgrill.com. Lunch entrees $12–$15; dinner entrees $26–$49; 3-course prix fixe menu $39. AE, DC, DISC, MC, V. Daily 10:30am–midnight.

Inexpensive

Cha Cha Cha MEXICAN/CARIBBEAN Its heroic margaritas, cheap happy-hour beer, *pupu,* excellent homemade chips, and all-around lovable menu make this a Waikiki treasure. From the beans to the salsa to the grilled Jamaican chicken, there's nothing wimpy about the flavors here. The lime, coconut, and Caribbean spices make Cha Cha Cha more than plain old Mex, adding zing to the blackened mahimahi and fresh-fish burritos, the jerk chicken breast, and the grilled veggies in a spinach tortilla. Tacos, tamales, quesadillas, soups, enchiladas, chimichangas, and a host of spicy pork, chicken, and fish ensembles are real pleasers—plus don't miss the blackened swordfish, shrimp fajitas, daily specials, and homemade desserts (including a creamy toasted coconut custard).

342 Seaside Ave. © **808/923-7797.** Breakfast $7–$10; complete dinners $10–$19. MC, V. Daily 6–10am and 11:30am–11pm; happy hour 4–6pm and 9–11pm.

Eggs 'n Things ★★ BREAKFAST After a terrible fire a few years ago, this popular breakfast-only eatery reopened just a few blocks from its former location. The eclectic place is famous for its tasty food served in humongous portions. You'll find the fluffiest omelets (which come with pancakes, potatoes, and toast), melt-in-your-mouth waffles (piled high with fruit and whipped cream), and hot coffee constantly being poured into your cup. It's worth waiting in line for the incredibly reasonable prices. In 2010, Eggs 'n Things also started serving dinner; the menu includes those famous breakfast items, plus things like chicken fried steak, fresh ahi steak, and loco moco (rice topped with a hamburger patty, a fried egg, and gravy).

343 Saratoga Rd. (at Kalakaua Ave.). © **808/949-0820.** www.eggsnthings.com. Breakfast $5–$12, dinner $9–$13. MC, V. Daily 6am–2pm and 5–10pm.

HONOLULU BEYOND WAIKIKI

Ala Moana & Kakaako

EXPENSIVE

Longhi's ITALIAN Bob Longhi, who opened Longhi's in Lahaina in 1976, runs this swank, open-air, Italian-Mediterranean restaurant with romantic sunset views of the ocean. It features the family's famous cooking—lobster Longhi over linguine, prawns Amaretto, and *puttana,* a spicy calamari pasta dish with 35 whole garlic cloves. Meals can be pricey, in part because everything comes a la carte, but the view is spectacular and the service is prompt. It also is a great place for breakfast (their French toast, with a "touch" of Grand Marnier, is wickedly divine, and their baked goods are delicious), with moderate prices and that terrific view. Lunch, which can get crowded, features yummy salads, sandwiches, pastas, and excellent fish entrees.

At the Ala Moana Center, 1450 Ala Moana Blvd. © **808/947-9899.** www.longhis.com. Reservations recommended for dinner. Main courses $8.50–$21 breakfast, $10–$38 lunch, $21–$80 dinner. AE, DISC, MC, V. Mon–Fri 8am–10pm; Sat–Sun 7:45am–10pm.

Mariposa ★★ PACIFIC RIM Past the gourmet food department of the new Neiman Marcus lies Mariposa. The popular lunch spot's high ceilings and tables on the deck with views of Ala Moana Park and its Art Deco bridges add up to a pleasing ambience, with or without the shopping. You'll find cordial service, nearly four dozen reasonably priced wines by the glass, and a menu of Pacific and American (called "heritage cuisine") specialties that include everything from a tiger prawn paella to pan-roasted Hawaiian snapper and rib-eye steak. Chef Mark Anthony Freiberg's creativity emerges with dishes such as the Laksa seafood curry, which is only available at lunch. Another lunchtime favorite is Mariposa's signature starter: the towering, eggy popover with *poha* (cape gooseberry) butter. But save room for our favorite dessert, the Valrhona chocolate fudge cake (four layers of devil's food cake with chocolate ganache and raspberry compote)— heaven on earth!

At Neiman Marcus, Ala Moana Center, 1450 Ala Moana Blvd. © **808/951-3420**. www.neiman marcushawaii.com. Reservations recommended. Main courses $14–$25 lunch, $27–$39 dinner, $55–$65 tasting menus. AE, DC, MC, V. Daily 11am–9pm; Sunday brunch 11am–3pm.

The Pineapple Room ★★ HAWAII REGIONAL Yes, this restaurant is in a department store, but the chef is Alan Wong, a culinary icon. The dishes are gastronomic masterpieces, particularly anything with fresh island fish or *kalua* pig (such as the kalua pig BLT). The dining room features an open kitchen with a lava-rock wall and abundant natural light, but the food takes center stage. The menu changes regularly, so keep an eye out for the fresh Big Island *moi* (a highly prized Hawaiian fish, in this case served whole and steamed Chinese-style); crispy Asian slaw (with cilantro and mac-nuts); miso-glazed salmon; black-pepper ahi (with risotto); and pineapple barbecued baby back ribs (with garlic mashed potatoes and sautéed corn). We adore the apple-curry-glazed pork chop with pumpkin and mascarpone purée and mango chutney.

At Macy's, 1450 Ala Moana Blvd. © **808/945-6573**. www.alanwongs.com. Reservations recommended for lunch and dinner. Main courses $14–$25 lunch, main courses $24–$38 dinner. AE, DC, MC, V. Mon–Fri 11am–8:30pm; Sat 8 10:30am and 11:30am–8:30pm; Sun 9–10:30am and 11am–3pm.

Sushi Sasabune ★★ 🏠 SUSHI This elegant sushi restaurant, tucked away among nondescript shops along a very busy street, is one of the marvels of the edible world. If you wish to order from the regular menu, by all means grab a table. But if you sit at the sushi bar, you must submit to the Japanese version of the *Seinfeld* "Soup Nazi," otherwise known as *omakase*. You obey the chef, eat what's served, and God help you if you drop a grain of rice or dip something in wasabi without permission. The payoff is that whatever you eat is freshly shipped in that day and often exotic. Whether it's salmon from Nova Scotia, sea urchin from Japan, halibut from Boston, Louisiana blue crab, or farmed oyster from Washington, Chef Seiji Kumagawa's sushi comes with a strict protocol: Dip only when permitted, and then with restraint. This is an extraordinary experience for

---

📑 Fix & Freeze Dinners

If you are staying in a condo or other accommodations with kitchen facilities, there is an alternative to eating out every night or slaving over a stove during your vacation, and its name is Dream Dinners. **Dream Dinners,** Niu Valley Shopping Center, 549 Halemaumau St. (© **808/373-1221;** www.dreamdinners. com), is a "meal assembly kitchen," where you gather all the ingredients for your own heat-and-serve meals, using the recipes and prepared ingredients they provide. After signing up online and booking an appointment, you go through an assembly line choosing various fixings for your entrees. You can freeze or just refrigerate the meals and serve a gourmet dinner for a fraction of the cost of eating out. As we went to press, entrees (which included chicken with honey, garlic, and orange; lemon fish filets; arroz con pollo; lasagna; steakhouse sirloin; and risotto primavera) ranged in price from $5 to $7 per serving. The downsides of this great money-saver are that it's only best for groups or families (you choose 3–6 servings per dinner), it's located in Niu Valley (away from most visitor accommodations), and you need at least 1 to 2 hours to do your "shopping."

Restaurants in Honolulu Beyond Waikiki

sushi aficionados—a journey into new tastes, textures, and sensations. It's expensive but well worth it.

1417 S. King St. ☎ **808/947-3800.** Reservations recommended. Sushi $5–$50; *omakase* can run $80–$100 per person. AE, DC, DISC, MC, V. Tues–Fri noon–2pm; Mon–Sat 5:30–10pm.

MODERATE

Akasaka ★ JAPANESE Akasaka is difficult to find and you enter through a back door, but this cozy, casual, and always-busy restaurant wins high marks for sushi, sizzling tofu and scallops, miso-clam soup, and the overall quality of its cuisine. Highlights include the *temaki* (spicy tuna) hand roll, scallop roll with flying-fish roe, hamachi, and soft-shell crab (when in season). Lunch and dinner specials help ease the bite of the bill, and ordering noodles or other less expensive a la carte items can also reduce the cost considerably. Don't expect geisha girls, or even friendly service—the staff is efficient but not necessarily accommodating.

1646B Kona St. ☎ **808/942-4466.** Reservations recommended. Main courses $12–$25 lunch, $15–$33 dinner, sushi $5–$16. AE, DC, DISC, MC, V. Mon–Sat 11am–2:30pm and 5pm–1am; Sun 5pm–1am.

Assaggio ★ ITALIAN This wildly popular chain, until recently the toast of suburban Oahu (see p. 149 for the Kailua location), moved into Ala Moana Center to a roar of approval and immediate success. Townies can now enjoy Assaggio's extensive, high-quality Italian offerings—at good prices. At dinner, a panoply of pastas and specialties streams out of the kitchen: at least nine chicken entrees, pasta dishes ranging from mushroom and clam to primavera, and eight veal choices. One of Assaggio's best features is its prodigious seafood selection: shrimp, scallops, mussels, calamari, and fresh fish in many preparations, ranging from simple garlic and olive oil to spicy tomato and wine sauces. Assaggio's excellent service paired with the option of large or small plates for most dinner items deserves applause.

At the Ala Moana Center, 1450 Ala Moana Blvd. ☎ **808/942-3446.** www.assaggiohi.com. Reservations recommended. Main courses $10–$26 lunch, $16–$34 dinner. AE, DC, DISC, MC, V. Daily 11am–3pm and 4:30–9:30pm (until 10pm Fri–Sat).

Kincaid's Fish, Chop, and Steakhouse ★ SEAFOOD/STEAKHOUSE

Kincaid's always wins surveys for one thing or another—best place for a business lunch, best seafood restaurant—because it pleases wide-ranging tastes and budgets. Brisk service, a harbor view, and an extensive seafood menu keep the large dining room full, while fresh-fish sandwiches, seafood chowders, and French onion soups top the menu. They also serve a memorable rack-salted prime rib, pepper-crusted steak, and, if you can't make up your mind, a combo plate of center-cut filet mignon with Australian lobster tail. You might want to save room for the true-blue Key lime pie. *Tip:* From 3 to 7pm everyday, drinks and selected pupus are 50% off.

At Ward Warehouse, 1050 Ala Moana Blvd. ☎ **808/591-2005.** www.kincaids.com. Reservations recommended. Lunch $11–$20; dinner main courses $20–$40. AE, DC, DISC, MC, V. Daily 11am–10pm, bar 11am–midnight.

INEXPENSIVE

Angelo Pietro ITALIAN/JAPANESE This restaurant has a quirky take on Italian food that could come only from Japan. You can order raw potato salad with any of four dressings—shoyu, ginger, *ume* (plum), and sesame-miso—and chase it with one of more than four dozen spaghetti choices. With sauces and toppings ranging from several types of mushroom, shrimp, chicken, spinach, and sausage to squid ink and eggplant, everything is grist for the spaghetti mill at the hands of Angelo Pietro. Garlic lovers adore the crisp garlicky chips that are heaped atop some of the selections.

1585 Kapiolani Blvd. © **808/941-0555.** www.angelopietro.com. Reservations recommended for groups of 5 or more; not accepted for smaller groups. Main courses $10–$15. AE, DC, DISC, MC, V. Sun–Thurs 11am–10pm; Fri–Sat 11am–11pm.

I Love Country Cafe ☺ INTERNATIONAL If you've splurged on a few too many calories, here's the place to make amends. The menu ranges from the virtually fatless vegetarian meal to a regular local-style, gravy-covered lunch special. (The small cafe is filled with families, athletes, and bodybuilder types, all in terrific shape.) Just give yourself time to peruse the lengthy list of specials posted on the menu board, as well as the prodigious printed menu. Then stand in line at the counter, place your order and pay, and find a Formica-topped table; after about 10 minutes your takeout order will appear on a Styrofoam plate heaped with salad and other accompaniments.

In Ala Moana Plaza, 451 Piikoi St. © **808/596-8108.** www.thecateringhotline.com. Main courses $6–$10. AE, DC, DISC, MC, V. Daily 8am–9pm.

Kaka'ako Kitchen ★★ 🍴 HAWAIIAN This popular industrial-style, plate-lunch haven in the trendy Ward Centre is busier than ever, with an expanded concept that includes dinner and breakfast service. You'll get excellent home-style cooking (it's owned by chef Russell Siu, of 3660 on the Rise) served on Styrofoam plates, in a warehouse ambience, at budget prices. The menu, which changes every 3 to 4 months, includes a seared ahi sandwich with *tobiko* (flying-fish roe) aioli, sandwiches, beef stew, five-spice shoyu chicken, the very popular meatloaf, and other multi-ethnic entrees. *Tip:* If they're serving brownies, buy two; their brownies are "da' best in da' islands."

At Ward Centre, 1200 Ala Moana Blvd. © **808/596-7488.** Breakfast $5.50–$9, lunch and dinner main courses $8–$13. AE, MC, V. Mon–Thurs 8am–9pm; Fri–Sat 8am–10pm; Sun 8am–5pm.

Kua Aina ★ 🥪 AMERICAN This popular branch of the ultimate sandwich shop (the original is a North Shore fixture) is in the Ward Centre area (near Starbucks). Phone in your order if you can. During lunch and dinner hours, people wait patiently in long lines for the famous sandwiches: the beef burgers with heroic toppings; mahimahi with Ortega chili and cheese (a legend); grilled egg-plant and peppers; roast turkey, tuna, and avocado; roast beef and avocado; and about a dozen other selections on kaiser rolls or multigrain wheat or rye breads. The sandwiches and fries are excellent, and the outdoor section with tables has grown (thank goodness)—but there still may be a wait during lunch hour. The takeout business is brisk.

At Ward Village, 1116 Auahi St. © **808/591-9133.** Sandwiches and burgers $7–$9. DISC, MC, V. Mon–Sat 10:30am–9pm; Sun 10:30am–8pm.

Panda Cuisine ★ DIM SUM/SEAFOOD/CHINESE This is dim sum heaven, not only for the selection but for the late-night (after 10pm) service, a rare thing for what is a morning and lunchtime tradition in Hong Kong. Panda's dim sum selection—spinach-scallop, chive, taro, shrimp dumplings, pork hash, and some 50-plus others—is a real pleaser. (The spinach-scallop and taro puff varieties are a cut above.) The reckless can spring for the live Maine lobster and Dungeness crab in season, or the king clam and steamed fresh fish, but the steaming bamboo carts yielding toothsome surprises are hard to resist. Noodles and sizzling platters make good accompaniments.

641 Keeaumoku St. ✆ **808/947-1688.** Main courses $11–$30, dim sum $3–$5. MC, V. Daily 10:30am–2:30pm; Mon–Sat 5:30pm–1am; Sun 5:30am–10pm.

Shokudo ★ 🏢 JAPANESE *Shokudo* means "dining room" in Japanese, and the large, beautifully designed but casual dining room here is the first U.S. restaurant of this popular Japanese chain. It attracts local families and hip 20-somethings more than tourists. The eatery is a cross between an *izakaya* (Japanese pub where people eat appetizers and have a beer or two) and a sushi bar. The place is huge and looks even bigger with its high ceiling, tiered seating, and central bar, but the food comes on small plates, so bring a crowd to taste several items. The 60-item menu (complete with vivid color photos and an English translation of the food, with detailed descriptions of each dish) includes appetizers, tofu, salad, fish and meat, rice, soup, sushi, sashimi, nabe, ishiyaki, noodles, and desserts. Here are our picks: deep-fried battered tofu ($7.50); tuna sashimi salad ($14); garlic scallop seared on a hot plate ($13); and the honey toast dessert ($7.50), a sumo-size serving of soft, toasted bread drizzled with honey and topped with vanilla ice cream. The waitstaff is extremely knowledgeable, but service suffers during the busy dinner hours.

At the Ala Moana Pacific Center, 1585 Kapiolani Blvd. (at Kaheka St.). ✆ **808/941-3701.** www. shokudojapanese.com. Entrees $12–$25; sushi $7–$15. MC, V. Sun–Thurs 11:30am–midnight; Fri–Sat 11:30am–1am.

Side Street Inn ★ 🏢 HAWAIIAN After their own fancy kitchens have closed, some of Honolulu's top chefs head to this off-the-beaten-track neighborhood bar with TVs on the walls and a back room with dartboard and neon beer signs— very camp. Down a small side street near Ala Moana Center—noted more for its seedy bars than for pesto-crusted ahi and gourmet Nalo greens—Side Street Inn is a pleasant surprise. The grinds (that's local slang for "eats") are fabulous, with no pretensions and a spirited local feel. The barbecued baby back ribs in *lilikoi* (yellow passion fruit) sauce are tender, flavorful, and a steal at $17. Our faves are the blackened ahi, pesto-crusted ahi, shrimp scampi, escargots, and tender fresh-steamed Manila clams in a wine-garlic broth. By the end of the meal, you'll be planning your return. A second location, called Side Street Inn on Da Strip, is located at 614 Kapahulu Ave. (✆ 808/739-3939); daily 3pm–midnight.

1225 Hopaka St. ✆ **808/591-0253.** www.sidestreetinn.com. Reservations recommended for groups of 4 or more. Main courses $10–$27. AE, DC, MC, V. Daily 2pm–midnight (bar 2pm–2am).

Aloha Tower Marketplace

Chai's Island Bistro PACIFIC RIM We give Chai's high marks for food but have less enthusiasm for its service and ambience, especially at dinner time, when the overamped music can detract from the dining experience (the nightly entertainment, usually live music, can be excruciatingly loud). Also, the dinner entree prices have risen significantly. But the food is generally high quality and creative. The 200-seat restaurant has high ceilings, a good location (though not on the waterfront), indoor and outdoor seating, and a discreetly placed open kitchen. Our favorite item on the menu is an appetizer that could be an entree:

The sampler for two appears on a boat-size platter—a feast of gravlax salmon roulade; macadamia-nut-crusted tiger prawns; and Alaskan king crab cakes. Fusion dishes include steamed, fresh, Asian-style moi, and an ample selection of vegetarian dishes. *Tip:* Before you go, print the "$25 off" coupon from their website, which is good for Sunday, Monday, and Tuesday evenings.

At the Aloha Tower Marketplace, 1 Aloha Tower Dr. (C) **808/585-0011.** www.chaisislandbistro. com. Reservations recommended. Main courses $13–$35 lunch, $28–$48 dinner. AE, DC, MC, V. Tues–Fri 11am–9pm; Sat–Mon 4–9pm.

Don Ho's Island Grill HAWAIIAN This shrine to Don Ho, who passed away in 2007, mixes a number of nostalgic interior elements: koa paneling, a thatched roof, split-bamboo ceilings, old pictures of Ho with celebrities, faux palm trees, and open sides looking out onto the harbor. It's kitschy and charming, down to the vinyl pareu-printed tablecloths and the flowers behind the servers' ears. The Hawaiian food is perfectly fine, but people come here more for the atmosphere than the cuisine.

At the Aloha Tower Marketplace, 1 Aloha Tower Dr. (C) **808/528-0807.** www.donhos.net. Reservations recommended. Main courses $12–$22 lunch, $15–$27 dinner. AE, DC, DISC, MC, V. Daily 11am–9pm, Sunday brunch 10am–2pm.

Gordon Biersch Brewery Restaurant NEW AMERICAN The German-style lagers brewed on the premises would be enough of a draw, but the food at Gordon Biersch—one of Honolulu's liveliest after-work hangouts, located in the Aloha Tower Marketplace—is also a lure. Fresh Pacific and Island seafood highlights the eclectic menu. The lanai bar and the brewery bar—open until 1am—are the brightest spots in the marketplace, teeming with downtown types who nosh on pot stickers, grilled steaks, baby back ribs, chicken pizza, garlic fries, and any number of American classics with deft cross-cultural touches. The stage area for live music is a popular weekend feature.

At the Aloha Tower Marketplace, 1 Aloha Tower Dr. (C) **808/599-4877.** Reservations recommended. Main courses $11–$29. AE, DC, DISC, MC, V. Sun–Thurs 11am–10pm; Fri–Sat 11am–11pm.

Downtown

Downtowners love the informal walk-in cafes lining one side of attractive **Bishop Square,** at 1001 Bishop St. (at King St.), in the middle of the business district, where free entertainment is offered every Friday during lunch hour. The popular **Che Pasta,** 1001 Bishop St., Suite 10 ((C) **808/524-0004;** www.chepasta.com), is a stalwart here, chic enough for business meetings but not too formal (or expensive) for a spontaneous rendezvous over minestrone. Some places in Bishop Square open for breakfast and lunch, others just for lunch, but most close when the offices around them empty.

Note: Keep in mind that **Restaurant Row** (Ala Moana Blvd., btw. Punchbowl and South St.), which features several hot new establishments, offers free validated parking in the evening.

Duc's Bistro ★★ 🍴 FRENCH/VIETNAMESE Surrounded by lei stands and marked by a cheery neon sign, this cozy 80-seater stands out at the *mauka* (toward the mountains) end of Maunakea Street in Chinatown. Narrow and quietly elegant, the restaurant has three components: the front room with windows looking out to Maunakea Street, the windowless back room, and the tiny bar. It has an edgy chic that's more Manhattan than Honolulu, and the food is beautifully prepared and presented. Duc's new menu leans more toward the Vietnamese roots of the owners (husband-and-wife team Duc Nguyen and Minh Nga Vu), with some French influences. Sauces for the meats hint of Grand Marnier (duck supreme), bordeaux (lamb Raymond Oliver), cognac (steak au poivre), Pernod (prawns and oysters), and fresh herbs and vegetables. From the seafood spring rolls with shrimp, taro, and mushrooms to the excellent "meal in a bowl" (rice noodles heaped with fresh herbs and julienned vegetables, topped with lime dressing), creative touches abound. Live music is featured Saturday nights and surprise vocalists and hula dancers have been known to join in the fun.

1188 Maunakea St., Chinatown. ✆ 808/531-6325. www.ducsbistro.com. Reservations recommended. Main dishes $12–$22. AE, DC, DISC, MC, V. Mon–Fri 11am–2pm and 5-10pm; Sat-Sun 5–10pm.

Hiroshi Eurasian Tapas ★★ EURASIAN Star chef Hiroshi Fukui opened this restaurant along with Hawaii's only master sommelier, Chuck Furuya. Part of the *tapas* (Spanish appetizers) trend, small plates make up most of the menu here. The result is fabulous, especially for foodies who want to sample several items off the menu (the staff recommends three dishes per person). The small plates offer a range of tastes, from sizzling Moi carpaccio with ginger, tomato, tofu, and truffled ponzu vinaigrette; to foie gras sushi with a teriyaki glaze; to Portuguese sausage pot stickers with sweet corn, garlic chili foam, and truffled ponzu sauce; to crab cannelloni with shiitake mushrooms, dill pesto, mozzarella cheese, and miso sauce. Go with a group so you can sample even more. They also serve larger plates, like the dreamy crab-stuffed mahimahi, crispy skin catch of the day, and a red wine steamed veal cheek. Try to hold out for desserts such as the delicious lemongrass crème brûlée, the wicked chocolate cake with molten chocolate, and the great panna cotta.

On Restaurant Row, 500 Ala Moana Blvd. ✆ 808/533-HIRO [533-4476]. www.dkrestaurants.com. Reservations recommended. Tapas $10–$17, larger plates $25–$37. AE, DISC, MC, V. Daily 5:30–9:30pm.

Indigo Eurasian Cuisine ★★ EURASIAN Hardwood floors, red brick, wicker, high ceilings, and an overall feeling of Indochine luxury give Indigo a stylish edge. You can dine indoors or in a garden setting on menu offerings such as pot stickers, Buddhist *bao* buns, savory brochettes, shrimp lumpia, curry- and Asian-style dumplings, plum-glazed baby back ribs, and cleverly named offerings from both East and West. Chef Glenn Chu is popular, but many claim that Indigo is more style than flavor. We disagree—this is a great restaurant.

1121 Nuuanu Ave. ✆ 808/521-2900. www.indigo-hawaii.com. Reservations recommended. Lunch buffet $16, dinner main dishes $20–$36. AE, DC, DISC, MC, V. Tues–Fri 11:30am–2pm; Tues–Sat 6–9pm; martini time in the Green Room Tues–Fri 4–8pm.

Legend Seafood Restaurant ★ DIM SUM/SEAFOOD This is a dining room straight out of Hong Kong, complete with Chinese-speaking clientele pouring over Chinese newspapers and the clatter of chopsticks punctuating conversations. Excellent dim sum comes in bamboo steamers that beckon seductively from carts. Although dining here is a form of assertiveness training (you must wave madly to catch the server's eye and then point to what you want), the system doesn't deter fans from returning. Among our favorites: deep-fried taro puffs, prawn dumplings, shrimp dim sum, vegetable dumplings, and the open-faced seafood (with shiitake, scallops, and a tofu product called *aburage*). Dim sum is served only at lunch, but dinnertime seafood dishes comfort sufficiently. Not a very elegant restaurant, but the food is serious and great.

At the Chinese Cultural Plaza, 100 N. Beretania St. *C* **808/532-1868.** Reservations recommended for dinner. Most items under $17. AE, DC, MC, V. Mon–Fri 10:30am–2pm and 5:30–9pm; Sat–Sun 8am–2pm and 5:30–9pm.

Little Village Noodle House CHINESE Don't let the decor throw you—the interior design here reminds us of a small French bistro in Provence. No matter, the food here is authentic Chinese (Northern, Cantonese, and Hong Kong–style), as well as "simple and healthy" (their motto). Our picks are the Shanghai noodles with stir-fried veggies, the walnut shrimp, and the butterfish in black-bean sauce. The menu is eclectic and offers some interesting selections you don't often see. The service is not only friendly (a rarity in Chinatown), but the wait-staff is quite knowledgeable about the dishes. Even more unique for the area, parking is offered in back! It's BYOB, but the excellent wine store just around the corner (the staff will point it out to you) delivers to the restaurant.

1113 Smith St. *C* **808/545-3008.** www.littlevillagehawaii.com. Most items under $15. AE, DISC, MC, V. Sun–Thurs 10:30am–10:30pm; Fri–Sat 10:30am–midnight.

To Chau ★★ *🍴* VIETNAMESE The two stars are strictly for the *pho* (noodle soup), which many think is the best in a city studded with pho (pronounced fur) houses. You'll have to stand in line, ambience is nil, and service can be brusque. But that's all part of the charm at this no-nonsense Formica-style restaurant, located in Chinatown in a stone building along a river and marked, without fail, by a queue of Asian diners. The anticipation is heightened by the view of diners relishing their steaming, long-awaited orders, visible through the windows as you wait your turn on the sidewalk. The menu includes shrimp, spring rolls, and chicken and pork chop plates, but we've never seen anyone order anything but pho. And what a soup this is! The broth is clear, hearty, and marvelously flavored with hints of cinnamon and spice. You can order it with several choices of steak, and it comes with a heaping platter of fresh bean sprouts, basil, hot green peppers, and an Asian green called *boke* (bo-*kay*). It's worth the wait, and so inexpensive.

1007 River St., Chinatown. *C* **808/533-4549.** Reservations not accepted. Pho $6–$8. No credit cards. Daily 8:30am–2:30pm (or until they run out of food).

Vino Italian Tapas & Wine Bar ★ *🏛* ITALIAN Two Japanese guys, D. K. Kodama (chef and owner of Sansei Seafood Restaurant and Sushi Bar, p. 130; and d.k Steakhouse, p. 128) and Chuck Furuya (Hawaii's top master sommelier, also of d.k Steakhouse and Hiroshi Eurasian Tapas, p. 140) teamed up to create this culinary adventure for foodies. The cozy room includes murals of a vine-yard and a kitchen with barrels of wine on the walls. Among the mouthwatering Italian creations, we'd recommend any ravioli on the menu. Signature dishes include roasted peppers with grilled focaccia, tender crispy calamari, seared foie gras, and petite osso buco. Don't pass up the house-made gnocchi or the daily pizza. Furuyu has put together an amazing array of wines by the glass, dispensed from a custom-crafted 20-spigot wine cruvinet.

On Restaurant Row, 500 Ala Moana Blvd. *C* **808/524-8466.** Reservations recommended. Tapas $8–$28. AE, DISC, MC, V. Wed–Thurs 5:30–9:30pm; Fri–Sat 5:30 -10:30pm.

Yanagi Sushi ★ JAPANESE We love the late-night hours, the sushi bar, and the extensive choices of combination lunches and dinners. But we also love the a la carte Japanese menu, which covers everything from *chazuke* (a comfort food of rice with tea, salmon, seaweed, and other condiments) to *shabu-shabu* (Japanese hotpot) and other steaming earthenware-pot dishes. Complete dinners come with choices of sashimi, shrimp tempura, broiled salmon, New York steak, and many other possibilities. You can dine here affordably or extravagantly, on $10 noodles or a $36 lobster *nabe* (cooked in seasoned broth). Consistently crisp tempura and fine spicy-ahi hand rolls also make Yanagi worth remembering.

762 Kapiolani Blvd. ✆ **808/597-1525.** www.yanagisushi-hawaii.com. Reservations recommended. Main courses $9–$36, complete dinners $21–$26. AE, DC, DISC, MC, V. Daily 11am–2pm; Mon–Sat 5:30pm–2am; Sun 5:30–10pm.

Kalihi/Sand Island

La Mariana AMERICAN   Just try to find a spot more evocative or nostalgic than this South Seas oasis at lagoon's edge in the bowels of industrial Honolulu. It's got carved tikis, glass balls suspended in fishing nets, shell chandeliers, and old tables made from koa trees, and in the back section, the entire ceiling is made of tree limbs. The unique, nearly 50-year-old restaurant is popular for lunch, sunset appetizers, and impromptu Friday- and Saturday-night singalongs at the piano bar, where a colorful crowd (including some Don Ho look-alikes) gathers to sing Hawaiian classics like a 1950s high school glee club. It is delightful. The seared Cajun-style ahi is your best bet as an appetizer or entree; La Mariana is more about spirit and ambience than food.

50 Sand Island Rd. ✆ **808/848-2800.** Reservations recommended, especially Sat-Sun. Main courses $7–$15 lunch, $12–$35 dinner. AE, MC, V. Daily 11am–9pm. Turn *makai* (toward the ocean) on Sand Island Rd. from Nimitz Hwy.; immediately after the first light on Sand Island, take a right and drive toward the ocean; it's not far from the airport.

Nico's at Pier 38 ★★ 🎁 SEAFOOD   This tiny takeout place produces gourmet French cuisine island-style on Styrofoam takeout containers at local plate-lunch prices. Order inside, then sit on plastic lanai chairs and tables under a deep green awning at the edge of the pier to munch on the delicious entrees. Of course, you'll have to wait: French-born chef Nicolas "Nico" Chize has cooked at such upscale eateries as Michel's and the Bistro at Century Center, but his small, oddly located eatery is so popular you'll have to stand in line during the crowded

---

Local Chains & Familiar Names

L & L Drive-Inn (www.hawaiianbarbecue. com) is a plate-lunch bonanza, with 45 locations in Hawaii—36 on Oahu alone. Meanwhile, **Zippy's Restaurants** ★, the maestros of quick meals, offer a surprisingly good selection of fresh seafood, saimin, chili, and local fare, plus the wholesome new low-fat, vegetarian "Shintani Cuisine" (based on the dietary principles of Hawaiian doctor Terry Shintani). Every restaurant (21 of them on Oahu, at last count) offers a daily Shintani special, and some locations (Kahala, Vineyard, Pearlridge,

Kapolei, Waipio) sell cold Shintani items in 2-pound portions to take home and heat up. Call ✆ **808/973-0880** or visit **www.zippys.com** to find the location nearest you.

It's hard to spend more than $9 on the French and Vietnamese specials (pho, croissants as good as the espresso, and wonderful taro/tapioca desserts) at the **Ba-Le Sandwich Shops** (www.latour bakehouse.com). Among Ba-Le's 20 locations are those at Ala Moana Center (✆ 808/944-4752) and 333 Ward Ave. (✆ 808/591-0935).

lunch hour, along with commercial fishermen, business executives, and a smattering of tourists. (They do take orders over the phone if you want to shorten your wait.) Our favorite dish is the furikake pan-seared ahi with an addictive ginger garlic cilantro dip, served with greens or macaroni salad for $9.50. They also have catch-of-the-day specials (grilled swordfish with a fennel-cream sauce was on the menu when we were there), a loco moco (hamburger steak and 2 eggs smothered in onion mushroom gravy) to die for, and a mean beef stew. Hearty breakfasts are served till 9:30am weekdays and 10am Saturdays.

Pier 38, 1133 N. Nimitz Hwy., Iwilei. ©**808/540-1377.** www.nicospier38.com. Reservations not accepted, but takeout orders accepted by phone. Main courses $8-$10. AE, DC, DISC, MC, V. Mon-Fri 6:30am-5pm; Sat 6:30am-2:30pm.

Sam Choy's Breakfast, Lunch, Crab & Big Aloha Brewery SEAFOOD This is a happy, carefree eatery—elegance and cholesterol be damned. Chef/restaurateur Sam Choy's crab house features great fun and gigantic meals (a Choy trademark). Imagine dining in an all-wood *sampan*—a type of boat that is the centerpiece of this 11,000-square-foot restaurant—and washing your hands in an oversize wok that was installed in the center of the room just for kicks. A 2,000-gallon tank containing a live assortment of seasonal crabs (Kona, Maryland, Samoan, Dungeness, Florida stone) lines the open kitchen. Clam chowder, seafood gumbos, oysters from the oyster bar, and assorted *poke* (chunks of marinated raw fish) are also offered at dinner, which comes complete with soup, salad, and entree. Children's menus are an attractive feature for families. Several varieties of Big Aloha beer, brewed on-site, go well with the crab and poke.

580 Nimitz Hwy., Iwilei. ©**808/545-7979.** Reservations recommended for lunch and dinner. Main courses $8-$15 breakfast, $12-$36 lunch, $12-$47 dinner. AE, DC, DISC, MC, V. Mon-Thurs 7am-2pm and 5-10pm; Fri-Sat 8am-2pm and 5-10pm; Sun 9am-1pm and 5-9:30pm. Located in the Iwilei industrial area near Honolulu Harbor, across the street from Gentry Pacific Design Center.

Yohei Sushi ★ 🎁 JAPANESE Yohei is difficult to find—it's tucked away in a small, nondescript complex just before Dillingham Boulevard crosses the bridge into Kalihi, Honolulu's industrial area. But it's well worth the hunt, especially for lovers of authentic Tokyo-style sushi. Try the *amaebi* (sweet shrimp), *akagai* (surf clam), hamachi, *negi toro temaki* (butterfly tuna), *kohada gari chiso temaki* (bluefish), and a wonderful assortment of seafood, fresh as can be.

1111 Dillingham Blvd., across from Honolulu Community College. ©**808/841-3773.** Reservations recommended. Main courses $8-$18 lunch, complete dinners $17-$75. DC, MC, V. Mon-Sat 11am-1:45pm and 5-9:30pm.

Manoa Valley/Moiliili/Makiki
VERY EXPENSIVE
Chef Mavro Restaurant ★★★ PROVENCAL/HAWAII REGIONAL Chef/owner George Mavrothalassitis—a native of Provence and formerly the creative force behind La Mer at Halekulani and Seasons at the Four Seasons Resort Wailea—was the winner of the 2003 James Beard "Best Chef: Northwest/Hawaii" award. His restaurant is also the only independently operated AAA Five-Diamond restaurant in Hawaii. But that doesn't mean it's stuffy: In fact, it's in a conveniently accessible, nontouristy neighborhood in McCully. The menu is prix fixe, with or without dazzling wine pairings; it includes the chef's signature

items (filet of moi with crisp scales, sautéed mushrooms, and saffron coulis; or award-winning onaga baked in Hawaiian-salt crust) as well as some new favorites: Keahole lobster in an Asian broth; a Hawaiian/Marseilles bouillabaisse; and cut-it-with-a-fork-tender filet of beef tenderloin crusted with red-wine confit onion. Hints of Tahitian vanilla, lemongrass, *ogo* (seaweed), rosemary, and Madras curry add exotic flavors to the French-inspired cooking and fresh island ingredients. The desserts are extraordinary, especially the all-American apple tart with Hawaiian vanilla ice cream. The split-level room is quietly cordial, and the menu changes monthly to highlight seasonal ingredients.

1969 S. King St. ℂ **808/944-4714.** www.chefmavro.com. Reservations recommended. Prix-fixe menu $75–$128 ($123–$191 with wine pairings). AE, DC, DISC, MC, V. Tues–Sun 6–9:30pm.

EXPENSIVE

Alan Wong's Restaurant ★★★ HAWAII REGIONAL Alan Wong is one of Hawaii's most sought-after chefs, but the service at his bustling eatery has often suffered because of his popularity. Long waits in front of the elevator have angered many. Still, worshipful foodies come from all over the state, drawn by the food—which is brilliant—and a menu that is irresistible. The 90-seat room has a glassed-in terrace and open kitchen. Sensitive lighting and curly koa wall panels accent an unobtrusively pleasing environment—casual, but not too much so. The menu's cutting-edge offerings sizzle with the Asian flavors of lemongrass, sweet-and-sour, garlic, and wasabi, deftly melded with the fresh seafood and produce of the islands. The California roll is a triumph, made with salmon roe, wasabi, and Kona lobster instead of rice—served warm. We love the opihi shooters, day-boat scallops, and fresh-fish preparations. But don't get attached to any one item, as the menu changes daily.

1857 S. King St., 3rd floor. ℂ **808/949-2526.** www.alanwongs.com. Reservations highly recommended. Main courses $25–$52, 5-course sampling menu $75 ($105 with wine), chef's 7-course tasting menu $95 ($135 with wine). AE, DC, MC, V. Daily 5–10pm.

MODERATE

Contemporary Museum Cafe ★ 🍴 INTERNATIONAL The surroundings are an integral part of the dining experience at this tiny lunchtime cafe, part of an art museum nestled on the slopes of Tantalus amid carefully cultivated Asian gardens, with a breathtaking view of Diamond Head and priceless contemporary artwork displayed indoors and out. The menu is limited to sandwiches, soups, salads, and appetizers, but you won't leave disappointed: They're perfect lunchtime fare. Try the day's crostini, hummus and pita, Moroccan chicken wrap, cold soba noodle salad with Asian slaw, or tuna salad with basil pesto. Crown your meal with flourless chocolate cake or fresh, locally made gelato. You can also buy a Lauhala picnic for two ($30) to enjoy in the gardens.

At the Contemporary Museum, 2411 Makiki Heights Dr. ℂ **808/523-3362.** www.tcmhi.org. Reservations recommended. Main courses $10–$12. AE, MC, V. Tues–Sat 11:30am–2:30pm; Sun noon–2:30pm.

Maple Garden CHINESE This Szechuan specialist hums like a top and rarely disappoints. Maple Garden is known for its garlic eggplant, Peking duck, and Chinaman's Hat, a version of mu shu pork, available in vegetarian form as well. The crisp green beans are out of this world. Other hits: braised scallops with Chinese mushrooms, sautéed spinach, and prawns in chili sauce. Vegetarian selections are ample, as are dozens of seafood entrees—everything from sea cucumbers and braised salmon to lobster with black-bean sauce. An ever-expanding visual feast adorns the dining-room walls, covered with original drawings, sketches, and murals by noted artist John Young. The staff is unbelievably friendly, service is top-notch, and most entrees are only $9 to $10.

909 Isenberg St. ℰ**808/941-6641.** www.maplegardenhawaii.com. Plates $9–$30, buffet $12 lunch, $16 dinner. AE, MC, V. Daily 11am–2pm and 5:30-9:30pm.

Spices ♦ SOUTHEAST ASIAN Located in a small building near the university, this tiny Asian bistro specializes in delicious traditional dishes from Vietnam, Laos, Thailand, and Burma (now known as Myanmar), re-created with local Hawaii ingredients. True to the restaurant's name, the smell of pungent spices greets you as you enter the restaurant. Walls are painted in saffron orange, mustard yellow, and green basil trim. A tantalizing cornucopia of Southeast Asian specialties (with plenty of vegetarian dishes) range from curries (green, yellow, Malaysian, and Laotian) to noodles (pad Thai) to soups. But the best is the homemade ice cream with such unusual flavors as durian, pandanus, or chili/lemongrass. Limited parking (about eight spots) behind the restaurant.

2671 S. King St. (at University Ave.) ℰ**808/949-2679.** www.spiceshawaii.com. Curries $14–$18, rice and noodle dishes $12–$15. MC, V. Tues-Fri 11:30am–2pm and 5:30-9:30pm; Sat 5:30-9:30pm; Sun 5-9pm. Limited parking (about 8 stalls) behind the restaurant.

Sushi King ♦ JAPANESE This is a top value for lovers of Japanese food. Brusque service can't deter the throngs that arrive for the excellent lunch specials. It's tricky to find, located in a small minimall (look for University Flower Shop). Don't pass up the jumbo platters that come with soup; pickles; a California roll; and your choice of chicken teriyaki, beef teriyaki, shrimp and vegetable tempura, or calamari and vegetable tempura, all at arrestingly low prices. Other combination lunches offer generous choices that include sashimi, tempura, butterfish, fried oysters, and noodles served hot and cold. Early-bird specials are offered daily from 5:30 to 7pm.

2700 S. King St. ℰ**808/947-2836.** Reservations recommended, especially for groups of 5 or more on weekends. Lunch $10–$17, dinner main courses $16–$25. AE, DC, DISC, MC, V. Daily 11:30am–2pm, and 5:30pm–2am.

Willows HAWAIIAN The food is more than adequate, but the ambience is the headliner here: There just aren't many places left in Hawaii with this kind of tropical setting. Shoes click on hardwood floors in rooms surrounded by lush foliage and fountains fed by the area's natural springs. The dining rooms are open-air, with private umbrella-topped tables scattered about. And though Willows will never fully regain the charm and nostalgia of its early *kamaaina* (old-time) days (despite the meticulous restoration), some of its Hawaiian dishes—like *laulau* (meat or fish steamed in taro or ti leaves), lomilomi salmon ("massaged" salmon, marinated with tomatoes, onion, and salt), and poke—are quite good. Everything is served buffet-style.

817 Hausten St. ℰ**808/952-9200.** www.willowshawaii.com. Reservations recommended. Lunch buffet $20 Mon-Fri, $25 Sat, $35 Sun; dinner buffet $35 daily. AE, DC, DISC, MC, V. Mon-Fri 11am–2pm and 5:30-9pm; Sat-Sun 10am–2:30pm and 5–9pm. No neighborhood parking; valet parking $3, self-parking $3.

INEXPENSIVE

Andy's Sandwiches & Smoothies ♦ HEALTH FOOD It started as a health-food restaurant, expanded into a juice bar, and today is a neighborhood fixture for fresh-baked bread, healthy breakfasts and lunches (its mango muffins are famous), and vegetarian fare. Andy's roadside stop always carries fresh papayas, sandwiches, and healthy snacks for folks on the run. The ahi deluxe sandwich is tops, and the fresh roasted turkey sandwiches are an acclaimed favorite.

2904 E. Manoa Rd., opposite Manoa Marketplace. ℂ **808/988-6161.** www.andyssandwiches.com. Most items less than $9. AE, MC, V. Mon–Thurs 7am–5pm; Fri 7am–4pm; Sun 7am–2:30pm.

Chiang Mai Thai Cuisine THAI Chiang Mai made sticky rice famous in Honolulu, serving it in bamboo steamers with fish and exotic curries. Menu items include toothsome red, green, and yellow curries; the signature Cornish game hen in lemongrass and spices; and a garlic-infused green papaya salad marinated in tamarind sauce. Spicy shrimp soup, eggplant with basil and tofu, and the vegetarian green curry are favorites.

2239 S. King St. ℂ **808/941-1151.** www.808chiangmai.com. Reservations recommended for dinner. Main courses $10–$36. AE, DC, DISC, MC, V. Mon–Fri 11am–2pm; daily 5:30–9:30pm.

Jimbo's Restaurant ★ 🍴 JAPANESE Jimbo's is the quintessential neighborhood restaurant—it's small, with a line of regulars outside, serves fantastic house-made noodles and broths, and everything is affordable. A must for any noodle lover, Jimbo's homemade *udon* (wide buckwheat noodles), in a flawless broth with a subtly smoky flavor, can be topped with shrimp tempura, chicken, eggs, vegetables, seaweed, roasted *mochi* (Japanese rice bun), and other accompaniments of your choice. Cold noodles (the Tanuki salad is wonderful!), stir-fried noodles, *donburi* (rice dishes with assorted toppings), and combination dinners are other delights, but for real value, the earthenware pot of noodles with shiitake mushrooms, vegetables, and udon, plus a platter of tempura on the side, is top of the line. But our favorite is the *nabeyaki* (a clay pot of udon with tempura on top). Owner Jimbo Motojima, a perfectionist, uses only the finest ingredients from Japan.

936 S. King St. ℂ **808/947-2211.** Reservations not accepted. Main courses $10–$20. AE, DC, MC, V. Daily 11am–2:45pm and 5–9:45pm; Fri–Sat 5–10:30pm.

Kaimuki/Kapahulu
EXPENSIVE

Ninniku-Ya Garlic Restaurant EURASIAN This great restaurant is a paean to the "stinking rose." Ninniku-Ya is located in a cozy old home, divided between a split-level dining room and outdoor seating under venerable trees. The menu titillates with many garlicky surprises and specials. (The seasonal specialties are fine but not necessary, as the staples are quite wonderful.) The four-mushroom pasta is sublime, the hot-stone filet mignon tender and tasty, and the garlic rice a meal in itself. Every garlic lover should experience the garlic toast and the roasted garlic with blue cheese. Everything contains garlic, even the house-made garlic gelato, which doesn't overpower. Yes, that's garlic gelato—and it gets high marks from us. Look for the festive fairy lights lining the building.

3196 Waialae Ave. ℂ **808/735-0784.** Reservations recommended. Main dishes $17–$39. AE, DC, DISC, MC, V. Tue–Sun 5:30–9:30pm.

3660 On the Rise ★★★ PACIFIC RIM Ever since *Wine Spectator* gave this 200-seat restaurant its "Award of Excellence," it's been packed, and with good reason. Chef Russell Siu adds an Asian or local touch to the basics: rack of lamb with macadamia nuts, filets of catfish in *ponzu* (a Japanese sauce), and seared ahi

WHERE TO EAT | Honolulu Beyond Waikiki

salad with grilled shiitake mushrooms, a local favorite. The ahi katsu, wrapped in nori and fried medium-rare, is a main attraction in the appetizer department. Diners rave over Chef Gilbert Crisostomo's desserts, especially the warm chocolate cake. *Tip:* 3660 offers smaller portions of some entrees.

3660 Waialae Ave. (C) **808/737-1177.** www.3660.com. Reservations suggested. Main courses $22–$59, prix-fixe menu $41. AE, DC, DISC, MC, V. Tues–Sun 5:30–8:30pm.

MODERATE

Genki Sushi ★ ☺ SUSHI Take your place in line for a seat at one of the U-shaped counters. Conveyor belts parade by with freshly made sushi, usually two pieces per color-coded plate, priced inexpensively. The possibilities are dizzying: spicy tuna topped with scallions, ahi, scallops with mayonnaise, a Canadian roll (same as a California roll, except with salmon), sea urchin, flavored octopus, sweet shrimp, surf clam, corn, tuna salad, and so on. Genki starts with a Japanese culinary tradition and takes liberties with it, so don't be a purist. By the end of the meal, the piled-high plates are tallied up by color, and presto, your bill appears. Combination platters are available for takeout.

900 Kapahulu Ave. (C) **808/735-7700.** A la carte sushi from $1.50 for 2 pieces; takeout combination platters $26–$50. AE, DC, DISC, MC, V. Sun–Thurs 11am–9pm; Fri–Sat 11am–10pm; takeout available daily 11am–9pm.

Town ★ ▮ CONTEMPORARY ITALIAN The latest hip restaurant along Waialae's miracle mile of "in" spots is a surprisingly delicious place to eat. (Generally the new hot spots, filled with beautiful young diners, tend toward pretense rather than lip-smacking food.) Ignore the metro high-tech atmosphere of highly polished concrete floors, stainless steel tables, and incredibly uncomfortable chairs, and ask for a table outside on the lanai (where the noise level will be bearable). The hand-typed (who the heck still has a typewriter these days?), incredibly creative menu changes daily, but promises "local first, organic whenever possible, with aloha always," and delivers. At last visit, we sampled the ahi tartar on risotto cakes and veggie frito misto, and an Italian tempura of scallops, celery, lemon, and white beans. Entrees range from braised lamb to crispy moi to excellent gnocchi. Desserts (in the $7 range) include the likes of buttermilk panna cotta and chocolate banini (panini of toast, chocolate, and bananas—yum). Lunches are along the lines of sandwiches, salads, and pastas. Breakfast (frittata of the day, eggs, wonderful baked goods) has recently been added.

3435 Waialae Ave. (at 9th St.). (C) **808/735-5900.** www.townkaimuki.com. Reservations required for dinner. Main courses $5–$9.50 breakfast, $13–$20 lunch, $19–$30 dinner. AE, MC, V. Mon–Thurs 7am–2:30pm and 5:30–9:30pm; Fri–Sat 5:30–10pm.

12th Avenue Grill ★ ▮ AMERICAN This tiny (14-table) upscale neighborhood diner is packed every night. If you've had your fill of Hawaii regional cuisine and long for some good ol' American food—though not quite like mom used to make—Chef Kevin Hanney whips up a gourmet version of macaroni and cheese (with smoked Parmesan) and a signature kim-chee steak (beef marinated in a sweet-hot sauce and grilled). A chalkboard menu lists the specials of the night (the smoked trout is a must). Diners are packed in close, so noise is a problem (you can easily find yourself screeching to be heard by your dinner partners), but the food more than makes up for this one flaw. Whatever you order, leave room for the desserts by Chef Samantha Choy (the baker for Sam Choy Restaurants), who always has a fruit crisp of the day on the menu. The most recent upgrade is their full bar.

1145-C 12th Ave. (at Waialae Ave.). ☎ **808/732-9469.** www.12thavegrill.com. Reservations recommended. Small plates $6–$12, large plates $18–$32. MC, V. Mon–Thurs 5:30–9pm; Fri–Sat 5:30–10pm.

INEXPENSIVE

Cafe Laufer ★ BAKERY This small, cheerful cafe features frilly decor and sublime pastries—apple scones, Linzer tortes, fruit flan, decadent chocolate mousse, carrot cake, and so on—to accompany the latte and espresso. Fans drop in for simple soups and deli sandwiches on fresh-baked breads; biscotti during coffee break; or a hearty loaf of seven-grain, rye, pumpernickel, or French bread. The place is a solid hit for lunch; the small but satisfying menu includes soup-salad-sandwich specials for a song, a fabulous spinach salad with dried cranberries and Gorgonzola, and gourmet greens with mango-infused, honey-mustard dressing. The orange-seared shrimp salad and the Chinese chicken salad are hits for the light eater, and the smoked Atlantic salmon with fresh pumpernickel bread and cream cheese, Maui onions, and capers is excellent. The special Saturday-night desserts draw a brisk postmovie business.

3565 Waialae Ave. ☎ **808/735-7717.** www.cafelaufer.com. Checks average $15–$20 per person. AE, DC, DISC, MC, V. Sun and Wed–Thurs 10am–9pm; Fri–Sat 10am–10pm.

Hale Vietnam VIETNAMESE Duck into this house of pho and brave the no-frills service for steaming noodle soups, the house specialty. The stock is simmered and skimmed for many hours and is accompanied by noodles, beef, chicken, and a platter of bean sprouts and fresh herbs. (But approach the green chiles with caution!) We love the chicken soup and shrimp vermicelli, as well as the seafood pho and spicy chicken with eggplant. Be advised that this restaurant, like most other Vietnamese eateries, uses MSG, and that the pho, although respectable, does not equal that of To Chau in Chinatown, the *ne plus ultra* of pho in Honolulu (p. 141).

1140 12th Ave. ☎ **808/735-7581.** Reservations recommended for groups. Main courses $12–$28. AE, DISC, MC, V. Daily 10am–9:45pm.

EAST OF WAIKIKI: KAHALA

Hoku's ★★★ HAWAII REGIONAL Elegant without being stuffy, creative without being overwrought, the upscale dining room of the Kahala Hotel & Resort combines European finesse with an island touch. This is fusion that really works. The setting is stellar, with its ocean view, open kitchen, and astonishing bamboo floor. Reflecting the restaurant's cross-cultural influences, the kitchen is equipped with a kiawe grill and Szechuan woks for the prawn, lobster, tofu, and other stir-fried specialties. The chef's daily selection of appetizers could include pan-seared Hudson Valley foie gras, sashimi, Chinese roast duck, and other dainty tastings, and is a good choice for the curious. Salt-crusted rack of lamb, avocado crusted seared halibut and the full range of East-West specialties appeal to many tastes, and the wok-fried whole fresh fish is worthy of a special occasion. Sunday brunch is also not to be missed. This is one of the few places in Hawaii that has a "dress code"—collared shirts with slacks or evening wear.

At the Kahala Hotel & Resort, 5000 Kahala Ave. ☎ **808/739-8780.** www.kahalaresort.com/dining/hoku.cfm. Reservations recommended. Collared shirts and long pants preferred for men. Main courses $30–$86. AE, DC, DISC, MC, V. Tues–Sat 5:30–10pm; Sun brunch 10:30am–2pm.

Olive Tree Cafe ★★ 🎪 MEDITERRANEAN Delectables at bargain prices stream out of the tiny open kitchen here. Recently voted "Best Restaurant in Hawaii Under $20" in a local survey, Olive Tree is every neighborhood's dream—a totally hip restaurant with divine fare and friendly prices. The mussel ceviche is broke-the-mouth fabulous, with lemon, lime, capers, herbs, and olive oil—a perfect blend of flavors. The creamy, tender chicken saffron, a frequent special, always elicits groans of pleasure, as does the robust and generous Greek salad, another Olive Tree attraction. We also love the souvlaki, ranging from fresh fish to chicken and lamb, spruced up with the chef's homemade yogurt-dill sauce. First, order and pay at the counter, then grab an umbrella table outside or at one of a few seats indoors. Larger parties now have an awning over the sturdy wooden tables on the Koko Head side. It's BYOB (for a small fee), and a group can dine here like sultans without breaking the bank and take in a movie next door, too.

4614 Kīlauea Ave., next to Kahala Mall. ☎ **808/737-0303.** Main courses $10–$15. No credit cards. Daily 5–10pm.

EAST OAHU

Roy's Restaurant ★★★ EURASIAN This is the first of Roy Yamaguchi's six signature restaurants in Hawaii (he has two dozen all over the world). It is still the flagship and many people's favorite, true to its Eurasian roots and Yamaguchi's winning formula: open kitchen, fresh ingredients, ethnic touches, and a good dose of nostalgia mingled with European techniques. The menu changes nightly, but you can generally count on individual pizzas; a varied appetizer menu (Szechuan spiced baby back ribs, blackened ahi); a small pasta selection; and entrees such as garlic-mustard short ribs, hibachi-style salmon in ponzu sauce, and several types of fresh catch. One of Hawaii's most popular restaurants, Roy's is lit up at night with tiki torches outside; the view from within is of scenic Maunalua Bay. Roy's is also renowned for its high-decibel style of dining—it's always full and noisy. Other Roy's restaurants in Hawaii are located in Ko Olina, Oahu; Poipu, Kauai; Waikoloa, Big Island; and Kihei and Napili, Maui. Patrons enjoy live music every evening from 6pm.

6600 Kalanianaole Hwy., Hawaii Kai. ☎ **808/396-7697.** www.roysrestaurant.com. Reservations recommended. Main courses $25–$45, 3-course prix-fixe $42. AE, DC, DISC, MC, V. Mon–Fri 5:30–9pm; Sat 5–9:30pm; Sun 5–9pm.

THE WINDWARD COAST

Assaggio ★ ITALIAN This was the mother ship of the Assaggio empire before the Ala Moana branch (p. 136) opened. The affordable prices, attentive service, and winning menu items have attracted loyal fans throughout the years. The homemade hot antipasto is a best-seller, with jumbo shrimp, fresh clams, mussels, and calamari in a sauce of cayenne pepper, white wine, and garlic. You can choose linguine, fettuccine, or ziti with 10 different sauces in small or regular portions, or any of nine chicken pastas (the chicken Assaggio, with garlic, peppers, and mushrooms, is especially flavorful). Equally impressive is the extensive list of seafood pastas, including the garlic and olive oil sauté. The half-price, half-portion dinner servings are a plus.

The best, sweetest, juiciest shrimp you are ever going to eat will be from a shrimp truck on Oahu's North Shore. Several trucks line up around the entry to Haleiwa, just off the Kamehameha Highway, but our favorite is **Giovanni's Original White Shrimp Truck** (📞 808/293-1839), which usually parks across the street from the Haleiwa Senior Housing (or McDonald's). It claims to be the first shrimp truck to serve the delicious aquaculture shrimp farmed in the surrounding area. The menu is simple: spicy, garlic, or lemon-and-butter shrimp. Skip the lemon-and-butter (boring), and go for the garlic (our fave) or the spicy (but beware—it really packs a punch). The battered white truck has picnic tables under its awning, so you can munch away right there.

354 Uluniu St., Kailua. 📞 **808/261-2772.** www.assaggiohi.com. Reservations recommended. Main courses $9–$26 lunch, $16–$34 dinner. AE, DC, DISC, MC, V. Mon–Fri 11:30am–2:30pm; Sun–Thurs 5–9:30pm; Fri–Sat 5–10pm.

Buzz's Original Steak House STEAKHOUSE/SEAFOOD A Lanikai fixture for nearly a half century, Buzz's is a few feet from Kailua Beach (windsurfing central), just past the bridge that leads into Lanikai. (Though it's on the beach, shirt and shoes are required.) A small deck, varnished koa bar, rattan furniture, and wood walls covered with snapshots and surf pictures will put you immediately at ease. Buzz's has the perfect Gauguinesque tropical ambience to accompany its offerings: great burgers at lunch (including a mushroom garden burger), fresh catch, a superb artichoke appetizer, and steak-and-lobster combos, all much loved by fans. Dinner offerings are pricier, but include Alaskan king crab legs, prime rib, fresh fish, and wonderful items at the soup and salad bar.

413 Kawailoa Rd., Lanikai. 📞 **808/261-4661.** www.buzzssteakhouse.com. Reservations required. Main courses $9–$15 lunch, $16–$38 dinner. DC, DISC, MC, V. Daily 11am–3pm and 4:30–9:30pm.

Lucy's Grill 'n Bar ★★ HAWAII REGIONAL This is one of Kailua's most popular restaurants, not just because of the open-air bar and the outdoor lanai seating, but because of the terrific food (which they are now serving as both large and small plates). The menu is eclectic Hawaii regional cuisine, with lots of choices and giant portions. The dress is casual, and the clientele is local. Be sure to order the spicy ahi tower with sushi rice, avocado, wasabi cream, and roasted nori to get you started. The fresh fish and seafood is wonderful, especially the Szechuan-spiced jumbo tiger prawns with black-bean cream and penne pasta, and the lemongrass-crusted scallops with yellow Thai curry. Save room for crème brûlée with Tahitian vanilla bean, dark chocolate soufflé cake, or their "damn fine" apple crisp—a la mode, of course.

33 Aulike St., Kailua. 📞 **808/230-8188.** Reservations recommended. Main courses $14–$30. MC, V. Daily 5–10pm.

THE NORTH SHORE

The following restaurants are located in the area shown on the "The North Shore Attractions" map on p. 243.

Expensive

21 Degrees North ★★★ PACIFIC RIM Foodie alert: It is well worth the drive from Waikiki (45–60 min.) to the North Shore to enjoy this impressive signature restaurant at Turtle Bay Resort (p. 115). Not only is it visually inspiring, with floor-to-ceiling windows overlooking the North Shore's famous rolling surf, but chef Hector Morales' Pacific Rim cuisine is outstanding. The chef has taken contemporary island cuisine and made it fresh and interesting, and the dishes emerging from the kitchen take Hawaiian dining to a new level. The ever-changing menu has such unusual combinations as crab-crusted Hawaiian sea bass with a lemongrass coulis, hamachi fillet with toasted orzo and ginger shoyu butter, and sautéed fois gras with vanilla pineapple and roasted pearl onions. The five-course tasting menu is a good way to tour numerous creations.

At Turtle Bay Resort, 57-091 Kamehameha Hwy., Kahuku. ℂ **808/293-8811.** www.turtlebay resort.com. Reservations required. Main courses $28–$50; 5-course tasting menu $76 without wine, $105 with wine. AE, DC, DISC, MC, V. Tues–Sat 6–9pm.

Moderate

Haleiwa Joe's AMERICAN/SEAFOOD There are only two Haleiwa restaurants close to the ocean, and this is one of them. Next to the Haleiwa bridge, with a great view of the harbor and sunset, Haleiwa Joe's serves up fresh local seafood such as whole Hawaiian moi, opakapaka, ahi, and whatever comes in fresh that day. This is a steak-and-seafood harborside restaurant with indoor-outdoor seating and a surf-and-turf menu that could include New York steak, coconut shrimp, and black-and-blue sashimi. Sandwiches and salads make it a great lunch stop, too.

66-011 Kamehameha Hwy., Haleiwa. ℂ **808/637-8005.** www.haleiwajoes.com. Reservations not accepted. Main courses $9–$18 lunch, $16–$30 dinner. MC, V. Mon–Thurs 11:30am–9:30pm (limited menu 4:15–5:30pm); Fri–Sat 11:30am–10pm (limited menu 4:15–5:30pm, bar until midnight); Sun 11:30am–9:30pm (limited menu 3:45–5pm).

Jameson's by the Sea SEAFOOD Duck into this roadside watering hole across the street from the ocean for cocktails, sashimi, and its celebrated salmon pâté, or for other hot and cold appetizers, salads, and sandwiches. The grilled crab-and-shrimp sandwich on sourdough bread is a perennial favorite, and it's hard to go wrong with the fresh-fish sandwich of the day, grilled plain and simple. The dinner menu offers the usual surf-and-turf choices: fresh opakapaka ulua (Hawaiian jackfish), mahimahi, scallops in lemon butter and capers, lobster tail, and steaks.

62-540 Kamehameha Hwy., Haleiwa. ℂ **808/637-4336.** www.jamesonshawaii.com. Reservations recommended. Main courses $10–$25 lunch, $20–$46 dinner. AE, DC, DISC, MC, V. Mon–Fri 11am–9:30pm; Sat–Sun 9am–9:30pm.

Ola at Turtle Bay Resort ★★ 🎁 SEAFOOD Even if you are staying in Waikiki, plan a day at the beach on the North Shore and eat here for dinner—you won't regret it. First, the location is literally on the beach, next door to the Turtle Bay Resort. Second, the restaurant is an open-air beach pavilion, made from ironwood trees harvested from the surrounding area; the view of the Pacific waves lapping onto the sand—and the tiki torches lit at sunset—is very, very romantic. But, wait, the best part is . . . the food! Chef Fred DeAngelo named his restaurant Ola, which means "alive" or "healthy" in Hawaiian, and he insists on only the freshest of ingredients. The menu is filled with creative selections (the ahi and lobster poke served with a wonton spoon) and some of the best food you will eat in Hawaii, such as the incredible slow-poached togarashi salmon with a sweet, sugar-cane crust served with Okinawan sweet potato and locally grown corn; the Lawai'a fishermen's stew with lobster, shrimp, scallops, and fresh fish; or the unreal kiawe-smoked beef tenderloin.

At Turtle Bay Resort, 57-091 Kamehameha Hwy., Kahuku. © **808/293-0801.** www.olaislife.com. Reservations recommended for dinner. Main courses $10–$24 lunch, $19–$60 dinner. AE, DC, DISC, MC, V. Daily 11am–3pm and 5:30–10pm (last seating).

Inexpensive

Cafe Haleiwa BREAKFAST Haleiwa's legendary breakfast joint is a big hit with surfers, urban gentry with weekend country homes, reclusive artists, and anyone who loves mahimahi plate lunches and heroic sandwiches. It's a wake-up-and-hit-the-beach kind of place, serving generous omelets with such names as Off the Wall, Off the Lip, and Breakfast in a Barrel. Surf pictures line the walls, and the ambience is Formica casual. Those needing a caffeine fix will appreciate the espresso bar.

66-460 Kamehameha Hwy., Haleiwa. © **808/637-5516.** Reservations not accepted. Main courses $7–$14. AE, MC, V. Daily 7am–1:45pm.

Cholos Homestyle Mexican II 🗡 MEXICAN There's usually a wait at this popular eatery, where some of the tables have leather stools without backs, and great home-style Mexican food is presented with so-so service. Still, this is the unhurried North Shore, and the biggest rush for most folks is getting to and from the beach. We recommend the spinach quesadilla, a generous serving filled with black beans, cheese, and fresh vegetables; the chicken fajita plate; and the fish taco plate, a steal at $13 (just $5.50 a la carte). Tables with stools preside outdoors; indoors, it's dark and cavelike, with loud music and Mexican handicrafts.

At the North Shore Marketplace, 66-250 Kamehameha Hwy. © **808/637-3059.** Combination plates $11–$14. AE, DISC, MC, V. Daily 10:30am–9 or 9:30pm.

Luau!

Before luaus existed, "there were '*aha 'aina*—feasts of food, *mele* (song), and hula," says Royal Hawaiian Hotel General Manager Kelly Hoen. And now you have the chance to take part in one: The Royal Hawaiian (© **808/921-4600**) re-creates an 'aha 'aina every Monday evening on the Ocean Lawn, with the Waikiki Beach and Diamond Head in the background. The 'aha 'aina (which translates to "gathering for a meal") is composed of three spectacular acts: Hawaii cultural activities, dinner, and entertainment. As guests enter the grounds, traditional Hawaii cultural activities such as *kapa*-making (cloth made of pounded bark),

poi-pounding, and *na lawai'a* (tending of fishing tools) are demonstrated. The sound of a *pu* (conch) calls guests to the feast, and the entertainment begins; a dramatic performance incorporating hula and song commemorates ancient islanders' rich history and culture.

This epicurean journey through time is held every Monday from 5:30 to 9pm; it's priced at $155 per person for nonresort guests, $145 per person for resort guests, $83 for nonresort-guest children ages 5 to 12 years old, and $75 resort-guest children; children under 5 years of age are free with a paying adult.

Kua Aina ★ 🍴 AMERICAN "What's the name of that sandwich shop on the North Shore?" We hear that often. After 29 years at the same spot, Kua Aina moved a few years ago down the street to a larger, 75-seat eatery. It's as busy as ever, though many diners get their burgers to go and head for the beach. Kua Aina's thin and spindly french fries are renowned islandwide and are the perfect accompaniment to its legendary burgers. Fat, moist, and homemade, the burgers can be ordered with avocado, bacon, and many other accompaniments, including Ortega chiles and cheese. The tuna/avocado, roast turkey, and mahimahi sandwiches are excellent alternatives to the burgers. Kua Aina is unparalleled on the island and is a North Shore must, eclipsing its fancier competitors at lunch.

66-160 Kamehameha Hwy., Haleiwa. ⓒ **808/637-6067.** Sandwiches and burgers $7-$9. No credit cards. Daily 11am-8pm.

Paradise Found Cafe VEGETARIAN A tiny cafe behind Celestial Natural Foods, Paradise Found is a bit of a hunt, but stick with it. For more than a few townies, the North Shore sojourn begins at Paradise, the only purely vegetarian restaurant in these parts. Breakfasts feature the "Up & At 'Em" (scrambled eggs, tempeh, veggies, and home fries wrapped in a cheese quesadilla) and the "Nanna Nutty" (peanut butter, banana, honey, granola, and cinnamon, wrapped in a flour tortilla and grilled). Their smoothies (especially the Waimea Shorebreak) are legendary, and their organic soups, fresh-pressed vegetable juices, sandwiches, and healthy plate lunches are a great launch to a Haleiwa day. Vegan substitutions are willingly made.

66-443 Kamehameha Hwy., Haleiwa. ⓒ **808/637-4540.** All items under $12. AE, MC, V. Mon-Sat 9am-5pm; Sun 9am-4pm.

LEEWARD OAHU

Roy's Ko Olina ★★★ 🍴 EURASIAN The latest in Roy's empire of excellent restaurants opened in 2004 in Ko Olina Resort on the leeward coast of Oahu, some 16 years after the flagship restaurant (p. 149) opened in Hawaii Kai. One of some nearly three dozen locations around the globe, Roy's Ko Olina perches in a peerless location overlooking the lagoon, waterfalls, and 18th hole of the Ko Olina Golf Club. The space, formerly home to the Niblick Restaurant, has been totally transformed to include Roy's famous display kitchen, and boasts floor-to-ceiling windows that showcase the view. Unlike other Roy's locations, the dining room is relaxing and romantic—quiet enough to have a conversation without shouting while enjoying the incredible cuisine. The menu changes daily, but you can generally count on Roy's classics: blackened ahi, hibachi salmon, and Szechuan baby back ribs. Some great additions include Asian pesto steamed fresh fish, cilantro-dusted *papio* (jack trevally), kiawe-grilled filet mignon, and roasted chicken with *huli-huli* sauce (sort of a Hawaiian barbecue sauce). Unlike the Hawaii Kai location, Ko Olina is also open for lunch; between lunch- and dinnertime, you can enjoy appetizers at the bar. It's worth the drive to participate in this incredible dining experience.

At the Ko Olina Resort, 92-1220 Aliinui Dr., Kapolei. ⓒ **808/676-7697.** www.roysrestaurant. com. Reservations recommended. Lunch $15-$25, appetizers at the bar $10-$20, dinner entrees $20-$50. AE, DC, DISC, MC, V. Daily 11am-2pm; Mon-Thurs 5:30-9:30pm; Fri-Sun 5-9:30pm (appetizers only 2-5:30pm).

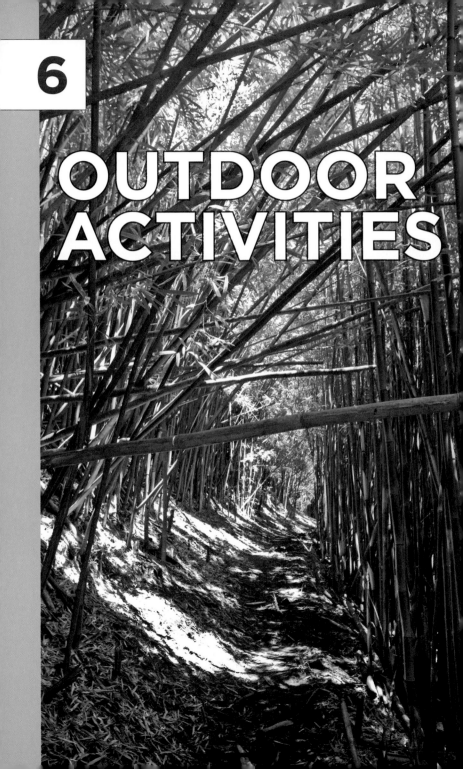

6

OUTDOOR ACTIVITIES

P ictures of hotels lining the shores of Waikiki Beach and canyons of tall buildings in downtown Honolulu have given Oahu a bad rap. The island is much more than an urban concrete jungle or a tropical Disneyland blighted by overdevelopment; it's also a haven for the nature lover and outdoor enthusiast.

With year-round temperatures in the upper 70s, and miles of verdant unspoiled landscape, Oahu is perfect for outdoor activities of all kinds, including hiking, golf, tennis, biking, and horseback riding. But the island's waters, which also enjoy year-round temperatures in the mid to upper 70s, are where the majority of residents and visitors head for relaxation, rejuvenation, and recreation. Locals don't think of their island or state boundaries as ending at land's edge—rather, they extend beyond the reefs, well out into the ocean.

All the activities in this chapter are organized geographically around the island in a counterclockwise direction. For camping information, see p. 177.

BEACHES

Oahu has more than 130 beaches of every conceivable kind—from legendary white-sand stretches to secluded rocky bays. Waikiki, of course, is the best known, but there are many others—some more beautiful, all less crowded. The following sample of Oahu's finest beaches was carefully selected to suit every need, taste, and interest, from the sunbather in repose to the most ardent diver.

The Waikiki Coast

ALA MOANA BEACH PARK ★★

Quite possibly America's best urban beach, gold-sand Ala Moana ("by the sea"), on sunny Mamala Bay, stretches for more than a mile along Honolulu's coast between downtown and Waikiki. This 76-acre midtown beach park, with spreading lawns shaded by banyans and palms, is one of the island's most popular playgrounds. It has a man-made beach, created in the 1930s by filling a coral reef with Waianae Coast sand, as well as its own lagoon, yacht harbor, tennis courts, music pavilion, bathhouses, picnic tables, and enough wide-open green spaces to accommodate four million visitors a year. The water is calm almost year-round, protected by black lava rocks set offshore. You can park in the large lot or at metered street parking.

WAIKIKI BEACH ★★★

No beach anywhere is so widely known or so universally sought after as this narrow, 1½-mile-long crescent of imported sand (from Molokai) at the foot of a string of high-rise hotels. Home to the world's longest-running beach party, Waikiki attracts nearly five million visitors a year from every corner of the planet. First-timers are always amazed to discover how small Waikiki Beach actually is, but everyone finds a place for themselves under the tropical sun here.

FACING PAGE: **The eerily beautiful Puu Ohia Trail.**

Waikiki is actually a string of beaches that extends between **Sans Souci State Recreational Area,** near Diamond Head to the east, and **Duke Kahanamoku Beach,** in front of the Hilton Hawaiian Village Beach Resort & Spa, to the west. Great stretches along Waikiki include **Kuhio Beach,** next to the Moana Surfrider, which provides the quickest access to the Waikiki shoreline; the stretch in front of the Royal Hawaiian Hotel known as **Grey's Beach,** which is canted so it catches the rays perfectly; and **Sans Souci,** the small, popular beach in front of the New Otani Kaimana Beach Hotel that's locally known as "Dig Me Beach" because of all the gorgeous bods who strut their stuff here. Grey's

TOP: **The end of a long surfing day at Waikiki Beach.** ABOVE: **Getting ready to dive into Hanauma Bay's underwater park.**

is probably the best spot for catching the rays—the beach is set at the perfect angle for sunning. It's also a great spot for people-watching. Get here early; by midday (when the rays are at their peak), it's towel-to-towel out there.

Waikiki is fabulous for swimming, board- and bodysurfing, outrigger canoeing, diving, sailing, snorkeling, and pole fishing. Every imaginable type of marine equipment is available for rent here. Facilities include showers, lifeguards, restrooms, grills, picnic tables, and pavilions at the **Queen's Surf** end of the beach (at Kapiolani Park, btw. the zoo and the aquarium). The best place to park is at Kapiolani Park, near Sans Souci.

East Oahu

HANAUMA BAY ★★

Oahu's most popular snorkeling spot is this volcanic crater with a broken sea wall; its small, curved, 2,000-foot gold-sand beach is packed elbow-to-elbow with

GOLF COURSES

Ala Wai Municipal Golf Course **3**
Hawaii Country Club **33**
Hawaii Kai Golf Course **6**
Kahuku Golf Course **17**
Ko Olina Golf Club **28**
Makaha Resort Golf Club **26**
Mililani Golf Club **32**
Olomana Golf Links **8**
Pali Golf Course **11**
Pearl Country Club **31**
Turtle Bay Resort **18**
West Loch Municipal Golf Course **30**

BEACHES

Ala Moana Beach Park **1**
Banzai/Pipeline/Ehukai
   Beach Park **20**
Haleiwa Beach Park **23**
Hanauma Bay **4**
Haula Beach Park **14**
Kahana Bay Beach Park **13**
Kailua Beach **10**
Ko Olina **29**
Kualoa Regional Park **12**
Lanikai Beach **9**
Makaha Beach Park **25**
Makapuu Beach Park **7**
Malaekahana Bay State
   Recreation Area **16**
Pokai Bay Beach Park **27**
Pounders Beach **15**
Pupukea Beach Park **21**
Sandy Beach **5**
Sunset Beach Park **19**
Waikiki Beach **2**
Waimea Beach Park **22**
Yokohama Bay **24**

Beaches & Golf
on Oahu

people year-round. The bay's shallow shoreline water and abundant marine life are the main attractions, but this good-looking beach is also popular for sunbathing and people-watching. Serious divers shoot "the slot" (a passage through the reef) to gain access to Witch's Brew, a turbulent cove, and then

brave strong currents in 70-foot depths at the bay mouth to see coral gardens, turtles, and—that's right—sharks. (Divers: Beware the Molokai Express, a strong current.) Snorkelers hug the safe, shallow (10 ft.) inner bay that, depending on when you go, is either like swimming in a fish-feeding frenzy or like bathing with 300,000 honeymooners. Because Hanauma Bay is a conservation district, you may look at but not touch or take any marine life here. Feeding the fish is also prohibited.

In 2004, a $13 million Marine Education Center opened with exhibits and a 7-minute video orienting visitors on this marine life sanctuary. The 10,000-square-foot center includes a training room, gift shop, public restrooms, snack bar, and staging area for the motorized tram, which will take you down the steep road to the beach. (Tram fees are 75¢ down to the beach, $1 up from the beach to the parking lot, or $2.50 all-day rides up and down.) Facilities include parking, restrooms, a pavilion, a grass volleyball court, lifeguards, barbecue grills, picnic tables, and food concessions. Alcohol is prohibited in the park; no smoking past the visitor center. Expect to pay $1 per vehicle to park and a $7.50-per-person entrance fee (active duty military personnel and their dependents, and children 12 and under are free). If you're driving, take Kalanianaole Highway to Koko Head Regional Park. Avoid the crowds by going early, about 8am, on a weekday morning; once the parking lot's full, you're out of luck. Or take TheBus (p. 278) to escape the parking problem: The Hanauma Bay Shuttle runs from Waikiki to Hanauma Bay every half-hour from 8:45am to 1pm; you can catch it at the Ala Moana Hotel, the Ilikai Hotel, or any city bus stop. It returns every hour from noon to 4:30pm. Hanauma Bay is closed on Tuesdays so the fish can have a day off. Park is open from 6am to 7pm Wednesday through Monday.

SANDY BEACH ★

Sandy Beach is one of the best bodysurfing beaches on Oahu; it's also one of the most dangerous. It's better to just stand and watch the daredevils literally risk their necks at this 1,200-foot-long gold-sand beach that's pounded by wild waves and haunted by a dangerous shore break and strong backwash. Weak swimmers and children should definitely stay out of the water here; Sandy Beach's heroic lifeguards make more rescues in a year than those at any other beach on Oahu. Visitors, easily fooled by experienced bodysurfers who make wave-riding look easy, often fall victim to the bone-crunching waves. Lifeguards post flags to alert beachgoers to the day's surf: Green means safe, yellow caution, and red indicates very dangerous water conditions; always check the flags before you dive in.

Facilities include restrooms and parking. Go weekdays to avoid the crowds, weekends to catch the bodysurfers in action. From Waikiki, drive east on the H-1, which becomes Kalanianaole Highway; proceed past Hawaii Kai, up the hill to Hanauma Bay, past the Halona Blow Hole, and along the coast. The next

Bodysurfing in tandem on Sandy Beach.

big, gold, sandy beach you see ahead on the right is Sandy Beach. TheBus no. 22 will also get you here.

MAKAPUU BEACH PARK ★

Makapuu Beach, the most famous bodysurfing beach in Hawaii, is a beautiful 1,000-foot-long gold-sand beach cupped in the stark black Koolau cliffs on Oahu's easternmost point. Even if you never venture into the water, it's worth a visit just to enjoy the great natural beauty of this classic Hawaiian beach. You've probably already seen it in countless TV shows, from *Hawaii Five-O* and *Magnum, P.I.* to *Lost*.

In summer, the ocean here is as gentle as a Jacuzzi, and swimming and diving are perfect; come winter, however, Makapuu is hit with big, pounding waves that are ideal for expert bodysurfers, but too dangerous for regular swimmers. Small boards—3 feet or less with no skeg (bottom fin)—are permitted; regular board surfing is banned by state law.

Facilities include restrooms, lifeguards, barbecue grills, picnic tables, and parking. To get here, follow Kalanianaole Highway toward Waimanalo, or take TheBus no. 57, 23, or 22.

The Windward Coast

LANIKAI BEACH ★★

One of Hawaii's best spots for swimming, gold-sand Lanikai's crystal-clear lagoon is like a giant saltwater swimming pool that you're lucky to share with the resident tropical fish and sea turtles. Too gorgeous to be real, this is one of Hawaii's postcard-perfect beaches: It's a mile long and thin in places, but the sand's as soft as talcum powder. Prevailing onshore trade winds make this an excellent place for sailing and windsurfing. Kayakers often paddle out to the two tiny offshore Mokulua islands, which are seabird sanctuaries. Because Lanikai is in a residential neighborhood, it's less crowded than other Oahu beaches, the perfect place to enjoy a quiet day. Sun worshipers should arrive in the morning, though, as the Koolau Range blocks the afternoon rays.

There are no facilities here, just off-street parking. From Waikiki, take the H-1 to the Pali Highway (Hwy. 61) through the Nuuanu Pali Tunnel to Kailua, where the Pali Highway becomes Kailua Road as it proceeds through town. At

159

Kalaheo Avenue, turn right and follow the coast about 2 miles to Kailua Beach Park; just past it, turn left at the T-intersection and drive uphill on Aalapapa Drive, a one-way street that loops back as Mokulua Drive. Park on Mokulua Drive and walk down any of the eight public-access lanes to the shore. Or, take TheBus no. 56 or 57 (Kailua), and then transfer to the shuttle.

KAILUA BEACH ★★★

Windward Oahu's premier beach is a 2-mile-long, wide golden strand with dunes, palm trees, panoramic views, and offshore islets that are home to seabirds. The swimming is excellent, and the azure waters are usually decorated with bright sails; this is Oahu's premier windsurfing beach as well. It's also a favorite spot to sail catamarans, bodysurf the gentle waves, or paddle a kayak. Water conditions are quite safe, especially at the mouth of Kaelepulu Stream, where toddlers play in the freshwater shallows at the middle of

Oahu's miles and miles of beaches.

the beach park. The water's usually about 78°F (26°C), the views are spectacular, and the setting, at the foot of the sheer, green Koolaus, is idyllic. Best of all, the crowds haven't found it yet.

The 35-acre beach park is intersected by a freshwater stream and watched over by lifeguards. Facilities include picnic tables, barbecues, restrooms, a volleyball court, a public boat ramp, free parking, and an open-air cafe. Kailua's new bike path weaves through the park, and windsurfer and kayak rentals are available as well. To get here, take Pali Highway (Hwy. 61) to Kailua, drive through town, turn right on Kalaheo Avenue, and go a mile until you see the beach on your left. Or take TheBus no. 56 or 57 into Kailua, then the no. 70 shuttle.

KUALOA REGIONAL PARK ★★

This 150-acre coconut palm–fringed peninsula is the biggest beach park on the windward side and one of Hawaii's most scenic. It's on Kaneohe Bay's north shore, at the foot of the spiky Koolau Ridge. The park has a broad, grassy lawn and a long, narrow, white-sand beach ideal for swimming, walking, beachcombing, kite flying, or sunbathing. Picnic and camping areas are available, too. In ancient Hawaii, this was a very sacred spot where Hawaiian chiefs brought their infant children to be raised and trained as rulers. Today, the park is listed on the National Register of Historic Places. It's easy to see why it was so revered: The curtain of the Koolau Mountains provides a spectacular backdrop in one direction. The waters are shallow and safe for swimming year-round, and at low tide, you can swim or wade out to the islet of Mokolii (popularly known as Chinaman's

Hat), which has a small sandy beach and is a bird preserve—so don't spook the red-footed boobies. Lifeguards are on duty.

Because both residents and visitors frequent this huge beach park, it's better to go on a weekday. The park is on Kamehameha Highway (Hwy. 83) in Kualoa; you can get here via TheBus no. 55.

KAHANA BAY BEACH PARK ★★

This white-sand, crescent-shaped beach is backed by a huge, jungle-cloaked valley with dramatic, jagged cliffs and is protected by ironwood and kamani trees. The bay's calm water and shallow, sandy bottom make it a safe swimming area for children. The bay is famous for the *akule* (bigeye scad), which come in seasonally; *papio* (skip jack) and goatfish are also found here. The surrounding park has picnic areas, camping, and hiking trails. The wide sand-bottom channel that runs through the park and out to Kahana Bay is one of the largest on Oahu—it's perfect for kayakers. Locals come here on weekends, so weekdays are less crowded. The beach park is on Kamehameha Highway in Kahana; take TheBus no. 55 (Circle Island) to get here.

HAUULA BEACH PARK

The town of Hauula and nearby Hauula Beach Park were named after the *hau* trees that were once abundant. Although less plentiful now, the trees continue to blossom here every July and August. The blossoms begin as a bright yellow flower in the morning, changing color as the day progresses, until they are reddish gold by dusk and dark red by night, when they fall to the ground. The cycle is repeated the next day.

Hauula Beach Park, which fronts Kamehameha Highway, is a straight and narrow stretch (about 1,000 ft. long), shaded by kamani and ironwood trees. An offshore reef protects the waters off the beach, but the shallow and rocky bottom makes the area unsafe for swimming. Snorkeling is good along the edge of the coral reef, and fishing for papio and goatfish can be fruitful. Picnic and camping facilities are available. Weekends tend to be more crowded here, too. TheBus no. 55 (Circle Island) will get you to Hauula Beach.

POUNDERS BEACH

Because of its easy access and great bodysurfing waves, Pounders is a popular weekend beach. The beach used to be called Pahumoa, after a local fisherman who arranged the local *hukilau* (the catching of fish in a net) and made sure that the elderly living in the area received a portion of the catch. The name change occurred in the 1950s, when a group of students at the Church College of the Pacific (now Brigham Young University–Hawaii) called the beach "Pounders" after the crushing shore break that provided brief but spectacular bodysurfing rides; the nickname stuck.

Pounders is a wide beach, extending a quarter-mile between two points. At the west end of the beach, next to the old landing, the waters usually are calm and safe for swimming. However, at the opposite end, near the limestone cliffs, there's a shore break that can be dangerous for inexperienced bodysurfers; there the bottom drops off abruptly, causing strong rip currents. The weekends and after-school hours are the busiest time for this beach; weekday mornings are the quietest. Park on Kamehameha Highway in Kailua, or take TheBus no. 55 (Circle Island) to get here.

The North Shore

BANZAI/PIPELINE/EHUKAI BEACH PARK ★

Because the sandy beach here is continuous, with only one sign—EHUKAI BEACH PARK—most people think of this area as one beach park, although it's actually three separate ones. Located near Pupukea, **Ehukai Beach Park** is 1 acre of grass with a parking lot. The long, broad, white-sand beach is known for its winter surfing action. Swimming is good during the spring and summer months, but currents and waves prohibit safe swimming in the winter. The surf in front of Ehukai Beach Park is excellent for body and board surfers.

The park also provides access to Pipeline and Banzai. **Pipeline** is actually about 100 yards to the left of Ehukai Beach Park. When the winter surf rolls in and hits the shallow coral shelf, the waves that quickly form are steep—so steep, in fact, that the crest of the wave falling forward forms a near-perfect tube, or "pipeline." Surfers have tried for years to master Pipeline; many have wiped out, suffering lacerations and broken bones on the shallow reef. The first surfer to ride Pipeline successfully was Phil Edwards in the early 1960s. Even today, Pipeline still causes its share of injuries and fatalities.

Just west of Pipeline is the area surfers call **"Banzai Beach."** The Japanese word *banzai* means "10,000 years"; it's given as a toast or as a battle charge, meaning "go for it." In the late 1950s, filmmaker Bruce Brown was shooting one of the first surf movies ever made, *Surf Safari,* when he saw a bodysurfer ride a huge wave. Brown yelled, "Banzai!" and the name stuck. In the winter, this is a very popular beach with surfers, surf fans, curious residents, and visitors; it's less crowded in the summer months. Again, access is via Ehukai Beach Park, off Kamehameha Highway, on Ke Nui Road in Pupukea. TheBus no. 52 (Circle Island) will drop you on the highway.

PUPUKEA BEACH PARK ★

This 80-acre beach park is a Marine Life Conservation District; as such, it has strict rules about taking marine life, sand, coral, shells, and rocks. Two major swimming areas are in the Marine Life Conservation District: **Shark's Cove** and **Three Tables.** Don't worry: Shark's Cove, near the northern end, is *not* named for an abundance of sharks that call this home (in fact, it's relatively uncommon to see a shark here); rather, it's a popular snorkeling and dive site. Diving is best outside the cove, where caves promise interesting night diving. During the calm summer months, this is a popular dive site both day and night.

At the southern end of the Marine Life Conservation District is Three Tables, which is named for the three flat sections of reef visible at low tide. Snorkeling is good around the tables where the water is about 15 feet deep. Diving outside the tables, where the water is 30 to 45 feet deep, is excellent— there are many ledges, arches, lava tubes, and a variety of marine life. Swimming, diving, and snorkeling are best from May to October, when the water is calm; nevertheless, watch out for surges. In the winter, when currents form and waves roll in, this area is very dangerous, even in the tide pools; a lifeguard is never present in

> ## Impressions
>
> *The boldness and address with which we saw them perform these difficult and dangerous maneuvers was altogether astonishing.*
>
> —Captain James Cook's observations of Hawaiian surfers

this area. Summers find this Marine Life Conservation District brimming with visitors weekdays and weekends; it's a popular site for local dive operators to take their clients. In the winter, it's nearly empty during the week. It's right on Kamehameha Highway in Pupukea and has a small parking lot. TheBus no. 52 (Circle Island) stops at the park.

MALAEKAHANA BAY STATE RECREATION AREA ★★★

This almost mile-long white-sand crescent lives up to just about everyone's image of the perfect Hawaiian beach. It's excellent for swimming. On a weekday, you may be the only one here; but should some net fisherman—or a kindred soul—intrude upon your delicious privacy, you can swim out to Goat Island (or wade across at low tide) and play Robinson Crusoe. (The islet is a sanctuary for seabirds and turtles, so no chase 'em, brah.) Facilities include restrooms, barbecue grills, picnic tables, outdoor showers, and parking.

To get here, take Kamehameha Highway (Hwy. 83) 2 miles north of the Polynesian Cultural Center; as you enter the main gate, you'll come upon the wooded beach park. Or you can take TheBus no. 52.

SUNSET BEACH PARK ★★

Surfers around the world know this famous site for its spectacular winter surf—the waves can be huge thundering peaks reaching 15 to 20 feet. This surfing spot wasn't really "discovered" until the 1940s; before that, surfers preferred Makaha on the leeward side of the island. During the winter surf season (Sept–Apr) swimming is very dangerous here, due to the alongshore currents and powerful rip currents. The "Sunset rip" has been the site of many rescues and has carried numerous surfboards out to sea. The only safe time to swim at Sunset is during the calm summer months. Sunset also features a huge sandy beach adjacent to the street. This is a great place to people-watch, but don't go too near the water when the lifeguards have posted the red warning flags. One of the most popular beaches on the island, Sunset attracts local surfers, sunbathing beauties, and visitors wanting to get a glimpse of this world-famous surf destination. To avoid the crowds, go during midweek. Because the beach is located right on Kamehameha Highway in Paumalu, TheBus no. 52 (Circle Island) will get you there if you'd rather not drive.

WAIMEA BEACH PARK ★★

This deep, sandy bowl has gentle summer waves that are excellent for swimming, snorkeling, and bodysurfing. To one side of the bay is a huge rock that local kids like to climb and dive from. In this placid scene, the only clues of what's to come in winter are those evacuation whistles on poles beside the road. But what a difference a season makes: From November to March, monstrous winter waves pound the narrow bay, sometimes rising to 50 feet high. The ground actually vibrates and everyone on the beach is covered with salt spray mist when they break onshore. When the surf's really up, very strong currents and shore breaks sweep the bay—and it seems like everyone on Oahu drives out to Waimea to get a look at the massive waves and those who paddle out to challenge these freight trains. This unforgettable activity won't cost you a dime, and you'll be amazed at how small the surfers appear in the lip of the giant waves. Weekends are great for watching the surfers; to avoid the crowds, go on weekdays. *Tip:* Don't get too distracted by the waves and forget to pay attention when parking or crossing the road.

Facilities include lifeguards, restrooms, showers, parking, and nearby restaurants and shops in Haleiwa town. The beach is on Kamehameha Highway (Hwy. 83); from Waikiki, you can take TheBus no. 52.

Leeward Oahu/The Waianae Coast

KO OLINA

The developer of the 640-acre Ko Olina Resort has created four white-sand lagoons to make the rocky shoreline more attractive and accessible. Nearly circular, the man-made lagoons offer calm, shallow waters and a powdery white-sand beach bordered by a broad, grassy lawn. No lifeguards are present, but the generally tranquil waters are great for swimming, are perfect for kids, and offer some snorkeling opportunities around the boulders at the entrance to the lagoons. Two lagoons have restrooms, and plenty of public parking is on-hand. Located off H-1 in Kapolei, Ko Olina has no local bus service; the closest bus stop is on Farrington Highway, more than 4 miles away.

MAKAHA BEACH PARK

When surf's up here, it's spectacular: Huge waves pound the beach from October through April. This is the original home of Hawaii's big-wave surfing championship; surfers today know it as the home of Buffalo's Big Board Surf Classic, where surfers ride the waves on old-Hawaiian-style 10-foot-long wooden boards. Nearly a mile long, the half-moon gold-sand beach is tucked between 231-foot Lahilahi Point, which locals call Black Rock, and Kepuhi Point, a toe of the Waianae mountain range. Summer is the best time to hit this beach—the waves are small, the sand abundant, and the water safe for swimming. Children hug the shore on the north side of the beach, near the lifeguard stand, while surfers dodge the rocks and divers seek an offshore channel full of big fish. *Note:* This is a "local" beach; you're welcome, of course, but you can expect "stink eye" (mild approbation) if you are not respectful of the beach and the local residents who use the facility all the time.

Facilities include restrooms, lifeguards, and parking. To get here, take the H-1 freeway to the end of the line, where it becomes Farrington Highway (Hwy. 93), and follow it to the beach; or you can take TheBus no. 40/40A.

The soft sands and cliffs of Yokohama Bay.

YOKOHAMA BAY ★

Where Farrington Highway (Hwy. 93) ends, the wilderness of Kaena Point State Park begins. It's a remote 853-acre coastline park of empty beaches, sand dunes, cliffs, and deep-blue water. This is the last sandy stretch of shore on the northwest coast of Oahu. Sometimes it's known as Keawalua Beach or Puau Beach, but everybody here calls it Yokohama, after the Japanese immigrants who came from that port city to work the cane fields and fish along this shoreline. When the surf's calm—mainly in summer—this is a good area for snorkeling, diving, swimming, shore fishing, and picnicking. When surf's up, board and bodysurfers are out in droves; don't go in the water then unless you're an expert. No lifeguards or facilities are available, except at the park entrance, where a restroom and lifeguard stand are positioned. No bus serves the park.

POKAI BAY BEACH PARK ★

This wonderful beach, off the beaten path for most visitors, offers excellent swimming year-round, even when the rest of the Waianae shoreline is getting battered by heavy surf. The waters inside this protected bay are calm enough for children and offer excellent snorkeling. The swimming area is marked by buoys. Waianae-area residents have a bit of a reputation for being xenophobic; however, they want the same things most people want. Just go with respect for local customs, be a good steward of the land, and appreciate the local resources. Do what the locals do: Pick up your garbage, don't play loud music, and be courteous and friendly. On weekdays, you can practically have the area to yourself. The beach park is on Waianae Valley Road, off Farrington Highway. TheBus no. 51 will drop you off on the highway, and you can walk the block to the park.

WATERSPORTS

Oahu has a wealth of watersports opportunities, whether you're a professional surfer braving giant winter waves on the North Shore, or a recreational water-skier enjoying the calm waters of Hawaii Kai. You can kayak from Lanikai Beach to the Mokulua Islands or float above Waikiki on a parasail as a speedboat tows you blissfully through the air. If you have something of an adventurous spirit, you might scuba dive the walls of Kahuna Canyon, swim with clouds of *ta'ape* (bluestripe snapper), or view an occasional shark from the comfort of a passenger submarine. No matter what your aquatic interests are, whether you're a beginner or an expert, you can find the right sport on Oahu.

If you want to rent beach toys (such as a mask, snorkel, and fins; boogie boards; surfboards; kayaks; and more), check out the following rental shops: **Snorkel Bob's,** on the way to Hanauma Bay at 700 Kapahulu Ave. (at Date St.), Honolulu (© **808/735-7944;** www.snorkelbob.com); and **Aloha Beach Service,** in the Sheraton Moana Surfrider Hotel, 2365 Kalakaua Ave. (© **808/922-3111,** ext. 2341), in Waikiki. On Oahu's windward side, try **Kailua Sailboards & Kayaks,** 130 Kailua Rd., a block from the Kailua Beach Park (© **808/262-2555;** www.kailuasailboards.com). On the North Shore, get equipment from **Surf-N-Sea,** 62-595 Kamehameha Hwy., Haleiwa (© **808/637-9887;** www.surfnsea.com).

Boating

A funny thing happens to people when they come to Hawaii: Maybe it's the salt air, the warm tropical nights, or the blue Hawaiian moonlight, but otherwise-rational people who have never set foot on a boat in their life suddenly want to go out to sea. You can opt for a "booze cruise" with a thousand loud, rum-soaked strangers, or you can sail on one of these special yachts, all of which will take you out **whale-watching** in season (roughly Dec–Apr). For fishing charters, see "Sportfishing," below.

Captain Bob's Adventure Cruises ★

See the majestic Windward Coast the way it should be seen—from a boat. Captain Bob will take you on a 4-hour, lazy-day sail of Kaneohe Bay aboard his 42-foot catamaran, which skims across the almost always calm water above the shallow coral reef, lands at the disappearing sandbar Ahu o Laka, and takes you past two small islands to snorkel spots full of tropical fish and, sometimes, turtles. The color of the water alone is worth

Dolphins help lead a Wild Side Tour.

the price. This is an all-day affair, but hey, getting out on the water is part of the reason you came to Hawaii, right? A shuttle will pick you up at your Waikiki hotel between 9 and 9:30am and bring you back at about 4pm—it's a lot quicker than taking TheBus.

Kaneohe Bay. © **808/942-5077.** All-day cruise $88 adults, $73 children 3–12. Rates include all-you-can-eat barbecue lunch and transportation from Waikiki hotels. No cruises Sun and holidays. Bus: 55 or 56.

Navatek I ★★ You've never been on a boat, you don't want to be on a boat, but here you are being dragged aboard one. Why are you boarding this weird-looking vessel? It guarantees that you'll be "seasick-free," that's why. The 140-foot-long *Navatek I* isn't even called a boat; it's actually a SWATH (Small Waterplane Area Twin Hull) vessel. That means the ship's superstructure—the part you ride on—rests on twin torpedolike hulls that cut through the water so you don't bob like a cork and spill your mai tai. It's the smoothest ride on Mamala Bay. In fact, *Navatek I* is the only dinner cruise ship to receive U.S. Coast Guard certification to travel beyond Diamond Head.

Sunset dinner cruises leave Pier 6 (across from the Hawaii Maritime Museum) nightly. If you have your heart set on seeing the city lights, take the Royal Sunset Dinner Cruise, which runs from 5:30 to 7:30pm. The best deal is the **lunch cruise,** with full buffet lunch and a great view of Oahu offshore. During the **whale season** (roughly Jan–Apr), you can whale-watch, too. The lunch cruise lasts from noon to 2:30pm. Both cruises include live Hawaiian music. Check website for Internet deals.

Aloha Tower Marketplace, Pier 6, c/o Hawaiian Cruises Ltd. © **808/973-1311.** www.atlantis adventures.com/oahu.cfm. Dinner cruises $121 adults, $69 children 2–12; lunch cruises $63 adults, $32 children 2–11. Validated parking is half price. Bus: 8, 19, 20, 55, 56, or 57.

Wild Side Tours Picture this: You're floating in the calm waters off the Waianae coast, where your 42-foot sailing catamaran has just dropped you off; below you in the reef are turtles; in the distance you see spinner dolphins, taking the high, spinning leaps for which they are known. Happens every day on the 4-hour tours operated by the Cullins family, who have been swimming in these waters for decades. In the winter, you may spot humpback whales on the morning cruise, which includes continental breakfast, refreshments, snorkel gear, instruction, and flotation device. They also have an afternoon/sunset whale-watching sail in the winter for $75 per person, and a sunset/full moon/star-gazing sail for $95.

Waianae Boat Harbor, 87-1286 Farrington Hwy., Waianae. ℭ **808/306-7273.** www.sailhawaii. com. Morning sail/snorkel $115 for ages 6 and up (not recommended for younger children); sunset sail $95. MC, V. Bus: 19 or 20 to Ala Moana Center, then 40 or 40A.

Bodyboarding (Boogie Boarding) & Bodysurfing

Good places to learn to bodyboard are in the small waves of **Waikiki Beach** and **Kailua Beach,** and **Bellows Field Beach Park,** off Kalanianaole Highway (Hwy. 72) in Waimanalo, which is open to the public on weekends (from noon on Fri to midnight on Sun and holidays). To get here, turn toward the ocean on Hughs Road, then right on Tinker Road, which takes you right to the park. See above for a list of rental shops where you can get a boogie board.

Ocean Kayaking

For a wonderful adventure, rent a kayak, arrive at Lanikai Beach just as the sun is appearing, and paddle across the emerald lagoon to the pyramid-shaped islands called Mokulua—it's an experience you won't forget. Kayak equipment rental starts at $12 an hour for a single kayak, $25 an hour for a double. In Waikiki try **Prime Time Sports,** Fort DeRussy Beach (ℭ **808/949-8952**); on the windward side, check out **Kailua Sailboards & Kayaks,** 130 Kailua Rd., a block from Kailua Beach Park (ℭ **808/262-2555;** www.kailuasailboards.com), where a single kayak rents for $39 for a half-day, and a double kayak rents for $55 for a half-day. On the North Shore, **Surf-N-Sea,** 62-595 Kamehameha Hwy., Haleiwa (ℭ **808/637-9887;** fax 808/637-3008; www.surfnsea.com), rents kayaks at $10 for the first hour, or $60 a day.

First-timers should go to **Kailua Sailboards & Kayaks** (see above). The company offers a guided tour ($69 adults and $59 children 8–12 years), with the novice in mind, in a safe, protected environment. Lunch, all equipment, and transportation from Waikiki hotels are included. Kayak lessons and self-guided trips are also available.

Check Out the Beach Before You Leave Home

Before you leave your hotel room, check out the **Hawaii Beach Safety** website, http://oceansafety.soest.hawaii.edu, a joint venture among various governmental agencies (the City and County of Honolulu, University of Hawaii, and Hawaii Lifeguard Association, among others). You can view the latest wind and wave conditions and other safety information for the beach you want to visit. The site is updated at 9am, 3pm, and 9pm, or if conditions change.

Scuba Diving

Oahu is a wonderful place to scuba dive, especially for those interested in wreck diving. One of the more famous wrecks in Hawaii is the **Mahi,** a 185-foot former minesweeper easily accessible just south of Waianae. Abundant marine life makes this a great place to shoot photos—schools of lemon

butterflyfish and taape are so comfortable with divers and photographers that they practically pose. Eagle rays, green sea turtles, manta rays, and white-tipped sharks occasionally cruise by as well, and eels peer out from the wreck.

For nonwreck diving, one of the best spots in summer is **Kahuna Canyon.** In Hawaiian, *kahuna* means priest, wise man, or sorcerer; this massive amphitheater, near Mokuleia, is a perfect example of something a sorcerer might conjure up. Walls rising from the ocean floor create the illusion of an underwater Grand Canyon. Inside the amphitheater, crabs, octopuses, slippers, and spiny lobsters abound (be aware that taking them in summer is illegal), and giant trevally, parrotfish, and unicorn fish gather as well. Outside the amphitheater, you might just see an occasional shark in the distance.

Because Oahu's most rewarding dives are offshore, your best bet is to book a two-tank dive from a dive boat. Hawaii's oldest and largest outfitter is **Aaron's Dive Shop,** 307 Hahani St., Kailua (✆ 808/262-2333; www.hawaii-scuba.com), which offers boat and beach dive excursions off the coast. Boat dives cost from $125 per person, including two tanks and transportation from the Kailua shop. The beach dive off the North Shore in summer or the Waianae Coast in winter is the same price as a boat dive, including all gear and transportation. Price includes pick up in Honolulu.

In Waikiki, **Dive Oahu,** 1085 Ala Moana (✆ 808/922-3483; www.diveoahu.com), offers everything from shipwreck dives in Waikiki to World War II Corsair plane dives in Hawaii Kai, for just $129 for a two-tank boat dive (friends or family members can tag along for just $35 each to snorkel). Captain Brian, who has a couple of decades under his dive belt, loves to help beginners feel comfortable scuba diving, as well as show experienced scuba divers what the Waikiki coast has to offer. On the North Shore, **Surf-N-Sea,** 62-595 Kamehameha Hwy., Haleiwa (✆ 808/637-9887; fax 808/637-3008; www.surfnsea.com), has dive tours from the shore (starting at $75 for one tank), from a boat ($140 for two tanks), and at night ($100 for one tank, summer only). Surf-N-Sea also rents equipment and can point you to the best dive sites in the area.

Another great resource for diving on your own is **HawaiiScubaDiving.com,** a great source listing dive companies, dive sites, and everything else you want to know about diving in Hawaii. If you are looking to find a dive buddy, want to post a dive experience, or have dive gear to sell, check it out.

Stand-Up Paddle Boarding

One of the new sports to hit Hawaii is stand-up paddle boarding, where you balance on a oversized surfboard and maneuver over the water with a very long paddle. Actually, it's quite easy to do and a great workout at the same time. You feel

UP CLOSE & PERSONAL WITH *jaws*

You're 4 miles out from land, which is just a speck on the horizon, with the open ocean all around you. Suddenly, from the blue depths, a shape emerges: the sleek, pale shadow of a 6-foot-long gray reef shark, followed quickly by a couple of 10-foot-long Galápagos sharks. Within a few heartbeats, you're surrounded by sharks on all sides. Do you panic? No, you paid $120 to be in the midst of these jaws of the deep. Of course, a 6 × 6 × 10-foot aluminum shark cage separates you from all those teeth.

It happens every day on **North Shore Shark Adventures** (© **808/228-5900;** www.hawaiisharkadventures.com), the dream of Captain Joe Pavsek, who decided, after some 30 years of surfing and diving, to share the experience of seeing a shark with visitors. His 32-foot boat, *Kailolo II,* attracts sharks (generally gray reef, Galápagos, and sandbars, ranging 5–15 ft.)—sometimes just a few, sometimes a few dozen—who associate the sound of the motor with neighboring fishing boats.

Depending on sea conditions and the weather, snorkelers can stay in the cage as long as they wish, with the sharks just inches away. The shark cage, connected to the boat with a line, floats several feet back and a little above the surface, holding two snorkelers comfortably and four snugly. You can stay on the boat and view the sharks from a more respectable distance for just $60. The brave and adventuresome will be down in that cage—it definitely will be a memory you won't forget. Check website for specials.

Divers and sharks face to face on North Shore Shark Adventures.

like you're walking on water and getting a great view of the aquatic world beneath the waves. If you are in Waikiki, call **Paddle Core Fitness** (✆ **808/723-5357;** www.paddlecorefitness.com); one-hour lessons and equipment start at $50 for a group or $75 private.

Snorkeling

Bordered by a 2,000-foot gold-sand beach, the shallow water (10 ft. in places) of **Hanauma Bay** ★★ is perfect for neophyte snorkelers. The bay is crowded —sometimes it seems there are more people than fish—but this former volcanic crater has clear, warm, protected waters and an abundance of friendly reef fish, including Moorish idols, scores of butterflyfish, damselfish, and wrasses. Hanauma Bay has two reefs, an inner and an outer—the first for novices, the other for experts. The inner reef is calm and shallow (less than 10 ft.); in some places, you can just wade and put your face in the water. Go early to beat the crowds: It's packed by 10am (and closed on Tues). There is a fee for entrance ($7.50) and for parking ($1 per vehicle). For details, see p. 156.

Braver snorkelers may want to head to **Shark's Cove,** on the North Shore just off Kamehameha Highway, between Haleiwa and Pupukea. Sounds risky, we know, but we've never seen any sharks in this cove, and in summer, this big, lava-edged pool is one of Oahu's best snorkel spots. Waves splash over the natural lava grotto and cascade like waterfalls into the pool full of tropical fish. To the right of the cove are deep-sea caves to explore. For directions, see p. 162.

Sportfishing

Kewalo Basin, between the Honolulu International Airport and Waikiki, is the main location for charter fishing boats on Oahu. From Waikiki, take Kalakaua Ewa (west) beyond Ala Moana Center; Kewalo Basin is on the left, across from Ward Centre. Look for charter boats all in a row in their slips; on lucky days, the captains display the catch of the day in the afternoon. You can also take TheBus no. 19 or 20 (toward the airport).

The best way to book a sportfishing charter is through the experts; the best booking desk in the state is **Sportfish Hawaii** ★ (✆ **877/388-1376** or 808/396-2607; www.sportfishhawaii.com), which not only reserves boats on Oahu, but on all islands. These fishing vessels have been inspected and must meet rigorous criteria to guarantee that you will have a great time. Prices range from $812 to $932 for a full-day exclusive charter (you, plus five friends, get the entire boat to yourself), $717 for a half-day exclusive, or from $191 for a full-day shared charter (you share the boat with five other people).

Submarine Dives

Here's your chance to play Jules Verne and experience the underwater world from the comfort of a submarine, which will take you on an adventure below the surface in high-tech comfort. If swimming's not your thing, this is a great way to see Hawaii's spectacular sea life; the entire trip is narrated as you watch tropical fish and sunken ships just outside the sub. Shuttle boats to the sub leave from Hilton Hawaiian Village Pier. The cost is $99 for adults, $45 for kids 12 and under (children must be at least 36 in. tall). *Tip:* Book online for discount rates of $90 for adults and $41 for kids. Call **Atlantis Submarines** ★ (✆ **800/548-6262** or 808/973-9811; www.atlantissubmarines.com) to reserve. *Note:* Skip this if you suffer from claustrophobia.

Surfing

In summer, when the water's warm and there's a soft breeze in the air, the south swell comes up. It's surf season, so—call a fire fighter? Yep, the **Hawaiian Fire Surf School** (② 888/955-7873 or 808/737-3473; www.hawaiianfire.com) is owned and operated by the Honolulu firefighters. The instructors (all firefighters) think safety first and transport their clients from Waikiki to a very safe, remote beach in Kalaeloa on West Oahu, where they can practically have the beach all to themselves. Prices are very reasonable: Two-hour group lessons (one teacher for every three students) are $99 for kids and $109 for adults. Expect to spend about 45 minutes on the beach learning the basics and then about 75 minutes in the water. You couldn't be in safer hands!

Now there's no excuse not to learn to surf in Hawaii: Hans Hedemann, a champion surfer for some 34 years, has opened the **Hans Hedemann Surf School** at the Turtle Bay Resort (② 808/924-7778; www.hhsurf.com). His classes range from one-on-one private sessions to group lessons (four students to one teacher) and begin at $75 for a 2-hour lesson. There's another location in Waikiki.

If you just want to rent a surfboard in Waikiki, **Waikiki Beach Activities,** on the beach fronting the **Hilton Hawaiian Village** (② 808/951-4088; www.waikikibeachactivities.com), at one end of Waikiki; and **Aloha Beach Service,** facing the Moana Surfrider Hotel (② 808/922-3111, ext. 2341), at the other end of Waikiki, both rent surfboards and other ocean toys. Surfboards are also available for rent on the North Shore at **Surf-N-Sea,** 62-595 Kamehameha Hwy., Haleiwa (② 808/637-9887; www.surfnsea.com), for $5 to $7 an hour. They offer lessons for $85 for 2 hours. (For the best surf shops, where you can soak in the culture as well as pick up gear, also see p. 258.)

On the windward side, call **Kimo's Surf Hut,** 151 Hekili St., across from Don Quijote, in Kailua (② 808/262-1644; www.kimossurfhut.com). Kimo and his wife, Ruth, couldn't be more friendly and helpful. In addition to surfboards that rent for $50 a day, Kimo has a personal collection of vintage surfboards lovingly displayed on the walls of his shop and will gladly tell you the pedigree and history of each board. Although Kimo doesn't offer formal surfing lessons, he'd be happy to give you pointers.

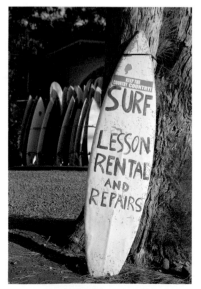

More experienced surfers should drop in on any surf shop around Oahu, or call the **Surf News Network Surfline** (② 808/596-SURF [596-7873]) to get the latest surf conditions. **The Cliffs,** at the base of Diamond Head, is a good spot for advanced surfers; 4- to 6-foot waves churn here, allowing high-performance surfing.

If you're in Hawaii in winter and want to see the serious surfers catch

Where better to learn to surf than Oahu?

Even the small waves are big in Oahu.

the really big waves, bring your binoculars and grab a front-row seat on the beach near **Kalalua Point.** To get here from Waikiki, take the H-1 toward the North Shore, veering off at H-2, which becomes Kamehameha Highway (Hwy. 83). Keep going to the funky surf town of Haleiwa and Waimea Bay; the big waves will be on your left, just past Pupukea Beach Park. Expect a traffic jam and be careful parking and crossing the highway. See p. 162 for more info.

Swimming

For a quiet, peaceful place to swim, **Malaekahana Bay ★**, near Kahuku, is one of the best Oahu beaches. This mile-long, white-sand, crescent-shaped beach is about a 90-minute drive and a million miles from the crowds at Waikiki. To get there, take Kamehameha Highway past Laie and follow the signs to Malaekahana State Recreational Area. Or take TheBus no. 52 (Circle Island). Another good swimming beach is **Lanikai;** secluded and calm, this beach is great for families. From Waikiki, take TheBus no. 56 or 57 (Kailua), and then transfer to the shuttle.

See also "Beaches," p. 155, where each description mentions the relative calmness of the waters.

Water-Skiing

To learn to water-ski, or to just go out and have a good time, call the oldest water-ski company in Hawaii, **Hawaii Water Sports,** Koko Marina Shopping Center (✆ **808/395-3773;** www.hawaiiwatersportscenter.com; TheBus no. 22). Lessons and boat rental are $49 for 20 minutes and $69 for a half-hour, including the boat and all equipment rental (maximum of five people).

Whale-Watching

From December to April, 45-foot humpback whales—Hawaii's most impressive visitors—come to spend the winter. They make the journey from Alaska to calve and mate in Hawaii's calm, warm waters. Once nearly hunted to extinction, humpback whales are now protected by federal law. The mammals may not be approached by any individual or watercraft within 300 ft.

Whales can frequently be seen off the island on calm days. If you spot the familiar spout of water—a sign the mammal is exhaling—there's a good chance you'll see the whale on the surface. If you're in a car, please pull over, as many accidents have occurred when visitors try to spot whales and drive at the same time.

For whale-watching cruises, see "Boating," p. 165.

Windsurfing

Windward Oahu's **Kailua Beach** is the home of champion and pioneer windsurfer Robbie Naish; it's also the best place to learn to windsurf. The oldest and most established windsurfing business in Hawaii is **Naish Hawaii/ Naish Windsurfing Hawaii,** 155-A Hamakua Dr., Kailua (✆ 800/767-6068 or 808/262-6068; www.naish.com). The company offers everything: sales, rentals, instruction, repair, and

Windsurfing instruction from Naish Hawaii on Kailua Beach.

free advice on where to go when the wind and waves are happening. Private 90-minute lessons start at $75 for one, $100 for two; beginner equipment rental is $40 for 4 hours and $45 for a full day. Kitesurfing lessons are also available ($125 for 1½ hr.). Kiteboard rentals are $25 a day (boards only). **Kailua Sailboards & Kayaks,** 130 Kailua Rd., a block from the Kailua Beach Park (✆ 808/262-2555; www.kailuasailboards.com), offers 3-hour small-group lessons in windsurfing ($129 per person, including all gear, plus lunch) and rentals of kitesurfing boards, windsurfing equipment, surfboards, snorkel gear, and ocean kayaks.

NATURE HIKES

People think Oahu is just one big urban island, so they're always surprised to discover that the great outdoors is less than an hour away from downtown Honolulu. Highlights of the island's 33 major hiking trails include razor-thin ridgebacks and deep waterfall valleys.

Check out Stuart Ball's *The Hikers Guide to Oahu* (1993) before you go. Another good source of hiking information on Oahu is the state's **Na Ala Hele (Trails to Go On) Program** (✆ 808/973-9782 or 808/587-0058).

For a free Oahu recreation map listing all 33 trails, write to the **Department of Land and Natural Resources,** 1151 Punchbowl St., Rm. 310, Honolulu, HI 96813 (✆ 808/587-0166; www.hawaiitrails.org). The department will also send free topographic trail maps on request and issue camping permits (applications for permits are on the website; allow 10 days' processing time).

Another good source of information is the *Hiking/Camping Information Packet,* which costs $10 (postage included); to order, contact **Hawaii Geographic**

Maps and Books, 49 S. Hotel St., Honolulu, HI 96813 (© 800/538-3950 or 808/538-3952; hawaiigeographicbooksandmaps@gmail.com). This store also carries a full line of United States Geographic Survey topographic maps, very handy for hikers. They prefer emails to phone calls.

Be sure to get a copy of *Hiking on Oahu: The Official Guide,* a hiking safety brochure that includes instructions on hiking preparation, safety procedures, emergency phone numbers, and necessary equipment; for a copy, contact the **Division of Forestry and Wildlife** (© 808/587-0166) or download it from **www2.hawaii.edu/~turner/hoo/hoo-main.htm**.

The **Hawaiian Trail and Mountain Club,** P.O. Box 2238, Honolulu, HI 96804 (www.htmclub.org), offers regular hikes on Oahu. You bring your own lunch and drinking water and meet up with the club at the Iolani Palace to join them on a hike. The club has information on hiking and camping in Hawaii, as well as a schedule of all upcoming hikes on their website.

Other organizations that offer regularly scheduled hikes are the **Sierra Club,** 1040 Richards St., Rm. 306, Honolulu, HI 96813 (www.hi.sierraclub. org); and the **Hawaii Nature Center,** 2131 Makiki Heights Dr. (© 888/955-0104; www.hawaiinaturecenter.org).

For camping information, see "Oahu's Campgrounds & Wilderness Cabins," p. 117.

Honolulu-Area Hikes

DIAMOND HEAD CRATER ★★★

Almost everyone can make the moderate but steep hike to the top of Hawaii's most famous landmark, Diamond Head Crater. The 1.4-mile round-trip goes to the top of the 750-foot volcanic cone, where you have a 360-degree view of Oahu up the leeward coast from Waikiki. Kids love the lookout. The hike takes about 1½ hours and the entry fee is $1 for pedestrians or $5 per car.

Diamond Head was created by a volcanic explosion about half a million years ago. The Hawaiians called the crater *Leahi* (meaning the brow of the ahi, or tuna, referring to the shape of the crater). Diamond Head was considered a sacred spot; King Kamehameha offered human sacrifices at a *heiau* (temple) on the

The challenging but rewarding hike to Diamond Head Crater.

western slope. It wasn't until the 19th century that Mount Leahi got its current name: A group of sailors found what they thought were diamonds in the crater; it turned out they were calcite crystals, but the Diamond Head moniker stuck.

Before you begin your journey to the top of the crater, put on some decent shoes (rubber-soled tennies are fine) and take a flashlight (you'll walk through several dark tunnels), binoculars (for better viewing at the top), water (very important), a hat to protect you from the sun, and a camera. You might want to put all your gear in a pack to leave your hands free for the climb. If you don't have a flashlight or your hotel can't lend you one, you can buy a small one for a few dollars as part of a Diamond Head climbers' "kit" at the gift shop at the **New Otani Kaimana Beach Hotel,** on the Diamond Head end of Kalakaua Avenue, just past the Waikiki Aquarium and across from Kapiolani Park.

Go early, preferably just after the 6am opening (park closes at 6pm), before the midday sun starts beating down. The hike to the summit of Diamond Head starts at Monsarrat and 18th avenues on the crater's inland (or *mauka*) side. To get there, take TheBus no. 58 from the Ala Moana Shopping Center or drive to the intersection of Diamond Head Road and 18th Avenue. Follow the road through the tunnel (which is closed 6pm–6am) and park in the lot. The trail head starts in the parking lot and proceeds along a paved walkway (with handrails) as it climbs up the slope. You'll pass old World War I and II pillboxes, gun emplacements, and tunnels built as part of the Pacific defense network. Several steps take you up to the top observation post on Point Leahi. The views are indescribable.

If you want to go with a guide, the **Clean Air Team** leads a guided hike to the top of Diamond Head the first Saturday of every month. The group gathers at 9am, near the front entrance to the Honolulu Zoo (look for the Mahatma Gandhi statue). Hikers should bring a flashlight and cash to pay Clean Air's $10 fee. Each person will be given a bag and asked to help keep the trail clean by picking up litter. For more information, call ✆ **808/948-3299.**

KANEALOLE TRAIL

This is the starting place for some of Oahu's best hiking trails; miles of trails converge through the Makiki Valley–Tantalus–Round Top–Nuuanu Valley area. To get a general feel for the hikes in the region, take the Kanealole 1.5-mile round-trip moderate hike, which climbs some 500 feet and takes less than an hour. If you're interested, stop at the **Hawaii Nature Center,** by the trail head at 2131 Makiki Heights Dr. (✆ **808/955-0100;** www.hawaiinaturecenter.org; Mon–Fri, 8am–4:30pm), where you can find information on the environmental and conservation needs of Hawaii, displays of plants and animals, hands-on exhibits, and numerous maps and pamphlets about this hiking area. They also sponsor organized hikes on weekends.

To get here, take McCully Avenue north out of Waikiki; cross over the H-1 Freeway and turn left on Wilder Avenue. Make a right turn on Makiki Street and continue until the road forks at the park. Take the left fork past the Makiki Pumping Station; the road is now called Makiki Heights Drive. Follow it up to the hairpin turn and make a right onto the small spur road that goes into Makiki Valley; park just beyond the green trailers that house the Hawaii Nature Center. If you are taking TheBus, it's a little trickier: From Waikiki, take TheBus no. E8, 19, 20, 23, 24, or 42 to the Ala Moana Shopping Center and transfer to TheBus no. 17. Tell your driver where you're going, and he'll let you off near the spur road just off Makiki Heights Drive; you'll have to walk the rest of the way.

After stopping at the Hawaii Nature Center, continue up the path, which wanders beneath the protection of kukui trees and lush vines. The path gets smaller and smaller until it's just a footpath. Along this narrow path, look for the tall, bushy, grasslike plant called Job's tears. It's considered a weed in Hawaii, but this is no ordinary grass; it can grow up to 5 feet high and produces a gray, tear-shaped seed. The trail continues through an abandoned valley where there once was a thriving Hawaiian community. Occasionally, you'll spot the remains of stone walls and even a few coffee plants—Makiki Valley supported a coffee plantation in the 19th century. When you meet the Makiki Valley Trail, you can retrace your steps or choose from the dozens of trails in the area.

MAKIKI-MANOA CLIFFS ★★

From rainforests to ridge-top views, this somewhat strenuous loop trail is one you'll never forget. The hike is just over 6 miles, gains 1,260 feet in elevation, and takes about 3 hours. To get to the trail—part of a labyrinth of trails—follow the directions for the Kanealole Trail (see above).

The trail starts by the restrooms of the Hawaii Nature Center. Look for the paved path that crosses Kanealole Stream via a footbridge (Maunalaha Trail). Stay on the trail, following it up the hill into the forest, where you'll pass bananas, Norfolk and Cook Island pines, ti (pronounced *tea*) plants, and even a few taro patches. Cross over Moleka Stream and look for the four-way junction with the Makiki Valley and Ualakaa trails; turn right on the **Makiki Valley Trail.** This takes you through a dense forest, past a giant banyan tree, and then joins the Moleka Trail. Turn left on the **Moleka Trail**—now you're in the rainforest: Ancient guava trees reach overhead, maidenhair ferns cling to rocks, and tiny, white-flowered begonias crop up.

Further on, the kukui and koa give way to a bamboo-filled forest, which opens up to a parking lot on Round Top Drive at the end of the Moleka Trail. Cross Round Top Drive to the **Manoa Cliffs Trail,** which emerges on Tantalus Drive. Turn right on Tantalus and walk about 100 yards down the street to the **Nahuina Trail** on the left side of Tantalus. As you walk downhill, you'll have breathtaking views of downtown Honolulu. At the junction of Kanealole Trail, turn right and continue back to where you started.

Outdoor Etiquette

Carry out what you carry in. Find a trash can for all your litter (including cigarette butts—it's very bad form to throw them out your car window). Observe *kapu* (forbidden) and no trespassing signs. And don't climb on ancient Hawaiian *heiau* walls or carry home rocks, all of which belong to the Hawaiian volcano goddess Pele. Some say it's just a silly superstition or coincidence, but each year the U.S. Park Service gets boxes of lava rocks sent back to Hawaii by visitors who've experienced unusually bad luck.

176

MANOA FALLS TRAIL ★★

In the misty sunbeams, colorful birds flit among giant ferns and hanging vines, while towering tropical trees form a thick canopy that shelters all below in cool shadows. This emerald world is a true Eden—and an easy walk. The .75-mile (one-way) hike is terrific for families; it takes less than an hour to reach idyllic Manoa Falls. The trail head, marked by a footbridge, is at the end of Manoa Road, past Lyon Arboretum. The staff at the arboretum prefers that hikers do not park in their lot, so the best place to park is in the residential area below Paradise Park; you can also get to the arboretum via TheBus no. 5. The often-muddy trail follows Waihi Stream and meanders through the forest reserve past guavas, mountain apples, and wild ginger. The forest is moist and humid and is inhabited by giant bloodthirsty mosquitoes, so bring repellent. If it has rained recently, stay on the trail and step carefully, as it can be very slippery (and it's a long way down if you slide off the side). As we went to press, the state of Hawaii was still assessing the safety of the trail after a series of landslides. Before you venture out, call ✆ 808/587-0166 to check if the trail is open.

PUU OHIA TRAIL TO NUUANU VALLEY VIEW ★

This moderate hike takes you through a rainforest, up to the top of Tantalus (Puu Ohia) cinder cone, and down through Pauoa Flats to view Nuuanu Valley. Plan about 2 hours for this 3.5-mile round-trip hike, which gains about 1,200 feet in altitude.

To get there, follow the directions for the Kanealole Trail, above, but turn to the right at the park fork in Makiki Street. The fork to the right is Round Top Drive. Drive to the top and park in the turnout on the ocean side of the street. Unfortunately, bus service is not available.

The Puu Ohia trail head is across the street from where you parked. As you head up (a series of switchbacks and, at the steepest part, hand-cut stairs in the dirt), you'll pass night-blooming jasmine, ginger, Christmas berry, and avocado trees. After dense guava trees and bamboo, the vegetation parts for a magnificent view of Honolulu and Diamond Head. Just as quickly, as you continue along the trail, the bamboo once again obstructs the view. At the next junction, stay on the main trail by bearing to the left; you'll pass through ginger, koa, and bamboo. At the next junction, bear left again, and climb up the steps around the trunk of an old koa tree. At the top is a paved road; turn right and walk downhill. The road leads to an old telephone relay station and then turns into a footpath. You'll pass through bamboo, koa, ti, and strawberry guava, and turn left onto the Manoa Cliffs Trail. At the next junction, turn right on the Puu Ohia Trail, which leads to Pauoa Flats and the view of the Nuuanu Valley. Retrace your steps for your return.

The serene view from Puu Ohia Trail.

UALAKAA LOOP ★

The same series of volcanic eruptions that produced Diamond Head and Koko Crater also produced the cinder cones of Round Top (Puu Ualakaa), Sugarloaf (Puu Kakea), and Tantalus (Puu Ohia). *Puu,* as you may have already guessed, means "hill"; these three hills overlook Honolulu and offer spectacular views. The easy Ualakaa Loop Trail is a half-hour hike of about a mile that traverses through woods, offering occasional panoramic views of Honolulu.

No bus serves this trail head. Follow the directions for the Puu Ohia hike, above, but instead of driving to the top of Round Top Drive, turn off on the fourth major hairpin turn (look for it after a long stretch of panoramic straightaway). The turn will go through the gate of **Puu Ualakaa State Wayside Park.** Continue a little more than 4 miles inside the park; look for a stand of Norfolk pine trees and park there. The trail head is on the right side of the Norfolk pines. The park is open 7am to 7:45pm from April 1 to Labor Day; in winter, the park closes at 6:45pm.

The loop trail, lined with impatiens, passes through Norfolk pines, palm trees, ironwoods, and Christmas berry trees. The once-native forest now has many foreign intrusions—including all of the foregoing—as well as ti, banana, banyan, guava, and mountain apple. At two points along the trail, you emerge on Round Top Drive; just walk about 100 feet to continue on the trail on the opposite side of the road. The loop will bring you back to where you started.

Pearl City Hikes
UPPER WAIMANO TRAIL

This is a strenuous, 14-mile round-trip with an altitude gain of nearly 2,000 feet. The rewards are worth the effort: magnificent views from the top of windward Oahu's Koolau Mountains and a chance to see rare native Hawaiian plants. Plan a full day for this 8-hour hike.

To get here from Waikiki, take H-1 to the Pearl City exit (exit 10) on Moanalua Road; head north and turn right on Waimano Home Road; follow it to the end, just over 22 miles. Park on the road. Or take TheBus no. E8, 19, 20, 23, 24, or 32 from Waikiki to the Ala Moana Shopping Center and transfer to TheBus no. 53. Tell your driver where you are going, and he will take you as far as he can on Waimano Home Road; you'll have to walk the rest of the way to the trail head (about 1½ miles).

You'll pick up the trail head at the dirt path to the left of the gate, outside the fence surrounding the Waimano

The famous and precarious Makapuu Lighthouse.

Home. Follow the trail through swamp mahogany trees to the first junction; turn right at the junction to stay on the upper Waimano Trail. At the second junction, turn right again to stay on the upper trail. Cross the streambed and climb the switchbacks on the eucalyptus-covered ridge. The trail ends on the sometimes rainy—and nearly always windy—peak of the Koolaus, where you'll have views of Waihee Valley and the entire windward side from Kahaluu to Kaneohe Bay. It's very clear that this is the end of the trail; retrace your steps to the trail head.

East Oahu Hikes
MAKAPUU LIGHTHOUSE TRAIL ★

You've seen this famous old lighthouse on episodes of *Magnum, P.I.* and *Hawaii Five-O*. No longer manned by the Coast Guard (it's fully automated now), the lighthouse is the goal of hikers who risk a precipitous cliff trail to gain an airy perch over the Windward Coast, Manana (Rabbit) Island, and the azure Pacific. It's about a 45-minute, mile-long hike from Kalanianaole Highway (Hwy. 72), along a paved road that begins across from Hawaii Kai Executive Golf Course and winds around the 646-foot-high sea bluff to the lighthouse lookout.

To get to the trail head from Waikiki, take Kalanianaole Highway (Hwy. 72) past Hanauma Bay and Sandy Beach to Makapuu Head, the southeastern tip of the island; you can also take TheBus no. 57. Look for a sign that says NO VEHICLES ALLOWED on a gate to the right, a few hundred yards past the entrance to the golf course. The trail isn't marked, but it's fairly obvious: Just follow the abandoned road that leads gradually uphill to a trail that wraps around Makapuu Point. It's a little precarious, but anyone in reasonably good shape can handle it.

Tip: When the south swell is running, usually in summer, a couple of blow-holes on the south side of Makapuu Head put the famous Halona blowhole to shame.

Windward Oahu Hikes
HAUULA LOOP ★

For one of the best views of the coast and the ocean, follow the Hauula Loop Trail on the windward side of the island. It's an easy, 2.5-mile loop on a well-maintained path that passes through a whispering ironwood forest and a grove of tall Norfolk pines. The trip takes about 3 hours and gains some 600 feet in elevation.

To get to the trail, take TheBus no. 55 or follow Highway 83 to Hauula Beach Park. Turn toward the mountains on Hauula Homestead Road; when it forks to the left at Maakua Road, park on the side of the road. Walk along Maakua Road to the wide, grassy trail that begins the hike into the mountains. The climb is fairly steep for about 300 yards but continues to easier-on-the-calves switchbacks as you go up the ridge. Look where you are stepping as you climb: You'll spot wildflowers and mushrooms among the matted needles. The trail continues up, crossing Waipilopilo Gulch, full of several forms of native plant life. Eventually, you reach the top of the ridge, where the views are spectacular.

Camping is permitted along the trail, but it's difficult to find a place to pitch a tent on the steep slopes or in the dense forest growth. A few places along the ridge, however, are wide enough for a tent. Contact the **Division of Forestry and Wildlife,** 1151 Punchbowl St., Honolulu, HI 96813 (www.dofaw. net; ✆ 808/587-0166), for information on camping permits.

Waimea Valley hides the secluded Waimea Falls.

KAHANA VALLEY

Spectacular views of this verdant valley and some clear swimming holes are the rewards of this 4.5-mile-loop trail. The downsides to this 2- to 3-hour, somewhat ardent adventure are mosquitoes (clouds of them) and some thrashing about in dense forest with a bit of navigation along the not-always-marked trail.

The trail starts behind the Visitor's Center at Kahana Valley State Park. To get there, take H-1 to the Pali Highway over to the windward side of Kailua-Kaneohe. Turn left onto Highway 83 (Kamehameha Hwy.) to Kahana Valley State Park. You can also take TheBus no. 55 and get off at the park entrance. Check in at the Visitor's Center for the latest trail conditions, warnings about stream flooding, and directions for the trail.

PALI (MAUNAWILI) TRAIL ★

For a million-dollar view of the Windward Coast, take this easy 11-mile (one-way) foothill trail. The trail head is about 6 miles from downtown Honolulu, on the windward side of the Nuuanu Pali Tunnel, at the scenic lookout just beyond the hairpin turn of the Pali Highway (Hwy. 61). Just as you begin the turn, look for the scenic overlook sign, slow down, and pull off the highway into the parking lot (sorry, no bus service available).

The mostly flat, well-marked, easy-to-moderate trail goes through the forest on the lower slopes of the 3,000-foot Koolau Mountain range and ends up in the backyard of the coastal Hawaiian village of Waimanalo. Go halfway to get the view and return to your car, or have someone meet you in 'Nalo.

North Shore Hikes

WAIMEA VALLEY

For nearly 3 decades, the 1,875-acre Waimea Valley park has lured visitors with activities from cliff diving and hula performances to kayaking and ATV tours. In 2008, the Office of Hawaiian Affairs took over and formed a new nonprofit corporation, **Hiipaka,** 59-864 Kamehameha Hwy., Haleiwa (✆ **808/638-7766;** www.waimeavalley.net), to run the park. Take TheBus no. 52. Admission is $13 for adults, $6 for seniors and children 4 to 12. Open daily 9am to 5pm. The current emphasis is now on perpetuating and sharing the "living Hawaiian culture." A visit here offers a lush walk into the past. The valley is packed with archaeological sites, including the 600-year-old Hale O Lono, a *heiau* dedicated to the Hawaiian god Lono, which you'll find to the left of the entrance. The botanical collection has 35 different gardens, including super-rare Hawaiian species such as the endangered *Kokia cookei* hibiscus. The valley is also home to fauna such as the endangered Hawaiian moorhen; look for a black bird with a red face cruising in the ponds. The 150-acre Arboretum and Botanical Garden contains more than 5,000 species of tropical plants. Walk through the gardens (take the paved paths or dirt trails) and wind up at 45-foot-high Waimea Falls—bring your bathing suit and you can dive into the cold, murky water. The public is invited to hike the trails and spend a day in this quiet oasis. There are several free cultural activities such as lei making, kappa demonstrations, hula lessons, Hawaiian games and crafts, music, and story telling.

Leeward Oahu Hikes

KAENA POINT ★

At the very western tip of Oahu lie the dry, barren lands of Kaena Point State Park: 853 acres consisting of a remote, wild coastline of jagged sea cliffs, deep gulches, sand dunes, endangered plant life, and a wind- and surf-battered coastline. *Kaena* means "red-hot" or "glowing" in Hawaiian; the name refers to the brilliant sunsets visible from the point.

Kaena is steeped in numerous legends. A popular one concerns the demigod Maui: Maui had a famous hook that he used to raise islands from the sea. He decided that he wanted to bring the islands of Oahu and Kauai closer together, so one day he threw his hook across the Kauai Channel and snagged Kauai (which

Kaena Point jutts into the Pacific.

is actually visible from Kaena Point on clear days). Using all his might, Maui was able to pull loose a huge boulder, which fell into the waters very close to the present lighthouse at Kaena. The rock is still called Pohaku o Kauai (the "Rock from Kauai"). Like Black Rock in Kaanapali on Maui, Kaena is thought of as the point on Oahu from which souls depart.

To hike out to the departing place, take the clearly marked trail from the parking lot of Kaena Point State Park. The moderate 5-mile round-trip to the point will take a couple of hours. The trail along the cliff passes tide pools abundant in marine life and rugged protrusions of lava reaching out to the turbulent sea; seabirds circle overhead. There are no sandy beaches, and the water is nearly always turbulent. In winter, when a big north swell is running, the waves at Kaena are the biggest in the state, averaging heights of 30 to 50 feet, rivaled only by Waimea Bay. Even when the water appears calm, offshore currents are powerful, so don't plan to swim. Go early in the morning to see the schools of porpoises that frequent the area just offshore.

To get to the trail head from Honolulu or Waikiki, take the H-1 west to its end; continue on Highway 93 past Makaha and follow Highway 930 to the end of the road. No bus service runs here.

GOLF

It *is* possible to play top-notch golf in Hawaii without having to take out a second mortgage on your home. Oahu has nearly three dozen golf courses, ranging from bare-bones municipal courses to exclusive country clubs with six-figure annual membership fees. Golfers unfamiliar with Hawaii's courses will be dazzled by some of the spectacular views, from shimmering ocean to majestic mountains.

Golfers will also come to know that the windward golf courses play much differently than the leeward courses. On the windward side, the prevailing winds blow from the ocean to the shore, and the grain direction of the greens tends to run the same way—from the ocean to the mountains. Leeward golf courses have the opposite tendency; the winds usually blow from the mountains to the ocean, and the grain direction on the greens matches. Below are a variety of courses, with greens fees (cart costs included) and notes on scenic views, challenges, and a taste of what golfing in paradise is like.

For last-minute and discount tee times, call **Stand-by Golf** (© **888/645-BOOK** [645-2665]; www.hawaiistandbygolf.com), which offers discounted and guaranteed tee times for same-day or next-day golfing. You can call from 7am to 2:30pm and 6 to 10pm Hawaii Standard Time to book one of the seven semiprivate and resort courses they handle and get a guaranteed tee time for the next day at up to a 30% discount.

TheBus does not allow golf bags onboard. If you don't have another means of transportation, you're going to have to rent clubs at the course.

Avoiding the Crowds & Saving Money

Oahu's golf courses tend to be crowded, so we suggest that you go during mid-week. Also, most island courses have twilight rates with substantial discounts if you're willing to tee off in the afternoon, usually between 1 and 3pm. Look for this feature in the golf listings that follow.

Waikiki

Ala Wai Municipal Golf Course *Guinness World Records* lists Ala Wai as the busiest golf course in the world; some 500 rounds a day are played on the 18-hole municipal course within walking distance of Waikiki's hotels. For years, we've held off recommending this par-70, 6,020-yard course because it was so busy (the tee times taken by local retirees), but a scandal involving telephone company employees tapping into the tee-time reservation system to get tee times for themselves and their friends has shaken up the old system, and visitors now have a better chance of playing here. It still is a challenge to get a tee time, and the computerized tee reservations system for all of Oahu's municipal courses will allow you to book only 3 days in advance, but keep trying. Ala Wai basically is a flat layout, bordered by the Ala Wai Canal on one side and the Manoa-Palolo Stream on the other. It's less windy than most Oahu courses, but pay attention to the 372-yard, par-4 1st hole, which demands a straight and long shot to the very tiny green. If you miss, you can make it up on the 478-yard, par-5 10th hole—the green is reachable in two, so with a two-putt, a birdie is within reach.

404 Kapahulu Ave., Waikiki. ☎ **808/733-7387** (golf course) or 808/296-2000 tee-time reservations. www.co.honolulu.hi.us/des/golf/alawai.htm. Greens fees: $46; twilight half-price; cart $20. From Waikiki turn left on Kapahulu Ave.; the course is on the *mauka* side of Ala Wai Canal. Bus: 13, 19, 20, or 22.

East Oahu

Hawaii Kai Golf Course This is actually two golf courses in one. The par-72, 6,222-yard **Hawaii Kai Championship Golf Course** is moderately challenging, with scenic vistas. The course is forgiving to high-handicap golfers, although it does have a few surprises. The par-3 **Hawaii Kai Executive Golf Course** is fun for beginners and those just getting back in the game after a few years. The course has lots of hills and valleys, with no water hazards and only a few sand traps. Lockers are available.

8902 Kalanianaole Hwy., Honolulu. ☎ **808/395-2358.** www.hawaiikaigolf.com. Greens fees: Championship Course $100 Mon–Fri, $110 Sat–Sun, twilight rates $70; Executive Course $39 Mon–Fri, $44 Sat–Sun. Take H-1 east past Hawaii Kai; it's immediately past Sandy Beach on the left. Bus: 23.

The Windward Coast

Olomana Golf Links Low-handicap golfers may not find this gorgeous course difficult, but the striking views of the craggy Koolau mountain ridge are worth the fees alone. The par-72, 6,326-yard course is popular with locals and visitors alike. It starts off a bit hilly on the front 9, but flattens out by the back 9. The back 9 have their own surprises, including tricky water hazards. The 1st hole, a 384-yard, par-4 that tees downhill and approaches uphill, is definitely a warmup. The next hole is a 160-yard, par-3 that starts from an elevated tee to an elevated green over a severely banked, V-shaped gully. Shoot long here—it's longer than you think—as short shots tend to roll all the way back down the fairway to the base of the gully. This course is very, very green; the rain gods bless it regularly with brief passing showers. You can spot the regular players here—they all carry umbrellas, wait patiently for the squalls to pass, and then resume play. Reservations are a must. Facilities include a driving range, practice greens, club rental, pro shop, and restaurant.

41-1801 Kalanianaole Hwy., Waimanalo. ☎ **808/259-7926.** www.olomanagolflinks.com. Greens fees: $95, second round $65; twilight fees $80. Take H-1 to the Pali Hwy. (Hwy. 61); turn right on Kalanianaole Hwy.; after 5 miles, it will be on the left. Bus: 57.

Pali Golf Course 🏌 This beautiful municipal course sits near Kaneohe, just below the historic spot where King Kamehameha the Great won the battle that united the islands of Hawaii. The par-72, 6,494-yard course, designed by Willard G. Wilkinson and built in 1953, makes use of the natural terrain (hills and valleys make up the majority of the 250 acres). The course does not have man-made traps, but a small stream meanders through it. If you're off-line on the 9th, you'll get to know the stream quite well. The challenge here is the weather—whipping winds and frequent rain squalls. Because of the potential for rain, you might want to pay for 9 holes and then assess the weather before signing up for the back 9. The views include Kaneohe Bay, the towns of Kailua and Kaneohe, and the verdant cliffs of the Koolau Mountains. Facilities include practice greens, club rental, locker rooms, and a restaurant.

45-050 Kamehameha Hwy., Kaneohe, HI 96744. ☎ **808/296-2000.** www.co.honolulu.hi.us/ des/golf/pali.htm. Greens fees: $46 ($20 extra for an optional cart, which carries 2 golfers); $23 twilight fees after 4pm (walking only, no carts). From Waikiki, take the H-1 freeway to the Pali Hwy. (Hwy. 61). Turn left at Kamehameha Hwy. at the 1st traffic light after going through the Pali Tunnels. The course is immediately on your left after you turn on Kamehameha Hwy. Bus: 85.

The North Shore

Kahuku Golf Course 🎁 This 9-hole budget golf course is a bit funky. There are no club rentals, no clubhouse, and no facilities other than a few pull carts that disappear with the first handful of golfers. But a round at this scenic oceanside

The stunning seaside Arnold Palmer Course at Turtle Bay.

course amid the tranquility of the North Shore is quite an experience nonetheless. Duffers will love the ease of the recreational course, and weight watchers will be happy to walk the gently sloping greens. Don't forget to bring your camera for the views (especially at holes 3, 4, 7, and 8, which are right on the ocean). No reservations are taken; tee times are first-come, first-served—with plenty of retirees happy to sit and wait, the competition is fierce for early tee times. Bring your own clubs and call ahead to check the weather. The cost for this experience? Twenty-four bucks!

56-501 Kamehameha Hwy., Kahuku. © **808/293-5842.** www.co.honolulu.hi.us/des/golf/kahuku. htm. Greens fees: $24. Take H-1 west to H-2; follow H-2 through Wahiawa to Kamehameha Hwy. (Hwy. 99, then Hwy. 83); follow it to Kahuku.

Turtle Bay Resort ★ This North Shore resort is home to two of Hawaii's top golf courses. The 18-hole **Arnold Palmer Course** (formerly the Links at Kuilima) was designed by golf legend Arnold Palmer and Ed Seay. Turtle Bay used to be labeled a "wind tunnel"; it still is one, though the *casuarina* (ironwood) trees have matured and dampened the wind somewhat. But Palmer and Seay never meant for golfers to get off too easy; this is a challenging course. The front 9, with rolling terrain, only a few trees, and lots of wind, play like a British Isles course. The back 9 have narrower, tree-lined fairways and water. The course circles Punahoolapa Marsh, a protected wetland for endangered Hawaiian waterfowl.

Another option is the **George Fazio Course**—the only one Fazio designed in Hawaii—a par-71, 6,200-yard course. Larry Keil, a pro at Turtle Bay, says that people like the Fazio course because it's more of a forgiving resort course, without the water hazards and bunkers of the more challenging Palmer course. The 6th hole has two greens, so you can play the hole as a par-3 or a par-4. The toughest hole has to be the par-3, 176-yard 2nd hole, where you tee off across a lake with the trade winds creating a mean crosswind. The most scenic hole is the 7th, where the ocean is on your left; if you're lucky, you'll see whales cavorting in the winter months. Facilities include a pro shop, driving range, putting and chipping green, and snack bar. Weekdays are best for tee times.

57-049 Kamehameha Hwy., Kahuku. © **808/293-8574** or 808/293-9094. www.turtlebay resort.com. Greens fees: Palmer Course $175; Fazio Course $175; $110 twilight. Take H-1 west past Pearl City; when the freeway splits, take H-2 and follow the signs to Haleiwa; at Haleiwa, take Hwy. 83 to Turtle Bay Resort. Bus: 52 or 55.

Leeward Oahu: The Waianae Coast

Ko Olina Golf Club ★★★ The Ted Robinson–designed 6,867-yard, par-72 Ko Olina course has rolling fairways and elevated tee and water features. The signature hole—the 12th, a par-3—has an elevated tee that sits on a rock garden with a cascading waterfall. Wait until you get to the 18th hole, where you'll see and hear water all around you—seven pools begin on the right side of the fairway and slope down to a lake. A waterfall is on your left off the elevated green. You'll have no choice but to play the left and approach the green over the water. Book in advance; this course is crowded all the time. Facilities include a driving range, locker rooms, Jacuzzi, steam rooms, and restaurant and bar. Lessons are available.

92-1220 Aliinui Dr., Kapolei. © **808/676-5300.** www.koolinagolf.com. Greens fees: $179 ($159 for Ihilani Resort guests); noon rates $149 ($129 for guests); twilight rates (after 2pm) $109 ($99 for resort guests). Ask about transportation package from Waikiki hotels. Collared shirts requested for men and women. Take H-1 west until it becomes Hwy. 93 (Farrington Hwy.); turn off at the Ko Olina exit; take the exit road (Aliinui Dr.) into Ko Olina Resort; turn left into the clubhouse. No bus service.

Makaha Resort Golf Club ★★ This challenging course—once named "The Best Golf Course on Oahu" by *Honolulu* magazine—sits some 45 miles west of Honolulu, in Makaha Valley. Designed by William Bell, the par-72, 7,091-yard course meanders toward the ocean before turning and heading into the valley. Sheer volcanic walls tower 1,500 feet above the course, which is surrounded by swaying palm trees and neon-bright bougainvillea; an occasional peacock will even strut across the fairways. The beauty here could make it difficult to keep your mind on the game if it weren't for the course's many challenges: 8 water hazards, 107 bunkers, and frequent brisk winds. This course is packed on weekends, so it's best to try weekdays. Facilities include a pro shop, bag storage, and snack shop.

84-627 Makaha Valley Rd., Waianae. ✆ **808/695-9544.** www.makaharesort.net. Greens fees: $160; twilight $95 (check for specials) Take H-1 west until it turns into Hwy. 93, which winds through the coastal towns of Nanakuli, Waianae, and Makaha. Turn right on Makaha Valley Rd. and follow it to the fork; the course is on the left. Buses: 13 to C to PH1.

West Loch Municipal Golf Course ⚑ This par-72, 6,615-yard course just 30 minutes from Waikiki, in Ewa Beach, offers golfers a challenge at bargain rates. The difficulties on this municipal course are water (lots of hazards), wind (constant trade winds), and narrow fairways. To help you out, the course features a "water" driving range (with a lake) to practice your stroke. After a few practice swings on the driving range, you'll be ready to take on this unusual course, designed by Robin Nelson and Rodney Wright. In addition to the driving range, West Loch has practice greens, a pro shop, and a restaurant.

91-1126 Okupe St., Ewa Beach. ✆ **808/675-6076.** www.co.honolulu.hi.us/des/golf/westloch. htm. Greens fees: $46; twilight rates (after 1pm) $23; cart $20. Book 3 days in advance. Take H-1 west to the Hwy. 76 exit; stay in the left lane and turn left at West Loch Estates, just opposite St. Francis Medical Center. To park, take 2 immediate right turns. Bus: 42 or 44.

Central Oahu

Hawaii Country Club This public course in Wahiawa is a modest course where golfers usually have no trouble getting a tee time. The 5,861-yard, par-71 course is not manicured like the resort courses, but it does offer fair play, with relatively inexpensive greens fees. Located in the middle of former sugar cane and pineapple fields, the greens and fairways tend to be a bit bumpy and you have to shoot around a number of tall monkeypod and pine trees, but the views of Pearl Harbor and Waikiki in the distance are spectacular. A few holes are challenging, such as the 7th (a 252-yard, par-4), which has a lake in the middle of the fairway and slim pickings on either side. With the wind usually blowing in your face, most golfers choose an iron to lay up short of the water and then pitch it over for par. Facilities include a driving range, practice greens, a club rental pro shop, and a restaurant.

98-1211 Kunia Rd., Wahiawa, HI 96786. ✆ **808/621-5654.** www.hawaiicc.com. Greens fees: $65 Mon–Fri; $75 Sat–Sun (cart included); book on the Internet for rates at $55 Mon–Fri and $65 Sat–Sun. From Waikiki, take the H-1 freeway west for about 20 min. Turn off at the Kunia exit (exit 5B) and follow it to the course. No bus service.

Mililani Golf Club This par-72, 6,455-yard public course is home to the Sports Shinko Rainbow Open, where Hawaii's top professionals compete. Located between the Koolau and Waianae mountain ranges on the Leilehua Plateau, this is one of Oahu's most scenic courses, with views of mountains from every hole. Unfortunately, due to lots of foliage— especially of eucalyptus, Norfolk pine, and coconut palm—it's a lesson in patience to stay on the fairways and away from the trees. The two signature holes, the par-4 number 4 (a classic middle hole with water, flowers, and bunkers) and the par-3 number 12 (a comfortable tee shot over a ravine filled with tropical flowers that jumps

Pearl Country Club's good looks are tempered by its difficulty.

to the undulating green with bunkers on each side) are so scenic, you'll forgive the challenges they pose.

95-176 Kuahelani Ave., Mililani. © **808/623-2222.** www.mililanigolf.com. Greens fees: $99; twilight $75. Take H-1 west past Pearl City; when the freeway splits, take H-2. Exit at Mililani (exit 5B) onto Meheula Pkwy.; go to the 3rd stoplight (about 2 miles from the exit) and turn right onto Kuahelani Ave. Bus: B to 52 or 13 to 84.

Pearl Country Club Looking for a challenge? You'll find one at this popular public course, just above Pearl City in Aiea. Sure, the 6,230-yard, par-72 looks harmless enough, and the views of Pearl Harbor and the USS *Arizona* Memorial are gorgeous, but around the 5th hole, you'll start to see what you're in for. That par-5, a blind 472-yard hole, doglegs seriously to the left (with a small margin of error between the tee and the steep out-of-bounds hillside on the entire left side of the fairway). A water hazard and a forest await your next two shots. Suddenly, this nice public course becomes not so nice. Oahu residents can't get enough of it, so don't even try to get a tee time on weekends. Stick to weekdays—Mondays are usually the best bet. Facilities include a driving range, practice greens, club rental, a pro shop, and a restaurant.

98-535 Kaonohi St., Aiea. © **808/487-3802.** www.pearlcc.com. Greens fees: $110 Mon–Fri; $120 Sat–Sun; after 4pm 9 holes are $45. Book at least a week in advance. Take H-1 past Pearl Harbor to the Hwy. 78 (Moanalua Fwy.), exit 13A; stay in the left lane where Hwy. 78 becomes Hwy. 99 (Kamehameha Hwy.); turn right on Kaonohi St., entry on the right. Buses: 8 to 53 to 71 (stops at Pearlridge Shopping Center at Kaonohi and Moanalua sts.; you'll have to walk about ½ mile uphill from here).

OTHER OUTDOOR ACTIVITIES
Bicycling

Bicycling is a great way to see Oahu. Most streets here have bike lanes. For information on biking trails, races, and tours, check out **www.honolulu.gov/dts/ bikepage.htm**. For information on bikeways and maps, contact the **Honolulu**

Every bike ride is stunning on Oahu.

City and County Bike Coordinator (℃ 808/768-8335; csayers@honolulu.gov).

If you're in Waikiki, you can rent a bike for as little as $10 for a half-day and $20 for 24 hours at **Big Kahuna Rentals,** 407 Seaside Ave. (℃ **888/451-5544** or 808/924-2736; www.bigkahunarentals.com).

For a bike-and-hike adventure, call **Bike Hawaii** (℃ **877/682-7433** or 808/734-4214; www.bikehawaii.com); this company offers a variety of group tours, including the "Rainforest to Reef" adventure, which gives you an overview of Oahu from 1,800 feet above Waikiki. The tour includes coasting down 5 miles of paved mountain road with scenic views above Waikiki, Honolulu, and Manoa Valley. Listen to the songs of birds, the wind through the trees, and learn about the culture, plants, and geology of the Hawaiian Islands. After that, leave your bike for a 2-mile round-trip hike to a 200-foot waterfall, followed by a relaxing catamaran sail and swim. The noon-to-5:30pm trip includes van transportation from your hotel, lunch, bike, helmet, snacks, water bottle, and guide ($160 adults, $100 children under 14).

If you'd like to join club rides, contact the **Hawaii Bicycle League** (℃ 808/735-5756; www.hbl.org), which offers rides every weekend, as well as several annual events. The league can also provide a schedule of upcoming rides, races, and outings.

Glider Rides

Imagine soaring through silence on gossamer-like wings, a panoramic view of Oahu below you. A glider ride is an unforgettable experience, and it's available at Dillingham Air Field, in Mokuleia, on Oahu's North Shore. The glider is towed behind a plane; at the proper altitude, the tow is dropped and you (and the glider pilot) are left to soar in the thermals. Three costs are involved in a glider ride: plane rental fee, instructor fee, and towing fee. We recommend Mr. Bill at **Honolulu Soaring** ★ (℃ 808/637-0207; www.honolulusoaring.com); he's been offering piloted glider rides since 1970. Rates start at $79 for 10 minutes for just one passenger (and go up to $215 for 60 min.).

Taking in the view of Kawela Beach, near Turtle Bay, on horseback.

Hang-Gliding

See things from a bird's-eye view (literally) as you and your instructor float high above Oahu on a tandem hang-glider. **Paradise Air Hawaii,** at the Dillingham Air Field (✆ **808/497-6033;** www.paradiseairhawaii.com), offers the opportunity to try out this daredevil sport. A tandem lesson of ground school plus 30 minutes in the air costs $150.

Horseback Riding

You can gallop on the beach at the **Turtle Bay Resort** (p. 115; ✆ **808/293-8811;** www.turtlebayresort.com), where 45-minute rides along sandy beaches with spectacular ocean views and through a forest of ironwood trees cost $65 for ages 7 years and up (they must be at least 4 ft., 4 in. tall). Romantic evening rides are $105 per person. Private rides for up to 4 people are $110 per person. Take TheBus no. 52 or 55.

Skydiving

Everything you need to leap from a plane and float to earth can be obtained from **SkyDive Hawaii,** 68-760 Farrington Hwy., Wahiawa (✆ **808/637-9700;** www.hawaiiskydiving.com). A tandem jump (where you're strapped to an expert who wears a chute big enough for the both of you) costs $225 (check the website for a coupon that gives you $75 off this rate). No doubt about it—this is the thrill of a lifetime. (Although, as SkyDive's website warns, "Skydiving is extremely dangerous.")

Tennis

In Waikiki, the **Waikiki Tennis Club** (**808/206-6735;** www.thewaikikitennis club.com) is operated by the USTA out of the Pacific Beach Hotel, 2490 Kalakaua Ave. The club offers private and group lessons and court and equipment rentals to visitors, all on clay courts, a rarity in Oahu. It's open Monday to Saturday 8am to 6pm, and Sunday 9am to 5pm. Private lessons are $75 per hour (plus tax) for

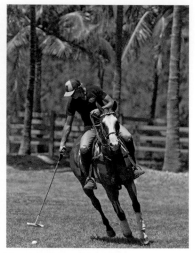

Waikiki Tennis Club's red clay courts.

The sport of kings at Mokuleia.

guests, group lessons are $20 per person (minimum of four people, maximum six), and courts alone are $30 per hour (less if you're a guest of the hotel or member of the club). Reserve in advance on the website.

Free city and county tennis courts on the mauka side of Paki Avenue are also open for play during daylight hours 7 days a week. See p. 227.

If you're on the North Shore, head to the **Turtle Bay Resort** (see above), which has 10 courts, four of which are lit for night play. You must reserve the night courts in advance; they're very popular. Court time is $10 per person per hour (complimentary for guests); equipment rental and lessons are also available.

SPECTATOR SPORTS

Although there aren't any major league sports teams in Hawaii, there are college teams and a handful of professional exposition games—many of them are immensely popular among the local residents. Check the schedule at the 10-story, 50,000-seat **Aloha Stadium,** near Pearl Harbor, 99-500 Salt Lake Blvd. (© **808/486-9300;** www.alohastadium.hawaii.gov), where high school and **University of Hawaii Warriors** (© **808/944-BOWS** [944-2697]; www.uh athletics.hawaii.edu) football games are also held from September to December. Other events at the stadium include: baseball, soccer, boxing, religious and music festivals, auto shows, motorcrosses, mud races, tractor pulls, and various concerts, plus the well-known weekly Aloha Swap Meet. Express buses often run to the stadium on game nights; they depart from Ala Moana Shopping Center (TheBus no. A), or from Monsarrat Avenue near Kapiolani Park (TheBus no. 2 to A or 2 to 11).

The **Neal Blaisdell Center,** at Kapiolani Boulevard and Ward Avenue (© **808/591-2211;** www.blaisdellcenter.com/calendar/index.cfm), features a variety of sporting events, such as professional boxing and Japanese sumo wrestling. In December, the annual **Rainbow Classic,** a collegiate basketball invitational tournament, takes place at the Blaisdell.

At the University of Hawaii, the **Rainbow Stadium,** 1337 Lower Campus Rd., and the **Rainbow Wahine Softball Stadium,** next door, are hosts to college baseball and softball from January through May. Information is available at ✆ **808/944-BOWS** (944-2697) or **www.uhathletics.hawaii.edu**. Collegiate volleyball, which is extremely popular in Hawaii, takes place at the **Stan Sheriff Center,** also on the UH campus, 1355 Lower Campus Rd., November through May. Information is available at the UH phone number and website listed above.

With Hawaii's cowboy history, **polo** is a popular sport, played every Sunday, starting in either April or May and lasting through late August or early September in Mokuleia or Waimanalo. Polo was introduced to Hawaii in 1886, but faded away during World War II. The games were revived in 1950 and moved out to Mokuleia, on the North Shore, in the 1960s. Bring a picnic lunch and enjoy the game. Call ✆ **808/250-0144** or visit **www.hawaii-polo.org** for schedule and admission information.

A sport you might not be familiar with is Hawaiian **outrigger canoe racing** or as residents call it, "paddling"—which is very big locally. If Hawaii were to have an "official" team sport, it would be this. Since the 1970's, Hawaii canoe racing has experienced a resurgence. On weekday evenings and weekend days from February to September, hundreds of paddlers gather at Ala Wai Canal and practice taking traditional Hawaiian canoes out to sea. (Find a comfortable spot at Ala Wai Park next to the canal and watch the canoe paddlers re-create this centuries-old sport.) Plus, every weekend from Memorial Day to Labor Day, canoe races are held around Oahu. Paddlers range from teenagers to grandmas, who turn out every year for the summer-long series of races.

The canoe played a very big part in Hawaii's culture. Not only was it the vehicle that got the Polynesians to Hawaii, but everything from the selection of the tree to carve the canoe to the launch was steeped in religious and cultural activities. When Captain James Cook arrived in Hawaii in 1779, he reported sighting some 1,500 canoes. The canoe races keep this aspect of the Hawaiian culture alive today. The races are free and draw huge crowds. Check the local papers for information on race schedules, or contact the **Oahu Hawaii Canoe Racing Association** (www.ohcra.com).

Some of the other spectator sports scheduled during the year, such as the NFL Pro Bowl, the Rainbow Classic, and major golf and surfing tournaments, are listed in the "Oahu Calendar of Events" on p. 44.

7

EXPLORING OAHU

W hile the rest of the Hawaiian Islands are fairly sleepy, Oahu is loaded with diversions. Honolulu itself is full of sights and activities. You might explore historic Honolulu—from the Queen's summer palace to the USS *Arizona* Memorial in Pearl Harbor. Or wander through exotic gardens, come face-to-face with brilliantly colored tropical fish, stand on the deck of a four-masted schooner that sailed 100 years ago, venture into haunted places where ghosts are said to roam, take in the spicy smells and sights of Chinatown, and participate in a host of cultural activities from flower lei making to hula dancing.

Of course, the moment always arrives—usually after a couple of days at the beach, swimming in the warm, blue-green waters of Waikiki Beach, enjoying sundown mai tais—when a certain curiosity kicks in about the rest of Oahu, largely unknown to most visitors. It's time to find the rental car in the hotel garage and set out around the island. You can also explore Oahu using **TheBus** (p. 278 for details on the transit system).

This chapter covers the sights in both Honolulu and beyond. For complete coverage of Oahu's best beaches and all kinds of outdoor activities, see p. 154.

HONOLULU & WAIKIKI ATTRACTIONS

You don't need a huge budget to experience Honolulu's best activities, and you don't really need a car. TheBus can get you where you need to go for $2, or you can hop on a moderately priced tour or trolley. Your only obstacle to enjoying all the activities here? Trying to fit everything you want to do into your schedule.

Aliiolani Hale Don't be surprised if this place looks familiar; you probably saw it on the old television show *Magnum, P.I.* This gingerbread Italianate building, designed by Australian Thomas Rowe in Renaissance revival style, was built in 1874 and was originally intended to be a palace. Instead, Aliiolani Hale ("chief unto heavens") became the Supreme Court and Parliament government office building. Inside, there's a **Judiciary History Center ★**, which features a multimedia presentation, a restored historic courtroom, and exhibits tracing Hawaii's transition from precontact Hawaiian law to Western law. Allow up to an hour to see it.

417 S. King St. (btw. Mililani and Punchbowl sts.). © **808/539-4999.** Fax 808/539-4996. www.jhchawaii.net. Free admission. Mon–Fri 9am–4pm; reservations for group tours only. Bus: B, 2, or 19. Limited meter parking on street.

FACING PAGE: The USS *Missouri,* bedecked in American flags.

Honolulu Attractions

1 ← Keehi Lagoon Beach Park

Bishop Museum 2

NUUANU

Royal Mausoleum 4

LILIHA

Keehi Lagoon

KALIHI

Kapalama Mil. Res.

Mokauea I.

Kapalama Basin

IWILEI

PAUOA

Nat. Mem. Cemetery of the Pacific

5

Punchbowl Crater 13

U.S. Coast Guard

Honolulu Harbor

7 State Capitol

6

8

9

Sand Island

Maritime Museum

10 11

12

Sand Island State Recreation Area

Sand Island Beach Park

Honolulu Channel

Thomas Sq.

Kakaako Waterfront State Recreation Area

ALA MOANA

Ala Moana Center

Mamala Bay

Ala Moana Beach

Ala Moana Park

Ala Wai Harbor

0 — 1/2 mi
0 — 1/2 km

Aloha Tower One of the reasons that the word *aloha* is synonymous with Hawaii is because of the Aloha Tower. Built in 1926 (for the then-outrageous sum of $160,000), this 184-foot, 10-story tower (until 1959, the tallest structure in Hawaii) has clocks on all four of its sides, with the word *aloha* under each clock. Aloha, which has come to mean both "hello" and "farewell," was the first thing steamship passengers saw when they entered Honolulu Harbor. In the days when tourists arrived by steamer, "boat days" were very big occasions. The Royal Hawaiian band would be on hand to play, crowds would gather, flower leis were freely given, and Honolulu came to a standstill to greet the visitors. Go up the elevator inside the Aloha Tower to the 10th-floor observation deck for a bird's-eye view that encompasses Diamond Head and Waikiki, the downtown and Chinatown areas, and the harbor coastline to the airport. On the ocean side you can see the harbor mouth, Sand Island, the Honolulu reef runway, and the Pearl Harbor entrance channel.

1 Aloha Tower Dr. ✆ **808/535-9377.** Free admission. Daily 9am–5pm. Bus: 2, 13, 19, or 20.

Bishop Museum ★★★ ☺ Even if you do not have kids, this is a must-see on your vacation. It's a great rainy-day diversion; plan to spend at least half a day here. The museum was founded by a Hawaiian princess, Bernice Pauahi, who collected priceless artifacts and, in her will, instructed her husband, Charles Reed Bishop, to establish a Hawaiian museum "to enrich and delight" the people of Hawaii. Not only does this multibuilding museum have the world's greatest collection of natural and cultural artifacts from Hawaii and the Pacific, but recently it has added a terrific new 16,500-square-foot Richard T. Mamiya Science Adventure Center, specializing in volcanology, oceanography, and biodiversity. You'll become a kid again in this interactive, fun environment: Walk down a "Hawaiian origins" tunnel into the deep ocean zone, stopping along the way to play with all the cool, high-tech toys, then explore the interior of a volcano and climb to the top to get a bird's-eye view of an erupting caldera that looks like the real thing.

Sea life on land at the Bishop Museum.

Paul Morrison's *Gamodeme* at the Contemporary Museum.

The Hawaiian Hall, the original cut-stone building (which dates from 1889) just completed a massive $20-millon renovation which updated the 19th-century-type displays with computer technology, installed new lighting and surround sound, and added recorded Hawaiian voices and chants. The renovated first floor tells the story of Hawaii before Westerners arrived. The importance of land and nature to Hawaiians is the focus on the middle level, and the top floor will have changing exhibits that center on issues relating to Hawaii.

Other buildings on the grounds are jampacked with acquisitions—from insect specimens and ceremonial spears to calabashes and old photos of topless hula dancers. A visit here will give you a good basis for understanding Hawaiian life and culture. You'll see the great feathered capes of kings, the last grass shack in Hawaii, pre-industrial Polynesian art, even the skeleton of a 50-foot sperm whale.

Hula performances ★ take place Wednesday through Monday at 2pm. This daily cultural event is worth making time for. Tours include the **Kai Akea,** at 11am, which tells the story of Hawaii in the beginning; the **Ola Na Mo Olelo,** at 1pm, an oral portrayal of the Museum's exhibits; **Plants of Paradise Garden Tour** (10:30am); and **Meet Me at the Hot Spot—Lava Melting Demo** (noon).

That said, given the choice, we would plan our trip around the shows in the planetarium: **The Sky Tonight** (10:30am), **Astronomy of Galileo** (3:30pm), and (our fave) **Explorers of Polynesia** (1:30pm).

1525 Bernice St., just off Kalihi St. (also known as Likelike Hwy.). ✆ **808/847-3511.** www.bishop museum.org. Admission $18 adults, $15 children 4–12 and seniors. Wed–Mon 9am–5pm. Bus: 2.

Contemporary Museum ★ Set on the slopes of Tantalus, one of Honolulu's upscale residential communities, the Contemporary Museum is renowned for its 3 acres of Asian gardens (with reflecting pools, sun-drenched terraces, views of Diamond Head, and stone benches for quiet contemplation). Its Cades Pavilion houses David Hockney's *L'Enfant et les Sortileges,* an environmental installation of his sets and costumes for Ravel's 1925 opera, and six galleries display significant works from the last 4 decades. Equally prominent is the presence of contemporary Hawaiian artists in the museum's programs and exhibitions. Ask about the daily docent-led tours, and look for an excellent cafe and shop. Depending on your passion for art, you could spend an hour to all day here. The Contemporary Museum is owned and run by the Academy of Arts (p. 199), so a single ticket to one or the other will gain you admission to both museums (on the same day).

2411 Makiki Heights Dr. © **808/526-0232.** www.tcmhi.org. Admission $10 adults, $5 seniors and students, free for children 12 and under; free to all 3rd Thurs of each month. Tues–Sat 10am–4pm; Sun noon–4pm. Docent-guided tours 1:30pm daily. Bus: 4 or 2 transfer to 15 to Makiki Heights Dr.

Diamond Head ★★★ ☺ 📷 The 360-degree view from atop Diamond Head Crater is worth the 560-foot ascent and should not be missed. You can see all the way from Koko Crater to Barbers Point and the Waianae Mountains. The 750-foot-tall volcano, which has become the symbol for Hawaii, is about 350,000 years old. The trail to the summit was built in 1910 to service the military installation along the crater; the hike to the top takes about 30 minutes but is quite manageable by anyone of any age. (For additional details, see p. 174.)

Diamond Head has always been considered a "sacred site" by Hawaiians. According to legend, Hi'iaka, the sister to the volcano goddess Pele, named the mountain Leahi (meaning the "brow of the ahi") when she saw the resemblance to the yellowfin tuna (called "ahi" in Hawaiian). Kamehameha the Great built a *luakini heiau* on the top where human sacrifices were made to the god of war, Ku.

The name *Diamond Head* came into use around 1825 when a group of British sailors (some say they were slightly inebriated) found some rocks sparkling in the sun. Absolutely sure they had struck it rich, the sailors brought these "diamonds" back into Honolulu. Alas, the "diamonds" turned out to be calcite crystals. The sailors didn't become fabulously rich, but the name Diamond Head stuck.

Diamond Head Rd. Admission $1 for walk-ins, $5 for cars. Daily 6am–6pm. To get here from Waikiki, take Kalakaua Ave. toward Kapiolani Park. Turn left onto Monsarrat Ave. at the Park.

Diamond Head dwarfs downtown Honolulu.

Monsarrat Ave. becomes Diamond Head Rd. after Campbell Ave. Continue on Diamond Head Rd. to turnoff to crater. Turn right into turnoff, follow to parking lot. Bus: 13, 23, or 24.

Foster Botanical Garden ★★ 🎁 You could spend days in this unique historic garden, a leafy oasis amid the high-rises of downtown Honolulu. Combine a tour of the garden with a trip to Chinatown (just across the street) to maximize your time. The giant trees that tower over the main terrace were planted in the 1850s by William Hillebrand, a German physician and botanist, on royal land leased from Queen Emma. Today the 14-acre public garden is a living museum of plants, some rare and endangered, collected from the tropical regions of the world. Of special interest are 26 "Exceptional Trees" protected by state law, a large palm collection, a primitive cycad garden, and a hybrid orchid collection.

50 N. Vineyard Blvd. (at Nuuanu Ave.). ℂ **808/522-7066.** www.co.honolulu.hi.us/parks/hbg/fbg.htm. Admission $5 adults, $1 children 6–12. Daily 9am–4pm; guided tours Mon–Sat at 1pm (reservations recommended). Bus: B or 13.

Hawaii State Art Museum ★★ Displaying an array of works that reflect a mix of Hawaii's ethnic and cultural traditions, this museum offers a real visual treat. It's housed in the original Royal Hawaiian Hotel built in 1872, during the reign of King Kamehameha V. The works of 284 artists—most of the pieces dating from the 1960s to the present—blend Western art forms with traditional forms. Allow at least an hour to view the current exhibit, which depicts Hawaii, its history, culture, and ideals through a variety of mediums.

250 S. Hotel St. (at Richards St.). ℂ **808/586-0900.** www.state.hi.us/sfca. Free admission. Tues–Sat 10am–4pm, and the First Friday of every month 5–9pm. Bus: E, 2, or 13.

Honolulu Academy of Arts ★★ This acclaimed museum's $28 million Henry R. Luce Pavilion Complex has wowed the state with its exhibition space, courtyard, expanded outdoor cafe, and gift shop (p. 254). The magnificent facility also includes two 4,000-square-foot galleries in addition to the original 30,

Helen Frankenthaler's *Sun Frame* (center), from the Honolulu Academy of Arts' European/American 20th century collection.

as well as the John Dominis and Patches Damon Holt Gallery, which displays the entire Hawaii regional collection in one space. Considered Hawaii's premier example of *kamaaina-* (old-time-) style architecture, the Academy is the state's only general fine-arts museum and boasts one of the top Asian art collections in the country, including James Michener's collection of Hiroshige's *ukiyo-e* (woodblock) prints. Also on exhibit are American and European masters and prehistoric works of Mayan, Greek, and Hawaiian art. The museum's award-winning architecture is a paragon of graciousness, featuring magnificent courtyards, lily ponds, and sensitively designed galleries. Spend a few hours or linger for a day here. The Academy of Arts merged with the Contemporary Museum (p. 197) in 2011, so a single ticket will gain you admission to both museums.

900 S. Beretania St. © **808/532-8700,** or 808/532-8701 for recorded information. www.honoluluacademy.org. Admission $10 adults; $5 students, seniors, and military personnel; free for children under age 12. Free admission on the 1st Wed of the month and 3rd Sun of every month. Tues–Sat 10am–4:30pm; Sun 1–5pm. Bus: B or 2.

Honolulu Zoo ★ ☺ Nobody comes to Hawaii to see an Indian elephant or African lions and zebras. Right? Wrong. This 43-acre municipal zoo in Waikiki attracts visitors in droves. If you've got kids, allot at least half a day. The highlight is the new African Savannah, a 10-acre exhibit with more than 40 African critters roaming around in the open. The zoo also has a rare Hawaiian nene goose, a Hawaiian pig, and mouflon sheep. (Only the goose, an evolved version of the Canadian honker, is considered to be truly Hawaiian; the others are imported from Polynesia, India, and elsewhere.)

For a real treat, take the **Zoo by Twilight Tour ★**, which offers a rare behind-the-scenes look into the lives of the zoo's nocturnal residents. Tours are Friday and Saturday from 5:30 to 7:30pm; the cost is $14 for adults and $10 for children ages 4 to 12 years. Other great family programs include **Snooze in the Zoo,** where kids can discover "who is roaring and who is snoring"—the sleepover includes pizza, tours, and campfire time with s'mores, plus breakfast and a morning stroll ($50 age 4 and up; check website for dates)—and **Star Gazing at the Zoo,** an evening tour of the zoo that also explores the night sky above Hawaii with astronomer Dr. Michael Chauvin ($16 adults, $12 children ages 4–12).

151 Kapahulu Ave. (btw. Paki and Kalakaua aves.), at entrance to Kapiolani Park. © **808/971-7171.** www.honoluluzoo.org. Admission $12 adults, $3 children 6–12, family pass $25. Daily 9am–4:30pm. The Zoo parking lot entrance is on Kapahulu Ave. and charges 25¢ per hour. The Shell parking lot across the street on Monsarrat Ave. has free parking. Bus: 2, 13, or 42.

Iolani Palace ★ If you want to really "understand" Hawaii, Oahu's royal palace is well worth the time. Iolani Palace was built by King David Kalakaua, who spared no expense. The 3-year project, completed in 1882, cost $360,000—and nearly bankrupted the Hawaiian kingdom. This four-story Italian Renaissance palace was the first electrified building in Honolulu (it had electricity before the White House and Buckingham Palace). Royals lived here for 11 years, until Queen Liliuokalani was deposed and the Hawaiian monarchy fell forever, in a palace coup (led by descendants of the original missionaries and American sugar planters), on January 17, 1893.

Cherished by latter-day royalists, the 10-room palace stands as an architectural statement of the monarchy period. Iolani attracts 60,000 visitors a year in groups of 15; everyone must don denim booties to scoot across the royal floors. Tours are either a comprehensive **grand tour ★**, which offers visitors a brief

Soccer with a view at Kapiolani Park.

video about the history of the palace, a docent-guided tour of the inside of the palace, and a self-guided tour of the basement; or an **audio tour** that provides guests with an audio wand for a tour through the first and second floors and concludes with a self-guided tour of the gallery; or a **gallery tour,** a self-guided tour for those with limited time, that includes the palace galleries, complete with crown jewels, the ancient feathered cloaks, the royal china, and more.

364 S. King St. (at Richards St.). ✆ **800/532-1051** or 808/522-0832. www.iolanipalace.org. Grand Tour $20 adults, $5 children 5–12; Audio Tour $13 adults, $6 children 5–12; Gallery Tour (offered Tue–Sat afternoons only) $12 adults, $3 children 5–12. Mon–Sat 9am–5pm. Call ahead to reserve the Grand Tour. Children under 5 not permitted. Extremely limited parking on palace grounds; try metered parking on the street. Bus: 2.

Kapiolani Park ★ ☺ In 1877, King David Kalakaua gave 130 acres of land to the people of Hawaii and named it after his beloved wife, Queen Kapiolani. This truly royal park has something for just about everyone: tennis courts, soccer and rugby fields, archery, picnic areas, wide-open spaces for kite flying and Frisbee throwing, and a jogging path with aerobic exercise stations. On Sundays in the summer, the Royal Hawaiian Band plays in the bandstand, just as they did during Kalakaua's reign. The Waikiki Shell, located in the park, is host to a variety of musical events, from old Hawaiian songs to rock and roll.

Bordered by Kalakaua Ave. on the ocean side, Monsarrat Ave. on the Ewa side, and Paki Ave. on the mountain side. Bus: 2.

Kawaiahao Church ★ In 1842, Kawaiahao Church stood complete at last, the crowning achievement of missionaries and Hawaiians working together for the first time on a common project. Designed by Rev. Hiram Bingham and supervised by Kamehameha III, who ordered his people to help build it, the project took 5 years. Workers quarried 14,000 coral blocks weighing 1,000 pounds each from the offshore reefs and cut timber in the forests for the beams.

This proud stone church, complete with bell tower and colonial colonnade, was the first permanent Western house of worship in the islands. It became the church of the Hawaiian royalty and remains in use today. Some fine portraits of Hawaiian royalty hang inside. We recommend seeing this edifice while **Hawaiian-language services** ★★ (which probably set old Rev. Bingham spinning in his grave) are being conducted, on Sundays at 9am.

957 Punchbowl St. (at King St.), entrance on the side of the church. © **808/522-1333.** www. kawaiahao.org. Free admission (donations appreciated). Mon–Fri 8am–4:30pm; Sun services 9am. Bus: 2.

Lyon Arboretum ★ The Lyon Arboretum dates back to 1918, when the Hawaiian Sugar Planters Association wanted to demonstrate the value of watershed for reforestation. In 1953 it became part of the University of Hawaii, where they continued to expand the extensive collection of tropical plants. Six-story-tall breadfruit trees, yellow orchids no bigger than bus tokens, ferns with fuzzy buds as big as human heads . . . these are just a few of the botanical wonders you'll find on the 194 acres. A whole different world opens up to you along the self-guided 20-minute hike through the arboretum to Inspiration Point. You'll pass more than 5,000 exotic tropical plants full of singing birds in this cultivated rainforest (a University of Hawaii research facility) at the head of Manoa Valley.

3860 Manoa Rd. (near the top of the road). © **808/988-0456.** www.hawaii.edu/lyon arboretum. No admission fee, but donations accepted ($5 is suggested). Mon–Fri 8am–4pm; Sat 9am-3pm. Bus: 2 transfer to 5.

A bromeliad in bloom at the Lyon Arboretum.

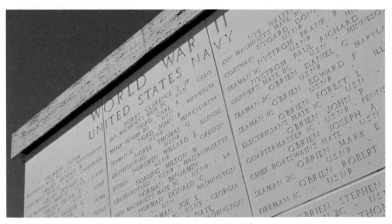

A memorial of fallen soldiers at the National Cemetery of the Pacific.

Mission Houses Museum This museum tells the dramatic story of cultural change in 19th-century Hawaii, when missionaries who landed on the island set about trying to convert the natives. American Protestant missionaries established their headquarters here in 1820. Included in the complex are a visitor center and three historic mission buildings, which have been restored and refurnished to reflect the daily life and work of the missionaries.

553 S. King St. (at Kawaiahao St.). *C* **808/531-0481.** www.missionhouses.org. Admission $10 adults, $8 military personnel and seniors, $6 students (age 6–college), free for children 5 and under. Tues–Sat 10am–4pm. Bus: 2.

National Cemetery of the Pacific The National Cemetery of the Pacific (also known as "the Punchbowl") is an ash-and-lava tuff cone that exploded about 150,000 years ago—like Diamond Head, only smaller. Early Hawaiians called it Puowaina, or "hill of sacrifice." The old crater is a burial ground for 35,000 victims of three American wars in Asia and the Pacific: World War II, Korea, and Vietnam. Among the graves, you'll find many unmarked ones with the date December 7, 1941, carved in stone. Some will be unknown forever; others are famous, like that of war correspondent Ernie Pyle, killed by a Japanese sniper in April 1945 on Okinawa; still others buried here are remembered only by family and surviving buddies. The white stone tablets, known as the Courts of the Missing, bear the names of 28,788 Americans missing in action in World War II.

Survivors come here often to reflect on the meaning of war and to remember those, like themselves, who stood in harm's way to win peace a half-century ago. Some fight back tears, remembering lost comrades, lost missions, and the sacrifices of those who died.

Punchbowl Crater, 2177 Puowaina Dr. (at the end of the road). *C* **808/532-3720.** Free admission. Daily 8am–5:30pm (Mar–Sept to 6:30pm). Bus: 15.

Pacific Aviation Museum Pearl Harbor Opened on the 65th anniversary of the bombing of Pearl Harbor, the first phase of this historical museum (in a 42,442-sq.-ft. hangar) tells the story of military aviation in the Pacific during

Grounded bombers at the Pacific Aviation Museum Pearl Harbor.

World War II via a collection of original, historical aircraft (Japanese Zero fighter, Navy Wildcat fighter, Army Air corps B-25 Michell bomber, and so on), documentary films, displays (the story of the little-known battle of Niihau, where the Hawaiian residents captured a crash-landed Japanese pilot), and (our favorite) the interactive simulated aircraft control where you can "experience" what it was like to fly either an American or Japanese plane. They recently have added an "Aviator's Guided Tour," where trained tour guides take you on a journey into aviation history, with stories about the planes and the battles they saw, plus you get a sneak peak into behind the scenes at the museum with access to parts of the collection not generally seen by the public (like aircraft being restored, a close-up of the F-14 Tomcat, the F-15 Eagle, Bell helicopters, and other vintage aircraft). *Note:* No bags of any kind are allowed on the shuttle bus to Ford Island.

Pearl Harbor Hangar 37, Ford Island, 319 Lexington Blvd. ℭ **808/441-1000.** www.pacific aviationmuseum.org. Tickets $20 adults, $10 children ages 4–12; Aviator's Guided Tour $30 adults, $20 children (ages 4–12); flight simulators $10. Daily 9am–5pm. From Waikiki take H-1 east to the USS *Arizona*/Stadium exit, no. 15A (the 2nd exit after the airport). Continue on H-99 (Kamehameha Hwy.) 1½ miles, at the 4th traffic light, turn left on Kalaloa St and go about 1/10th of a mile. The visitor center will be on your left. Tickets may be purchased at the USS *Bowfin* Ticket Office. Bus: 20 or 42.

Puu Ualakaa State Park ★ 📷 The best **sunset view** of Honolulu is from a 1,048-foot-high hill named for sweet potatoes. (It's more romantic than it sounds.) The poetic Hawaiian name means "rolling sweet potato hill," which is how early planters used gravity to harvest their crop. The panorama is sweeping and majestic. On a clear day—which is almost always—you can see from Diamond Head to the Waianae Range, almost the length of Oahu. At night, several scenic overlooks provide romantic spots for young lovers who like to smooch under the stars with the city lights at their feet. It's a top-of-the-world experience—the view, that is.

At the end of Round Hill Dr. Daily 7am–6:45pm (to 7:45pm in summer). From Waikiki, take Ala Wai Blvd. to McCully St., turn right, and drive mauka (inland) beyond the H-1 on-ramps to Wilder St.; turn left and go to Makiki St.; turn right, and continue onward and upward about 3 miles.

Queen Emma Summer Palace Hanaiakamalama, the name of the country estate of Kamehameha IV and Queen Emma, was once in the secluded uplands of Nuuanu Valley; these days it's adjacent to a six-lane highway full of speeding cars. This simple, seven-room New England–style house, built in 1848 and restored by the Daughters of Hawaii, is worth about an hour of your time to see the interesting blend of Victorian furniture and hallmarks of Hawaiian royalty, including feather cloaks and *kahili,* the feathered standards that mark the presence of *alii* (royalty). Other royal treasures include a canoe-shaped cradle for Queen Emma's baby, Prince Albert, who died at the age of 4. (Kauai's ultraritzy Princeville Resort is named for the little prince.)

2913 Pali Hwy. (at Old Pali Rd.). ℭ **808/595-6291.** www.daughtersofhawaii.org. Admission $6 adults, $1 children 11 and under. Daily 9am–4pm. Bus: 4, 55, 56, 57, or 65.

Royal Mausoleum In the cool uplands of Nuuanu, on a 3.7-acre patch of sacred land dedicated in 1865—and never surrendered to the United States—stands the Royal Mausoleum, the final resting place of King Kalakaua, Queen Kapiolani, and 16 other Hawaiian royals. Only the Hawaiian flag flies over this grave, a remnant of the kingdom. Allow about an hour for your visit.

Relaxing on the veranda of Queen Emma Summer Palace.

2261 Nuuanu Ave. (btw. Wyllie and Judd sts.). ℭ **808/587-2590.** Free admission. Mon–Fri 8am–4:30pm. Bus: 4.

U.S. Army Museum Built in 1909 and formerly used in defense of Honolulu and Pearl Harbor, the Army Museum houses military memorabilia ranging from ancient Hawaiian warfare items to modern-day high-tech munitions. On the upper deck, the Corps of Engineers Pacific Regional Visitors Center shows how the corps works with the civilian community to manage water resources in an island environment. Plan to spend an hour perusing the place.

Fort DeRussy Park, Waikiki. ℭ **808/438-2822.** Free admission. Tues–Sun 10am–4:30pm. Bus: 8 or 19.

USS *Arizona* Memorial at Pearl Harbor ★★★ On December 7, 1941, the USS *Arizona,* while moored here in Pearl Harbor, was bombed in a Japanese air raid. The 608-foot battleship sank in 9 minutes without firing a shot, taking 1,177 sailors and Marines to their deaths—and catapulting the United States into World War II.

Nobody who visits the memorial will ever forget it. The deck of the ship lies 6 feet below the surface of the sea. Oil still oozes slowly up from the Arizona's engine room to stain the harbor's calm, blue water; some say the ship still weeps for its lost crew. The memorial is a stark, white, 184-foot rectangle that spans the sunken hull of the ship; it was designed by Alfred Pries, a German architect interned on Sand Island during the war. It contains the ship's bell, recovered from the wreckage, and a shrine room with the names of the dead carved in stone.

Try to arrive at the visitor center, operated by the National Park Service, no later than 1:30pm to avoid the huge crowds; waits of 1 to 3 hours are common, and they don't take reservations at this time. While you're waiting for the free launch (operated by the U.S. Navy) to take you out to the ship—get the **audio tour ★★★**. This will make the trip even more meaningful. The tour (on an MP3 player), which runs about 2½ hours, is like having your own personal park ranger as your guide; the $5 fee is one of Hawaii's best deals. Narrated by Ernest Borgnine, it features stories told by actual Pearl Harbor survivors, both American and Japanese—not to be missed! Plus, while you are waiting for the boat, the tour guides you step by step through the museum's personal mementos, photographs, and historic documents. You can pause the recording for the moving 20-minute film which precedes your journey to the ship. The tour continues on the launch, describing the shore line and the memorial itself and continues at the site, giving you a clear picture of that fateful day; it continues through your boat ride back. Allow a total of at least 4 hours for your visit.

Due to increased security measures, visitors cannot carry on purses, handbags, fanny packs, backpacks, camera bags (but you can carry your camera or video camera with you), diaper bags, or other items that offer concealment. However, there is a storage facility to store carry-on-size items (no bigger than 30 x 30 x 18 in.), for a fee.

Note: Parents, note that baby strollers, baby carriages, and baby backpacks are not allowed in the theater, on the boat, or on the USS *Arizona* Memorial. All babies must be carried. Unfortunately, the USS *Arizona* is a high-theft area—leave your valuables in your hotel safe.

The shipshape deck of the USS *Bowfin* submarine.

Pearl Harbor. ☎ **808/422-0561** (recorded info) or 808/422-2771. www.nps.gov/usar. Free admission. Daily 7am–5pm (programs run 8am–3pm). Children under 12 should be accompanied by an adult. Shirts required; swimsuits and flip-flops highly discouraged (shorts acceptable). Wheelchairs gladly accommodated. Drive west on H-1 past the airport; take the USS *Arizona* Memorial exit and follow the green-and-white signs; there's ample free parking. Bus: 20; or *Arizona* Memorial Shuttle Bus VIP (☎ **808/839-0911**), which picks up at Waikiki hotels 7am–11:30pm ($9 per person round-trip).

USS *Bowfin* Submarine Museum & Park ★ The USS *Bowfin* is one of only 15 World War II submarines still in existence today. You can go below deck of this famous submarine—nicknamed the "Pearl Harbor Avenger" for its successful attacks on the Japanese—and see how the 80-man crew lived during wartime. The *Bowfin* Museum has an impressive collection of submarine-related artifacts. The Waterfront Memorial honors submariners lost during World War II.

11 Arizona Memorial Dr. (next to the USS *Arizona* Memorial Visitor Center). ☎ **808/423-1341.** www.bowfin.org. Admission $10 adults, $7 active-duty military personnel and seniors, $4 children 4–12 (children under 4 are not permitted for safety reasons). Daily 7am–5pm. See USS *Arizona* Memorial, above, for driving, bus, and shuttle directions.

USS *Missouri* Memorial ★ On the deck of this 58,000-ton battleship (the last one the navy built), World War II came to an end with the signing of the Japanese surrender on September 2, 1945. The *Missouri* was part of the force that carried out bombing raids over Tokyo and provided firepower in the battles of Iwo Jima and Okinawa. In 1955, the navy decommissioned the ship and placed it in mothballs at the Puget Sound Naval Shipyard, in Washington State. But the *Missouri* was modernized and called back into action in 1986, eventually being deployed in the Persian Gulf War, before retiring once again in 1992. Here it sat until another battle ensued, this time over who would get the right to keep this living legend. Hawaii won that battle and brought the ship to Pearl Harbor in 1998. The 887-foot ship is now open to visitors as a museum memorial.

If you have the time, take the 1-hour tour, which begins at the visitor center. Guests are shuttled to Ford Island on military-style buses while listening to a 1940s-style radio program (complete with news clips, wartime commercials, and music). Once on the ship, guests watch an informational film and are then free to explore on their own or take a guided tour. Highlights of this massive (more than 200-ft. tall) battleship include the forecastle (or *fo'c's'le*, in Navy talk), where the 30,000-pound anchors are "dropped" on 1,080 feet of anchor chain; the 16-inch guns (each 65 ft. long and weighing 116 tons), which can accurately fire a 2,700-pound shell some 23 miles in 50 seconds; and the spot where the Instrument of Surrender was signed as Douglas MacArthur, Chester Nimitz, and "Bull" Halsey looked on.

Battleship Row, Pearl Harbor. © **877/MIGHTY-MO** [644-4896]. www.ussmissouri.com. Admission $20 adults, $10 children 4–12. Mighty Mo Tour (35 min.), Battle Stations Tour (90 min.) $25 extra. Daily 8am–5pm; guided tours 9:30am–4:30pm. Check in at the USS *Bowfin* Submarine Museum, next to the USS *Arizona* Memorial Visitor Center. Drive west on H-1 past the airport, take the USS *Arizona* Memorial exit, and follow the brown-and-white signs; there's ample free parking. Bus: 20.

Waikiki Aquarium ★★★ ☺ Do not miss this! Half of Hawaii is its underwater world, so plan to spend at least 2 hours discovering it. Behold the chambered nautilus, nature's submarine and inspiration for Jules Verne's *20,000 Leagues Under the Sea.* You may see this tropical spiral-shelled cephalopod mollusk—the only living one born in captivity—any day of the week here. Its natural habitat is the deep waters of Micronesia, but aquarium director Bruce Carlson not only succeeded in trapping the pearly shell in 1,500 feet of water (by dangling chunks of raw tuna), but also managed to breed this ancient relative of the octopus. Plenty of other

A trainer gets up close and personal with a seal at Waikiki Aquarium.

fish also inhabit this small but first-class aquarium, located on a live coral reef. The Hawaiian reef habitat features sharks, eels, a touch tank, and habitats for the endangered Hawaiian monk seal and green sea turtle. There's also a rotating biodiversity exhibit and interactive displays focusing on corals and coral reefs.

2777 Kalakaua Ave. (across from Kapiolani Park). © **808/923-9741.** www.waquarium.org. Admission $9 adults; $6 active military, seniors, and college students; $4 children 13–17; $2 children 5–12; and free for children 4 and under. Daily 9am–5pm. Bus: 2.

Waikiki Historic Trail ★ The Waikiki you see today bears no resemblance to the Waikiki of yesteryear, a place of vast taro fields extending from the ocean to

☺ ESPECIALLY FOR kids

See an Erupting Volcano It looks like the real thing—a real molten-spewing, roaring, rock-launching volcano—only you are standing just a few feet away. It's the Bishop Museum's 16,500-square-foot Science Adventure Center, specializing in volcanology, oceanography, and biodiversity. Children are spellbound as they wander through the "Hawaiian origins" tunnel into the deep ocean, stopping along the way to play with all the cool, high-tech toys, then exploring the interior of a volcano and climbing to the top to get a bird's-eye view of an erupting caldera. See p. 196.

Take a Walk on the Wild Side Visit Africa in Hawaii at the Honolulu Zoo. The lions, giraffes, zebras, and elephants delight youngsters and parents alike. But the great new thrill is the Zoo by Moonlight tour—so kids can see what really goes bump (or roar) in the night. See p. 200.

Shop Aloha Flea Market Most kids hate to shop. But the Aloha Flea Market, a giant outdoor bazaar at Aloha Stadium every Wednesday, Saturday, and Sunday, is more akin to a carnival, full of strange food, odd goods, and bold barkers. Nobody ever leaves this place empty-handed—or without having had lots of fun. See p. 17.

Fly a Kite at Kapiolani Park Great open expanses of green and constant trade winds make this urban park one of Hawaii's prime locations for kite flying. Watch the pros fly dragon kites and stage kite-fighting contests, or join in the fun after checking out the convenient kite shop across the street in New Otani's arcade. See p. 201.

Eat Shave Ice at Haleiwa No visit to Hawaii is complete without an authentic shave ice. You can find shave ice in all kinds of tropical flavors throughout the islands, but for some reason, it tastes better in this funky North Shore surf town. See p. 241.

Beat Bamboo Drums in a Fijian Village The Polynesian Cultural Center introduces kids to the games played by Polynesian and Melanesian children. The activities, which range from face painting to Hawaiian bowling, go on every day from 12:30 to 5:30pm. See p. 235.

Splash Down at Wet 'n' Wild This 29-acre water park features a wave pool for bodysurfing, two 65-foot-high free-fall slides, two water-toboggan bullet slides, inner-tube slides, body flume slides, a continuous river for floating inner tubes, and separate pools for adults, teens, and children. See p. 241.

deep into Manoa Valley, dotted with numerous fishponds and gardens tended by thousands of people. This picture of old Waikiki can be recaptured by following the emerging Waikiki Historic Trail, a meandering 2-mile walk with 20 bronze surfboard markers (each standing 6 ft., 5 in. tall—you can't miss 'em), complete with descriptions and archival photos of the historic sites. The markers note everything from Waikiki's ancient fishponds to the history of the Ala Wai Canal.

The trail begins at Kuhio Beach and ends at the King Kalakaua statue, at the intersection of Kuhio and Kalakaua avenues. www.waikikihistorictrail.com. Bus: 2.

Explore the Bishop Museum

There are some 1,180,000 Polynesian artifacts; 13,500,000 different insect specimens; 6,000,000 marine and land shells; 490,000 plant specimens; 130,000 fish specimens; and 85,000 birds and mammals, all in the Bishop Museum. Kids can explore interactive exhibits, see a 50-foot sperm whale skeleton, and check out a Hawaiian grass hut—the museum has something for everyone. See p. 196.

Walk Through a Submarine

At the USS *Bowfin* Submarine Museum Park, an interactive museum offers children the chance to experience a real submarine—one that served in some of the fiercest naval battles in World War II. Kids can explore the tightly packed interior that housed some 90 to 100 men, and see the stacked shelves where they slept, the radar and electronics in the command center, and where the torpedoes are stored. See p. 206.

Watch the Fish and Sharks at the Waikiki Aquarium

Much more than a big fish tank, the Waikiki Aquarium will astound and educate your youngsters. They can probably sit for hours staring at the sharks, turtles, eels, rays, and fish swimming in the main tank. For a few laughs, wander out to the monk seal area and watch the antics of these seagoing clowns. See p. 207.

Snorkel in Hanauma Bay

Kids will be enthralled with the teeming tropical fish and the underwater world at this marine park. The shallow waters near the beach are perfect for neophyte snorkelers, and the long (2,000-ft.) beach has plenty of frolicking room. Get there early; it can get very crowded. See p. 156.

Hike to the Top of Diamond Head Crater

The entire family can make this easy 1.4-mile round-trip walk to the top of the 750-foot volcanic cone with its rewarding view of Oahu. Bring a flashlight for the entry tunnel and a camera for the view. See p. 174.

Explore the Depths in a Submarine Dive

Better than a movie, more exciting than a video game, the *Atlantis* or *Voyager* submarines journey down 100 feet below the water's surface to explore the Neptunian world of tropical reef fish and even an occasional shark or two. See p. 170.

See Sea Creatures at Sea Life Park

Kids love this 62-acre ocean-theme park that features orca whales, dolphins, seals, and penguins. It also offers a Hawaiian reef tank full of native tropical fish, a "touch" pool, and the world's only "wholphin"—a cross between a false killer whale and an Atlantic bottle-nosed dolphin. See p. 232.

WALKING TOUR 1: **CHINATOWN**

GETTING THERE:	**From Waikiki, take TheBus no. 2 or 20 toward downtown; get off on North Hotel Street (after Maunakea St.). If you're driving, take Ala Moana Boulevard and turn right on Smith Street; make a left on Beretania Street and a left again at Maunakea. The city parking garage (50¢ per hr.) is on the Ewa (west) side of Maunakea Street, between North Hotel and North King streets.**
START & FINISH:	**North Hotel and Maunakea streets.**
TIME:	**1 to 2 hours, depending on how much time you spend browsing.**
BEST TIME:	**Daylight hours.**

Chinese laborers from Guangdong Province first came to work on Hawaii's sugar and pineapple plantations in the 1850s. They quickly figured out that they would never get rich working in the fields; once their contracts were up, a few of the ambitious started small shops and restaurants in the area around River Street.

Chinatown was twice devastated by fire, once in 1886 and again in 1900. The second fire still intrigues historians. In December 1899, bubonic plague broke out in the area, and the Board of Health immediately quarantined its 7,000 Chinese and Japanese residents. But the plague continued to spread. On January 20, 1900, the board decided to burn down plague-infected homes, starting at the corner of Beretania Street and Nuuanu Avenue. But the fire department wasn't quite ready; a sudden wind quickly spread the flames from one wooden building to another in the densely built area, and soon Chinatown's entire 40 acres were leveled. Many historians believe that the "out-of-control" fire may have been purposely set to drive the Chinese merchants—who were becoming economically powerful and controlled prime real estate—out of Honolulu. If this was indeed the case, it didn't work: The determined merchants built a new Chinatown on the same spot.

Chinatown reached its peak in the 1930s. In the days before air travel, visitors arrived here by cruise ship. Just a block up the street was the pier where they disembarked—and they often headed straight for the shops and restaurants of Chinatown, which mainlanders considered an exotic treat. In the 1940s, military personnel on leave flocked here looking for different kinds of exotic treats—in the form of pool halls, tattoo joints, and brothels.

Today, Chinatown is again rising from the ashes. After deteriorating over the years into a tawdry district of seedy bars, drug dealing, and homeless squatters, the neighborhood recently underwent extensive urban renewal. Just enough sleaze still flourishes on the fringes (a few peep shows and a couple of topless bars) to keep it from being a theme park–style tourist attraction, but Chinatown is poised to relive its glory days.

It's not exactly a microcosm of China, however. What you'll find is a mix of Asian cultures, all packed into a small area where tangy spices rule the cuisine, open-air markets have kept out the minimalls, and the way to good health is through acupuncture and herbalists. The jumble of streets comes alive every day with bustling residents and visitors from all over the world; a cacophony of sounds, from the high-pitched bleating of vendors in the market to the lyrical dialects of the retired men "talking story" over a game of mah-jongg; and brilliant reds, blues, and greens trimming buildings and goods everywhere you look. No trip to Honolulu is complete without a visit to this exotic, historic district.

Start your walk on the Ewa (west) side of Maunakea Street at:

1 Hotel Street

During World War II, Hotel Street was synonymous with good times. Pool halls and beer parlors lined the blocks, and prostitutes were plentiful. Nowadays, the more nefarious establishments have been replaced with small shops, from art galleries to specialty boutiques, and urban professionals and recent immigrants look for bargains where the sailors once roamed.

Once you're done wandering through the shops, head to the intersection with Smith Street. On the Diamond Head (east) side of Smith, you'll notice stones in the sidewalk; they were taken from the sandalwood ships, which came to Hawaii empty of cargo except for these stones, which were used as ballast on the trip over. The stones were removed and the ships' hulls were filled with sandalwood for the return to the mainland.

From Hotel Street, turn left on Maunakea and proceed to the corner of King Street to the:

2 Bank of Hawaii

This unusual-looking bank is not the conservative edifice you'd expect—it's guarded by two fire-breathing dragon statues.

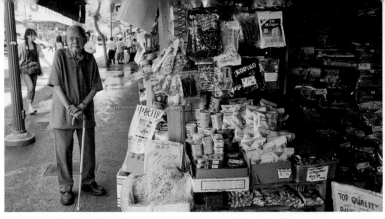

The authentically Chinese Hotel Street.

Turn right onto King Street, where you'll pass the shops of various Chinese herbalists. Stop at 150 N. King St., where you'll find the:

3 Yat Tung Chow Noodle Factory

The delicious, delicate noodles that star in numerous Asian dishes are made here, ranging from threadlike noodles (literally no thicker than embroidery thread) to fat udon noodles. Tours of the factory are not offered, but you can look through the window, past the white cloud of flour that hangs in the air, and watch as dough is fed into rollers at one end of the noo-

An herbalist measuring at the Viet Hoa Chinese Herb Shop.

dle machines; perfectly cut noodles emerge at the other end.

Proceed to 162 N. King St., to the:

4 Viet Hoa Chinese Herb Shop

At this location, Chinese herbalists act as both doctors and dispensers of herbs. Patients come in and tell the herbalist what ails them; the herbalist then decides which of the myriad herbs to mix together. Usually, there's a wall of tiny drawers labeled in Chinese characters; the herbalist quickly pulls from the drawers various objects that range from dried flowers and ground-up roots to such exotics as mashed antelope antler. The patient then takes the concoction home to brew into a strong tea.

Cross to the south side of King Street, where, just west of Kekaulike Street, you'll come to the most visited part of Chinatown, the open-air market known as:

5 Oahu Market Place

Those interested in Asian cooking will find all the necessary ingredients here, including pig's heads, poultry (some still squawking), fresh octopi,

7

Chinatown

EXPLORING OAHU

salted jellyfish, pungent fish sauce, fresh herbs, and thousand-year-old eggs. The friendly vendors are happy to explain their wares and give instructions on how to prepare these exotic treats. The market, which has been at this spot since 1904, is divided into meats, poultry, fish, vegetables, and fruits. Past the open market are several grocery stores with fresh produce on display on the sidewalk. You're bound to spot some varieties here that you're not used to seeing at your local supermarket.

Offbeat meat at Oahu Market Place.

Follow King Street down to River Street and turn right toward the mountains.

A range of inexpensive restaurants lines River Street from King to Beretania. You can get the best Vietnamese and Filipino food in town in these blocks, but go early—lines for lunch start at 11:15am. Beyond Beretania Street is the:

6 River Street Pedestrian Mall

Here, River Street ends and the pedestrian mall begins with the **statue of Chinese revolutionary leader Sun Yat-sen.** The wide mall, which borders the Nuuanu Stream, is lined with shade trees, park benches, and tables where seniors gather to play mah-jongg and checkers. Plenty of takeout restaurants are nearby if you'd like to eat lunch outdoors. If you're up early (5:30am in summer and 6am in winter), you'll see senior citizens practicing tai chi.

Along the River Street Mall, extending nearly a block over to Maunakea Street, is the:

Bargaining: A Way of Life in Chinatown

In Chinatown, nearly every purchase—from chicken's feet to an 18-carat gold necklace—is made by bargaining. It's the way of life for most Asian countries—and part of the fun and charm of shopping in Chinatown.

The main rule of thumb when negotiating a price is **respect.** The customer must have respect for the merchant and understand that he's in business to make money. This respect is coupled with the understanding that the customer does not want to be taken advantage of and would like the best deal possible.

Keep in mind two rules when bargaining: **cash** and **volume.** Don't even

begin haggling if you're not planning to pay cash. The second you pull out a credit card (if the merchant or vendor will even accept it), all deals are off. And remember, the more you buy, the better the deal the merchant will extend to you.

Significant savings can be realized for high-ticket items like jewelry. The price of gold in Chinatown is based on the posted price of the tael (a unit of weight, slightly more than an ounce), which is listed for 14-, 18-, and 24-carat gold, plus the value of the labor. The tael price is non-negotiable, but the cost of the labor is where the bargaining begins.

Colorful and spiritual: Kuan Yin Temple.

7 Chinatown Cultural Plaza

This modern complex is filled with shops featuring everything from tailors to calligraphers (most somewhat more expensive than their street-side counterparts), as well as numerous restaurants—a great idea, but in reality, people seem to prefer wandering Chinatown's crowded streets to venturing into a modern mall. A couple of interesting shops here specialize in Asian magazines; there's also a small post office tucked away in a corner of the plaza, for those who want to mail cards home with the "Chinatown" postmark. The best feature of the plaza is the **Moongate Stage** in the center, the site of many cultural presentations, especially around the Chinese New Year.

Continue up the River Street Mall and cross the Nuuanu Stream via the bridge at Kukui Street, which will bring you to the:

8 Izumo Taisha Mission Cultural Hall

This small, wooden Shinto shrine, built in 1923, houses a male deity (look for the X-shaped crosses on the top). Members of the faith ring the bell out front as an act of purification when they come to pray. Inside the temple is a 100-pound sack of rice, symbolizing good health. During World War II, the shrine was confiscated by the city of Honolulu and wasn't returned to the congregation until 1962.

If temples interest you, walk a block toward the mountains to Vineyard Boulevard; cross back over Nuuanu Stream, past the entrance of Foster Botanical Gardens, to:

9 Kuan Yin Temple

This Buddhist temple, painted in a brilliant red with a green ceramic-tiled roof, is dedicated to Kuan Yin Bodhisattva, the goddess of mercy, whose statue towers in the prayer hall. The aroma of burning incense is your clue that the temple is still a house of worship, not an exhibit, so enter with respect and leave your shoes outside. You may see people burning paper "money" for prosperity and good luck, or leaving flowers and fruits at the altar (gifts to the goddess). A common offering is the *pomelo,* a grapefruit-like fruit that's a fertility symbol as well as a gift, indicating a request for the blessing of children.

Continue down Vineyard and then turn right (toward the ocean) on:

10 Maunakea Street

In the several-square-block area between Beretania and King streets are numerous **lei shops** (with lei-makers working away right on the premises). The air is heavy with the aroma of flowers being woven into beautiful treasures. Not only is this the best place in all of Hawaii to get a deal on leis, but the size, color, and design of the leis made here are exceptional—and the finest might go for as little as $3.50. Wander through the shops before you decide which lei you want.

11 Take a Break ☕

If you have a sweet tooth, stop in at **Shung Chong Yuein ★**, 1027 Maunakea St. (near Hotel St.), for delicious Asian pastries such as moon cakes and almond cookies, all at very reasonable prices. The shop also has a wide selection of dried and sugared candies (such as ginger, pineapple, and lotus root) that you can eat as you stroll or give as an exotic gift to friends back home.

Turn left on Hotel Street and walk in the Diamond Head (east) direction to:

12 Nuuanu Avenue

You may notice that the sidewalks on Nuuanu are made of granite blocks; they came from the ballasts of ships that brought tea from China to Hawaii in the 1800s. On the corner of Nuuanu Avenue and Hotel Street is **Lai Fong Department Store,** a classic Chinatown store owned by the same family for more than 75 years. Walking into Lai Fong is like stepping back in time. The old store sells everything from precious antiques to god-awful knickknacks to rare turn-of-the-century Hawaiian postcards—but it has built its reputation on its fabulous selection of Chinese silks, brocades, and custom dresses.

Between Hotel and Pauahi streets is the **Pegge Hopper Gallery** (p. 247), 1164 Nuuanu Ave., where you can admire Pegge's well-known paintings of beautiful Hawaiian women.

At Pauahi Street, turn right (toward Diamond Head) and walk up to Bethel Street and the:

13 Hawaii Theatre

This restored 1920 Art Deco theater is a work of art in itself. It hosts a variety of programs, from the Hawaii International Film Festival to beauty pageants (see "Oahu After Dark," p. 262, for how to find out what's on).

Turn right onto Bethel and walk toward the ocean. Turn right again onto Hotel Street, which will lead you back to where you started.

WALKING TOUR 2: **HISTORIC HONOLULU**

GETTING THERE: **From Waikiki, take Ala Moana Boulevard in the Ewa direction. Ala Moana Boulevard ends at Nimitz Highway. Turn right on the next street on your right (Alakea St.). Park in the garage across from St. Andrews Church after you cross Beretania Street. TheBus: 1, 2, 3, 4, 11, 12, or 50.**

START: **St. Andrew's Church, Beretania and Alakea streets.**

FINISH: **Same place.**

TIME: **2 to 3 hours, depending on how long you linger in museums.**

BEST TIME: **Tuesday through Saturday, daytime, when the Iolani Palace has tours.**

The 1800s were a turbulent time in Hawaii. By the end of the 1790s, Kamehameha the Great had united all the islands. Foreigners then began arriving by ship—first explorers, then merchants, and in 1820, missionaries. The rulers of Hawaii were hard-pressed to keep up. By 1840 it was clear that the capital had shifted from Lahaina, Maui, where the Kingdom of Hawaii was actually centered, to Honolulu, where the majority of commerce and trade was taking place. In 1848, the Great Mahele (division) enabled commoners and eventually foreigners to own crown land, and in two generations, more than 80% of all private lands had shifted to foreign ownership. With the introduction of sugar as a crop, the foreigners prospered, and in time they put more and more pressures on the government.

By 1872, the monarchy had run through the Kamehameha line and in 1873 David Kalakaua was elected to the throne. Known as the "Merrie Monarch," Kalakaua redefined the monarchy by going on a world tour, building Iolani Palace, having a European-style coronation, and throwing extravagant parties. By the end of the 1800s, however, the foreign sugar growers and merchants had become extremely powerful in Hawaii. With the assistance of the U.S. Marines, they orchestrated the overthrow of Queen Liliuokalani, Hawaii's last reigning monarch, in 1893. The United States declared Hawaii a territory in 1898.

You can witness the remnants of these turbulent years in just a few short blocks.

Cross the street from the church parking lot and venture back to 1858 when you enter:

1 St. Andrew's Church

The Hawaiian monarchs were greatly influenced by the royals in Europe. When King Kamehameha IV saw the grandeur of the Church of England, he decided to build his own cathedral. He and Queen Emma founded the Anglican

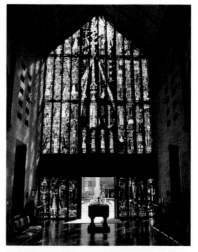

St. Andrew's brilliant stained glass.

1 St. Andrew's Church
2 Washington Place
3 Father Damien Statue
4 Hawaii State Capitol
5 Iolani Palace
6 Iolani Palace Grounds
7 Hawaii State Art Museum
8 King Kamehameha Statue
9 Aliiolani Hale
10 Kawaiahao Church
11 Mission Houses Museum
12 Honolulu Hale
13 State Library
14 Kalanimoku

Walking Tour 2: Historic Honolulu

Church of Hawaii in 1858. The king, however, didn't live to see the church completed; he died on St. Andrew's Day, 4 years before King Kamehameha V oversaw the laying of the cornerstone in 1867. The church was named St. Andrew's in honor of King Kamehameha IV's death. This French-Gothic structure was shipped in pieces from England and reassembled here. Even if you aren't fond of visiting churches, you have to see the floor-to-eaves hand-blown stained-glass window that faces the setting sun. In the glass is a mural of Rev. Thomas Staley, the first bishop of Hawaii; King Kamehameha IV; and Queen Emma. The church's excellent thrift shop has some real bargains and is open Monday, Wednesday, and Friday 9:30am to 4pm and Saturday 9am to 1pm.

Next, walk down Beretania Street in the Diamond Head direction to the gates of:

2   Washington Place

Once the residence of the Governor of Hawaii (sorry, no tours; just peek through the iron fence), this Greek revival–style home nevertheless occupies a distinguished place in Hawaii's history. Built in 1842 by a U.S. sea captain named John Dominis, it got its name from the U.S. ambassador who once stayed there and told so many stories about President George Washington that people started calling the home Washington Place. The sea captain's son, also named John, married a beautiful Hawaiian princess, Lydia Kapaakea, who later became Hawaii's last queen, Liliuokalani. When the queen was overthrown by U.S. businessmen in 1893, she moved out of Iolani Palace and into her husband's inherited home, Washington Place, where she lived until her death in 1917. On the left side of the building, near the sidewalk, is a plaque inscribed with the words to one of the most popular songs written by Queen Liliuokalani, "Aloha Oe" ("Farewell to Thee").

Cross the street and walk to the front of the Hawaii State Capitol, where you'll find the:

3 Father Damien Statue

The people of Hawaii have never forgotten the sacrifice this Belgian priest made to help the sufferers of leprosy when he volunteered to work with them in exile on the Kalaupapa Peninsula on the island of Molokai. After 16 years of service, Father Damien died of leprosy, at the age of 49. The statue is frequently draped in leis in recognition of Father Damien's humanitarian work. Recently the Catholic Church made Father Damien a saint.

Behind Father Damien's statue is the:

4 Hawaii State Capitol

Here's where Hawaii's state legislators work from mid-January to the end of April every year. This is not your typical white dome structure, but a building symbolic of Hawaii. Unfortunately, it symbolizes more of Hawaii than the architect and the state legislature probably bargained for. The building's unusual design has palm-tree-shaped pillars, two cone-shaped chambers (representing volcanoes) for the legislative bodies, and in the inner courtyard, a 600,000-tile mosaic of the sea (Aquarius) created by a local artist. A reflecting pool (representing the sea) surrounds the entire structure. Like a lot of things in Hawaii, it was a great idea, but no one considered the logistics. The reflecting pond also draws brackish water, which rusts the hardware; when it rains, water pours into the rotunda, dampening government business; and the Aquarius floor mosaic became so damaged by the elements that it became a hazard. In the 1990s, the entire building (built in 1969) was closed for a couple of years for renovations, forcing the legislature to set up temporary quarters in several buildings. It's open again, and you are welcome to go into the rotunda and see the woven hangings and murals at the entrance, or take the elevator up to the fifth floor for a spectacular view of the city's historical center.

Walk down Richards Street toward the ocean and stop at:

5 Iolani Palace

Hawaii is the only state in the U.S. to have not one but two royal palaces; one in Kona (on Big Island), where the royals went during the summer, and Iolani Palace (*Iolani* means "royal hawk"). Don't miss the opportunity to see this grande dame of historic buildings. Tours are limited—see p. 200 for details on tour hours and admission prices.

In ancient times a *heiau* stood in this area. When it became clear to King Kamehameha III that the capital should be transferred from Lahaina

The coat of arms of the Kingdom of Hawaii displayed at Iolani Palace reads, "The life of the land is perpetuated in righteousness."

to Honolulu, he moved to a modest building here in 1845. The construction of the palace was undertaken by King David Kalakaua and was begun in 1879; it was finished 3 years later at a cost of $350,000. The king spared no expense: You can still see the glass and iron work imported from San Francisco. The palace had all the modern conveniences of its time: Electric lights were installed 4 years before the White House had them; every bedroom had its own full bathroom with hot and cold running water and copper-lined tub, a flush toilet, and a bidet. The king had a telephone line from the palace to his boathouse on the water a year after Alexander Graham Bell introduced it to the world.

It was also in this palace that Queen Liliuokalani was overthrown and placed under house arrest for 9 months. Later, the territorial and then the state government used the palace until it outgrew it. When the legislature left in 1968, the palace was in shambles and has since undergone a $7-million overhaul to restore it to its former glory. See p. 200 for more information.

After you visit the palace, spend some time on the:

6 Iolani Palace Grounds

You can wander around the grounds at no charge. (The ticket window to the palace and the gift shop are in the former barracks of the Royal Household Guards.) The domed pavilion on the grounds was originally built as a coronation stand by King Kalakaua; 9 years after he took the throne, he decided to have a formal European-style coronation ceremony where he crowned himself and his queen, Kapiolani. Later he used it as a **Royal Bandstand** for concerts (Kalakaua, along with Herni Berger, the first Royal Hawaiian Bandmaster, wrote "Hawaii Pono'i," the state anthem). Today the Royal Bandstand is still used for concerts by the Royal Hawaiian Band. The more modern building on the grounds is the **State Archives,** built in 1953, which holds records, documents, and photos of Hawaii's people and its history.

From the palace grounds, turn in the Ewa direction, cross Richards Street, and walk to the corner of Richards and Hotel streets to the:

7 Hawaii State Art Museum

Opened in 2002, the Hawaii State Art Museum is housed in the original Royal Hawaiian Hotel built in 1872, during the reign of King Kamehameha V. All of the 360 works currently displayed were created by artists who live in Hawaii. The pieces were purchased by the state thanks to a 1967 law that says that 1% of the cost of state buildings will be used to acquire works of art. Nearly 4 decades later, the state has amassed some 5,000 pieces. The current exhibit depicts Hawaii, its history, culture, and ideals, through a variety of mediums. It's open Tuesday to Saturday 10am to 4pm and is free.

Walk makai down Richards Street and turn left (toward Diamond Head) on S. King Street to the:

8 King Kamehameha Statue

At the juncture of King, Merchant, and Mililani streets stands a replica of the man who united the Hawaiian Islands. The striking black-and-gold bronze statue is magnificent. The best day to see the statue is on June 11 (King Kamehameha Day), when it is covered with leis in honor of Hawaii's favorite son.

The statue of Kamehameha I was cast by Thomas Gould in 1880 in Paris. However, it was lost at sea somewhere near the Falkland Islands. Subsequently, the insurance money was used to pay for a second statue, but in the meantime, the original statue was recovered. The original was eventually sent to the town of Kapaau on the Big Island, the birthplace of Kamehameha, and the second statue was placed in Honolulu in 1883, as part of King David Kalakaua's coronation ceremony. A third statue (all three are very different, but they were supposedly all cast from the same mold) was sent to Washington, D.C., when Hawaii became a state in 1959.

King Kamehameha still gets dressed up on King Kamehameha Day.

9 Aliiolani Hale

This "House of Heavenly Kings," with its distinctive clock tower, now houses the State Judiciary Building. King Kamehameha V originally wanted to build a palace here and commissioned the Australian architect Thomas Rowe in 1872. However, it ended up as the first major government building for the Hawaiian monarchy. Kamehameha V didn't live to see it completed, and King David Kalakaua dedicated the building in 1874. Ironically, less than 20 years later, on January 17, 1893, Stanford Dole, backed by other prominent sugar planters, stood on the steps to this building and proclaimed the overthrow of the Hawaiian monarchy and the establishment of a provisional government. Tours are conducted Tuesday through Thursday, 10am to 3pm (no charge). See p. 193 for more information.

Walk toward Diamond Head on King Street; at the corner of King and Punchbowl, stop in at:

10 Kawaiahao Church

When missionaries came to Hawaii, the first thing they did was build churches. Four thatched grass churches (one measured 54 ft. x 22 ft. and could seat 300 people on lauhala mats; the last thatched church held 4,500 people) had been built on this site through 1837 before Rev. Hiram Bingham began building what he considered a "real" church—a New England–style congregational structure with Gothic influences. Between 1837 and 1842, the building of the church required some 14,000 giant coral slabs (some weighing more than 1,000 lb.). Hawaiian divers literally raped the reefs, digging out huge chunks of coral and causing irreparable environmental damage.

Kawaiahao is Hawaii's oldest church, and it has been the site of numerous historical events, such as a speech made by King Kamehameha III in 1843, an excerpt from which became Hawaii's state motto *("Ua mau ke ea o ka aina i ka pono,"* which translates as, "The life of the land is preserved in righteousness").

This is the Westminster Abbey of Hawaii; the vestibule is lined with portraits of the Hawaiian monarchy, many of whom were coronated in this very building. The coral church is also a perfect setting to experience an all-Hawaiian service, complete with Hawaiian song. (Hawaiian-language services are held every Sunday at 9am and admission is free—let your conscience be your guide as to a donation.)

The clock tower in the church, which was donated by King Kamehameha III and installed in 1850, continues to tick today. The church is open Monday through Saturday, from 8am to 4pm; you'll find it to be very cool in temperature. Don't sit in the pews in the back, marked with kahili feathers and velvet cushions; they are still reserved for the descendants of royalty. See p. 201 for more information.

Cross the street, and you'll see the:

11 Mission Houses Museum

On the corner of King and Kawaiahao streets stand the original buildings of the Sandwich Islands Mission Headquarters: the **Frame House** (built in

The Frame House, at the Mission Houses Museum.

1821), the **Chamberlain House** (1831), and the **Printing Office** (1841). The complex is open Tuesday through Saturday from 10am to 4pm; admission is $10 for adults, $8 for military personnel and seniors, $6 for children ages 6 to college. The tours are often led by descendants of the original missionaries to Hawaii.

Believe it or not, the missionaries brought their own prefab house along with them when they came around Cape Horn from Boston in 1819. The Frame House was designed for frigid New England winters and had small windows. (It must have been stiflingly hot inside.) Finished in 1921 (the interior frame was left behind and didn't arrive until Christmas 1920), it is Hawaii's oldest wooden structure. The Chamberlain House, built in 1931, was used by the missionaries as a storehouse.

The missionaries believed that the best way to spread the Lord's message to the Hawaiians was to learn their language and then to print literature for them to read. So it was the missionaries who gave the Hawaiians a written language. The Printing House on the grounds was where the lead-type Ramage press (brought from New England, of course) printed the Hawaiian Bible. See p. 203 for more information.

Cross King Street and walk in the Ewa direction to the corner of Punchbowl and King to:

12 Honolulu Hale

The **Honolulu City Hall,** built in 1927, was designed by Honolulu's most famous architect, C. W. Dickey. His Spanish mission–style building has an open-air courtyard, which is used for art exhibits and concerts. Open weekdays.

Cross Punchbowl Street and walk mauka to the:

13 State Library

Anything you want to know about Hawaii and the Pacific can be found here, the main branch of the state's library system. Located in a restored historic building, it has an open garden courtyard in the middle, great for stopping for a rest on your walk.

Head mauka up Punchbowl to the corner of Punchbowl and Beretania streets, to:

14 Kalanimoku

The beautiful name "Ship of Heaven" has been given to this dour state office building. Here you can get information on hiking and camping (from the Department of Land and Natural Resources) in state parks.

Retrace your steps in the Ewa direction down Beretania to Alakea back to the parking garage.

WALKING TOUR 3: **KAPIOLANI PARK**

GETTING THERE:	**From Waikiki, walk toward Diamond Head on Kalakaua Avenue. If you're coming by car, the cheapest parking is metered street parking on Kalakaua Avenue adjacent to the park. TheBus: 19 or 20.**
START:	**Waikiki Beach Center, Kalakaua Avenue, Diamond Head side of the Moana Surfrider hotel, across the street from the Hyatt Regency and Uluniu Avenue.**
FINISH:	**Kapiolani Beach Park.**
TIME:	**4 to 5 hours. Allow at least an hour each for walking around the park, wandering around the zoo, and exploring the aquarium, plus all the time you want for the beach.**
BEST TIME:	**Weekday mornings.**

On June 11, 1877, King Kamehameha Day, then-king David Kalakaua donated some 140 acres of land to the people of Hawaii for Hawaii's first park. He asked that the park be named after his beloved wife, Queen Kapiolani, and he celebrated the opening of this vast grassy area with a free concert and "high stakes" horse races (the king loved gambling) on the new horse-racing oval he had built below Diamond Head.

The horse races, and the gambling that accompanied it, were eventually outlawed, but the park—and the free concerts—live on. Just a coconut's throw from the high-rise concrete jungle of Waikiki lies this 133-acre grassy park (the Paki playground and a fire station make up the remaining acreage) dotted with spreading banyans, huge monkeypod trees, blooming royal poincianas, and swaying ironwoods. Throughout the open spaces are jogging paths, tennis courts, soccer and cricket fields, and even an archery range. People come to the park to listen to music, watch ethnic dancing, exercise, enjoy team sports, take long meditative walks, picnic, buy art, smell the roses, and just relax. The park is the site of international kite-flying contests, the finishing line for the Honolulu marathon, and the home of yearly Scottish highland games, Hawaiian cultural festivals, and about a zillion barbecues and picnics.

Start at the:

1 Waikiki Beach Center

On the ocean side of Kalakaua Avenue, next to the Moana Surfrider hotel, is a complex of restrooms, showers, surfboard lockers, rental concessions, and the Waikiki police substation.

On the Diamond Head side of the police substation are the:

2 Wizard Stones/Healing Stones

These four basalt boulders, which weigh several tons apiece and sit on a lava rock platform, are held sacred by the Hawaiian people. The story goes that sometime before the 15th century, four powerful healers named Kapaemahu, Kahaloa, Kapuni, and Kihohi, from Moaulanuiakea in the Society Islands, lived in the Ulukoa area of Waikiki. After years of healing the people and the *alii* (chiefs) of Oahu, they wished to return home. They asked the people to erect four monuments made of bell stone, a basalt rock that was found in a Kaimuki quarry and that produced a bell-like ringing when struck. The healers spent a ceremonious month transferring their spiritual healing power, or *mana,* to the stones, so the natives could access it after the healers departed.

The great mystery is how the boulders were transported from Kaimuki to the marshland near Kuhio Beach in Waikiki. Over time a bowling alley was built on the spot, and the stones got buried beneath the structure. After the bowling alley was torn down in the 1960s, tourists used the stones for picnicking or drying their wet towels. In 1997, the stones were once again given a place of prominence with the construction of a $75,000 shrine that includes the platform and a wrought-iron fence. Since then the stones have become something of a mecca for students and patients of traditional healing.

Further down the beach in the Diamond Head direction you'll find the:

3 Duke Kahanamoku Statue

Here, cast in bronze, is Hawaii's most famous athlete, also known as the father of modern surfing. Duke (1890–1968) won Olympic swimming medals in 1912, 1920, 1924, and 1928. He was enshrined in both the Swimming Hall of Fame and the Surfing Hall of Fame. He also traveled around the world promoting surfing. When the city of Honolulu first erected the statue of this lifelong ocean athlete, they placed it with his back to the water.

Duke Kahanamoku stands with his back to the water, but that doesn't deter his fans.

**Walking Tour 3:
Kapiolani Park**

*M a m a l a
B a y*

*Honolulu
Zoo*

*K A P I O L A N I

P A R K*

1 Waikiki Beach Center
2 Wizard Stones/
  Healing Stones
3 Duke Kahanamoku Statue
4 Kuhio Beach Park
5 Kapiolani Park Kiosk
6 Honolulu Zoo
7 Kapiolani Park Bandstand
8 Art on the Zoo Fence
9 Waikiki Shell
10 Queen Kapiolani Garden
11 People's Open Market
12 Diamond Head
   Tennis Courts
13 Sans Souci Beach
14 Natatorium
15 Waikiki Aquarium
16 Kapiolani Beach Park

There was public outcry, because no one familiar with the ocean would ever stand with his back to it. To quell the outcry, the city moved the statue closer to the sidewalk.

Continuing in the Diamond Head direction, you'll come to:

4   Kuhio Beach Park

The two small swimming spots here are great, but heed the warning sign: Watch out for holes. Deep holes are in the sandy bottom, and you may suddenly find yourself in over your head. The best pool for swimming is the one on the Diamond Head end, but the water circulation is questionable—there sometimes appears to be a layer of suntan lotion floating on the surface. If the waves are up, watch the boogie boarders surf by the seawall. They ride toward the wall and at the last minute veer away with a swoosh.

After watching the surfers, walk down Kalakaua Avenue (toward Diamond Head) to the entrance of Kapiolani Park, where you'll see the:

5 Kapiolani Park Kiosk

On the corner of Kalakaua and Kapahulu avenues, this small display stand contains brochures and actual photos of the park's history. It also carries information on upcoming events at the various sites within the park (Aquarium, Zoo, Waikiki Shell, and Kapiolani Bandstand). An informative map will orient you to the park grounds.

Continue up Kapahulu Avenue to the entrance of the:

6 Honolulu Zoo

The city's 42-acre zoo is open every day from 9am to 4:30pm, but the best time to go is as soon as the gates open; the animals seem to be more active then, and we agree—it is a lot cooler than in the hot midday sun. See p. 200 for more information.

Trace your steps back to Kapahulu and Kalakaua avenues and head mauka down Monsarrat Avenue to the:

7 Kapiolani Park Bandstand

Once upon a time, from 1937 to 2002, the **Kodak Hula Show** presented the art of hula to visitors, with some 3,000 people squeezed into the bleachers around a grassy stage area every day. The Kodak Hula Show is gone now, but the bandstand is still used for concerts and special events.

Back on Monsarrat Avenue, on the fence facing the zoo, you'll find the:

8 Art on the Zoo Fence

Formerly known as **Art Mart** or the **Artists of Oahu Exhibit** (www.artonthezoofence.com); local artisans hang their artwork on a fence for the public to view and buy. Not only do you get to meet the artists, but you also have an opportunity to purchase their work at a considerable discount from the prices you'll see in galleries. Exhibits are Saturday, Sunday, and Wednesday 10am to 4pm.

Cross Monsarrat Avenue, and you'll see the:

9 Waikiki Shell

This open-air amphitheater hosts numerous musical shows, from the Honolulu Symphony to traditional Hawaiian music.

Continue walking down till the end of the block (corner of Monsarrat and Paki aves.) to the:

A glut of choices at Art on the Zoo Fence.

10 Queen Kapiolani Garden

You'll see a range of hibiscus plants and dozens of varieties of roses, including the somewhat rare Hawaiian rose. The tranquil gardens are always open and are a great place to wander and relax.

Across the street, on a Wednesday morning, you'll find the:

11 People's Open Market

Open from 10 to 11am on Wednesdays, the farmers' market with its open stalls is an excellent spot to buy fresh produce and flowers. See p. 250 for more information.

After you make your purchases, continue in the Diamond Head direction down Paki Avenue to the:

12 Diamond Head Tennis Courts

Located on the mauka side of Paki Avenue, the free city and county tennis courts are open for play during daylight hours 7 days a week. Tennis etiquette suggests that if someone is waiting for a court, limit your play to 45 minutes.

After watching or playing, turn onto Kalakaua Avenue and begin walking back toward Waikiki to:

13 Sans Souci Beach

Located next to the New Otani Kaimana Beach Hotel (p. 107), this is one of the best swimming beaches in Waikiki. The shallow reef, which is close to shore, keeps the waters calm. Farther out is good snorkeling in the coral reef by the Kapua Channel. Facilities include outdoor showers and a lifeguard. See p. 156 for more information.

After a brief swim, keep walking toward Waikiki until you come to the:

14 Natatorium

This huge concrete structure next to the beach is both a memorial to the soldiers of World War I and a 100-meter saltwater swimming pool. Opened in 1927, when Honolulu had hopes of hosting the Olympics, the ornate swimming pool fell into disuse and disrepair after World War II, and was finally closed in 1979. The last mayor of the City and County of Honolulu wanted to reopen the saltwater pool and poured $4.4 million into restoring the outside arches to the building, construction of modern restrooms and showers, and refurbishment of the bleacher seating. The subsequent administration balked at spending the estimated $6.4 million more needed to make the saltwater swimming pool usable again, and the money was released back into the city's general fund—though volunteers continue to fight for its restoration. Stop by and take a peek at this once-magnificent site.

After a brief stop here, continue on to the:

15 Waikiki Aquarium

The Aquarium is located at 2777 Kalakaua Ave. Try not to miss this stop—the tropical aquarium is worth a look if only to see the only living **chambered nautilus** born in captivity. See p. 207 for more information.

Only the freshest produce is available at the People's Open Market.

The young and the beautiful flock to Sans Souci Beach.

Your final stop is:

16 Kapiolani Beach Park

Relax on the stretch of grassy lawn alongside the sandy beach, one of the best-kept secrets of Waikiki. This beach park is much less crowded than the beaches of Waikiki, plus it has adjacent grassy lawns, barbecue areas, picnic tables, restrooms, and showers. The swimming is good here year-round, a surfing spot known as "Public's" is offshore, and there's always a game going at the volleyball courts. The middle section of the beach park, in front of the pavilion, is known as Queen's Beach or Queen's Surf and is popular with the gay community.

EAST OAHU ATTRACTIONS

From the high-rises of Waikiki, venture down Kalakaua Avenue through tree-lined Kapiolani Park to take a look at a different side of Oahu, the arid south shore. The landscape here is more moonscape, with prickly cacti onshore and, in winter, spouting whales cavorting in the water. Some call it the South Shore, others refer to it as Sandy's (after the mile-long beach here), but Hawaiians call it **Ka Iwi,** which means "the bone"—no doubt because of all the bone-cracking shore breaks along this popular bodyboarding coastline. The beaches here are long, wide, and popular with local daredevils.

This open, scenic coast is the best place on Oahu to watch sea, shore, and even land birds. It's also a good whale-watching spot in season, and the night sky is ideal for amateur astronomers on the lookout for meteors, comets, and stars.

To get to this coast, follow Kalakaua Avenue past the multitiered Dillingham Fountain and around the bend in the road, which now becomes Poni Moi Road. Make a right on Diamond Head Road and begin the climb up the side of the old crater. At the top are several lookout points, so if the official Diamond Head Lookout is jammed with cars, try one of the other lookouts just down the road. The view of the rolling waves is spectacular; take the time to pull over.

Diamond Head Road rolls downhill now into the ritzy community of **Kahala.** At the V in the road at triangular Fort Ruger Park, veer to your right and continue on palm-tree-lined Kahala Avenue. Make a left on Hunakai Street, then a right on Kilauea Avenue, and look for the sign H-1 WEST—WAIMANALO. Turn right at the sign, although you won't get on the H-1 Freeway; get on the Kalanianaole Highway, a four-lane highway interrupted every few blocks by a stoplight. This suburban bedroom community to Honolulu is marked by malls on the left and beach parks on the right.

About a half-hour outside of Waikiki, you'll see the turnoff to **Hanauma Bay ★★** (p. 156) on the right. This marine preserve is a great place to stop for a swim; you'll find the friendliest fish on the island here. *Note:* The beach park is closed on Tuesdays.

Around mile marker 11, the jagged lava coast itself spouts sea foam at the **Halona Blowhole.** Look out to sea from Halona over Sandy Beach and across the 26-mile gulf to neighboring Molokai and the faint triangular shadow of Lanai on the far horizon. **Sandy Beach** (p. 158) is Oahu's most dangerous beach; it's the only one with an ambulance always standing by to whisk injured wave catchers to the hospital. Bodyboarders just love it.

The coast looks raw and empty along this stretch, but the road weaves past old Hawaiian fishponds and the famous formation known as **Pele's Chair,** just off Kalanianaole Highway (Hwy. 72) above Queen's Beach. From a distance, the lava-rock outcropping looks like a mighty throne; it's believed to be the fire goddess's last resting place on Oahu before she flew off to continue her work on other islands.

Ahead lies 647-foot-high **Makapuu Point,** with a lighthouse that once signaled safe passage for steamship passengers arriving from San Francisco. The automated light now brightens Oahu's south coast for passing tankers, fishing boats, and sailors. You can take a short hike up here for a spectacular vista (p. 179).

Turn the corner at Makapuu, and you're on Oahu's windward side, where cooling trade winds propel windsurfers across turquoise bays; the waves at **Makapuu Beach Park** are perfect for bodysurfing (p. 159).

Ahead, the coastal vista is a profusion of fluted green mountains and strange peaks, edged by golden beaches and the blue, blue Pacific. The 3,000-foot-high sheer green Koolau Mountains plunge almost straight down, presenting an irresistible jumping-off spot for hang-glider pilots, who catch the thermals on hours-long rides.

Winding up the coast, Kalanianaole Highway (Hwy. 72) leads through rural **Waimanalo,** a country beach town of nurseries and stables, fresh-fruit stands, and some of the island's best conch and triton shell

Sea spray from the Halona Blowhole.

The craggy and probably uncomfortable Pele's Chair.

specimens at roadside stands. Nearly 4 miles long, **Waimanalo Beach** is Oahu's longest beach and the most popular for bodysurfing. Take a swim here or head on to **Kailua Beach ★★**, one of Hawaii's best (p. 160).

If it's still early in the day, you can head up the lush, green Windward Coast by turning right at the Castle Junction, Highway 72 and Highway 61 (which is also Kailua Rd. on the makai, or seaward, side of the junction, and Kalanianaole Hwy. on the mauka, or inland, side of the junction), and continuing down Kailua Road (Hwy. 61). After Kailua Road crosses the Kaelepulu Stream, the name of the road changes to Kuulei Road. When Kuulei Road ends, turn left onto Kalaheo Avenue, which becomes Kaneohe Bay Drive after it crosses the Kawainui Channel. Follow this scenic drive around the peninsula until it crosses Kamehameha Highway (Hwy. 83); turn right and continue on Kamehameha Highway for a scenic drive along the ocean.

If you're in a hurry to get back to Waikiki, turn left at Castle Junction and head over the Pali Highway (Hwy. 61), which becomes Bishop Street in Honolulu and ends at Ala Moana. Turn left for Waikiki; it's the second beach on the right.

Lanikai Beach ★★ This is one of the best places on Oahu to greet the sunrise. Watch the sky slowly move from pitch black to wisps of gray to burnt orange as the sun rises over the two tiny offshore islands of Mokulua. Use your five senses for this experience: hear the birds sing, feel the gentle breezes on your face, taste the salt in the air, smell the ocean, and see the kaleidoscope of colors as another day dawns.

Mokulua Dr., Kailua. To get here from Honolulu, take Hwy. 61 (Pali Hwy.) into Kailua. Follow the street (which becomes Kailua Rd., then becomes Kuulei Rd.) until it ends. Turn right on Kalaheo Ave. (which will become Kawailoa Rd. in a few blocks). Follow the road over the canal. At the stop sign, turn left on Kaneapu Place. At the fork in the road, bear left on one-way Aalapapa Dr. Turn right at any cross street onto Mokulua Dr. No bus service.

Nuuanu Pali Lookout ★ 📷 Gale-force winds sometimes howl through the mountain pass at this 1,186-foot-high perch guarded by 3,000-foot peaks, so hold onto your hat—and small children. But if you walk up from the parking lot to the precipice, you'll be rewarded with a view that'll blow you away. At the edge, the dizzying panorama of Oahu's windward side is breathtaking: Clouds low enough to pinch scoot by on trade winds; pinnacles of the *pali* (cliffs), green with ferns,

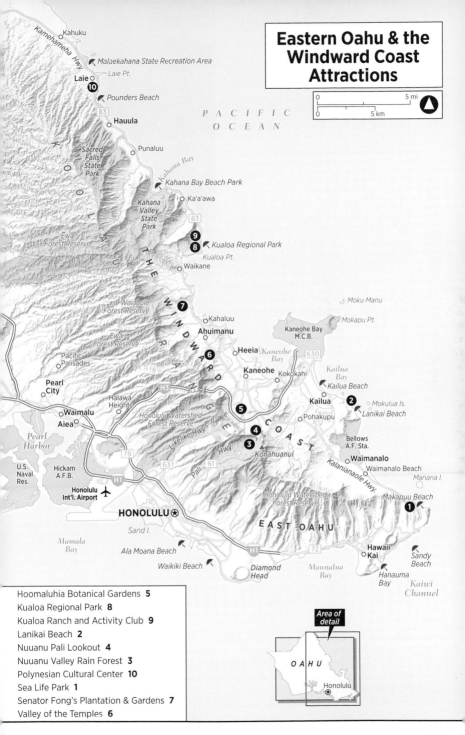

Eastern Oahu & the Windward Coast Attractions

PACIFIC OCEAN

Kahuku

Kamehameha Hwy

Malaekahana State Recreation Area

Laie Pt.

Laie ○
10

Pounders Beach

83

Hauula ○

Punaluu

Sacred Falls State Park

Kahana Bay

Kahana Bay Beach Park

Ka'a'awa

Kahana Valley State Park

83

Ewa Forest Reserve

9
8 Kualoa Regional Park

Kualoa Pt.

Waikane ○

Moku Manu

Waiahole Forest Reserve

7

○ Kahaluu

Ahuimanu

Mokapu Pt.

Kaneohe Bay M.C.B.

Ewa Forest Reserve

6

Heeia

Kaneohe Bay

630

Kaneohe ○ Kokokahi

Pacific Palisades

Kailua Bay

Pearl City

Halawa Heights

H3

Honolulu Watershed Forest Reserve

Kailua Beach

2 Mokulua Is.

Waimalu ○

Aiea ○

5

Kailua ○

Lanikai Beach

Pohakupu

Pearl Harbor

Likelike Hwy.

4
3

Konahuanui

Bellows A.F. Sta.

U.S. Naval Res.

78

63

Pali Hwy.

61

Waimanalo

Kalanianaole Hwy.

Waimanalo Beach

Hickam A.F.B.

Manana I.

H1

Honolulu Int'l. Airport

Honolulu Watershed Forest Reserve

Makapuu Beach

1

HONOLULU ✪

Sand I.

EAST OAHU

Mamala Bay

Ala Moana Beach

H1

72

Hawaii Kai ○

Sandy Beach

Waikiki Beach

Diamond Head

Maunalua Bay

Hanauma Bay

Kaiwi Channel

0 ——— 5 mi
0 ——— 5 km

Hoomaluhia Botanical Gardens **5**
Kualoa Regional Park **8**
Kualoa Ranch and Activity Club **9**
Lanikai Beach **2**
Nuuanu Pali Lookout **4**
Nuuanu Valley Rain Forest **3**
Polynesian Cultural Center **10**
Sea Life Park **1**
Senator Fong's Plantation & Gardens **7**
Valley of the Temples **6**

Area of detail

O A H U

Honolulu ✪

231

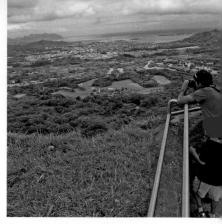

The expansive views from Nuuanu Pali.

often disappear in the mist; the vertical slopes of the Koolaus end in lush green valleys that become the town of Kaneohe; and the Pacific, a magnificent blue, dotted with whitecaps, beckons in the distance. Definitely take a jacket with you; it can be quite misty and cool at the lookout. On very windy days, you'll notice that the waterfalls look as though they are flowing up rather than down.

In 1898, John Wilson built the road up to the lookout using 200 laborers. Even before the road existed, the Nuuanu Pali (which translates as "cool heights") was infamous because legend claims it as the location of Kamehameha the Great's last battle. Although some academic scholars scoff at this, the story alleges that in 1795, Kamehameha pursued Oahu's warriors up Nuuanu to these cliffs and waged a battle in his attempt to unite the Hawaiian islands. Supposedly, the Oahu warriors were driven over the cliffs by Kamehameha's men. Some say the battle never happened, some say it happened but with only a few men fighting, and some say thousands were forced over the cliff, plunging to their deaths. Others say at night you can still hear the cries of these long-dead warriors coming from the valley below.

From on high, the tropical palette of green and blue runs down to the sea. Combine this 10-minute stop with a trip over the Pali to the windward side.

Near the summit of Pali Hwy. (Hwy. 61); take the Nuuanu Pali Lookout turnoff.

Nuuanu Valley Rain Forest 🎁 It's not the same as a peaceful nature walk, but if time is short and hiking isn't your thing, Honolulu has a rainforest you can drive through. It's only a few minutes from downtown Honolulu in verdant Nuuanu Valley, where it rains nearly 300 inches a year. And it's easy to reach: As the Pali Highway leaves residential Nuuanu and begins its climb though the forest, the last stoplight is the Nuuanu Pali Road turnoff; turn right for a junglelike detour of about 2 miles under a thick canopy strung with liana vines, past giant bamboo that creaks in the wind, Norfolk pines, and wild shell ginger. The road rises and the vegetation clears as you drive, blinking in the bright light of day, past a small mountain reservoir.

Soon the road rejoins the Pali Highway. Kailua is to the right and Honolulu to the left—but it can be a hair-raising turn. Instead, turn right, go a half-mile to the Nuuanu Pali Lookout (see above), stop for a panoramic view of Oahu's windward side, and return to the town-bound highway on the other side.

Take the Old Nuuanu Pali Rd. exit off Pali Hwy. (Hwy. 61).

Sea Life Park ★ ☺ This 62-acre park in East Oahu is one of the island's top attractions. It features whales from Puget Sound, Atlantic bottle-nosed dolphins, California sea lions, and penguins going through their motions to the delight of kids of all ages. With children, allow all day to take in the sights. Also popular are the Hawaiian reef tank full of tropical fish; the "touch" pool, where you can feel a real sea cucumber (commonly found in tide pools); and a bird sanctuary, where you can see such birds as the red-footed booby and the frigate bird. The chief curiosity, though, is the world's only "wholphin"—a cross between a false killer whale and an Atlantic bottle-nosed dolphin. On-site, marine biologists operate a recovery center for endangered marine life; during your visit, you'll be able to see rehabilitated Hawaiian monk seals and seabirds.

41-202 Kalanianaole Hwy. (at Makapuu Point), Honolulu. © **808/259-7933.** www.sealifepark hawaii.com. Admission $30 adults, $20 children 3–12. Daily 10:30am–5pm. Parking $5. Shuttle buses from Waikiki $21. Bus: 22 or 23.

WINDWARD COAST ATTRACTIONS

From the **Nuuanu Pali Lookout ★**, near the summit of the Pali Highway (Hwy. 61), you get the first hint of the other side of Oahu, a region so green and lovely that it could be an island sibling of Tahiti. With its many beaches and bays, the scenic 30-mile Windward Coast parallels the corduroy-ridged, nearly perpendicular cliffs of the Koolau Range, which separates the windward side of the island from Honolulu and the rest of Oahu. As you descend on the serpentine Pali Highway beneath often gushing waterfalls, you'll see the nearly-1,000-foot spike of **Olomana,** the bold pinnacle that always reminds us of Devil's Tower National Monument in Wyoming, and beyond, the Hawaiian village of **Waimanalo.**

From the Pali Highway, to the right is **Kailua,** Hawaii's biggest beach town, with more than 50,000 residents and two special beaches, Kailua and Lanikai, begging for visitors. Funky little Kailua is lined with million-dollar houses next to tarpaper shacks, antiques shops, and bed-and-breakfasts. Although the Pali Highway (Hwy. 61) proceeds directly to the coast, it undergoes two name changes, becoming first Kalanianaole Highway—from the intersection of Kamehameha Highway (Hwy. 83)—and then Kailua Road as it heads into Kailua town; but the road remains Highway 61 the whole way. Kailua Road ends at the T-intersection at Kalaheo Drive, which follows the coast in a northerly and southerly direction. Turn right on South Kalaheo Drive to get to Kailua Beach Park and Lanikai Beach. No signs point the way, but you can't miss the beaches.

If you spend a day at the beach here, stick around for sunset, when the sun sinks behind the Koolau Range and tints the clouds pink and orange. After a hard day at the beach, you'll work up an appetite, and Kailua has several great, inexpensive restaurants (p. 149).

If you want to skip the beaches this time, turn left on North Kalaheo Drive, which becomes Kaneohe Bay Drive as it skirts Kaneohe Bay and leads back to Kamehameha Highway (Hwy. 83), which then passes through Kaneohe. The suburban maze of Kaneohe is one giant strip mall of retail excess that mars one of the Pacific's most picturesque bays. After clearing this obstacle, the place begins to look like Hawaii again.

The imposing and sharp Olomana.

Incredibly scenic Kaneohe Bay is spiked with islets and lined with gold-sand beach parks like **Kualoa,** a favorite picnic spot (p. 160). The bay has a barrier reef and four tiny islets, one of which is known as Moku o loe, or Coconut Island. Don't be surprised if it looks familiar—it appeared in *Gilligan's Island.*

At Heeia State Park is **Heeia Fish Pond,** which ancient Hawaiians built by enclosing natural bays with rocks to trap fish on the incoming tide. The 88-acre fishpond, which is made of lava rock and had four watchtowers to observe fish movement and several sluice gates along the 5,000-foot-long wall, is now being restored.

Stop by **Heeia Pier,** which juts onto Kaneohe Bay. You can take a snorkel cruise here, or sail out to a sandbar in the middle of the bay for an incredible view of Oahu that most people, even those who live here, never see. If it's Tuesday or Thursday through Sunday between 7am and 4pm, stop in at the **Deli on Heeia Kea Pier** (✆ **808/235-2192**). They have served fishermen, sailors, and kayakers the beach town's best omelets and plate lunches at reasonable prices since 1979.

Everyone calls it **Chinaman's Hat,** but the tiny island off the eastern shore of Kualoa Regional Park is really named **Mokolii.** It's a sacred *puu honua,* or place of refuge, like the restored Puu Honua Honaunau on the Big Island of Hawaii. Excavations have unearthed evidence that this area was the home of ancient *alii.* Early Hawaiians believed that Mokolii ("fin of the lizard") is all that remains of a *mo'o,* or lizard, slain by Pele's sister, Hi'iaka, and hurled into the sea. At low tide, you can swim out to the island, but keep an eye on the changing tide, which can sweep you out to sea. The islet has a small, sandy beach and is a bird preserve, so don't spook the red-footed boobies.

Little poly-voweled beach towns, such as **Kaaawa, Hauula, Punaluu,** and **Kahaluu,** pop up along the coast, offering passersby shell shops and art galleries to explore. Famed hula photographer **Kim Taylor Reece** lives on this coast; his gallery at 53-866 Kamehameha Hwy., near Sacred Falls (✆ **808/293-2000**), is open Thursday to Saturday, noon to 6pm. You'll also see working cattle ranches, fishermen's wharves, and roadside fruit and flower stands vending ice-cold coconuts (to drink) and tree-ripened mangoes, papayas, and apple bananas.

Sugar, once the sole industry of this region, is gone. But **Kahuku,** the former sugar-plantation town, has found new life as a small aquaculture community with prawn farms that supply island restaurants.

From here, continue along Kamehameha Highway (Hwy. 83) to the North Shore.

Hoomaluhia Botanical Gardens ★ At the foot of the steepled Koolau Mountains, this 400-acre botanical garden is the perfect place for a picnic. Its name means "a peaceful refuge," and that's exactly what the Army Corps of Engineers created when they installed a flood-control project here, which resulted in a 32-acre freshwater lake and garden. Just unfold a beach mat, lie back, and watch the clouds race across the rippled cliffs of the majestic Koolau Range. This is one of Oahu's few public places that provides a close-up view of the steepled cliffs. The park has hiking trails and—best of all—the island's only free inland campground (p. 118). If you like hiking and nature, plan to spend at least a half-day here. ***Note:*** Be prepared for rain, mud, and mosquitoes.

45-680 Luluku Rd., Kaneohe. ✆ **808/233-7323.** www.co.honolulu.hi.us/parks/hbg/hmbg.htm. Free admission. Daily 9am–4pm. Guided nature hikes Sat 10am and Sun 1pm. Take H-1 to the Pali Hwy. (Hwy. 61); turn left on Kamehameha Hwy. (Hwy. 83); at the 4th light, turn left onto Luluku Rd. Bus: 55 or 56 will stop on Kamehameha Hwy.; it's a 2-mile walk to the visitor center.

A craftsman whittles a sculpture on Kaaawa's main street.

Senator Fong's lush flora.

Kualoa Ranch and Activity Club This once-working ranch now has various adventure packages covering numerous activities on its 4,000 acres, including horseback riding, ATV rides, ranch tours, and more.

49-560 Kamehameha Hwy., Kaaawa. ✆ **800/231-7321** or 808/237-7321. www.kualoa.com. Reservations required. Various activity packages: single activities $23–$95. Daily 8am–5pm. Take H-1 to the Likelike Hwy. (Hwy. 63), turn left at Kahekili Hwy. (Hwy. 83), and continue to Kaaawa. Bus: 52.

Polynesian Cultural Center ★ ☺ Experience the natural beauty and culture of the entire vast Pacific in a single day at the Polynesian Cultural Center, a kind of living museum of Polynesia. Here you can see firsthand the lifestyles, songs, dance, costumes, and architecture of seven Pacific islands or archipelagos—Fiji, New Zealand, the Marquesas, Samoa, Tahiti, Tonga, and Hawaii—in the re-created villages scattered throughout the 42-acre lagoon park. A $1.1 million renovation project remodeled the front entrance and added an exhibit on the story of the Polynesian immigration.

You travel through this museum by foot or in a canoe on a man-made freshwater lagoon. Each village is "inhabited" by native students from Polynesia who attend Hawaii's Brigham Young University. The park, which is operated by the Mormon Church, also features a variety of stage shows celebrating the music, dance, history, and culture of Polynesia. A luau takes place every evening. Because a visit can take up to 8 hours, it's a good idea to arrive before 2pm. Just beyond the center is the **Hawaii Temple** of the Church of Jesus Christ of Latter-Day Saints, which is built of volcanic rock and concrete in the form of a Greek cross and includes reflecting pools, formal gardens, and royal palms. Completed in 1919, it was the first Mormon temple built outside the continental United States. An optional tour of the Temple Visitors Center, as well as neighboring Brigham Young University Hawaii, is included in the package admission prices.

55-370 Kamehameha Hwy., Laie. ✆ **800/367-7060,** 808/293-3333, or 808/923-2911. www.polynesia.com. Various packages available for $50–$229 adults, $36–$179 children 3–11. Parking $8. Mon–Sat Noon–9:30pm. Take H-1 to Pali Hwy. (Hwy. 61) and turn left on Kamehameha Hwy. (Hwy. 83). Bus: B or 8 transfer to 55. Polynesian Cultural Center coaches $22 round-trip; call numbers above to book.

Senator Fong's Plantation & Gardens Senator Hiram Fong, the first Chinese-American elected to the U.S. Senate, served 17 years before retiring to this 725-acre tropical garden years ago. This land originally belonged to King Lunalilo. In 1950, Senator Fong purchased it. The landscape you see today is relatively the same as what early Polynesians saw hundreds of years ago, with forests of kukui, hala, koa, and *ohia-'ai* (mountain apple). Ti and pili grass still cover the slopes. It's definitely worth an hour—if you haven't already seen enough flora to last a lifetime.

47-285 Pulama Rd., Kaneohe. ✆ **808/239-6775.** www.fonggarden.net. Admission $15 adults, $13 seniors, $9 children 5–12. Daily 10am–2pm; guided walking tours daily 10:30am and 1pm. Take the H-1 to the Likelike Hwy. (Hwy. 63); turn left at Kahekili Hwy. (Hwy. 83); continue to Kaneohe and turn left on Pulama Rd. Bus: 8 or B then transfer to 55; it's a 1-mile walk uphill from the stop.

Valley of the Temples This famous cemetery in a cleft of the pali is stalked by wild peacocks and about 700 curious people a day, who pay to see the 9-foot meditation Buddha, 2 acres of ponds full of more than 10,000 Japanese koi carp, and Byodo-In, a replica of Japan's 900-year-old Buddhist temple. The original, made of wood, stands in Uji, on the outskirts of Kyoto; the Hawaiian version, made of concrete, was erected in 1968 to commemorate the 100th anniversary of the arrival of the first Japanese immigrants to Hawaii. It's not the same as seeing the original, but it's worth a detour. A 3-ton brass temple bell brings good luck to those who can ring it—although the gongs do jar the Zen-like serenity of this little bit of Japan. If you're in a rush, you can sail through here in an hour, but you'll probably want to stay longer.

47-200 Kahekili Hwy. (across the street from Temple Valley Shopping Center), Kaneohe. ✆ **808/239-8811.** Admission $3 adults, $2 children under 12 and seniors 65 and over. Daily 9am–5pm. Take the H-1 to the Likelike Hwy. (Hwy. 63); after the Wilson Tunnel, get in the right lane and take the Kahekili Hwy. (Hwy. 63); at the 6th traffic light is the entrance to the cemetery (on the left). Bus: B, then transfer to 65.

Byodo-In graces the Valley of the Temples.

CENTRAL & LEEWARD OAHU ATTRACTIONS

If you can afford the splurge, rent a bright, shiny convertible—the perfect car for Oahu, since you can tan as you go—and head for the North Shore (p. 73) and Hawaii's surf city: Haleiwa, a quaint turn-of-the-20th-century sugar-plantation town designated a historic site. A collection of faded clapboard stores with a picturesque harbor, Haleiwa has evolved into a surfer outpost and major road-side attraction with art galleries, restaurants, and shops that sell hand-decorated clothing, jewelry, and sports gear.

But getting to the North Shore is half the fun. You have two choices: The first is to meander north along the lush Windward Coast, through country ham-lets with roadside stands selling mangoes, bright tropical pareus, fresh corn, and pond-raised prawns. For attractions along that route, see p. 233.

The second choice is to cruise up the H-2 through Oahu's broad and fer-tile central valley, past Pearl Harbor and the Schofield Barracks of *From Here to Eternity* fame, and on through the red-earthed heart of the island, where pine-apple and sugar-cane fields stretch from the Koolau to the Waianae mountains, until the sea reappears on the horizon. If you take this route, the tough part is get-ting on and off the H-1 freeway from Waikiki, which is done by way of convoluted routing on neighborhood streets. Try McCully Street off Ala Wai Boulevard, which is always crowded but usually the most direct route.

Once you're on H-1, stay to the right side; the freeway tends to divide abruptly. Keep following the signs for the H-1 (it separates off to Hwy. 78 at the airport and reunites later on; either way will get you there), then the H-1/H-2. Leave the H-1 where the two "interstates" divide; take the H-2 up the middle of the island, heading north and following signs directing you toward the town of Wahiawa.

The H-2 runs out and becomes a two-lane country road about 18 miles outside downtown Honolulu, near Schofield Barracks (p. 240). The highway be-comes Kamehameha Highway (Hwy. 99 and later Hwy. 83) at Wahiawa. Just past Wahiawa, about a half-hour out of Honolulu, the **Dole Pineapple Plantation,** 64-1550 Kamehameha Hwy. (© **808/621-8408;** www.dole-plantation.com; bus no. 52), offers a rest stop with pineapples, pineapple history, pineapple trinkets, and pine-apple juice, open daily from 9:30am to 5pm. This agricultural exhibit/re-tail area also features a maze kids will love to wander through, open daily from 9am to 5pm; admission is free. However there are fees for the tours: the Pineapple Express is a single-en-gine diesel locomotive with four cars that takes a 22-minute tour around 2¼ miles of the plantation's grounds, with an educational spiel on the legacy of the

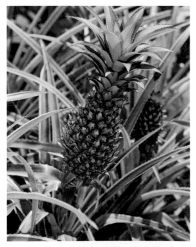

The Dole Plantation's signature pineapples.

pineapple and agriculture in Hawaii. The first tour departs at 9:30am, and the last tour gets back to the station at 5pm. Cost is $8 for adults, $6 for children 4 to 12 (free for ages 3 and under). The Plantation Garden tour is a self-guided tour through the various crops that have been grown on Oahu's North Shore. The tour costs $5 for adults and $4.25 for children. The Maze Garden Tour is $6 for adults and $4 for children ages 4 to 12, free for children under 4 years old. "Kam" Highway, as everyone calls it, will be your road for most of the rest of the trip to Haleiwa.

An old-time Hawaiian Railway train (with requisite old-time conductor).

On the central plains of Oahu, tract homes and malls with factory-outlet stores are now spreading across abandoned sugar cane fields, where sandalwood forests used to stand at the foot of Mount Kaala, the mighty summit of Oahu. Hawaiian chiefs once sent commoners into the thick sandalwood forests to cut down trees, which were then sold to China traders for small fortunes. The scantily clad natives caught cold in the cool uplands, and many died.

Also on these plains, in 1908, the U.S. Army pitched a tent that later became a fort. And on December 7, 1941, Japanese pilots came screaming through Kolekole Pass to shoot up the Art Deco barracks at Schofield, sending soldiers running for cover, and then flew on to sink ships at Pearl Harbor.

Hawaiian Railway ☺ All aboard this train ride back into history! Between 1890 and 1947 the chief mode of transportation for Oahu's sugar mills was the Oahu Railway and Land Co.'s narrow-gauge trains. The line carried not only equipment, raw sugar, and supplies, but also passengers from one side of the island to the other. You can relive those days every Sunday with a 1½-hour narrated ride through Ko Olina Resort and out to Makaha. As an added attraction, on the second Sunday of the month, you can ride on the nearly 100-year-old, custom-built, parlor-observation car belonging to Benjamin F. Dillingham, founder of the Oahu Railway and Land Co. The fare for this treat is $20 (no kids under 13), and you must reserve in advance.

Ewa Station, Ewa Beach. ✆ **808/681-5461.** www.hawaiianrailway.com. Admission $10 adults, $7 seniors and children 2–12. Departures Sun at 1pm and 3pm; Mon–Fri by appointment. Take H-1 west to Exit 5A; take Hwy. 76 south for 2½ miles to Tesoro Gas; turn right on Renton Rd. and drive 1½ miles to end of paved section. The station is on the left. Bus: E to Ft. Weaver Rd., then transfer to no. 44, which goes through Ewa and drops you off outside the gate.

Hawaii's Plantation Village The hour-long tour of this restored 50-acre village offers a glimpse back in time to when sugar planters shaped the land, economy, and culture of Hawaii. From 1852, when the first contract laborers arrived here from China, to 1947, when the plantation era ended, more than 400,000 men, women, and children from China, Japan, Portugal, Puerto Rico, Korea, and the Philippines came to work the sugar cane fields. The "talk story" tour brings the old village alive with 30 faithfully restored camp houses, Chinese and Japanese temples, the Plantation Store, and even a sumo-wrestling ring.

Central & Leeward Oahu Attractions

Kauai Channel

Kahuku Pt.

THE NORTH SHORE

Kawela
Waialee

Kahuku

Kamehameha Hwy.

83

Sunset Beach
Ehukai Beach
Pupukea Beach
Waimea
Waimea Beach Park

Pupukea-Paumalu
Forest Reserve

83

Kaiwikoele Str.

Kaena Pt.

Kaena Point State Park

Kuaokala Game Mgmt. Area

Dillingham Airport ✈

Farrington 930 *Hwy.*

Haleiwa

Waialua

Opaeula Str.

Kamehameha Hwy.

99

Poamoho Str.

Dole Pineapple Plantation

Wahiawa Naval Res.

Ewa Forest Reserve

Makua Valley Mil. Res.

Mokuleia Forest Reserve

803

Whitmore Village

Schofield Barracks Mil. Res.

CENTRAL OAHU (EWA PLAIN)

❶ Wahiawa
❷

Kaala

Makua Keaau Forest Reserve

Waianae Kai Forest Reserve

Kahanaunu Str.

H2

Waipio Acres

Makaha Beach Park
Makaha
Lahilahi Pt.

WAIANAE RANGE

LEEWARD OAHU (WAIANAE COAST)

Farrington Hwy.

Lualualei Naval Res.

Kaua

Mililani

99

Nanakuli Forest Reserve

750

Waipio

Pacific Palisades

Waianae

Maili

Pearl City

Nanakuli

93

Village Park

❸ Waipahu

Waimalu

Aiea

Waipo Pen.

Pearl Harbor

H1

Makakilo

Ewa Villages

U.S. Naval Res.

Hickam A.F.B.

Ko Olina Lagoons

❺
❹ Kapolei

76

95

✈ Kalaeloa Airport

Ewa Beach

Mamala Bay

Area of detail

OAHU

Honolulu ✪

0 _____ 5 mi
0 _____ 5 km

Hawaii's Plantation Village	**3**
Hawaiian Railway	**4**
Kukaniloko Birthing Stones	**1**
U.S. Army Schofield Barracks	**2**
Wet 'n' Wild	**5**

EXPLORING OAHU | Central & Leeward Oahu Attractions

Hawaii's long-dormant Plantation Village fields.

Waipahu Cultural Garden Park, 94-695 Waipahu St. (at Waipahu Depot Rd.), Waipahu. © 808/677-0110. www.hawaiiplantationvillage.org. Admission (including escorted tour) $13 adults; $10 seniors; $7 military personnel; $5 children 4–11; children 3 and under free. Mon–Sat 10am–2pm. Take H-1 west to the Waikele-Waipahu exit (exit 7); get in the left exit lane and turn left on Paiwa St.; at the 5th light, turn right onto Waipahu St.; after the 2nd light, turn left. Bus: E or 13 transfering to 43.

Kukaniloko Birthing Stones This is the most sacred site in central Oahu. Two rows of 18 lava rocks once flanked a central birthing stone, where women of ancient Hawaii gave birth to potential *alii.* The rocks, according to Hawaiian belief, held the power to ease the labor pains of childbirth. Birth rituals involved 48 chiefs who pounded drums to announce the arrival of newborns likely to become chiefs. Children born here were taken to the now-destroyed Holonopahu Heiau in the pineapple field, where chiefs ceremoniously cut the umbilical cord.

Used by Oahu's *alii* for generations of births, the *pohaku* (rocks), many in bowl-like shapes, now lie strewn in a grove of trees that stands in a pineapple field. Some think the site also may have served ancient astronomers—like a Hawaiian Stonehenge. Petroglyphs of human forms and circles appear on some of the stones. The Wahiawa Hawaiian Civic Club recently erected two interpretive signs, one explaining why this was chosen as a birth site and the other telling how the stones were used to aid in the birthing process.

Off Kamehameha Hwy., btw. Wahiawa and Haleiwa, on Plantation Rd., opposite the road to Whitmore Village.

U.S. Army Schofield Barracks James Jones, author of *From Here to Eternity,* called Schofield Barracks "the most beautiful army post the U.S. has or ever had." The *Honolulu Star Bulletin* called it a country club. More than a million soldiers just called Schofield Barracks home. With its broad, palm-lined boulevards and Art Deco buildings, this old army cavalry post is still the largest operated by the U.S. Army outside the continental United States. And it's still one of the best places to be a soldier.

The artfully arranged Kukaniloko Birthing Stones.

You can no longer visit the barracks themselves, but the history of Schofield Barracks and the 25th Infantry Division is told in the small **Tropic Lightning Museum.** Displays range from a 1917 bunker exhibit to a replica of Vietnam's infamous Cu Chi tunnels.

Schofield Barracks, Building 361, Waianae Ave. © **808/655-0438.** www.25idl.army.mil/tropic%20lightning%20museum/main.asp. Free admission. Tues–Sun 10am–4pm. Bus: 19 to Ala Moana center then 52 to Wahiawa; transfer at California Ave. to no. 72, Schofield Barracks Shuttle.

Wet 'n' Wild ★ ☺ Formerly called the Hawaiian Waters Adventure Park, kids love this 29-acre water-theme amusement park, which opened in 1999 with some $14 million in attractions. Plan to spend the day. Highlights are a football-field-size wave pool for bodysurfing, two 65-foot-high free-fall slides, two water-toboggan bullet slides, inner-tube slides, body-flume slides, a continuous river for floating inner tubes, and separate pools for adults, teens, and children. In addition, there are restaurants, Hawaiian performances, and shops.

400 Farrington Hwy., Kapolei. © **808/674-WAVE** [674-9283]. www.hawaiiwetnwild.com. Admission $42 adults, $32 children 3–11, free for children 2 and under (check website for special offers). Hours vary, but generally hours are daily 10:30am–4 or 5pm in peak season (summer); during off-season 10:30am–3:30 or 4pm; closed some weekdays. Take H-1 west to Exit 1 (Campbell Industrial Park). Make an immediate left to Farrington Hwy.; you will see the park on your left.

NORTH SHORE ATTRACTIONS

Only 28 miles from Waikiki is surf city: **Haleiwa ★**, the funky ex-sugar-plantation town that's the world capital of big-wave surfing. This beach town really comes alive in winter, when waves rise up, light rain falls, temperatures dip into the 70s, and practically every surfer in the world is here to see and be seen.

Officially designated a historic cultural and scenic district, Haleiwa thrives in a time warp recalling the turn of the 20th century, when it was founded by sugar baron Benjamin Dillingham, who built a 30-mile railroad to link his Honolulu and North Shore plantations in 1899. He opened a Victorian hotel overlooking

Jameson's iconic mai tai.

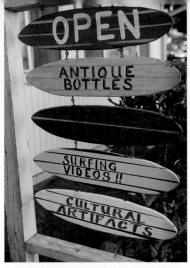

Surfboards everywhere at the North Shore Surf and Cultural Museum.

Kaiaka Bay and named it Haleiwa, or "House of the Iwa," the tropical seabird often seen here. The hotel and railroad are gone, but Haleiwa, which was rediscovered in the late 1960s by hippies, resonates with rare rustic charm. Tofu, not taro, is a staple in the local diet. Arts and crafts, boutiques, and burger stands line both sides of the town. Haleiwa's busy fishing harbor is full of charter boats and captains who hunt the Kauai Channel daily for tuna, mahimahi, and marlin. The bartenders at **Jameson's ★**, 62-540 Kamehameha Hwy. (p. 151; ✆ **808/637-6272**), make the best mai tais on the North Shore; they use the original recipe by Trader Vic Bergeron.

Once in Haleiwa, the hot and thirsty traveler should report directly to the nearest shave-ice stand, usually **Matsumoto Shave Ice ★★**, 66-087 Kamehameha Hwy. (p. 41; ✆ **808/637-4827**). For 40 years, this small, humble shop operated by the Matsumoto family has served a popular rendition of the Hawaii-style snow cone flavored with tropical tastes. The local favorites are *li hing mui* (lee hing moo-*ee*, which is sweet, sour, and salty), or with sweet Japanese adzuki beans hidden inside.

Just down the road are some of the fabled shrines of surfing—**Waimea Beach, Banzai Pipeline, Sunset Beach**—where some of the world's largest waves, reaching 30 feet and more, rise between November and January. They draw professional surfers as well as reckless daredevils and hordes of onlookers, who jump in their cars and head north when word goes out that "surf's up." Don't forget your binoculars. (For more details on North Shore beaches, see p. 162.)

North Shore Surf and Cultural Museum Even if you've never set foot on a surfboard, you'll want to visit Oahu's only surf museum to learn the history of this Hawaiian sport of kings. This collection of memorabilia traces the evolution of surfboards from an enormous, weathered redwood board made in the 1930s for Turkey Love, one of Waikiki's legendary beach boys, to the modern-day equivalent—a light, sleek, racy, foam-and-fiberglass board made for big-wave surfer Mark Foo, who drowned while surfing in California in 1994. Other items include classic 1950s surf-meet posters, 1960s surf-music album covers, old beach-movie posters with Frankie Avalon and Sandra Dee, the early black-and-white photos by legendary surf photographer LeRoy Grannis, and trophies won

Area of detail

OAHU

Honolulu

Kahuku Pt.

Kawela

Waialee

Sunset Beach

Ehukai Beach

Pupukea Beach

Waimea

Waimea Beach Park

THE NORTH SHORE

Pupukea-Paumalu Forest Reserve

Kamehameha Hwy.

Kahuku

Mokuauia I.

Malaekahana State Recreation Area

Laie

Laie Pt.

Pounders Beach

KOOLAU RANGE

Haleiwa Beach Park

Haleiwa

Kanewkoele Str.

Opaeula Str.

Waialua

Kamehameha Hwy.

CENTRAL OAHU (EWA PLAIN)

Mokuleia Forest Reserve

Wahiawa Naval Res.

Whitmore Village

Schofield Barracks Mil. Res.

Wahiawa

Hauula

Punaluu

Sacred Falls State Park

Kahana Bay Beach Park

Kahana Valley State Park

Ewa Forest Reserve

0   2mi
0   2 km

North Shore Surf and Cultural Museum 1
Puu o Mahuka Heiau 2

by surfing's greatest. Curator Steve Gould is working on a new exhibit of surfing in the ancient Hawaiian culture, complete with Hawaiian artifacts.

North Shore Marketplace, 66-250 Kamehameha Hwy. (behind KFC), Haleiwa. ℂ **808/637-8888.** www.captainrick.com/surf_museum.htm. Free admission. Tue–Sun noon–6pm (unless the surf is up).

Puu o Mahuka Heiau ★ 📷 Go around sundown to feel the *mana* (sacred spirit) of this ancient Hawaiian site. The largest sacrificial temple on Oahu, it's associated with the great *kahuna* (priest) Kaopulupulu, who sought peace between Oahu and Kauai. The prescient Kaopulupulu predicted that the island would be overrun by strangers from a distant land, and in 1794, three of Captain George Vancouver's men of the *Daedalus* were sacrificed here. In 1819, the year before New England missionaries landed in Hawaii, King Kamehameha II ordered all idols here to be destroyed.

A national historic landmark, the 18th-century temple, known as the "hill of escape," sits on a 5-acre, 300-foot bluff overlooking Waimea Bay and 25 miles of Oahu's wave-lashed North Coast—all the way to Kaena Point, where the Waianae Range ends in a spirit leap to the other world. The *heiau* (temple) appears as a huge rectangle of rocks twice as big as a football field (170 ft. x 575 ft.), with an altar often covered by the flower and fruit offerings left by native Hawaiians.

1 mile past Waimea Bay. Take Pupukea Rd. mauka (inland) off Kamehameha Hwy. at Foodland, and drive ⁷⁄₁₀ miles up a switchback road. Bus: 52, then walk up Pupukea Rd.

8

SHOPPING

t's a no-brainer: Honolulu is a shopping destination. Shopping competes with golf, surfing, and sightseeing as a bona fide Honolulu attraction. The proliferation of top-notch made-in-Hawaii products, the vitality of the local crafts scene, and the unquenchable thirst for mementos of the islands lend respectability to shopping here. More than 1,000 stores occupy the 11 major shopping centers on this island, with a tsunami of new retail stores to come.

From T-shirts to Versace, posh European to down-home local, avant-garde to unspeakably tacky, Oahu's offerings are wide-ranging indeed. Nestled amid the Louis Vuitton, Chanel, and Tiffany boutiques on Waikiki's Kalakaua Avenue are plenty of booths hawking airbrushed T shirts, gold by the inch, and tasteless aloha shirts.

But this chapter won't help you discover cheap souvenirs or tony items from designer fashion chains; you can find these things on your own. Rather, we offer a guide to finding the special treasures that lie somewhere in between. Be aware that small shops and boutiques have their own hours. Some don't open until 10am, some close for lunch, and some close their doors at 5pm, while others are open until 9pm. To make sure, call the store before you go.

IN & AROUND HONOLULU & WAIKIKI

Aloha Wear

One of Hawaii's lasting afflictions is the penchant tourists have for wearing loud, matching aloha shirts and muumuus. We applaud such visitors' good intentions, but no local resident would be caught dead in such a getup. Muumuus and aloha shirts are wonderful, but the real thing is what island folks wear on Aloha Friday (every Fri), to the Brothers Cazimero Lei Day Concert (every May 1), or to work (where allowed). It's what they wear at home and to special parties where the invitation reads "Aloha Attire."

Aside from the vintage Hawaiian wear (1930s–50s) found in collectibles shops and at swap meets, our favorite contemporary aloha-wear designer is Hawaii's **Tori Richards. Tommy Bahama,** which never calls its shirts "aloha shirts" but claims, instead, a Caribbean influence, is another Hawaii shirt icon, and so is the up-and-coming **Tiki** brand, quirky and distinctive, with elements that hark back to the 1950s.

The best aloha shirts are pricey these days, going for $80 to $125. For the vintage look, **Avanti** has a corner on the market with its line of silk shirts and dresses in authentic retro patterns. **Kahala Sportswear,** a well-known local company established in 1936, is also popular. Kahala has faithfully reproduced, with

FACING PAGE: **Shopping in Chinatown sometimes feels like shopping in China.**

astounding success, the linoleum-block prints of noted Maui artist Avi Kiriaty and the designs of other contemporary artists. Kahala is sold in department stores, surf shops, and stylish boutiques throughout Hawaii and the mainland.

For the most culturally correct aloha wear, and for a graphic identity that is rare in the aloha shirt realm, check out the shirts, dresses, and pareus of **Sig Zane Designs** (www.sigzane.com), found in many department stores (with one dedicated outlet on the Big Island, in Hilo). Zane, an accomplished hula dancer married to one of Hawaii's most revered hula masters, has an unmistakable visual style and a profound knowledge of Hawaiian culture that brings depth and meaning to his boldly styled renditions. Each Sig Zane pareu and aloha shirt, in pure cotton, tells a story. No wonder it's the garb of cultural connoisseurs, who also buy fabrics by the yard for interior accents.

Reyn Spooner is another source of attractive aloha shirts and muumuus in traditional and contemporary styles, with stores in Ala Moana Center and Kahala Mall. Reyn has popularized the reverse-print aloha shirt—the uniform of downtown boardrooms—and has also jumped aboard the vintage-look bandwagon with Old Hawaii cotton prints, some of them in attractive two-color pareu patterns.

Well-known muumuu labels in Hawaii include **Princess Kaiulani** and **Bete** for the dressier muumuus, sold along with many other lines at Macy's and other department stores. **Hilo Hattie's** Ala Moana store (✆ **808/973-3266**) is a goldmine for affordable aloha wear. Hilo Hattie also offers free daily shuttle service from Waikiki to its retail outlet, 700 N. Nimitz Highway (✆ **808/535-6500**). You'll also find macadamia nuts, Hawaiian coffees, and other souvenirs at these Hilo Hattie's stores, as well as live Hawaiian entertainment. Quality and selection have improved noticeably in recent years.

See also "Fashion Boutiques," p. 252.

Avanti Fashion This leading retro aloha shirt label turns out stunning silk shirts and dresses in authentic 1930s to 1950s fabric patterns. The shirts, though made of thin silk, are hip and nostalgic, without the web-thin fragility of authentic antique shirts. The line is distributed in better boutiques and department stores throughout Hawaii, but the best selections are at its Waikiki retail store. 2164 Kalakaua Ave. ✆ **808/924-3232**. www.avantishirts.com.

Bailey's Antiques & Aloha Shirts 🎁 A large selection (that is, thousands) of vintage, secondhand, and nearly new aloha shirts and other collectibles fills this eclectic emporium. It looks as though the owners regularly scour Hollywood movie costume departments for odd ball gowns, feather boas, fur stoles, leather jackets, 1930s dresses, and scads of other garments from periods past. Bailey's has one of the largest vintage aloha-shirt collections in Honolulu, with prices ranging from inexpensive to sky-high. Old Levi's jeans, mandarin jackets, vintage vases, household items, shawls, purses, and an eye-popping assortment of barkcloth fabrics (the real thing, not repros) are among the other mementos in this monumental collection. 517 Kapahulu Ave. ✆ **808/734-7628.**

Hilo Hattie 🏄 Hilo Hattie, the largest manufacturer of Hawaiian fashions, attracts more than a million visitors to its ever-expanding empire throughout the state. Its Ala Moana store is a leap in image, quality, range of merchandise, and overall shopping options. You can find great gifts here, from coconut utensils to food products, and aloha shirts in all price ranges and motifs. There are some inexpensive silk aloha shirts, as well as brand-name aloha shirts from Tommy

Bahama and the store's own Hilo Hattie label, among others. Ala Moana Center, 1450 Ala Moana Blvd. ℂ 808/973-3266. 700 N. Nimitz Hwy. ℂ 808/535-6500.

Macy's If it's aloha wear, Macy's has it. The aloha shirt and muumuu departments here feature every label you can conjure, with a selection—in all price ranges—that changes with the times. 1450 Ala Moana Blvd., Ala Moana Center. ℂ 808/941-2345.

Reyn's Reyn's used to be a prosaic line but has stepped up its selection of women's and men's aloha wear with contemporary fabric prints and styles that appeal to a hipper clientele. Ala Moana Center, 1450 Ala Moana Blvd. ℂ 808/949-5929. Kahala Mall, 4211 Waialae Ave. ℂ 808/737-8313. Sheraton Waikiki, 2255 Kalakaua Ave. ℂ 808/923-7396. Downtown Rack, 125 Merchant St. ℂ 808/524-1885.

Antiques & Collectibles

For the best in collectible aloha wear, see "Aloha Wear," above (especially the listing for **Bailey's Antiques & Aloha Shirts**).

Anchor House Antiques This highly eclectic collection of Hawaiian, Asian, and European pieces sprawls over thousands of square feet. You'll find wooden calabashes, camphor chests, paintings, Hawaiian artifacts, and trinkets, priced from $10 to $2,000. 471 Kapahulu Ave. ℂ 808/732-3884.

Antique Alley This narrow shop is chockablock with the passionate collections of several vendors under one roof. With its expanded assortment of Old Hawaii artifacts and surfing and hula memorabilia, it's a sure winner for eclectic tastes. The showcases include estate jewelry, antique silver, Hawaiian bottles, collectible toys, pottery, cameras, Depression glass, linens, plantation photos and ephemera,

---

THE gallery SCENE

Like restaurants, galleries come and go in Chinatown, where efforts to revitalize the area have moved in fits and spurts. The **Pegge Hopper Gallery,** 1164 Nuuanu Ave. (ℂ 808/524-1160; www.peggehopper.com) is an exception, housed in a historic Chinatown building that's been renovated and transformed into a stunning showplace. Pegge Hopper, one of Hawaii's most popular artists, displays her widely collected paintings (usually of Hawaiian women with broad, strong features) here; the gallery has also become quite the gathering place for exhibits ranging from Tibetan sand-painting by saffron-robed monks to the most avant-garde printmaking in the islands.

The **Gallery at Ward Centre,** 1200 Ala Moana Blvd. (ℂ 808/597-8034), a cooperative gallery of Oahu artists, features fine works in all media, including paper, clay, scratchboard, oils, watercolors, collages, woodblocks, lithographs, glass, jewelry, and more.

Art lovers now have a wonderful new resource: a 34-page full-color brochure offering an overview of the music, theater, history, and visual arts of Oahu. The free brochure, which includes a map, phone numbers, websites, and more information, is put out by Arts with Aloha, which represents 11 major Honolulu cultural organizations. For current info download the brochure from the website (www.artswithaloha.com).

and a wide selection of nostalgic items from Hawaii and across America. At the rear is a small, attractive selection of Soiree clothing, made by Julie Lauster out of antique kimonos and obis. 1347 Kapiolani Blvd. ✆ **808/941-8551.**

Robyn Buntin This is Honolulu's most stellar source for museum-quality Asian art and contemporary and traditional Hawaiian art. The 5,000-square-foot gallery and picture-framing department, along with another gallery strictly for Hawaiian art nearby, at 820 S. Beretania St., are among the features of the burgeoning art resource, located three doors from the Honolulu Academy of Arts. 848 S. Beretania St. ✆ **808/523-5913.**

T. Fujii Japanese Antiques This long-standing icon in Hawaii's antiques world is an impeccable source for *ukiyo-e* (wood-block) prints, scrolls, obis, Imari porcelain, tansus, tea-ceremony bowls, and screens, as well as contemporary ceramics from Mashiko and Kasama. Prices range from $25 to $18,000. 1016 Kapahulu Ave. ✆ **808/732-7860.** Call for current store hours as they travel to Japan often.

Bookstores

Barnes & Noble With more than 150,000 titles; a respectable music department; and strong Hawaiiana, fiction, and new-release departments, as well as a popular coffee bar, Barnes & Noble has become the second home of Honolulu's casual readers and bibliophiles. Kahala Mall, 4211 Waialae Ave. ✆ **808/737-3323.**

Bill's Bookmobile Think back to your childhood when the library's bookmobile would come around the neighborhood. That is exactly what Bryde Cestare, executive director of the Friends of the Library Hawaii, wanted to create with this 12 x 27-foot RV, refitted to be an air-conditioned, well-lit bookstore on wheels. All profits support the state's 51 public libraries. 690 Pohukaina St. (next to Mother Waldron Park). ✆ **808/536-4174.**

Borders Borders is a beehive of literary activity, with weekly signings, prominent local and mainland musicians at least monthly, and special events almost daily that make this store a major Honolulu attraction. Borders has six branches on Oahu, including those listed here. Victoria Ward Centre. ✆ **808/591-8995.** Royal Hawaiian Hotel. ✆ **808/922-4154.** Kaneohe, 46-056 Kamehameha Hwy. ✆ **808/235-8803.**

Friends of Kailua Library Bookstore Located in the community meeting rooms of the Kailua Library, this bargain bookstore has a range of books from that perfect beach read to college textbooks and bestselling nonfiction. Every used book is either 50¢ or $1. Call for hours, as staffing is done by volunteers. Kailua Library, 239 Kuulei Rd., Kailua. ✆ **808/266-9911.**

Rainbow Books and Records A little weird but totally lovable, especially among students and eccentrics (and insatiable readers), Rainbow Books is notable for its selection of popular fiction, records, and Hawaii-themed books, secondhand and reduced. Because it's located in the university area, it's always bulging with textbooks, Hawaiiana, and popular music. It's about the size of a large closet, but you'll be surprised by what you'll find. 1010 University Ave. ✆ **808/955-7994.**

Edibles

In addition to the stores listed below, we recommend **Executive Chef,** in the Ward Warehouse (✆ **808/596-2433**), and **Islands' Best,** in the Ala Moana Center (✆ **808/949-5345**). Both shops contain wide-ranging selections that include Hawaii's specialty food items.

Asian Grocery Asian Grocery supplies many of Honolulu's Thai, Vietnamese, Chinese, Indonesian, and Filipino restaurants with authentic spices, rice, noodles, produce, sauces, herbs, and adventurous ingredients. Browse among the kaffir lime leaves, tamarind and fish pastes, red and green chiles, curries, chutneys, lotus leaves, gingko nuts, jasmine and basmati rice, and shelf upon shelf of medium to hot chili sauces. The chefs for most of Honolulu's Asian and ethnic restaurants shop here. 1319 S. Beretania St. ☏ **808/593-8440.** www.asianfood.com.

Chocolate-covered pineapple, a staple of the Honolulu Chocolate Co.

Don Quijote Stands offering takeout sushi, Korean *kal bi,* pizza, Chinese food, flowers, Mrs. Fields cookies, and other items for self and home surround this huge emporium. Inside, you'll find household products, a pharmacy, and inexpensive clothing, but it's the prepared foods and produce that excel. The fresh-seafood section is one of Honolulu's best, not far from where regulars line up for the bento lunches and individually wrapped sushi. When Kau navel oranges, macadamia nuts, Kona coffee, Chinese taro, and other Hawaii products are on sale, savvy locals arrive in droves to take advantage of the high quality and good value. 801 Kaheka St. ☏ **808/973-4800.** 345 Hahani St., Kailua. ☏ **808/266-4400.** 850 Kam Hwy., Pearl City. ☏ **808/453-5500.** 94-144 Farrington Hwy., Waipahu. ☏ **808/678-6800.**

Fujioka's Wine Merchants Oenophiles flock here for a mouthwatering selection of excellent wines, single-malt Scotches, and affordable, farm-raised caviar—food and libations for all occasions. Everyday wines, special-occasion wines, and esoteric wines are priced lower here than at most places. The wine-tasting bar at the rear of the store is a new attraction. Market City Shopping Center, 2919 Kapiolani Blvd., lower level. ☏ **808/739-9463.**

Honolulu Chocolate Co. Life's greatest pleasures are dispensed here with abandon: expensive gourmet chocolates made in Honolulu, Italian and Hawaiian biscotti, boulder-size turtles (caramel and pecans covered with chocolate), truffles, chocolate-covered coffee beans, and jumbo apricots in white and dark chocolate, to name a few. You pay dearly for them, but the dark-chocolate-dipped macadamia-nut clusters are beyond compare. Ward Centre, 1200 Ala Moana Blvd. ☏ **808/591-2997.**

Maunakea Marketplace Food Court Hungry patrons line up for everything from pizza and plate lunches to quick, authentic, and inexpensive Vietnamese, Thai, Italian, Chinese, Japanese, and Filipino dishes. The best seafood fried rice comes from the woks of **Malee Thai/Vietnamese Cuisine**—it's perfectly flavored, with morsels of fish, squid, and shrimp. **Tandoori Chicken Cafe** serves Indian culinary pleasures, from curries and jasmine-chicken rice balls to spiced rounds of curried potatoes and a wonderful lentil dal. **Masa's** serves bento and Japanese dishes, such as miso eggplant, which are famous. You'll find the best dessert at **Pho Lau,** which serves *haupia* (coconut pudding), tapioca, and taro in individual baskets made of pandanus. Join in the spirit of discovery at the produce stalls (pungent odors, fish heads, and chicken feet on counters—not for the squeamish). Vendors sell everything from fresh ahi and whole snapper to yams and taro, seaweed, and fresh fruits and vegetables. 1120 Maunakea St., Chinatown. ℂ 808/524-3409.

People's Open Markets Truck farmers from all over the island bring their produce to Oahu's neighborhoods in regularly scheduled, city-sponsored open markets, held Monday through Saturday at various locations. Among the tables of ong choy, choi sum, Okinawan spinach, opal basil, papayas, mangoes, seaweed, and fresh fish, you'll find homemade banana bread, Chinese pomelo (like large grapefruit), fresh fiddleheads (fern shoots) when available, and colorful, bountiful harvests from land and sea. Various sites around town. Call to find the open market nearest you. ℂ 808/522-7088. http://hfbf.org/markets.

R. Field Wine Co. Foodland supermarket has won countless new converts since Richard Field—oenophile, gourmet, and cigar aficionado—moved his wine shop here. The thriving gourmet store offers gemlike vine-ripened tomatoes and juicy clementines, sparkling bags of Nalo gourmet greens, designer cheeses, caviar, Langenstein Farms macadamia nuts, vegetarian and salmon mousses, vinegars, and all manner of epicurean delights, including wines and single-malt Scotches. The warm, just-baked breads (rosemary–olive oil, whole-wheat, organic wheat, and others) baked on the premises with dough flown in from Los Angeles' famous La Brea Bakery, are a huge hit. Foodland, 1460 S. Beretania St. ℂ 808/596-9463.

Sushi Company It's not easy to find premium-grade *hamachi* (yellowtail), ahi, *ikura* (salmon roe), *ika* (cuttlefish), and other top-grade fresh ingredients in anything but a bona-fide sit-down sushi bar. But here it is, a small, sparkling gem of a sushi maker that sells fast-food sushi of non-fast-food quality, at great prices. Order ahead or wait while they make it. The combinations range from minisets (27 pieces) to large-variety sets (43–51 pieces), ideal for picnics and potlucks. Sushi Company has one small two-person table; most of the business is takeout. 1111 McCully St. (at Young St.). ℂ 808/947-5411.

BAKERIES

If you're looking for a bakery, **Saint-Germain,** in Shirokiya, at Ala Moana Shopping Center (ℂ 808/955-1711), and near Times Supermarket, 1296 S. Beretania St. (ℂ 808/593-8711), sells baguettes, country loaves, and oddball delicacies such as mini mushroom-and-spinach pizzas. The reigning queen of bakers, though, is

---

Pampered Pedicure

In Hawaii, where going barefoot is as common as breathing, and open-toed sandals and slippers are the shoes of necessity, a pedicure is a must. Most resort spas will offer pedicures among their list of services, but our favorite pedicure is from **Honolulu Nails Salon,** 2570 S. Beretania St (ℂ 808/949-1600). We recommend the Special Spa Pedicure, a five-step process of soaking, scrubs, rubs, masks, and a wonderful refreshing gel before you get down to the polish (OPI and Essie). Allow an hour. The entire relaxing experience is $25 to $35 (and worth every penny).

In & Around Honolulu & Waikiki

SHOPPING

Cafe Laufer, 3565 Waialae Ave. (℃ **808/735-7717**); see p. 148. Nearby, old-timers still line up at **Sconees,** 1117 12th Ave. (℃ **808/734-4024**), formerly Bea's Pies. Sconees has fantastic scones, pumpkin-custard pies, and danishes. For warm bread, nothing can beat **Foodland,** 1460 S. Beretania St. (℃ **808/949-4365** for the bakery department), where R. Field (see above) is located. The Foodland bakery flies in dough from Los Angeles' famous La Brea bakery and bakes it fresh at this location, so you can pick up fresh-from-the-oven organic wheat, rosemary–olive oil, roasted garlic, potato-dill, and other spectacular breads.

Cake Works If creating cakes is an art form, former Hilo native, Chef Abigail "Abi" Langlas, the chef/owner of Cake Works, is a genius. This wonderful bakery, which specializes in custom wedding cakes, can also produce a specialty cake for any occasion. 2820 S. King St., across from the Hawaiian Humane Society. ℃ **808/946-4333.** www.cakeworks.org.

FISH MARKETS

Safeway on Beretania Street has a seafood counter with fresh choices and a staff that takes pride in its deftness with prepared foods. (Don't be shy about asking for a taste.) The prepared foods (fresh ahi poke, seaweed salad, marinated crab) are popular among busy working folks heading home. **Foodland,** on Beretania Street, occasionally offers good buys on live lobster and Dungeness crab, fresh ahi and aku poke, ahi sashimi and steaks, and a wide variety of fresh fish and shellfish, including whole snappers and oysters when available.

Honolulu Fish Auction If you want to experience the high drama of fish buying, head to this auction at the United Fishing Agency. The fishermen bring their fresh catch in at 5:30am (sharp) Monday through Saturday, and buyers bid on a variety of fish, from fat tunas to weird-looking hapupu. Don't be surprised if you don't recognize much of the language the bidders are using; it is an internal dialect developed over decades, which only the buyers and the auctioneer understand. You'll be happy you woke up so early! Pier 38, 1131 N. Nimitz Highway. ℃ **808/536-2148.**

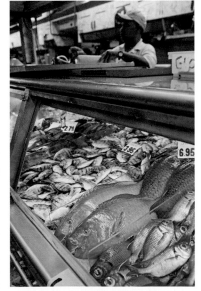

Tamashiro Market This is the grand-daddy of fish markets and the ace in the hole for home chefs with bouillabaisse or paella in mind. A separate counter sells seaweed salad, prepared poke, Filipino and Puerto Rican ti-wrapped steamed rice, and dozens of other ethnic foods. You'll think you're in a Fellini movie amid the tanks of live lobsters and crabs, and the dizzying array of counters glistening with fresh slabs of ahi, whole opakapaka, and *on-aga* and *ehu* filets. Point and ask if you don't know what you're looking at, and one of the fish cutters will explain and then clean and fillet your selection.

A rainbow of fresh fish on sale at Tamashiro Market.

Good service and the most extensive selection in Honolulu make Tamashiro a Honolulu treasure. 802 N. King St., Kalihi. ℂ **808/841-8047.**

Yama's Fish Market Neighbor islanders have been known to drive directly from the airport to Yama's for one of the best plate lunches in Honolulu. Robust Hawaiian plates with pork or chicken *lau lau* (20 combinations!), baked ahi, chili, beef stew, shoyu chicken, and dozens of other varieties stream out to those who line up at the counter. Many Honolulu businesses order by the dozen for their offices. But Yama's is also known for its inexpensive fresh fish (mahimahi is always less expensive here than in the supermarkets), tasty poke (ahi, aku, Hawaiian-style, Oriental-style, with seaweed), lomi salmon, and many varieties of prepared seafood. Chilled beer, boiled peanuts, and fresh ahi they'll slice into sashimi are popular for local-style gatherings, sunset beach parties, and festive *pau hana* (end of work) celebrations. At its new, larger location just a few hundred feet away, Yama's is offering more prepared foods and bakery items than ever before; their chocolate-chip/mac-nut cookies are peerless. 2332 Young St., Moiliili. ℂ **808/941-9994.**

HEALTH FOOD

Down to Earth This university district shop sells organic vegetables and bulk foods, with a strong selection of supplements, herbs, and cosmetic products. Everything here is vegetarian, down to the last drop of tincture. Cereals, bulk grains and nuts, breads, many varieties of honey, nonalcoholic beer, teas, snacks, environment-friendly paper and household products, and a vegetarian juice and sandwich bar are among the reasons shoppers of all ages come here. 2525 S. King St., Moiliili. ℂ **808/947-7678.**

House of Health Tiny, with a loyal clientele that has stuck by it through management and name changes and a hefty dose of parking problems, House of Health has competitive prices and a wide and user-friendly selection of health-food supplements. The supplements are good enough reason to shop here. No produce, but there are frozen vegetarian foods, cosmetics, bulk grains, and healthy snacks. 1541 S. Beretania St. ℂ **808/955-6168.**

Kokua Market Kokua is Honolulu's best source for healthy provisions in all categories but vitamin supplements. The market is trying, however, and the vitamin selection is expanding noticeably. Voluminous, leafy organic vegetables; an excellent variety of cheeses; pastas and bulk grains; sandwiches, salads, and prepared foods; poi as fresh as can be; organic coffee beans; breads and pastries; and a solid selection of organic wines give Kokua a special place in the hearts of health-minded shoppers. There's ample parking behind the store. 2643 S. King St., Moiliili. ℂ **808/941-1922.**

Whole Foods Market This national chain (the king of organic and health food stores) finally has come to Hawaii, and not in a small way. At 28,670 square feet, it is one of the largest grocery stores on Oahu. Kahala Mall, 4211 Waialae Ave. ℂ **808/738-0820.**

Fashion Boutiques

For those looking for unique, personal style, these hot new boutiques offer exclusive (and somewhat unexpected) fashions you won't find anywhere else.

House of Flys This is the place of extremes, both the retail and the retail outlet. Selling clothes isn't the only draw; events such as DJ nights or a skateboard-a-thon in the nearby parking lot periodically take place here, too. Owned by local surfers and sports enthusiasts Saree Chirayunion and Sci Fly, this boutique features their own line, Black Flys, which includes sunglasses, cargo pants, T-shirts, skateboards, caps, and high-tech backpacks. International Market Place, 2330 Kalakaua Ave. upstairs across from the Food Court. © **808/923-3597.**

In4mation This is a boutique for guys who are tired of seeing the same old stuff in every men's store. This hip, hot boutique has the latest clothes, unusual baseball caps, limited-release Nike and DC shoes, collectible toys, and a great collection of T-shirts. 226 Lewers St., upstairs. © **808/923-0888.** Ward Warehouse, 1050 Ala Moana Blvd. © **808/597-1447.**

Kicks Attention sneaker aficionados, collectors, and those looking for shoes as a fashion statement—this is your store. Limited editions and classic footwear by Nike and Adidas can be found here. Owners Edward Haus and Ian Ginoza carry clothing lines produced by their friends, as well as Anx, Freshjive, Creative, Subase, and Poetree. The store looks like a gallery, with the clothes and shoes as art. 1530 Makaloa St., Suite 211 (upstairs, across from Walgreens). © **808/941-9191.**

Valerie Joseph Word is getting out about this newcomer on the fashion scene. This small store has some unique clothing lines (BCBG Girls, French Connection, and its own private label), featuring everything from ultracasual to very, very dressy. Be sure to check the table in the back for earrings, necklaces, and other well-priced bling. Ala Moana Shopping Center, 1450 Kapiolani Blvd. © **808/942-5258.**

Flowers & Leis

At most lei shops, simple leis sell for $10 and up, deluxe leis for $25 and up. For a special-occasion designer bouquet or lei, you can't do better than Michael Miyashiro of **Rainforest Plantes et Fleurs** (© **808/738-0999**). He's an ecologically aware, highly gifted lei maker—his leis are pricey, but worth it. He custom-designs the lei for the person and occasion. Order by phone or stop by the Kilohana Square shop, 1016 Kapahulu Ave., an oasis of green and beauty.

Leis come in every shape and size on Maunakea Street.

Upon request, Miyashiro's leis will come in ti-leaf bundles called *pu'olo,* custom gift baskets (in woven green coconut baskets), and special arrangements. You can even request the card sentiments in Hawaiian, with English translations.

The other primary sources for flowers and leis are the shops lining the streets of Moiliili and Chinatown. Moiliili favorites include **Rudy's Flowers,** Isenburg Street at S. King Street (© **808/944-8844**), a local institution with the best prices on roses, Micronesian ginger lei, and a variety of cut blooms. Across the street, **Flowers for a Friend,** 2739 S. King St. (© **808/955-4227**), has good prices on leis, floral arrangements, and cut flowers. Nearby, **Flowers by Jr. and Lou,** 2652 S. King St. (☎ **808/941-2022**), offers calla lilies, Gerbera daisies, a riot of potted orchids, and the full range of cut flowers along with its lei selection.

In Chinatown, lei vendors line Beretania and Maunakea streets, and the fragrances of their wares mix with the earthy scents of incense and ethnic foods. Our top picks are **Lita's Leis,** 59 N. Beretania St. (☎ **808/521-9065**), which has fresh puakenikeni, gardenias that last, and a supply of fresh and reasonable leis; **Lin's Lei Shop,** 1017-A Maunakea St. (☎ **808/537-4112**), with creatively fashioned, unusual leis; and **Cindy's Lei Shoppe,** 1034 Maunakea St. (☎ **808/536-6538**), with terrific sources for unusual leis, such as feather dendrobiums and firecracker combinations, as well as everyday favorites like ginger, tuberose, orchid, and pikake. "Curb service" is available with phone orders. Just give them your car's color and model, and you can pick up your lei curbside—a great convenience on this busy street.

Hawaiiana & Gift Items

Our top recommendations are the fabulous, newly expanded **Academy Shop,** at the Honolulu Academy of Arts, 900 S. Beretania St. (☎ **808/523-8703**), and the **Contemporary Museum Gift Shop** (also owned by the Academy of Arts), 2411 Makiki Heights Rd. (☎ **808/523-3447**), two of the finest shopping stops on Oahu—worth a special trip whether or not you want to see the museums themselves. (And you will want to see the museums, especially the recently expanded Honolulu Academy of Arts, p. 199.) The Academy Shop offers a brilliant selection of art books, jewelry, basketry, ethnic fabrics and native crafts from all over the world, posters and books, and fiber vessels and accessories. The Contemporary Museum (p. 197) shop focuses on arts and crafts such as avant-garde jewelry, cards and stationery, books, home accessories, and gift items made by artists from Hawaii and across the country. We love the glammy selection of jewelry and novelties, such as the twisted-wire wall hangings.

Other good sources for quality gift items are the **Little Hawaiian Craft Shop,** in the Royal Hawaiian Shopping Center.

Hula Supply Center Hawaiiana meets kitsch in this shop's marvelous selection of Day-Glo cellophane skirts, bamboo nose flutes, T-shirts, hula drums, shell leis, feathered rattle gourds, lauhala accessories, fiber mats, and wide assortment of pareu fabrics. Although hula dancers shop here for their dance accoutrements, it's not all serious shopping. This is fertile ground for souvenirs and memorabilia of Hawaii, rooted somewhere between irreverent humor and cultural integrity. 1008 Isenberg St. (at S. King St.), Moiliili. ☎ **808/941-5379.**

Mana Hawaii Get some authentic Hawaiian culture in the heart of Waikiki at this unusual store, where the owners are five successful Native Hawaiians who have combined their talents. Their partners include Native Books (see below), which sells books, CDs, and educational material about Hawaii; Na Mea Hawaii, featuring Hawaiian-made gifts, clothing, jewelry, and art; Hula Supply Center (see above) with everything for hula from fabric to implements; Ukulele House, offering ukuleles; and the Lomi Shop Va'a, specializing in health and wellness through massage. They also offer free cultural activities; call for schedule. Waikiki Beach Walk, 226 Lewers St., 2nd level. ☎ **808/923-2220.**

Native Books & Beautiful Things 🎁 This *hui* (association) of artists and craftspeople is a browser's paradise featuring a variety of Hawaiian items from musical instruments to calabashes, jewelry, leis, and books. You'll find contemporary Hawaiian clothing; handmade koa journals; Hawaii-themed home accessories; lauhala handbags and accessories; jams, jellies, and food products; etched glass; hand-painted fabrics and clothing; stone poi pounders; and other high-quality gift items. Some of Hawaii's finest artists in all craft media have their works available here on a regular basis, and the Hawaiian-book selection is tops. Ward Warehouse, 1050 Ala Moana Blvd. © **808/596-8885.**

Nohea Gallery A fine showcase for contemporary Hawaii art, Nohea celebrates the islands with such thoughtful, attractive selections as pit-fired raku, finely turned wood vessels, jewelry, handblown glass, paintings, prints, fabrics (including Hawaiian-quilt cushions), and furniture. Nohea's selection is always evolving and growing, with 90% of the works by Hawaii artists. Ward Warehouse, 1050 Ala Moana Blvd. © **808/596-0074.** Sheraton Waikiki, 2255 Kalakaua Blvd. © **808/931-8843.** Westin Moana Surfrider, 2365 Kalakaua Ave. © **808/923-6644.** www.noheagallery.com.

Shop Pacifica Local crafts, lauhala and Cook Island woven coconut wares, Hawaiian music tapes and CDs, pareu, and a vast selection of Hawaii-themed books anchor this gift shop. Hawaiian quilt cushion kits, jewelry, glassware, seed and Niihau shell leis, cookbooks, and many other gift possibilities will keep you occupied between stargazing in the planetarium and pondering the shells and antiquities of the esteemed historical museum. In the Bishop Museum, 1525 Bernice St. © **808/848-4158.**

Kids

Baby Emporium Parents will be grateful that Tom Kim opened this one-stop shopping mecca for everything you could possibly need, from breast pumps and a range of strollers in a variety of styles and sizes, to clothes, blankets, and even tiny T-shirts with a selection of sayings that will leave you laughing. 614 Cooke St. © **808/596-4868.**

Zuke's Magic & Jokes You don't have to be Harry Potter to enter here, but you may feel like him as you enter the store with the soda sign proclaiming C. ZUKEMURA STORE GENERAL MERCHANDISE. Amateur and professional magicians from around the island stream into this magic store, and kids love the place. It's filled with shelves packed with tricks: candles that magically become flowers, a sponge ball that morphs into two balls, then three balls. . . . Go early, when it opens (call for hours), for a chance to "talk story" with 73-year-old owner Jimmy Zukemura, who doesn't just tell his young patrons how to do a trick, but how to make the trick into real magic. Open Saturdays only. 1516 Auld Lane (off Halona St.). © **808/847-7788.**

Shopping Centers

Ala Moana Center Many of the shops here are the familiar names of mainland chains, such as **DKNY, Macy's, Neiman Marcus, Nordstrom, Sears,** and **Old Navy.** The three-story, superluxe **Neiman Marcus,** opened in 1998, was a bold move in Hawaii's troubled economy and has retained its position as the shrine of the fashionistas. But there are practical touches in the center, too, such as banks, a U.S. Post Office, several optical companies (including 1-hr. service by **LensCrafters**), **Longs Drugs,** and a handful of photo-processing services. The smaller locally owned stores are scattered among the behemoths, mostly on the ground floor. Nearly 400 shops and restaurants sprawl over several blocks (and 1.8 million sq. ft. of store space), catering to every imaginable need, from over-the-top upscale (**Tiffany, Chanel, St. John**) to mainland chains such as **Gap** and **Banana Republic.** Department stores, such as **Macy's,** sell fashion, food, cosmetics, shoes, and household needs. Need shoes? They're a kick at **Nordstrom,** and **Walking Co.** has first-rate comfort styles by Mephisto, Ecco, and Naot.

A good stop for gifts is **Islands' Best,** which spills over with Hawaiian-made foodstuffs, ceramics, fragrances, and more. **Splash! Hawaii** has women's swimwear, and for aloha shirts and men's swimwear, try **Macy's, Town & Country Surf, Reyn's,** or the terminally hip **Hawaiian Island Creations.** The **food court** is abuzz with dozens of stalls purveying Cajun food, ramen, pizza, plate lunches, vegetarian fare, green tea and fruit freezes (such as frozen yogurt), panini, and countless other treats. Hours are Monday through Saturday 9:30am to 9pm, Sunday 10am to 7pm. You can take bus no. 8, 19, or 20 to get there, or try the Ala Moana Shuttle Bus or the trolley (p. 279). 1450 Ala Moana Blvd. © **808/955-9517.** www.alamoanacenter.com. Bus: 8, 19, or 20.

Aloha Tower Marketplace In the early 1990s, city officials came up with the idea to renovate and restore the waterfront to bring back the feeling of "boat days." The shops, restaurants, and bars inside the resulting two-story Aloha Tower Marketplace offer an array of cuisines, one-of-a-kind shops, and even a microbrewery. Most shops open at 9am daily and the restaurants and bars don't shut down until the wee hours of the morning. There is a perpetual parking shortage here, and if you do manage to find a parking spot, the rates are sky-high. Take the trolley (p. 279) if you can. The refurbished Aloha Tower, once the tallest structure in Honolulu, still stands high over the complex.

Dining and shopping prospects abound: **Hawaiian Ukulele Company, Don Ho's Island Grill** (p. 139), **Chai's Island Bistro** (p. 138), and **Gordon Biersch Brewery Restaurant** (p. 139). Retail shops are open Monday through Saturday 9am to 9pm, Sunday 9am to 6pm; dining and entertainment, daily 8am to midnight. Various Honolulu trolleys stop here; if you want a direct ride from Waikiki, take the free Hilo Hattie trolley or the Waikiki Red Line trolley, which continues on to Hilo Hattie in Iwilei. 1 Aloha Tower Dr., on the waterfront btw. piers 8 and 11, Honolulu Harbor. © **808/528-5700.** Aloha Tower Entertainment Hotline: © **808/566-2333.** www.alohatower.com.

DFS Galleria "Boat days" is the theme at this Waikiki emporium, a three-floor extravaganza of shops ranging from the superluxe (such as **Givenchy** and **Coach**) to the very touristy. Great Hawaii food products range from the incomparable **Big Island Candies'** shortbread cookies to a spate of coffees and preserves. There are multitudes of aloha shirts and T-shirts, a virtual golf course, surf and skate equipment, a terrific Hawaiian music department, and a labyrinth of fashionable stores once you get past the Waikiki Walk. Fragrances and cosmetics make a big splash at **DFS. Starbucks** serves up coffee and smoothies. *Note:* Some sections are duty-free and therefore restricted to international travelers only. Daily 9am to 11pm. 330 Royal Hawaiian Ave. (corner of Kalakaua and Royal Hawaiian aves.). © **808/931-2655.** www.dfsgalleria.com.

Kahala Mall Chic, manageable, and unfrenzied, Kahala Mall is home to some of Honolulu's best shops. Located east of Waikiki in the posh neighborhood of Kahala, the mall has everything from a small **Macy's** to chain stores such as **Banana Republic** and **Barnes & Noble**—nearly 100 air-conditioned specialty shops (including dozens of eateries and eight movie theaters) in all. Java-magnet **Starbucks** sits a stone's throw from **Godiva Chocolatier,** with its sinfully wonderful treats. Smoothie lovers form long lines at **Jamba Juice.** For gift, fashion, and specialty stores, our picks of the mall's best and brightest are **Riches Kahala,** a tiny kiosk with a big, bold selection of jewelry; the **Compleat Kitchen;** and **Aveda,** with its lotions and potions. Monday through Saturday 10am to 9pm, Sunday 10am to 5pm. 4211 Waialae Ave., Kahala. 𝒞 **808/732-7736.** www.kahalamall center.com.

Royal Hawaiian Shopping Center The Royal Hawaiian Shopping Center recently spent 2 years and $115 million renovating; the result is a new, larger, upscale shopping center with 110 shops, restaurants, a nightclub and theater, and a garden grove of 70 coconut trees with an entertainment area. Totaling 310,000 square feet (17,000 sq. ft. larger than before), and with activities on four levels, including shopping and dining (the second level has a nine-restaurant food court), the mall stretches three blocks in the heart of Waikiki. But instead of clusters of stores, one right next to another, the renovated open-air mall is filled with space, lots of light, big windows, and breezeways between shops. The most exciting addition is the $15 million, 760-seat theater, with moving stages and acrobatic rigging. (The central performance area also features a landscaped courtyard with a pond, artesian fountain, stream, and a statue of Princess Bernice Pauahi Bishop.) Perhaps the biggest change, though, is the exterior finish, with a Polynesian-kapa look and an open-air bridge that connects the central area to the wings of the mall (with a panoramic view of the Royal Hawaiian hotel). *Upscale* is the operative word here. Although there are drugstores, lei stands, restaurants, and food kiosks, the most conspicuous stores are the European designer boutiques (**Cartier, Hermès, L'Occitane, Fendi, Kate Spade, Bvlgari, Salvatore Ferragamo,** and more) that cater largely to visitors from Japan. Daily 10am to 10pm. 2201 Kalakaua Ave., Honolulu. 𝒞 **808/922-0588.** www.shopwaikiki.com.

Sampling ukeleles at the Royal Hawaiian Shopping Center.

Waikele Premium Outlets Just say the word *Waikele* and our eyes glaze over. So many shops, so little time! There are two sections to this sprawling discount shopping mecca: the **Waikele Premium Outlets,** some 51 retailers offering designer and name-brand merchandise; and the **Waikele Value Center** across the street, with another 25 stores that are more practical than fashion-oriented (**Eagle Hardware, Sports Authority**). The 64-acre complex has made discount shopping a travel pursuit in itself, with tours for visitor groups and carloads of neighbor islanders and Oahu residents making pilgrimages from all corners of the state. They come to hunt down bargains on everything from perfumes, luggage, and hardware to sporting goods, fashions, vitamins, and

257

china. Examples: **Armani Exchange, Saks Fifth Avenue, Brooks Brothers, Calvin Klein, Izod, Polo Ralph Lauren, Banana Republic,** and the ultrachic **Barneys.** Monday through Friday 9am to 9pm, Sunday 10am to 6pm. Take H-1 west toward Waianae and turn off at exit 7. Or take bus no. 42 from Waikiki to Waipahu Transit Center, then 433 from Transit Center to Waikele. 94-790 Lumiaina St., Waikele (about 20 miles from Waikiki). ℂ **808/678-0786** or 808/676-5656. www.premiumoutlets.com/waikele.

Ward Centre Although it has a high turnover and a changeable profile, Ward Centre is a standout for its concentration of restaurants and shops. **Ryan's** and **Kakaako Kitchen** are as popular as ever, the former (with a Hawaiian grill menu) looking out over Ala Moana Park and the latter (which serves plate lunches) with lanai views of the sprawling **Pier 1 Imports** across the street. **Nordstrom Rack** and **Office Depot** have sprouted in a new development area that includes a 16-theater movie megaplex (p. 271). All these establishments are part of developer Victoria Ward's Kakaako projects, which take up several blocks in this area: Ward Centre, Ward Farmers' Market, Ward Village Shops, Ward Gateway Center, and Ward Warehouse.

Ward Centre's gift shops and galleries include **Crazy Shirts Factory Outlet** for T-shirts, and **Honolulu Chocolate Co.** (p. 249). Monday through Saturday 10am to 9pm, Sunday 10am to 5pm. 1200 Ala Moana Blvd. ℂ **808/591-8411.** www.victoriaward.com.

Ward Entertainment Center This large, multiblock complex includes Ward Centre, mentioned above, and Ward Warehouse, mentioned below, at the corner of Auahi and Kamakee streets. The centerpiece is a new 16-movie megaplex, and a new retail-and-restaurant complex, with such eateries as **Dave & Buster's** (with virtual golf, games, interactive entertainment, bars, and a restaurant), **Buca di Beppo,** and **Cold Stone Creamery.** Monday through Saturday 10am to 9pm, Sunday 10am to 6pm. Auahi and Kamakee sts. ℂ **808/591-8411.** www. victoriaward.com.

Ward Warehouse Older than its sister property, Ward Centre, and endowed with an endearing patina, Ward Warehouse remains a popular stop for dining and shopping. **Native Books & Beautiful Things** (p. 254) and the **Nohea Gallery** (p. 255) are excellent sources for quality Hawaii-made arts and crafts.

Other recommended stops include **C. June Shoes** for designer footwear; **Noa Noa** for distinctive island wear; and **Quiksilver Youth,** brimming with tasteful gifts for kids and babies. For T-shirts, swimwear, and an excellent selection of sunglasses, knapsacks, and footwear, check out the **T&C Surf Shop.** Monday through Saturday 10am to 9pm, Sunday 10am to 5pm. 1050 Ala Moana Blvd. ℂ **808/591-8411.** www.victoriaward.com.

Surf & Sports

The surf-and-sports shops scattered throughout Honolulu are a highly competitive lot, with each trying to capture your interest (and dollars). But we can't live without them.

The Bike Shop Excellent for cycling and backpacking equipment for all levels, with major camping lines such as North Face, MSR, and Kelty. 1149 S. King St., near Piikoi St. ℂ **808/596-0588.**

Hawaiian Island Creations HIC is a super-cool surf shop offering sunglasses, sun lotions, surf wear, surfboards, skateboards, and accessories galore. In the Ala

Moana Center, 1450 Ala Moana Blvd. ✆ **808/973-6780.** Pearlridge. ✆ **808/483-6700.** Waikiki Beach Walk. ✆ **808/923-0442.** Kailua. ✆ **808/266-6730.** Haleiwa. ✆ **808/637-0991.**

McCully Bicycle & Sporting Goods Find everything from bicycles and fishing gear to athletic shoes and accessories and a stunning selection of sunglasses. 2124 S. King St. ✆ **808/955-6329.**

The Sports Authority This discount mega-outlet offers a huge variety of sporting equipment, including cycles, all sorts of fishing gear, camping gear, beach chairs, and everything else you can imagine for life outside the office—plus clothing and shoes. 333 Ward Ave. ✆ **808/596-0166.** Waikele Center. ✆ **808/677-9933.**

WINDWARD OAHU

Windward Oahu's largest shopping complex is the **Windward Mall,** 46-056 Kamehameha Hwy., in Kaneohe (✆ **808/235-1143**), open Monday through Saturday from 10am to 9pm and Sunday from 10am to 5pm. The big draw here is the 10-screen theater complex. The 100 stores and services at this standard suburban mall include **Macy's** and **Sears,** health stores, airline counters, and surf shops. A small food court serves pizza, Chinese fare, tacos, and other morsels, and the new theaters are a big draw for Windwardites.

In Kailua, **Longs Drugs** and **Macy's** department store, located side-by-side on Kailua Road in the heart of this windward Oahu community, form the shopping nexus of the neighborhood.

Agnes Portuguese Bake Shop 🎁 This Kailua treasure is the longtime favorite of Hawaii's *malassada* mavens. *Malassadas*—sugary Portuguese dumplings that look and taste like doughnuts without holes—fly out of the bakery, infusing the entire neighborhood with an irresistible aroma. The Bake Shop also offers a variety of pastries, cookies, scones, Portuguese bean and other soups, and local- and European-style breads. 46 Hoolai St., Kailua. ✆ **808/262-5367.**

Alii Antiques of Kailua II Abandon all restraint, particularly if you have a weakness for vintage Hawaiiana. Koa lamps and rattan furniture from the 1930s and 1940s, hula bobbleheads, rare 1940s koa tables, Roseville vases, Don Blanding dinnerware, and a breathtaking array of vintage etched-glass vases and trays are some of the items in this unforgettable shop. Across the street, the owner's wife runs **Alii Antiques of Kailua,** which is chockablock with jewelry, clothing, Bauer and Fiesta Ware, linens, Bakelite bracelets, and floor-to-ceiling collectibles. 21-A Maluniu Ave., Kailua. ✆ **808/261-1705.**

BookEnds BookEnds is the quintessential neighborhood bookstore, run by a pro who buys good books and knows how to find the ones she doesn't have. There are more than 60,000 titles here, new and used, from *Celtic Mandalas* to C. S. Lewis's *Chronicles of Narnia* and the full roster of current bestsellers. Volumes on child care, cooking, and self-improvement; a hefty periodicals section; and mainstream and offbeat titles are among the treasures to be found. 600 Kailua Rd., Kailua. ✆ **808/261-1996.**

Heritage Antiques & Gifts This Kailua landmark is known for its selection of Tiffany-style lamps (ranging from $200–$2,000). The mind-boggling inventory also includes European, Asian, American, local, and Pacific Island collectibles. The shop is fun, the people friendly, and the selection diverse enough to appeal to the casual as well as serious collector. Glassware; china; and estate, costume, and fine jewelry are among the items of note. Heritage has its own jeweler who does custom designs and repairs, plus a stable of woodworkers who turn out custom-made koa rockers and hutches to complement the antique furniture selection. 670 Kailua Rd., Kailua. ℂ **808/261-8700.**

THE NORTH SHORE: HALEIWA

Haleiwa means serious shopping for those who know that the unhurried pace of rural life can conceal vast material treasures. Ask the legions of townies who drive an hour each way just to stock up on wine and clothes at Haleiwa stores. Below are our Haleiwa highlights.

Art, Gifts & Crafts

Haleiwa's shops and galleries display a combination of marine art, watercolors, and sculptures, as well as a plethora of crafts trying to masquerade as fine art. This is the town for gifts, fashions, and surf stuff—mostly casual, despite some very high price tags. **Haleiwa Gallery** in the North Shore Marketplace displays a lot of local art of the non-marine variety, and some of it is appealing.

Global Creations Interiors Global Creations offers casual clothing as well as international imports for the home, including Balinese bamboo furniture and colorful hammocks for the carefree life. There are gifts and crafts by 115 local potters, painters, and artists of other media. 66-079 Kamehameha Hwy. ℂ **808/637-1505.**

Oceans in Glass You can watch as local artists create beautiful sea-life sculptures of dolphins, sea turtles, humpback whales, sharks, and colorful reef fish all blown from glass in their studios within the gallery. North Shore Marketplace, 66-252 Kamehameha Hwy. ℂ **808/637-3366.**

Edibles

Haleiwa is best known for its roadside shave-ice stands: the famous **Matsumoto Shave Ice ★** (p. 242), with the perennial queue snaking along Kamehameha Highway, and nearby **Aoki's.** Shave ice is the popular island version of a snow cone, topped with your choice of syrups, such as strawberry, rainbow, root beer, vanilla, or passion fruit. Aficionados order it with a scoop of ice cream and sweetened black adzuki beans nestled in the middle.

Tiny, funky **Celestial Natural Foods,** 66-445 Kamehameha Hwy. (ℂ **808/637-6729**), is the health foodie's one-stop shop for everything from wooden spine-massagers to health supplements, produce, cosmetics, and bulk foods.

Fashion

Although Haleiwa used to be an incense-infused surfer outpost, where zoris and tank tops were the regional uniform and the Beach Boys and Ravi Shankar the music of the day, today it's one of the top shopping destinations for those with unconventional tastes. Specialty shops abound.

Top-drawer **Silver Moon Emporium,** North Shore Marketplace, 66-250 Kamehameha Hwy. (ℂ **808/637-7710**), features the terrific finds of owner Lucie Talbot-Holu. Exquisite clothing and handbags, reasonably priced footwear, hats straight out of *Vogue,* jewelry, scarves, and a full gamut of other treasures pepper the attractive boutique. The entire line of chic Brighton accessories—shoes, handbags, fragrance, belts, and jewelry—are a prized addition.

Other highlights of the prominent North Shore Marketplace include **Patagonia** (☎ 808/637-1245) for high-quality surf, swim, hiking, kayaking, and all-around adventure wear; **North Shore Swimwear** (☎ 808/637-6859) for excellent mix-and-match bikinis and one-piece suits, custom-ordered or off the rack; and **Jungle Gems** (☎ 808/637-6609), the mother lode of gemstones, crystals, silver, and beadwork.

Nearby **Oogenesis Boutique,** 66-249 Kamehameha Hwy (☎ 808/637-4422), in the southern part of Haleiwa, features a storefront lined with vintage-looking dresses that flutter prettily in the North Shore breeze.

A cone of Matsumoto shave ice goes a long way on a warm day.

Surf Shops

Surfers say Haleiwa's ubiquitous surf shops are the best on earth. These are our picks.

Barnfield's Raging Isle Sports Barnfield's is the surf center of the area, with everything from wet suits and surfboards to surf gear and clothing for men, women, and children. The adjoining surfboard factory puts out custom-built boards of high renown. In the North Shore Marketplace, 66-250 Kamehameha Hwy. ☎ 808/637-7707.

Northshore Boardriders Club The cream of the crop. This is the mecca of the board-riding elite, with sleek, fast, elegant, and top-of-the-line boards designed by North Shore legends such as long board shaper Barry Kanaiaupuni, John Carper, Jeff Bushman, and Pat Rawson. This is a Quicksilver "concept store," which means that it's the testing ground for the newest and hottest trends in surf wear put out by the retail giant. In the North Shore Marketplace, 66-250 Kamehameha Hwy. ☎ 808/637-5026.

Surf & Sea Surf Sail & Dive Shop A longtime favorite among old-timers is this newly expanded, flamboyant roadside structure just over the bridge, with old wood floors and blowing fans. It sports a tangle of surf and swimwear, T-shirts, surfboards, boogie boards, fins, watches, sunglasses, and miscellaneous goods; you can also rent surf and snorkel equipment here. 62-595 Kamehameha Hwy. ☎ 808/637-9887.

Tropical Rush Tropical Rush has a huge inventory of surf and swim gear: surfboards, long boards, bodyboards, Sector 9 skateboards, and all the accessories to go with an ocean-minded life, such as slippers and swimwear for men and women. T-shirts, hats, sunglasses, and visors are among the scads of cool gear, and you can rent equipment and arrange surf lessons, too. An added feature is the shop's surf report line, for the up-to-the-minute lowdown on wave action (☎ 808/638-7874); it covers the day's surf and weather details for all of Oahu. 62-620-A Kamehameha Hwy. ☎ 808/637-8886.

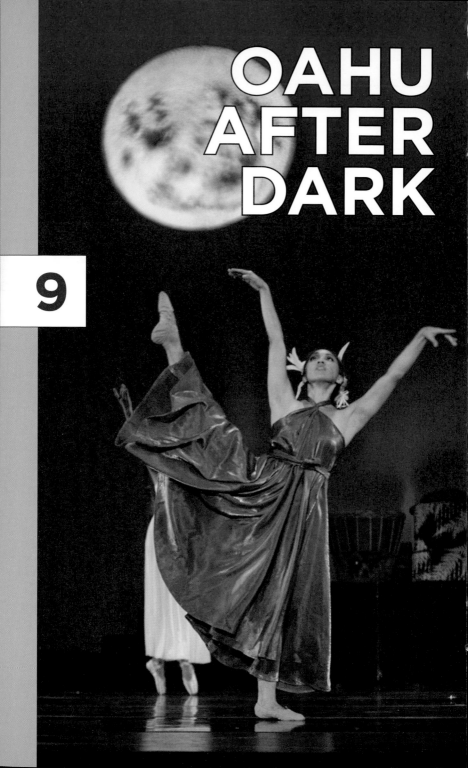

OAHU AFTER DARK

9

A must-do on your Hawaii vacation: Take the time every day to stop and enjoy the sunset. You can watch the big yellow ball descend slowly into the blue water of the Pacific from anywhere on the Waikiki-Honolulu-Leeward side of the island.

Some insist on viewing the sunset with a locally made tropical mai tai, a combination of fresh lime juice, fresh lemon juice, fresh orange juice, passion-orange-guava juice, and fresh grapefruit juice, if possible. Pour this concoction on ice in tall, frosty glasses, then add Meyer's rum that Tahitian vanilla beans have been soaking in for days. (Add cinnamon, if desired, or soak a cinnamon stick with the rum and vanilla beans.) A dash of Angostura bitters, a few drops of Southern Comfort as a float, a sprig of mint, a garnish of fresh lime, and voilà!—you have a tropical, homemade mai tai, a cross between planter's punch and the classic Trader Vic's mai tai. As the sun sets, lift your glass and savor the moment, the setting, and the first sip—not a bad way to end the day.

In Hawaii, the mai tai is more than a libation. It's a festive, happy ritual that signals holiday, vacation, or a time of play, not work. Computers and mai tais don't mix. Mai tais and hammocks do. Mai tais and sunsets go hand in hand.

Speaking of which, nightlife in Hawaii begins at sunset, when all eyes turn westward to see how the day will end. Like seeing the same pod of whales or school of spinner dolphins, sunset viewers seem to bond in the mutual enjoyment of a natural spectacle.

On Tuesdays, Thursdays, and Saturdays at 6:30pm, as the sun casts its golden glow on the beach, and surfers and beach boys paddle in for the day, **Kuhio Beach,** where Kalakaua Avenue intersects with Kaiulani, eases into evening with hula dancing and a torch-lighting ceremony. Start off earlier with a picnic basket and your favorite libations and walk along the oceanside path fronting **Queen's Surf,** near the Waikiki Aquarium. (You can park along Kapiolani Park or near the Honolulu Zoo.) There are few more pleasing spots in Waikiki than the benches at the water's edge at the **Diamond Head** end of Kalakaua Avenue, where lovers and families of all ages stop to peruse the sinking sun. A short walk across the intersection of Kalakaua and Kapahulu avenues takes you to the Duke Kahanamoku statue on Kuhio Beach and the nearby Wizard Stones.

THE BAR & CLUB SCENE
On the Beach

Waikiki's beachfront bars offer many possibilities, from the Royal Hawaiian Hotel's (p. 95) **Mai Tai Bar** (© 808/923-7311), a few feet from the sand, to the unfailingly enchanting **House Without a Key** (© 808/923-2311), at the Halekulani (p. 92), where the breathtaking former Miss Hawaii, Kanoelehua Miller, dances hula to the riffs of Hawaiian steel pedal guitar under a century-old kiawe tree. With the sunset and ocean glowing behind her and

FACING PAGE: Tau Dance Theater's production of *Poliahu* at the Hawaii Theater.

Drinks and dance at House Without a Key.

Diamond Head visible in the distance, the scene is straight out of Somerset Maugham—romantic, evocative, nostalgic. It doesn't hurt, either, that the Halekulani happens to make the best mai tais in the world. Halekulani has the after-dinner hours covered, too, with light jazz by local artists in the **Lewers Lounge** from 7:30pm to 1am nightly.

Another great bar for watching the sun sink into the Pacific is **Duke's Waikiki** (© 808/922-2268; www.dukeswaikiki.com), in the Outrigger Waikiki on the Beach (p. 97). The outside **Barefoot Bar** is perfect for sipping a tropical drink, watching the waves and sunset, and listening to music. It can get crowded, so get here early. Hawaii sunset music is usually from 4 to 6pm daily, and there's live entertainment nightly from 9:30pm to midnight.

In the Aloha Tower Marketplace

Unlike in Waikiki, palm trees don't sway at the **Aloha Tower Marketplace,** on the waterfront between piers 8 and 11, 1 Aloha Tower Dr., Honolulu Harbor (© 808/528-5700). But the landmark Aloha Tower, once Oahu's tallest building, does occupy a prime downtown location—on the water, at a naturally sheltered bay, near the business and civic center of Honolulu. Which means that since its construction, the Aloha Tower Marketplace has gained popularity as an entertainment and nightlife spot, with more than 100 shops and restaurants, including several venues for Honolulu's leading musical groups.

In the **Gordon Biersch Brewery Restaurant** (p. 139; © 808/599-4877; www.gordonbiersch.com), diners swing to jazz, blues, and island riffs with a changing slate of entertainers from sunset through the evening Wednesday through Saturday. The food and beer are great, too. The roster of performers includes the cream of the local contemporary music crop, and the **Atrium Center Court** features ongoing programs of foot-stomping good times. Hours at the Marketplace are daily 8am to midnight.

Most notable, however, is **Don Ho's Island Grill** (© 808/528-0807), a local hotspot, with Willie K. and other musical icons taking the stage throughout the year. It's worth calling to see who's playing. Also check out **Chai's Island Bistro** (© 808/585-0011), one of Honolulu's hottest nightspots (p. 138).

Downtown

The downtown scene is awakening from a long slumber, thanks to the performances at the **Hawaii Theatre** and the popular Nuuanu Avenue block parties, courtesy of some tenacious entrepreneurs who want everyone to love Nuuanu as much as they do. **Hank's Café** on Nuuanu, between Hotel and King streets (**℃ 808/526-1410;** www.hankscafehonolulu.com), is a tiny, kitschy, friendly pub with nightly live music, open-mic nights, and special events that attract great talent and a supportive crowd. On some nights, the music spills out into the streets and it's so packed you have to press your nose against the window to see what you're missing. At the *makai* end of Nuuanu, toward the pier, **Murphy's Bar & Grill** (**℃ 808/531-0422;** www.gomurphys.com) is a downtown ale house and media haunt that has kept Irish eyes smiling for years.

Chinatown

Bar 35, 35 N. Hotel St. (**℃ 808/537-3535;** www.bar35hawaii.com), is a great watering hole/grill with full bar (110 beers), eats (from pizza to oysters on the half shell), and rock-n-roll music in the background. Happy hour (Mon–Fri 4–8pm) features excellent prices, with beers discounted.

At the edge of Chinatown is something straight out of 1940s film noir: **Indigo's,** 1121 Nuuanu Ave. (**℃ 808/521-2900;** www.indigo-hawaii.com), which serves sizzling food during the day, and dishes up entertainment Tuesday through Friday nights from 4 to 8pm.

Another Chinatown "in" spot is **thirtyninehotel,** 29 N. Hotel St., between Smith Street and Nuuanu Avenue (**℃ 808/599-2552;** www.thirtynine hotel.com), where live jazz and visiting and resident DJs rock from 4pm to 2am Tuesday to Saturday. (During the day, Tues–Sat noon–6pm, it morphs into an art gallery, featuring contemporary local artists.) The door is unmarked, with only the address to tell you where you are. Enter and walk up the stairs to the second floor. The cover is $8 to $10.

Waikiki & the Surrounding Area

If you are looking for dancing, darts, pool, and a sports bar with huge TVs, the **Pipeline,** 805 Pohukaina St., in Kakaako (**℃ 808/589-1999;** www.pipeline cafehawaii.com), is your place. Patrons here tend to be younger (you can get in at 18 years old, but some events specify 21 and over) and dressed to go clubbing. The cover is generally $10 to $20; concerts are around $20 to $40 plus service charges.

The 20-something crowd, visitors, and military personnel head to **Moose McGillycuddy's,** 310 Lewers St., in Waikiki (**℃ 808/923-0751;** www.moose restaurantgroup.com). Downstairs is a cafe serving breakfast, lunch, and dinner; upstairs is a happening entertainment and dance club. Tuesday is $2 drink night, but with a $5 cover (it's the busiest night of the week).

Rumours Nightclub, in the lobby of the Ala Moana Hotel, 410 Atkinson Dr. (**℃ 808/955-4811**), is the disco of choice for those who remember Paul McCartney as something other than Stella's father. Friday 5 to 9pm and Saturday 9pm to 3:30am the music is strictly retro; on Sundays from 9pm to 3:30am, Top 40 music is played. A spacious dance floor, a good sound system, and the music draw a mix of generations.

Gay Bars & Clubs

The reigning queen of gay bars and clubs in Waikiki is **Hula's Bar & Lei Stand,** Waikiki Grand, 134 Kapahulu Ave., second floor (✆ **808/923-0669;** www.hulas. com), still going strong after 35 years. Overlooking Kapiolani Park, Queen's Surf Beach, and the Honolulu Zoo, it's packed from the 10am opening until last call at 2am the next day. Drag queens gather at **Fusion Waikiki,** 2260 Kuhio Ave., near Seaside Ave., second floor (✆ **808/924-2422;** www.fusionwaikiki.com), for the Gender Bender Lip Gloss Revue on Fridays and the Paper Doll Revue on Saturdays, plus a male strip show both nights (cover charge). The clientele tends toward local Hawaii residents at this only after-hours (till 4am) gay bar. **The In-Between,** 2155 Lauula St., near Lewers St. (✆ **808/926-7060;** www.in betweenonline.com), is a neighborhood gay bar with a great karaoke sound system. (You can belt out everything from contemporary hits and Broadway to Hawaiian and country & western.)

MUSIC
Hawaiian Music

"Aloha shirt to Armani" is what we call the night scene in Honolulu—mostly casual, but with ample opportunity to dress up if you can bear to part with your flip-flops.

Oahu has several key spots for Hawaiian music. A delightful (and powerful) addition to the Waikiki music scene is Hawaii's queen of falsetto, **Genoa Keawe,** who fills the Lobby Bar of the **Hawaiian Regent Hotel** (✆ **808/922-6611**) with her larger-than-life voice. You'll find her here from 5:30 to 8:30pm every Thursday; the rest of the week, except Monday, other contemporary Hawaiian musicians fill in.

Brothers Cazimero remains one of Hawaii's most gifted duos (Robert on bass, Roland on 12-string guitar), appearing every Wednesday at 7pm at **Chai's Island Bistro** (p. 138; ✆ **808/585-0011**), in the Aloha Tower Marketplace. Also at Chai's: Robert Cazimero plays by himself on the piano on Tuesdays at 7pm; and **Jerry Santos and Hula** performs on Mondays at 7pm.

Impromptu hula and spirited music from the family and friends of the performers are an island tradition at places such as the **Hilton Hawaiian Village** (✆ **808/949-4321**), which has live music nightly at the Tapa Bar and at the Tropics Bar and Grill. Plus every Friday night is the Rocking Hawaiian Rainbow Review with fireworks starting at 7pm. Its **Waikiki Style Luau** features Hawaiian entertainment with dinner five nights a week (Sun–Thurs) for $120. The **Royal Hawaiian** also has its own form of luau; see p. 95 for more details.

At **Duke's Canoe Club** at the Outrigger Waikiki (✆ **808/923-0711**), it's always three deep at the beachside bar as the sun sets; extra-special entertainment is a given here, from 4 to 6pm and again from 9:30pm to midnight every night.

Nearby, the Moana Surfrider offers a regular nightly program of live Hawaiian music and piano in its **Beach House** (✆ **808/922-3111**), which surrounds an islet-size canopy of banyan tree and roots where Robert Louis Stevenson loved to linger. The Veranda serves afternoon tea and cocktails.

Our best advice for Hawaiian music lovers is to scan the local dailies (especially Friday's pull-out TGIF section in the *Honolulu Star Advertiser;* www.star advertiser.com) or the *Honolulu Weekly* (www.honoluluweekly.com) to see if and where the following Hawaiian entertainers are appearing: **Kekuhi Kanahele,** an accomplished, award-winning chanter and *kahiko* (ancient hula) dancer; **Hookena,** a symphonically rich quintet featuring **Manu Boyd,** one of the most prolific songwriters and chanters in Hawaii; **Kealii Reichel,** premier chanter, dancer, and award-winning recording artist; **Robbie Kahakalau,** another award-winning musician; **Kapena,** for contemporary Hawaiian music; **Na Leo Pilimehana,** a trio of angelic Hawaiian singers; the **Makaha Sons of Niihau,** pioneers in the Hawaiian cultural renaissance; **Fiji,** a performer whose music is classified as Hawaiian soul; and slack-key guitar master **Raymond Kane.**

Consider the gods beneficent if you happen to be here when the hula *halau* (school) of **Frank Kawaikapuokalani Hewett** is holding its annual fundraiser. It's a rousing, inspired, family effort that always features the best in ancient and contemporary Hawaiian music. For the best in hula, check the dailies for halau fundraisers, which are always authentic, enriching, and local to the core.

The **Waikiki Improvement Association** also puts on free hula performances every Tuesday, Thursday, Saturday, and Sunday, from 6:30 to 7:30pm, at Kuhio Beach Park.

The Blues

The blues are alive and well in Hawaii, with quality acts both local and from the mainland drawing enthusiastic crowds. **Junior Wells, Willie & Lobo, War,** and surprise appearances by the likes of **Bonnie Raitt** are among the past

GET down WITH ARTAFTERDARK

The last Friday of every month (except Nov and Dec), the place to be after the sun goes down is the **Honolulu Academy of Arts' ARTafterDark ★★★,** a *pau-hana* (after-work) mixer in the art museum that brings residents and visitors together around a theme combining art with food, music, and dancing. In addition to the exhibits in the gallery, ARTafterDark also features visual and live performances. Themes range from "Plant Rice"—with rice and sake tastings, Asian beers, live Asian fusion music, and a tour of the "Art of Rice" exhibit—to "'80s Night," "Turkish Delights," "Cool Nights," "Hot Jazz and Blues," and "Havana Heat."

The party gets going about 6pm and lasts until 9pm. The crowd—ranging in age from their 20s to 50s—dresses in everything from jeans and T-shirts to designer cocktail party attire. Entry fee is $10. For more information, call ✆ 808/532-6091 or visit www.artafterdark.org.

The funky crowd at ARTafterDARK.

successes of this genre of big-time licks. The best-loved Oahu venue is **Anna Bannanas,** 2440 S. Beretania St., between University Avenue and Isenberg Street (**℃ 808/946-5190**), still rocking after 30 years in the business with reggae, blues, and rock—plus video games and darts.

Jazz

To find out what's happening in the jazz scene while you're in town, check out **www.honolulujazzscene.net**. **Duc's Bistro** (p. 139; **℃ 808/531-6325**), downtown, presents live jazz on Saturday nights.

In Waikiki, tops in taste and ambience is the perennially alluring **Lewers Lounge,** in the Halekulani, 2199 Kalia Rd. (p. 92; **℃ 808/923-2311;** www.halekulani.com). Recently renovated (with a higher ceiling, a contemporary color scheme, and comfy intimate seating around the pillars), this is a great spot for contemporary jazz nightly from 7:30pm to 1am. Be sure to try the "Hpnotiq" liqueur, a blend of premium vodka, cognac, and fruit juices from France, served over ice or in various concoctions.

Outside of Waikiki, the **Veranda,** at the Kahala Resort, 5000 Kahala Ave. (p. 111; **℃ 808/739-8888;** www.kahalaresort.com), is a popular spot for the over-40 crowd, with nightly jazz music and a dance floor.

In Honolulu, jazz fans will love **Jazz Wednesdays** at the **Honolulu Club,** 932 Ward Ave. (**℃ 808/543-3900**), where the seventh-floor lounge of this ultraupscale fitness center turns into a jazz nightclub with a wall of windows overlooking the Honolulu skyline. Music begins at 7pm (and lasts until 11:30pm), but the tables start filling up at 6pm. The cover is $10 and the crowd, often from the surrounding offices, generally ranges from people in their mid-20s to 50s. Skip the high-priced *pupu* (appetizers), but the local jazz musicians are well worth the price of drinks (martinis, ranging from $7 to $9, are your best bet).

Around town, watch for **Sandy Tsukiyama,** a gifted singer (Brazilian, Latin, jazz) and one of Honolulu's great assets, as well as for jazz singers **Rachel Gonzales** and **Loretta Ables.** Other noteworthy groups in jazz, blues, and R&B include **Blue Budda, Bongo Tribe, Secondhand Smoke, Bluzilla, Piranha Brothers,** and the **Greg Pai Trio.**

THE PERFORMING ARTS

Audiences have stomped to the big Off-Broadway percussion hit *Stomp* and have enjoyed the talent of *Tap Dogs,* Momix, the Hawaii International Jazz Festival, the American Repertory Dance Company, and John Kaimikaua's *halau*—all at the **Hawaii Theatre,** 1130 Bethel St. (**℃ 808/528-0506;** www.hawaiitheatre. com). It's the Carnegie Hall of the Pacific, still basking in its renaissance following a 4-year, $22-million renovation (it was built in 1922). The neoclassical Beaux Arts landmark features an original 1922 dome, 1,400 plush seats, and a hydraulically elevated organ. Breathtaking murals create an atmosphere that's making the theater a leading multipurpose center.

Other smaller theaters on Oahu are: the **Manoa Valley Theatre,** 2833 E. Manoa Rd. (**℃ 808/988-6131;** www.manoavalleytheatre.com), Honolulu's equivalent of Off-Broadway, with well-known shows performing; **Diamond Head Theatre,** 520 Makapuu Ave. (**℃ 808/733-0274;** www.diamondhead theatre.com), hosting a variety of performances from musicals to comedies to classical dramas; **Kumu Kahua Theatre,** 46 Merchant St. (**℃ 808/536-4222;**

www.kumukahua.org), producing plays dealing with the island experience, often written by residents; **Army Community Theatre,** Richardson Theatre, Fort Shafter (© 808/438-5230; www.army theatre.com), offering revivals of Broadway musicals; and **Leeward Community College Theatre,** 96-045 Ala Ike St. (© 808/455-0385; www.LCCtheatre.hawaii. edu), featuring an eclectic slate of productions, from visiting performing companies to local students' work.

The highly successful **Hawaii Opera Theatre** (© 808/596-7858; www. hawaiiopera.org) takes to the stage from January to March. Started in 1960 (past hits have included *La Bohème, Carmen, Turandot, Romeo and Juliet, Rigoletto,* and *Aïda*), the Opera still draws fans to the Neal Blaisdell Concert Hall. In the summer during July, the Hawaii Opera Theatre puts on a lighter performance, such as *South Pacific.* Dance also makes the list at the center with **Ballet Hawaii** (© 808/521-6514; www.ballethawaii.org) performing twice a year in August (in 2007, Tchaikovsky's *Sleeping Beauty* was presented) and December (the annual *Nutcracker* ballet, generally sold out).

Showroom Acts & Revues

One showroom act that has maintained a following is the **Society of Seven's** nightclub act (a blend of skits, Broadway hits, popular music, and costumed musical acts), in the **Outrigger Waikiki on the Beach** (p. 97; © 808/922-6408; www.societyofseven.com). Shows are Tuesday through Saturday at 8pm; direct admission is $39 adults and $17 children 4 to 20. If you buy your tickets from the hotel, it will run you $45 and $26 respectively. **"The Magic of Polynesia,"** at the **Waikiki Beachcomber** (© 808/971-4321 or 877/971-4321; www.magic ofpolynesia.com), starring illusionist **John Hirokana** (Michael Villoria fills in on Sun and Mon nights), is performed nightly at 6:45pm (with dinner: $85–$139 adults, children $57–$68 ages 4–11; without dinner, starting at 7:30pm: $53 adults, $35 children ages 4–11.) *Tip:* Book on the website for a 20% discount.

Also on Kalakaua Avenue is the still-sizzling Polynesian revue **"Creation—A Polynesian Odyssey"** in the **Sheraton Princess Kaiulani**'s second-floor Ainahau Showroom (p. 102; © 808/931-4660; www.princess-kaiulani.com/ dining/creation). Produced by **Tihati** (pronounced tea-*hot*-tea), the state's largest entertainment company, the show is a theatrical journey of fire dancing, special effects, illusions, hula, and Polynesian dances from Hawaii and the South Pacific. Dinner shows are Tuesday, Thursday, Friday, Saturday, and Sunday and cost $95 to $145 adults and $72 to $109 for children 5 to 12 years; show only is $55 adults, $42 children.

The best in comedy is **Andy Bumatai,** who performs local stand-up sketches that will have you not only understanding local residents, but also screaming with laughter. Another excellent comic is **Frank Delima.** If he's playing anywhere on Oahu, it's worth the drive to see this comic genius, who sings, dances, and performs comic routines that will have you laughing until your sides hurt.

Luau!

The sun is setting, the tiki torches are lit, the pig is taken from the *imu* (an oven in the earth), the drums begin pounding—it's luau time. Recently, three new luau have started: in Waikiki, on the North Shore, and in windward Oahu at Sea Life Park. Regrettably, there's no commercial luau on Oahu that comes close to Maui's Old Lahaina Luau, or Hawaii Island's legendary Kona Village Luau. In Waikiki, the **Royal Hawaiian Hotel,** 2259 Kalakaua Ave., at Seaside Ave. (p. 95; ℂ **888/808-4668;** www.honuhawaiiactivities.com), holds Waikiki's only oceanfront luau. Upon arrival, you'll be greeted with a Hawaiian flower lei and a refreshing drink, followed by a feast: a variety of traditional Hawaiian as well as continental American dishes. The buffet menu features delicacies such as roasted kalua pig, mahimahi, teriyaki steak, poi, sweet potatoes, rice, vegetables, *haupia* (coconut pudding), and a selection of delicious cakes. It all ends with the Royal Polynesian Extravaganza, which features songs and dances from Hawaii and other Polynesian island nations. Luau is Monday at 5:30pm; the cost is $155 adults and $80 for children (ages 5–12).

The largest luau venues are **Germaine's** (ℂ **800/367-5655** or 808/941-3338; www.germainesluau.com) and **Paradise Cove Luau** (ℂ **800/775-2683** or 808/842-5911; www.paradisecovehawaii.com), both about a 40-minute drive away from Waikiki on the Leeward Coast. Bus pickups and drop-offs in Waikiki are part of the deal.

Germaine's tries awfully hard and is a much more intimate affair than those legendary shows on Maui or Hawaii, but the experience is not as complete. Cost for Germaine's is $72 per adult, $62 for 14- to 20-year-olds, and $52 for 6- to 13-year-olds (5-year-olds and younger are free)—the prices include tax and transportation. The shows are held nightly from 6 to 9pm.

Paradise Cove, too, is a mixed bag, with 600 to 800 guests a night. The small thatched village feels more like a Hawaiian theme park, with Hawaiian

The elaborate luau at the Royal Hawaiian Hotel.

games, *hukilau* net throwing and gathering, craft demonstrations, and a beautiful shoreline looking out over what is usually a storybook sunset. Tahitian dance and ancient and modern hula make this a fun-filled evening for those spirited enough to join in. The food is safe, though not breathtaking: Hawaiian *kalua* pig, lomi salmon, poi, and coconut pudding and cake, as well as more traditional fare. Paradise Cove is extremely popular because of its idyllic setting and good entertainment quality. Tickets, including transportation and taxes, are $82 to $142 for adults, $72 to $127 for ages 13 to 20, $62 to $115 for ages 4 to 12, and free for those 3 and under. Shows are nightly from 5 to 9pm.

On the North Shore, the **Polynesian Cultural Center** (p. 235) presents **"Ali'i Luau,"** featuring a traditional luau buffet and entertainment during the meal. You can add to your luau package the **"Ha Breath of Life"** evening show. Tickets for the dinner only are $35 adults and $27 children ages 5 to 11. The luau plus the evening show are $76 adults and $62 children, and include transportation from Waikiki. *Note:* The Polynesian Cultural Center does not serve or allow alcohol on the property. To book, call © **800/367-7060** or go to **www. polynesia.com**.

On the North Shore, the **Turtle Bay Resort** (p. 115) presents **"Voyages of Luau,"** on the lawn overlooking the ocean. It includes a "Taste of the Islands" luau buffet and a Polynesian revue featuring the songs and dances of the Tuamotu Islands, Samoa, Tahiti, Fiji, and Hawaii. Tickets for the dinner and show are $95 adults and $55 children ages 4 to 11. To book, call © **808/293-6000** or go to **www.turtlebayresort.com/activities/luau.asp**.

FILM

A new 16-theater megaplex has opened in the **Victoria Ward** entertainment center, at the corner of Auahi and Kamakee streets, and the **Windward Mall's** 10-screen megaplex is also bringing movies to the masses more conveniently. Honolulu's film scene continues to sprawl with more screens, more seats, and more multiplexes.

A quick check in both dailies and the *Honolulu Weekly* will tell you what's playing where in the world of feature films. For film buffs and esoteric movie lovers, **The Movie Museum,** 3566 Harding Ave. (© **808/735-8771;** www. kaimukihawaii.com/businesses/current/956.html), has special screenings of vintage films and rents a collection of hard-to-find and classic films. The **Honolulu Academy of Arts Theatre,** 900 S. Beretania St. (© **808/532-8768;** www. honoluluacademy.org/cmshaa/academy/index.aspx?id=2402), is the film-as-art center of Honolulu, offering special screenings, guest appearances, and cultural performances, as well as noteworthy programs in the visual arts.

The Kahala Mall's **Kahala 8-Plex** (© **808/593-3000** www.consolidated theatres.com) and the 16-theater **Kapolei Megaplex** (© **808/593-3000;** www. consolidatedtheatres.com) are now eclipsed by the 18-screen **Dole Cannery** (© **808/526-3653;** www.regmovies.com), at Nimitz Highway and Pacific.

Free parking in the evenings, discount matinees, and special discounted midnight shows make the movies at the nine-screen **Wallace Theatres** on Restaurant Row, 500 Ala Moana Blvd., near downtown Honolulu (© **808/263-4171**), more affordable.

PLANNING YOUR TRIP TO OAHU

10

With so many places to explore, things to do, and sights to see in Oahu, where do you start? That's where we come in. In the pages that follow, we'll help you plan your ideal trip, providing information on airlines, seasons, a calendar of events, how to make camping reservations . . . even how to tie the knot.

Oahu is a relatively small island, measuring 26 miles long and some 44 miles across at its widest, totaling 608 square miles of land, with 112 miles of coastline. From outer space, Oahu looks somewhat like a frayed Indian arrowhead with two mountain ridges shoring up each side: the 4,000-foot Waianae Mountains on the leeward (western) coast and the 3,000-foot Koolau Mountains on the windward (eastern) side. At night you can see the lights of suburban Oahu pouring down the mountain valleys and reaching toward the shoreline.

To many, Oahu and its most famous city, Honolulu, are synonymous. In fact, some people think the name of the island is Honolulu, a misnomer further compounded by the island-wide county calling itself the "City and County of Honolulu." Honolulu's best-known neighborhood, Waikiki, is actually quite small, but its spectacular beach and array of resort hotels are what originally put Hawaii on the tourist map.

GETTING THERE
By Plane

Most major U.S. and many international carriers fly to Honolulu International Airport.

United Airlines (✆ 800/225-5825; www.ual.com) offers the most frequent service from the U.S. mainland. **American Airlines** (✆ 800/433-7300; www.americanair.com) offers flights from Dallas, Chicago, San Francisco, San Jose, Los Angeles, and St. Louis to Honolulu. **Continental Airlines** (✆ 800/231-0856; www.continental.com) offers the only daily nonstop from the New York area (Newark) to Honolulu. **Delta Air Lines** (✆ 800/221-1212; www.delta.com) flies nonstop from the West Coast and one-stop itineraries from Houston and Cincinnati. **Hawaiian Airlines** (✆ 800/367-5320; www.hawaiian air.com) offers nonstop flights to Honolulu from several West Coast cities (including new service from San Diego). **Alaska Airlines** (✆ 800/252-7522; www.alaskaair.com) has direct flights to Honolulu from Seattle and Anchorage.

Airlines serving Hawaii from places other than the U.S. mainland include **Air Canada** (✆ 800/776-3000; www.aircanada.ca); **Air New Zealand** (✆ 0800/737-000 in Auckland, 643/379-5200 in Christchurch, 800/926-7255 in the U.S.; www.airnewzealand.com); **Qantas** (✆ 008/177-767 in Australia, 800/227-4500 in the U.S.; www.qantas.com.au); **Japan Air Lines** (✆ 03/5489-1111 in Tokyo, 800/525-3663 in the U.S.; www.japanair.com); **All Nippon Airways** (**ANA;** ✆ 03/5489-1212 in Tokyo, 800/235-9262 in the U.S.;

FACING PAGE: The most elegant way to travel: Oahu by glider plane.

273

THE WELCOMING lei

The tropical beauty of the delicate garland, the deliciously sweet fragrance of the blossoms, the sensual way the flowers curl softly around your neck—there's no doubt about it: Getting lei'd in Hawaii is a sensuous experience.

Leis are one of the nicest ways to say hello, goodbye, congratulations, I salute you, my sympathies are with you, or I love you. Giving leis is a historic custom: According to chants, the first lei was given by Hiiaka, the sister of the volcano goddess, Pele. Hiiaka presented Pele with a lei of lehua blossoms on a beach in Puna.

During ancient times, leis given to *alii* (royalty) were accompanied by a bow, as it was *kapu* (forbidden) for a commoner to raise his arms higher than the king's head. The presentation of a kiss with a lei didn't come about until World War II; it's generally attributed to an entertainer who kissed an officer on a dare, then quickly presented him with her lei, saying it was an old Hawaiian custom. It wasn't then, but it sure caught on fast.

Lei-making is a tropical art form. All leis are fashioned by hand in a variety of traditional patterns; some are sewn of hundreds of tiny blooms or shells, or bits of ferns and leaves. Some are twisted, some braided, some strung. Every island has its own special flower lei. On Oahu, the choice is *ilima,* a small orange flower. Big Islanders prefer the *lehua,* a large, delicate red puff. Maui likes the *lokelani,* a small rose. On Kauai, it's the *mokihana,* a fragrant green vine and berry. Molokai prefers the *kukui,* the white blossom of a candlenut tree. And Lanai's lei is made of *kaunaoa,* a bright yellow moss, while Niihau uses its abundant seashells to make leis that were once prized by royalty and are now worth a small fortune.

Leis are available at lei stands at Honolulu International Airport. Other places to get creative, inexpensive leis are the half-dozen lei shops on **Maunakea Street** in Honolulu's Chinatown, and **Flowers by Jou & T Jr.,** 2652 S. King St. (near University Ave.), Honolulu (☎ **808/941-2022**). They're also available from florists, and even at supermarkets.

Leis are the perfect symbol of Hawaii: They're given in the moment, their fragrance and beauty are enjoyed in the moment, and when they fade, their spirit of aloha lives on. Welcome to the islands!

www.fly-ana.com); **China Airlines** (☎ **02/715-1212** in Taipei, 800/227-5118 in the U.S.; www.china-airlines.com); **Air Pacific** (☎ **800/227-4446;** www.air pacific.com), serving Fiji, Australia, New Zealand, and the South Pacific; **Korean Air** (☎ **02/656-2000** in Seoul, 800/223-1155 on the U.S. East Coast, 800/421-8200 on the U.S. West Coast, 800/438-5000 from Hawaii; www.koreanair.com); and **Philippine Airlines** (☎ **631/816-6691** in Manila, 800/435-9725 in the U.S.; www.philippineair.com).

Operated by the European Travel Network, **www.discount-tickets.com** is a great online source for regular and discounted airfares to destinations around the world. Compare rates and book accommodations, car rentals, and tours.

If you're traveling in the United States beyond Hawaii, some large American airlines—such as **American, Delta,** and **United**—offer travelers on transatlantic or transpacific flights special discount tickets under the name **Visit USA,** allowing travel between U.S. destinations at reduced rates. These tickets must be purchased before you leave your foreign point of departure. This system is the best, easiest, and fastest way to see the United States at low cost. You should obtain information well in advance from your travel agent or the airline office, as the conditions attached to these discount tickets can change without advance notice.

Locally, **Hawaiian Airlines** (✆ **800/367-5320;** www.hawaiianair.com) flies nonstop to Sydney, Australia; Tahiti; American Samoa; and Seoul, Korea.

AGRICULTURAL SCREENING

At Honolulu International Airport, baggage and passengers bound for the mainland must be screened by agricultural officials. Officials will confiscate local produce, such as fresh avocados, bananas, and mangoes, in the name of fruit-fly control. Pineapples, coconuts, and papayas inspected and certified for export, boxed flowers, leis without seeds, and processed foods (macadamia nuts, coffee, jams, dried fruit, and the like) will pass.

ARRIVAL AT HONOLULU INTERNATIONAL AIRPORT

Honolulu International Airport sits on the south shore of Oahu, west of downtown Honolulu and Waikiki, near Pearl Harbor.

While the airport is large and constantly expanding, the layout is quite simple and easy to navigate. You can walk or take the **Wiki-Wiki Bus,** a free airport shuttle, from your arrival gate to the main terminal and baggage claim, which is on the ground level. After collecting your bags, exit to the palm-lined street, where uniformed attendants flag down taxis, Waikiki shuttles, and rental car vans; they can also direct you to **TheBus** (p. 278).

GETTING TO & FROM THE AIRPORT

BY RENTAL CAR All major rental companies have cars available at Honolulu International Airport (p. 276). Rental agency vans pick you up at the middle curbside outside baggage claim and take you to their off-site lot.

Coping with Jet Lag

Jet lag is a pitfall of traveling across time zones. If you're flying north–south, your symptoms will be the result of dehydration and the general stress of air travel. When you travel east–west, however, your body becomes disoriented about what time it is, and everything from your digestive system to your brain is knocked for a loop. Traveling east, say from Maui to Boston, is more difficult on your internal clock than traveling west, say from Atlanta to Oahu, because most peoples' bodies are more inclined to stay up late than fall asleep early.

Here are some tips for combating jet lag:

○ **Reset your watch** to your destination time before you board the plane.

○ **Drink lots of water** before, during, and after your flight. Avoid alcohol.

○ **Exercise and sleep well** for a few days before your trip.

○ If you have trouble sleeping on planes, **fly eastward on morning flights.**

○ **Natural light** resets your body clock. **Outside In** (www.bodyclock.com) can provide a customized plan of when to seek and avoid daylight.

BY TAXI Oahu's major cab companies offer island-wide, 24-hour radio-dispatched service, with multilingual drivers, air-conditioned cars, limos, vans, and vehicles equipped with wheelchair lifts. Fares are standard for all taxi firms; from the airport, expect to pay about $35 to $45 (plus tip) to Waikiki, about $25 to $35 to downtown, about $60 to $75 to Kailua, about $60 to $70 to Hawaii Kai, and about $90 to $125 to the North Shore.

For a flat fee of $30, **Star Taxi** (✆ 800/671-2999 or 808/942-STAR [942-7827]) will take up to four passengers from the airport to Waikiki (with no extra charges for baggage); however, you must book in advance. After you have arrived and picked up your luggage, call Star for directions on where to meet the car.

BY AIRPORT SHUTTLE Shuttle vans operate 24 hours a day, every day of the year, between the airport and all 350 hotels and condos in Waikiki. The cheapest shuttle service is **Airport Waikiki Express** (✆ 800/831-5541; www.robertshawaii.com/airport-shuttle), with 24-hour service in air-conditioned vans for just $9 from the airport to Waikiki ($15 round-trip). You can board with two pieces of luggage and a carry-on at no extra charge; surfboards and bicycles are prohibited for safety reasons. Tips are welcome.

BY BUS **TheBus** (✆ 808/848-4500; www.thebus.org) is by far the cheapest way to get to Waikiki—a one-way fare is $2.50 (exact change only)—but you've got to be traveling light to use it. You can board TheBus with a carry-on or small suitcase as long as it fits under the seat and doesn't disrupt other passengers. TheBus nos. 19 and 20 (Waikiki Beach and Hotels) run from the airport to downtown Honolulu and Waikiki (travel time: 1 hr.). The first bus from Waikiki to the airport is at 4:55am on weekdays and 5:10am on weekends; the last bus departs the airport for Waikiki at 1:22am on weekdays, 1:24am on weekends. Two bus stops are on the main terminal's upper level; a third is on the second level of the interisland terminal. See p. 278 for more information on TheBus.

GETTING AROUND
By Car

To **rent a car** in Hawaii, you must be at least 21 years of age and have a valid U.S. or international driver's license and credit card. The average nondiscounted, unlimited-mileage rate for a 1-day rental for a midsize car in Honolulu was $44 to $67 in 2011.

At Honolulu International Airport, you'll find most major rental-car agencies, including **Avis** (✆ 800/321-3712; www.avis.com), **Budget** (✆ 800/527-0700; www.budget.com), **Dollar** (✆ 800/800-4000; www.dollar.com), **Enterprise** (✆ 800/325-8007; www.enterprise.com), **Hertz** (✆ 800/654-3011; www.hertz.com), **National** (✆ 800/227-7368; www.nationalcar.com), and **Thrifty** (✆ 800/367-2277; www.thrifty.com). It's almost always cheaper to rent a car at the airport than in Waikiki or through your hotel (unless there's one already included in your package deal); however, it's best to book in advance.

We no longer recommend **Alamo,** which tends to overbook their cars. Despite confirmed reservations, many loyal Frommer's readers have been forced to wait 1 to 2 hours at the start of their vacation (after sitting on an airplane for 5-plus hours) for cars to be returned.

Hawaii is a no-fault state, which means that if you don't have **collision-damage insurance,** you are required to pay for all damages before you leave the state, whether or not the accident was your fault. Your personal car insurance back home may provide rental-car coverage; read your policy or call your insurer before you leave home. Bring your insurance identification card if you decline the optional insurance, which usually costs from $12 to $20 a day. Obtain the name of your company's local claim representative before you go. Some credit card companies also provide collision-damage insurance to customers; check with yours before you rent.

TAXIS

See p. 276 for information on taxi cabs on the island of Oahu.

RUSH HOUR

Oahu residents own 600,000 registered vehicles, but they have only 1,500 miles of mostly two-lane roads. That's 400 cars for every mile, a fact that becomes abundantly clear during morning and evening rush hours. You can avoid the gridlock by driving between 9am and 3pm or after 6pm.

DRIVING RULES

Hawaii state law mandates that all car passengers must wear a **seat belt,** and all infants must be strapped into car seats. The fine is enforced with vigilance, so buckle up—you'll pay a $95 to $150 fine if you don't. **Pedestrians** always have the right of way, even if they're not in the crosswalk. You can turn **right on red** from the right lane after a full and complete stop, unless there's a sign forbidding you to do so.

MAIN STREETS & HIGHWAYS

Navigating around Oahu is actually easy as there are relatively few roads—some circle the perimeter of the island and a handful cut across the island.

TO & FROM THE AIRPORT The main thoroughfare that runs from the airport to Honolulu and Waikiki is the **H-1 Freeway.** The H-1 also runs in the opposite direction to Pearl Harbor and Ewa. The artery that runs from the airport to Honolulu and Waikiki is **Nimitz Highway** (which has stoplights). In downtown Honolulu, Nimitz Highway becomes **Ala Moana Boulevard.**

Easy Ridin' on Oahu

If your dream is to go screaming down the highway on the back of a big Harley, here's your chance. **Cruzin Hawaii Motorcycles,** 1980 Kalakaua Ave., at Kuhio Avenue, next to Tony Roma's, Waikiki (© 808/945-9595; www.cruzinhawaii.com), has a range of bikes starting at $79 (some insurance is included in the price). Also try **Big Kahuna Motorcycle Rentals,** 407 Seaside Ave., Waikiki (© 808/924-2736; www.bigkahunarentals.com), which specializes in Harley-Davidson, BMW, Yamaha, and Honda; or **Coconut Cruisers,** 2301 Kalakaua Ave., across from the International Market Place, Honolulu (© 808/924-1644; www.coconut cruisers.netfirms.com). You must have a valid motorcycle license to rent a bike.

IN HONOLULU The myriad of one-way streets in Honolulu can be confusing and frustrating. If you want to travel in the Diamond Head direction, **King Street** is one-way going toward Diamond Head. **Beretania Street** is one-way in the opposite direction, toward Ewa. **Punchbowl** and **Bishop streets** run toward the ocean (in the *makai* direction, as locals say; p. 71), and **Alakea** and **Bethel streets** run toward the mountains (in the *mauka* direction).

There are three parallel main streets in **Waikiki: Kalakaua Avenue** (which is one-way going toward Diamond Head and eventually fronts Waikiki Beach), **Kuhio Avenue** (1 block *mauka* of Kalakaua Ave., which has two-way traffic), and **Ala Wai Boulevard** (which fronts the Ala Wai Canal and runs one-way in the Ewa direction).

AROUND OAHU From Waikiki, **Highway 72** (the **Kalanianaole Hwy.**) takes you around Makapuu Point into Kailua and Kaneohe. From Kailua and Kaneohe, **Highway 83** (the **Kamehameha Hwy.**) traverses the North Shore to Haleiwa, where it is still called the Kamehameha Highway, but the number of the highway changes to 99, and the highway then cuts through mid-Oahu past Schofield Barracks and Wahiawa, and swings out to Pearl City.

On the leeward coast, H-1 Freeway becomes two-lane **Highway 93** (the **Farrington Hwy.**); after Makaha, the number changes to Highway 930, but it is still called Farrington Highway all the way out to Kaena Point. Although you cannot drive around Kaena Point, Farrington Highway (still called Hwy. 930) picks up on the north side of the point and goes through Mokuleia and Waialua.

ACROSS OAHU Highways that cut across the island are **Highway 99** (see above), the **Likelike Highway** (also called Hwy. 63, which goes from Honolulu to Kaneohe), and the **Pali Highway** (also called Hwy. 61, which goes from Honolulu to Kailua). The **H-3 Freeway,** which starts at Pearl Harbor, is the fastest way to get to Kaneohe and Kailua.

MAPS

One of the best general maps of the island is the ***Map of Oahu,*** cartography by James A. Bier, published by the University of Hawaii Press, available at bookstores or online at www.uhpress.hawaii.edu.

The best street map we have found is *TMK Maps: Oahu Streets and Condos,* published by Hawaii TMK Service, Inc. (☎ **808/536-0867**).

The best and most detailed maps for activities are published by **Franko's Maps** (www.frankosmaps.com); they feature a host of island maps, plus a terrific "Hawaiian Reef Creatures Guide," for snorkelers curious about what fish they spotted underwater. Free road maps are published by *This Week Magazine,* a free visitor publication available on Oahu, the Big Island, Maui, and Kauai.

For topographic and other maps of the islands, go to the **Hawaii Geographic Society,** 49 S. Hotel St., Honolulu; or hawaiigeographicsociety@gmail.com (☎ **800/538-3950** or 808/538-3952).

By Bus

One of the best deals anywhere, **TheBus** (☎ **808/848-5555,** or 808/296-1818 for recorded information; www.thebus.org) will take you around the whole island for $2.50. In fact, on a daily basis, more than 260,000 people use the system's 68 lines and 4,000 bus stops.

TRAVELER'S online TOOLBOX

Veteran travelers usually carry some essential items to make their trips easier. Following is a selection of handy online tools to bookmark and use.

- **Airplane Food** (www.airlinemeals. net)

- **Airplane Seating** (www.seatguru. com)

- **Hawaii Visitors and Convention Bureau** (www.gohawaii.com)

- **State of Hawaii** (www.hawaii.gov)

- **City and County of Honolulu** (www. co.honolulu.hi.us)

- **Helpful Hawaii Websites and Links** (www.hawaiiradiotv.com)

- **Honolulu Daily Newspaper** (www. staradvertiser.com)

- **Honolulu Weekly Guide to Activities** (www.honoluluweekly.com)

- **Foreign Languages for Travelers** (www.travlang.com)

- **The Hawaiian Language Website** (www.olelo.hawaii.edu)

- **Maps** (http://maps.google.com)

- **Oahu Visitors Bureau** (www.visitoahu. com)

- **Time and Date** (www.timeanddate. com)

- **Universal Currency Converter** (www. xe.com/ucc)

- **Visa ATM Locator** (www.visa.com)

- **MasterCard ATM Locator** (www. mastercard.com)

- **Weather** (www.weather.gov)

TheBus goes almost everywhere almost all the time. The most popular route is no. 8 (Waikiki/Ala Moana), which shuttles people between Waikiki and Ala Moana Center every 10 minutes or so (the ride is 15–20 min.). The no. 19 (Airport/Hickam), no. 20 (Airport/Pearlridge), no. 42 (Ewa Beach), and no. 23 (Waikiki/Ala Moana) cover the same stretch. Waikiki service begins daily at about 5am and runs until midnight; buses run about every 15 minutes during the day and every 30 minutes in the evening.

The Circle Island–North Shore route is no. 52 (Wahiawa/Circle Island); it departs Ala Moana Center every 30 minutes and takes about 4½ hours to circle the island. The Circle Island–South Shore route is no. 55 (Kaneohe/Circle Island); it also leaves Ala Moana every half-hour and takes about 3 to 4½ hours to circle the island.

You can buy a **Visitors Pass** for $25 at any ABC store in Waikiki (ABC stores are literally everywhere in Waikiki). It's good for unlimited rides anywhere on Oahu for 4 days.

By Trolley

It's fun to ride the 34-seat, open-air, motorized **Waikiki Trolley** (© 800/824-8804 or 808/593-2822; www.waikikitrolley.com), which looks like a San Francisco cable car. It loops around Waikiki and downtown Honolulu, stopping every 40 minutes at 12 key places: Hilton Hawaiian Village, Iolani Palace, Wo Fat's in Chinatown, the State Capitol, King Kamehameha's Statue, the Mission

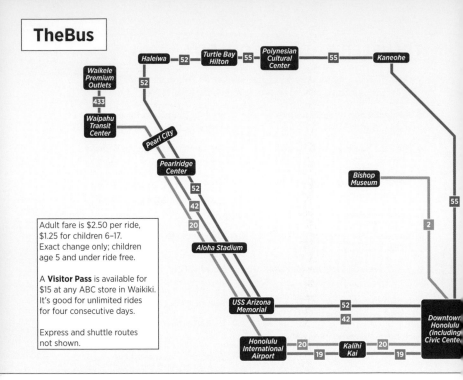

TheBus

Adult fare is $2.50 per ride, $1.25 for children 6–17. Exact change only; children age 5 and under ride free.

A **Visitor Pass** is available for $15 at any ABC store in Waikiki. It's good for unlimited rides for four consecutive days.

Express and shuttle routes not shown.

Getting There on TheBus:

Academy of Arts Take #2 bus (School/Middle St) to Beretania St. and Ward Ave.

Ala Moana Center Take bus #19 & #20 AIRPORT. Return via #19 WAIKIKI, or cross Ala Moana Blvd. for #20.

Bishop Museum Take #2 SCHOOL STREET. Get off at Kapalama St., cross School St., walk down Bernice St. Return to School St. and take #2 WAIKIKI.

Byodo-In Temple Take bus #2 to Hotel-Alakea St. (TRF) to #55 KANEOHE-KAHALUU. Get off at Valley of the Temple cemetery. Also #19 and #20 AIRPORT to King-Alakea St., (TRF) on Alakea St. to #55 KANEOHE-KAHALUU.

Circle Island Take a bus to ALA MOANA CENTER (TRF) to #52 WAHIAWA CIRCLE ISLAND or #55 KANEOHE CIRCLE ISLAND. This is a 4-hour bus ride.

Chinatown or Downtown Take any #2 bus going out of Waikiki to Hotel St. Return, take #2 WAIKIKI on Hotel St., or #19 or #20 on King St.

The Contemporary Museum & **Punchbowl (National Cemetery of the Pacific)** Take #2 bus (TRF) at Alapai St. to #15 MAKIKI-PACIFIC HGTS. Return, take #15 and get off at King St., area (TRF) #2 WAIKIKI.

Diamond Head Crater Take #22 HAWAII KAI-SEA LIFE PARK to the crater. Take a flashlight. Return to the same area and take #22 WAIKIKI.

Dole Plantation Take bus to ALA MOANA CENTER (TRF) to #52 WAHIAWA CIRCLE ISLAND.

Foster Botanical Garden Take #2 bus to Hotel-Riviera St. Walk to Vineyard Blvd. Return to Hotel St. Take #2 WAIKIKI, or take #4 NUUANU and get off at Nuuanu-Vineyard. Cross Nuuanu Ave. and walk one block to the gardens.

Hanauma Bay Take #22 Beach Bus.

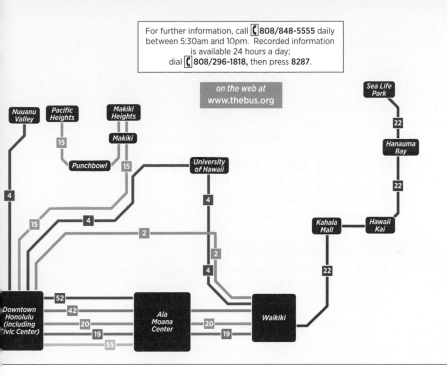

For further information, call ☎ **808/848-5555** daily between 5:30am and 10pm. Recorded information is available 24 hours a day; dial ☎ **808/296-1818,** then press **8287**.

on the web at
www.thebus.org

Aloha Tower Marketplace & **Hawaii Maritime Center** Take #19–#20 AIRPORT and get off at Alakea–Ala Moana. Cross the street to the Aloha Tower.

Honolulu Zoo Take any bus on Kuhio Ave. going DIAMOND HEAD direction to Kapahulu Ave.

Iolani Palace (also **State Capitol, Honolulu Hale, Kawaihao Church, Mission Houses, Queen's Hospital, King Kamehameha Statue, State Judiciary Bldg.**) Take any #2 bus and get off at Punchbowl and Beretania St. Walk to King St. Return #2 WAIKIKI on King St.

Kahala Mall Take #22 HAWAII KAI–SEA LIFE PARK to Kilauea Ave. Return, #22 WAIKIKI.

Pearl Harbor (*Arizona* **Memorial)** Take #20 AIRPORT. Get off across from Memorial, or take a bus to ALA MOANA CENTER (TRF) to #52.

Polynesian Cultural Center Take a bus to ALA MOANA CENTER (TRF) to #55 KANEOHE CIRCLE ISLAND. Bus ride takes 2 hours one-way.

Queen Emma's Summer Home Take #4 NUUANU, or board a bus to ALA MOANA CENTER (TRF) to #55 KANEOHE.

Sea Life Park Take #22 HAWAII KAI–SEA LIFE PARK. #22 will stop at Hanauma Bay en route to the park.

University of Hawaii Take #4 NUUANU. The bus will go to the University en route to Nuuanu.

Waimea Valley Audobon Center Take a bus to ALA MOANA CENTER (TRF) to #52 WAHIAWA CIRCLE ISLAND or #55 KANEOHE CIRCLE ISLAND.

Waikele Premium Outlets Take bus #42 from Waikiki to Wapahu Transit Center, then bus #433 to Waikele.

House Museum, Aloha Tower, Honolulu Academy of Arts, Hawaii Maritime Museum, Ward Centre, Fisherman's Wharf, and Restaurant Row. The driver provides commentary along the way. Stops on the new 2-hour, fully narrated Ocean Coast Line (the blue line) of the southeast side of Oahu include Sea Life Park, Diamond Head, and Waikiki Beach. A 1-day trolley pass ($19–$25 for adults, $15–$20 for seniors, and $9–$13 for kids ages 4–11) allows you to jump off all day long (8:30am–11:35pm). Four-day passes cost $52 for adults, $31 for seniors, and $20 for kids 4 to 11 (check online for discounts).

TIPS ON ACCOMMODATIONS

Hawaii offers everything from simple rooms in restored plantation homes and quaint cottages on the beach to luxurious oceanview condo units and opulent suites in beachfront resorts. Each has its pluses and minuses, so before you book, make sure you know what you're getting into.

Types of Accommodations

HOTELS In Hawaii "hotel" can indicate a wide range of options, from few or no on-site amenities to enough extras to qualify as a miniresort. Generally, a hotel offers daily maid service and has a restaurant, on-site laundry facilities, a pool, and a sundries/convenience–type shop. Top hotels have activities desks, concierge and valet service, room service, business centers, airport shuttles, bars and/or lounges, and perhaps a few more shops.

The advantages of a hotel stay are privacy and convenience; the disadvantage is generally noise (either thin walls between rooms or loud music from a lobby lounge late into the night). Hotels are often a short walk from the beach rather than right on the beachfront (although there are exceptions).

RESORTS In Hawaii, a resort offers everything a hotel does—and more. You can expect direct beach access, with beach cabanas and lounge chairs; pools and a Jacuzzi; a spa and fitness center; restaurants, bars, and lounges; a 24-hour front desk; concierge, valet, and bellhop services; room service (often round-the-clock); an activities desk; tennis and golf; ocean activities; a business center; kids' programs; and more.

The advantages of a resort are that you have everything you could possibly want in the way of services and things to do; the disadvantage is that the price generally reflects this. And don't be misled by a name—just because a place is called "ABC Resort" doesn't mean it actually *is* a resort. Make sure you're getting what you pay for.

CONDOS The roominess and convenience of a condo—which is usually a fully equipped, multiple-bedroom apartment—makes this a great choice for families. Condominium properties in Hawaii generally consist of several apartments set in either a single high-rise or a cluster of low-rise units. Condos usually have amenities such as some maid service (ranging from daily to weekly; it may or may not be included in your rate), a pool, and an on-site front desk or a live-in property manager. Condos tend to be clustered in resort areas. Some are very high-end, but most are quite affordable, especially if you're traveling in a group.

The advantages of a condo are privacy, space, and conveniences—which usually include a full kitchen, a washer and dryer, and a private phone. Downsides are the lack of an on-site restaurant and the density of the units.

BED & BREAKFASTS Hawaii has a wide range of places that call themselves B&Bs: everything from a traditional B&B—several bedrooms in a home, with breakfast served in the morning—to what is essentially a vacation rental on an owner's property that comes with fixings for you to make your own breakfast. Make sure that the B&B you're booking matches your own mental picture. Note that laundry facilities and private phones are not always available. We've reviewed lots of wonderful B&Bs in chapter 4. If you have to share a bathroom, we've spelled it out in the listings; otherwise, you can assume that you will have your own.

The advantages of a traditional B&B are its individual style and congenial atmosphere, with a host who's often happy to act as your own private concierge. In addition, they're usually an affordable way to go. The disadvantages are lack of privacy, usually a set time for breakfast, few amenities, and generally no maid service. Also, B&B owners usually require a minimum stay of 2 or 3 nights, and it's often a drive to the beach.

VACATION RENTALS This is another great choice for families and for long-term stays. "Vacation rental" usually means that there will be no one on the property where you're staying. The actual accommodations can range from an apartment to an entire fully equipped house. Generally, vacation rentals allow you to settle in and make yourself at home for a while. They have kitchen facilities (at least a kitchenette), on-site laundry facilities, and phone; some come with such extras as a TV, VCR, and stereo.

The advantages of a vacation rental are complete privacy, your own kitchen (which can save you money on meals), and lots of conveniences. The disadvantages are a lack of an on-site property manager and generally no maid service; often, a minimum stay is required (sometimes as much as a week). If you book a vacation rental, be sure that you have a 24-hour contact to call if the toilet won't flush or you can't figure out how to turn on the air-conditioning.

Bargaining on Prices

Rates can sometimes be bargained down, but it depends on the place. The best bargaining can be had at **hotels** and **resorts.** If business is slow and you book directly, both places may give you at least part of the commission they'd normally pay a travel agent. Most hotels and resorts also have local rates for islanders, which they may extend to visitors during slow periods. It never hurts to ask about discounted or local rates; a host of special rates are available for the military, seniors, members of the travel industry, families, corporate travelers, and long-term stays. Also ask about **package deals,** which might include a car rental or free breakfast for the same price as a room by itself. Hotels and resorts offer packages for everyone: golfers, tennis players, families, honeymooners, and more. We've found that it's worth the extra few cents to make a local call to the hotel; sometimes the local reservations person knows about package deals that the toll-free operators are unaware of. If all else fails, try to get the hotel or resort to upgrade you to a better room for the same price as a budget room, or waive the parking fee or extra fees for children. Persistence and polite inquiries can pay off.

It's harder to bargain at **bed-and-breakfasts.** You may be able to negotiate down the minimum stay or get a discount if you're staying a week or longer. But generally, a B&B owner has only a few rooms and has already priced the property at a competitive rate; expect to pay what's asked.

You have somewhat more leeway to negotiate at **vacation rentals** and **condos.** In addition to asking for a discount on a multinight stay, ask if they can throw in a rental car to sweeten the deal; believe it or not, they often will.

Booking with an Agency vs. Doing It Yourself

If you don't have the time to call places yourself, you might consider a booking agency.

A statewide booking agent for B&B's is **Bed & Breakfast Hawaii** (© **800/733-1632** or 808/822-7771; fax 808/822-2723; www.bandb-hawaii. com), offering a range of accommodations from vacation homes to B&Bs, starting at $65 a night. For vacation rentals, contact **Hawaii Beachfront Vacation Homes** (© **808/247-3637;** fax 808/235-2644). **Hawaii Condo Exchange** (© **800/442-0404;** www.hawaiicondoexchange.com) acts as a consolidator for condo and vacation-rental properties.

In the past we have gotten letters from our readers asking about the website **Vacation Rentals by Owner** (www.vrbo.com). It is a great website, but we do not recommend it because several of the owners do not have property managers on site or someone on call—in case the plumbing goes out at 3am or you cannot figure out how to get the television to work. If you decide to use this site, be sure to contact the owner and ask if they have someone on call if there is a problem. If they do have someone on call, find out the details of how quickly that person will respond: Is the handyman or manager on some kind of retainer so he'll respond immediately, or will you be just another customer in line and he'll get to you when he gets to you? This is a small point but it could ruin your vacation.

[FastFACTS] HONOLULU, WAIKIKI & OAHU

Area Code   All the Hawaiian Islands are in the **808** area code. Note that if you're calling one island from another, you'll have to dial 1-808 first.

Business Hours   Most offices are open Monday through Friday from 8am to 5pm. Bank hours are Monday through Thursday from 8:30am to 3pm and Friday from 8:30am to 6pm; some banks are open on Saturday as well. Shopping centers are open Monday through Friday 10am to 9pm, Saturday 10am to 5:30pm, and Sunday noon to 5 or 6pm.

Car Rentals   See p. 276.

Customs   Every visitor older than 21 years of age may bring in, free of duty, the following: 1 liter of wine or hard liquor; 200 cigarettes, 100 cigars (but not from Cuba), or 3 pounds of smoking tobacco; and $100 worth of gifts. These exemptions are offered to travelers who spend at least 72 hours in the United States and who have not claimed them within the preceding 6 months. It is forbidden to bring into the country almost any meat products (including canned, fresh, and dried meat products such as bullion, soup mixes, and so on). Generally, condiments including vinegars, oils, spices, coffee, tea, and some cheeses and baked goods are permitted. Avoid rice products, as rice can often harbor insects. Bringing fruits and vegetables is not advised, though not prohibited. Customs will allow produce depending on where you got it and where you're going after you arrive in the U.S. (Also see p. 275 for information on bringing produce from Hawaii to the U.S. mainland.) International visitors may carry in or out up to $10,000 in U.S. or foreign currency with no formalities; larger sums must be declared to U.S. Customs on entering or leaving, which includes filing form CM 4790. For details regarding U.S. Customs and Border Protection, consult your nearest U.S. embassy or consulate, or **U.S. Customs** (www.customs.gov).

For information on what you're allowed to bring home, contact one of the following agencies:

U.S. Citizens: U.S. Customs & Border Protection (CBP), 1300 Pennsylvania Ave., NW, Washington, DC 20229 (✆ **877/287-8667;** www.cbp.gov).

Canadian Citizens: Canada Border Services Agency (✆ **800/622-6232** in Canada, or 204/983-3500; www.cbsa-asfc.gc.ca).

U.K. Citizens: HM Customs & Excise at ✆ **0845/010-9000** (from outside the U.K., 020/8929-0152), or consult their website at **www.hmce.gov.uk**.

Australian Citizens: Australian Customs Service at ✆ **1300/363-263,** or log on to **www.customs.gov.au**.

New Zealand Citizens: New Zealand Customs, The Customhouse, 17–21 Whitmore St., Box 2218, Wellington (✆ **04/473-6099** or 0800/428-786; www.customs.govt.nz).

Disabled Travelers   Most disabilities shouldn't stop anyone from traveling to Hawaii. Thanks to provisions in the Americans with Disabilities Act, most public places are required to comply with disability-friendly regulations. There are more options and resources out there than ever before.

Travelers with disabilities are made to feel very welcome in Hawaii. There are more than 2,000 ramped curbs in Oahu alone, hotels are usually equipped with wheelchair-accessible rooms, and tour companies provide many special services. The **Hawaii Center for Independent Living,** 414 Kauwili St., Ste. 102, Honolulu, HI 96817 (✆ **808/522-5400;** fax 808/586-8129; www.hawaii-cil.org), can provide information.

The only travel agency in Hawaii specializing in needs for travelers with disabilities is **Access Aloha Travel** (✆ **800/480-1143;** www.accessalohatravel.com), which can book anything, including rental vans, accommodations, tours, cruises, airfare, and anything else you can think of.

The **America the Beautiful—National Park and Federal Recreational Lands Pass— Access Pass** (formerly the **Golden Access Passport**) gives visually impaired or permanently disabled persons (regardless of age) free lifetime entrance to federal recreation sites administered by the National Park Service, including the Fish and Wildlife Service, the Forest Service, the Bureau of Land Management, and the Bureau of Reclamation. This may include national parks, monuments, historic sites, recreation areas, and national wildlife refuges.

The America the Beautiful Access Pass can be obtained only in person at any NPS facility that charges an entrance fee. You need to show proof of medically determined disability. Besides free entry, the pass offers a 50% discount on some federal-use fees charged for such facilities as camping, swimming, parking, boat launching, and tours. For more information, go to **www.nps.gov/fees_passes.htm** or call the United States Geological Survey (USGS), which issues the passes, at ✆ **888/275-8747.** For more on organizations that offer resources to disabled travelers, go to frommers.com.

Doctors If you get sick in Oahu, you can get medical attention in Waikiki from **Doctors on Call** (☎ **808/971-6000;** www.ohwy.com/hi/d/doconcal.htm). They are located at the following hotels in Waikiki: **Outrigger Waikiki on the Beach** (open 24 hr.), 2335 Kalakaua Ave.; **Hilton Hawaiian Village,** 2005 Kalia Rd.; and **Royal Hawaiian Hotel,** 2259 Kalakaua Ave.

If you suffer from a chronic illness, consult your doctor before your departure. Pack prescription medications in your carry-on luggage, and carry them in their original containers, with pharmacy labels—otherwise, they won't make it through airport security. Visitors from outside the U.S. should carry generic names of prescription drugs. For U.S. travelers, most reliable health-care plans provide coverage if you get sick away from home. Foreign visitors may have to pay all medical costs up front and be reimbursed later. Also see "Hospitals," p. 290.

Drinking Laws The legal drinking age in Hawaii is 21. Bars are allowed to stay open daily until 2am; places with cabaret licenses are able to keep the booze flowing until 4am. Grocery and convenience stores are allowed to sell beer, wine, and liquor 7 days a week. Proof of age is required and often requested at bars, nightclubs, and restaurants, so bring ID when you go out.

Do not carry open containers of alcohol in your car or any public area that isn't zoned for alcohol consumption. The police can fine you on the spot. And nothing will ruin your trip faster than getting a citation for DUI ("driving under the influence"), so don't even think about driving while intoxicated.

Driving Rules See "Getting Around," p. 276.

Electricity Like Canada, the United States uses 110 to 120 volts AC (60 cycles), compared with 220 to 240 volts AC (50 cycles) in most of Europe, Australia, and New Zealand. Downward converters that change 220 to 240 volts to 110 to 120 volts are difficult to find in the United States, so bring one with you.

Embassies & Consulates All embassies are located in the nation's capital, Washington, D.C. Some consulates are located in major U.S. cities, and most nations have a mission to the United Nations in New York City. If your country isn't listed below, call for directory information in Washington, D.C. (☎ **202/555-1212**) or log on to **www.embassy.org/embassies**.

The embassy of **Australia** is at 1601 Massachusetts Ave. NW, Washington, DC 20036 (☎ **202/797-3000;** www.usa.embassy.gov/au). There are consulates in New York, Honolulu, Houston, Los Angeles, and San Francisco.

The embassy of **Canada** is at 501 Pennsylvania Ave. NW, Washington, DC 20001 (☎ **202/682-1740;** www.canadianembassy.org). Other Canadian consulates are in Buffalo (New York), Detroit, Los Angeles, New York, and Seattle.

The embassy of **Ireland** is at 2234 Massachusetts Ave. NW, Washington, DC 20008 (☎ **202/462-3939;** www.embassyofireland.org). Irish consulates are in Boston, Chicago, New York, San Francisco, and other cities. See website for complete listing.

The embassy of **New Zealand** is at 37 Observatory Circle NW, Washington, DC 20008 (☎ **202/328-4800;** www.nzembassy.com). New Zealand consulates are in Los Angeles, Salt Lake City, San Francisco, and Seattle.

The **United Kingdom**'s embassy is at 3100 Massachusetts Ave. NW, Washington, DC 20008 (☎ **202/588-6500;** www.britainusa.com). Other British consulates are in Atlanta, Boston, Chicago, Cleveland, Houston, Los Angeles, New York, San Francisco, and Seattle.

Emergencies Dial © **911** for police, fire, or ambulance. The **Poison Control Center** is © **800/222-1222.**

Family Travel Hawaii is paradise for children: beaches to run on, water to splash in, and unusual sights to see. To locate accommodations, restaurants, and attractions that are particularly child-friendly, refer to the Kids icon throughout this guide (see an example on p. viii). Be sure to check out the "Especially for Kids" box on p. 208. And look for *Frommer's Hawaii with Kids.*

The larger hotels and resorts offer supervised programs for children and can refer you to qualified babysitters. By state law, hotels can accept only children ages 5 to 12 in supervised activities programs, but they often accommodate younger kids by simply hiring babysitters to watch over them. You can also contact **People Attentive to Children (PATCH),** which can refer you to babysitters who have taken a training course on child care. On Oahu, call © **808/839-1988** or visit **www.patchhawaii.org**.

Baby's Away (© **800/496-6386** or 808/497-2009; www.babysaway.com) rents cribs, strollers, highchairs, playpens, infant seats, and the like on Oahu. The staff will deliver whatever you need to wherever you're staying and pick it up when you're done.

Recommended family travel websites include **Family Travel Forum** (www.familytravel forum.com), a comprehensive site that offers customized trip planning; **Family Travel Network** (www.familytravelnetwork.com), an online magazine providing travel tips; and **TravelWithYourKids.com** (www.travelwithyourkids.com), a comprehensive site written by parents for parents offering sound advice for long-distance and international travel with children. For a list of more family-friendly travel resources, turn to the experts at **www.frommers.com**.

Gasoline (Petrol) At press time, the cost of gasoline in Hawaii was abnormally high. Taxes are already included in the printed price. One U.S. gallon equals 3.8 liters or .85 imperial gallons. Fill-up locations are known as gas stations or service stations. As we went to press, "regular" gas was averaging $4.15 a gallon and premium gas was $4.95.

Health Like any tropical climate, Hawaii is home to lots of bugs. Most of them won't harm you. However, watch out for mosquitoes, centipedes, and scorpions, which do sting and may cause anything from mild annoyance to severe swelling and pain.

Mosquitoes are not native to Hawaii but arrived as larvae stowed away in water barrels on the ship *Wellington* in 1826, when it anchored in Lahaina. There's not a whole lot you can do about them, except to apply commercial repellent, which you can pick up at any drugstore.

Centipedes, those segmented bugs with a jillion legs, come in two varieties: 6- to 8-inch-long brown ones and 2- to 3-inch-long blue guys. Both can really pack a wallop with their sting. Centipedes are generally found in damp, wet places, such as under wood piles or compost heaps; wearing closed-toe shoes can help prevent stings. If you're stung, apply ice at once to prevent swelling. See a doctor if you experience extreme pain, swelling, nausea, or any other severe reaction.

Rarely seen, **scorpions** are found in arid, warm regions; their stings can be serious. Campers in dry areas should always check their boots before putting them on and shake out sleeping bags and bed rolls. Symptoms of a scorpion sting include shortness of breath, hives, swelling, and nausea. In the unlikely event that you're stung, apply diluted household ammonia and cold compresses to the area of the sting and seek medical help immediately.

In addition to taking the appropriate precautions regarding Hawaii's bug population, **hikers** should always let someone know where they're heading, when they're going, and when they plan to return; too many hikers get lost in Hawaii because they don't let others know their basic plans.

Before you head out, always check weather conditions with the **National Weather Service** (© **808/973-4380** on Oahu; www.weather.gov). Hike with a pal, never alone. Wear hiking boots, a sun hat, clothes to protect you from the sun and from getting scratches, and high-SPF sunscreen on all exposed areas of skin. Take water. Stay on the trail. Watch your step. It's easy to slip off precipitous trails and into steep canyons. Many experienced hikers and boaters today pack a cellphone in case of emergency; just dial © **911.**

The volcanic haze dubbed *vog* is caused by gases released when molten lava—from the continuous eruption of Kilauea volcano on the Big Island—pours into the ocean. Some people claim that long-term exposure to the hazy, smoglike air has caused bronchial ailments, but it's highly unlikely to cause you any harm in the course of your visit.

There actually is a vog season in Hawaii: the fall and winter months, when the trade winds that blow the fumes out to sea die down. The vog is felt not only on the Big Island, but also as far away as Oahu.

Because most people coming to Hawaii are unfamiliar with the **ocean environment,** they're often unaware of the natural hazards it holds. With just a few precautions, your ocean experience can be a safe and happy one. An excellent book is *All Stings Considered: First Aid and Medical Treatment of Hawaii's Marine Injuries,* by Craig Thomas and Susan Scott (1997).

Note that **sharks** are not a big problem in Hawaii; in fact, they appear so infrequently that locals look forward to seeing them. Since records have been kept, starting in 1779, there have been only about 100 shark attacks in Hawaii, of which 40% have been fatal. Most attacks occurred after someone fell into the ocean from the shore or from a boat; in these cases, the sharks probably attacked after the person was dead. But general rules for avoiding sharks are: Don't swim at sunrise, at sunset, or where the water is murky due to stream runoff—sharks may mistake you for one of their usual meals. And don't swim where there are bloody fish in the water, as sharks become aggressive around blood.

The waters in Hawaii can range from as calm as glass to downright frightening (in storm conditions); they usually fall somewhere in between. In general, expect rougher conditions in winter than in summer. Some 90% of the population tends toward seasickness. If you've never been out on a boat, or if you've had **seasickness** in the past, you might want to heed the following suggestions:

- The day before you go out on the boat, avoid alcohol, caffeine, citrus and other acidic juices, and greasy, spicy, or hard-to-digest foods.

- Get a good night's sleep the night before.

- Take or use whatever seasickness prevention works best for you—medication, an acupressure

> ### Everything You've Always Wanted to Know About Sharks
>
> **The Hawaii State Department of Land and Natural Resources has launched a website, www.hawaiisharks.com,** that covers the biology, history, and culture of these carnivores. It also provides safety information and data on shark bites in Hawaii.

wristband, gingerroot tea or capsules, or any combination. But do it *before* you board; once you set sail, it's generally too late.

o   While you're on the boat, stay as low and as near the center of the boat as possible. Avoid the fumes (especially if it's a diesel boat); stay out in the fresh air and watch the horizon. Do not read.

o   If you start to feel queasy, drink such clear fluids as water, and eat something bland, such as a soda cracker.

The most common **stings** in Hawaii come from jellyfish, particularly Portuguese man-of-war and box jellyfish. Because the poisons they inject are very different, you need to treat each type of sting differently.

A bluish-purple floating bubble with a long tail, the **Portuguese man-of-war** is responsible for some 6,500 stings a year on Oahu alone. These stings, although painful and a nuisance, are rarely harmful; fewer than 1 in 1,000 requires medical treatment. The best prevention is to watch for these floating bubbles as you snorkel (look for the hanging tentacles below the surface). Get out of the water if anyone near you spots these jellyfish.

Reactions to stings range from mild burning and reddening to severe welts and blisters. *All Stings Considered* recommends the following treatment: First, pick off any visible tentacles with a gloved hand, a stick, or anything handy; then rinse the sting with salt- or fresh water, and apply ice to prevent swelling and to help control pain. Avoid folk remedies, such as vinegar, baking soda, or urinating on the wound, which may actually cause further damage. Most Portuguese man-of-war stings will disappear by themselves within 15 to 20 minutes if you do nothing at all to treat them. Still, be sure to see a doctor if pain persists or a rash or other symptoms develop.

Transparent, square-shaped **box jellyfish** are nearly impossible to see in the water. Fortunately, they seem to follow a monthly cycle: 8 to 10 days after the full moon, they appear in the waters on the leeward side of each island and hang around for about 3 days. Also, they seem to sting more in the morning hours, when they're on or near the surface.

The stings can cause anything from no visible marks to hivelike welts, blisters, and pain lasting from 10 minutes to 8 hours. *All Stings Considered* recommends the following

DON'T GET burned: SMART TANNING TIPS

Hawaii's Caucasian population has the highest incidence of malignant melanoma (deadly skin cancer) in the world. And nobody is completely safe from the sun's harmful rays: All skin types and races can burn. To ensure that your vacation won't be ruined by a painful sunburn, be sure to wear a strong sunscreen that protects against both UVA and UVB rays at all times (look for zinc oxide, benzophenone, oxybenzone, sulisobenzone, titanium dioxide, or avobenzone in the list of ingredients). Wear a wide-brimmed hat and sunglasses. Keep infants under 6 months out of the sun completely, and slather older babies and children with strong sunscreen frequently.

If you do get a burn, aloe vera, cool compresses, cold baths, and benzocaine can help with the pain. Stay out of the sun until the burn is completely gone.

treatment: First, pour regular household vinegar on the sting; this will stop additional burning. Do not rub the area. Pick off any vinegar-soaked tentacles with a stick. For pain, apply an ice pack. Seek additional medical treatment if you experience shortness of breath, weakness, palpitations, muscle cramps, or any other severe symptoms. Most box jellyfish stings disappear by themselves without any treatment.

Most **sea-related punctures** come from stepping on or brushing against the needle-like spines of **sea urchins** (known locally as *wana*). Be careful when you're in the water; don't put your foot down (even if you have booties or fins on) if you can't clearly see the bottom. Waves can push you into *wana* in a surge zone in shallow water. The spines can even puncture a wet suit.

A sea urchin puncture can result in burning, aching, swelling, and discoloration (black or purple) around the area where the spines entered your skin. The best thing to do is to pull any protruding spines out. The body will absorb the spines within 24 hours to 3 weeks, or the remainder of the spines will work themselves out. Again, contrary to popular wisdom, do not urinate or pour vinegar on the embedded spines—this will not help.

All **cuts** obtained in the marine environment must be taken seriously because the high level of bacteria present in the water can quickly cause the cut to become infected. The best way to prevent cuts is to wear a wet suit, gloves, and reef shoes. Never touch coral; not only can you get cut, but you can also damage a living organism that took decades to grow.

The symptoms of a coral cut can range from a slight scratch to severe welts and blisters. *All Stings Considered* recommends gently pulling the edges of the skin open and removing any embedded coral or grains of sand with tweezers. Next, scrub the cut well with fresh water. If pressing a clean cloth against the wound doesn't stop the bleeding, or the edges of the injury are jagged or gaping, seek medical treatment.

Hospitals Hospitals offering 24-hour emergency care include **Queens Medical Center,** 1301 Punchbowl St. (✆ 808/538-9011); **Kuakini Medical Center,** 347 Kuakini St. (✆ 808/536-2236); **Straub Clinic and Hospital,** 888 S. King St. (✆ 808/522-4000); **Kaiser Moanalua,** 3288 Moanalua Rd. (✆ 808/432-0000); **Kapiolani Medical Center for Women and Children,** 1319 Punahou St. (✆ 808/983-8633); and **Kapiolani Medical Center,** at Pali Momi, 98-1079 Moanalua Rd. (✆ 808/486-6000). Central Oahu has **Wahiawa General Hospital,** 128 Lehua St. (✆ 808/621-8411). On the windward side is **Castle Medical Center,** 640 Ulukahiki St., Kailua (✆ 808/263-5500).

Insurance If you think your travel plans may change, you might want to look into travel insurance. For information on traveler's insurance, trip-cancellation insurance, and medical insurance while traveling, please visit **www.frommers.com/planning**.

Internet & Wi-Fi If you do not have your computer with you, find a cybercafe close to where you are staying: check **www.cybercaptive.com** and **www.cybercafe.com**. If your hotel doesn't have Web access, head to **Web Site Story Café,** 2555 Cartwright Rd. (in the Hotel Waikiki), Waikiki (✆ 808/922-1677). It's open daily from 7am to 11pm and serves drinks. Or, go to **www.shaka.net** for locations of their Internet kiosks.

Aside from formal cybercafes, all **public libraries** on Oahu offer free access if you have a library card, which you can purchase for a $10 fee. The closest library is the **Waikiki-Kapahulu Library,** 400 Kapahulu St. (across from the Ala Wai Golf Course; ✆ **808/733-8488**). Most hotels in Waikiki have business centers where you can rent computers and get on line access for a fee. If you have your computer with you most hotels (and even small B&Bs) on Oahu have **in-room Wi-Fi connection,** but the charges can be exorbitant ($11–$14 per day).

Enjoying the Ocean & Avoiding Mishaps

The Pacific Whale Foundation has a free brochure called *Enjoying Maui's Unique Ocean Environment* that introduces visitors to Hawaii's ocean, beaches, tide pools, and reefs. Although written for Maui (with maps showing Maui's beaches), it's a great general resource on how to stay safe around the ocean, with hints on how to assess weather before you jump into the water and the best ways to view marine wildlife. To get the brochure, call ☎ 808/856-8316 or visit www.pacific whale.org.

ShakaNet (www.shaka.net), Hawaii's largest wireless provider, has completed the first phase of its free Wireless Waikiki network. Phase I covers a significant portion of Waikiki and includes an estimated 1,000 hotel rooms, portions of the Honolulu Zoo, Kapiolani Park, Queens Beach, Kuhio Beach, and the adjacent shoreline. The boundaries of Phase I are on their website.

Remember to bring a **connection kit** of the right power adapters, or find out whether your hotel supplies them to guests.

Legal Aid If you are "pulled over" for a minor infraction (such as speeding), never attempt to pay the fine directly to a police officer; this could be construed as attempted bribery, a much more serious crime. Pay fines by mail, or directly into the hands of the clerk of the court. If accused of a more serious offense, say and do nothing before consulting a lawyer. Here the burden is on the state to prove a person's guilt beyond a reasonable doubt, and everyone has the right to remain silent, whether he or she is suspected of a crime or actually arrested. Once arrested, a person can make one telephone call to a party of his or her choice. International visitors should call your embassy or consulate. Call the **Legal Aid Society of Hawaii,** 924 Bethel St., Honolulu, HI 96813 (☎ **808/536-4302**).

LGBT Travelers Hawaii is known for its acceptance of all groups. The number of gay- or lesbian-specific accommodations on the islands is limited, but most properties welcome gays and lesbians like any other travelers. **Out in Honolulu** (www.outin honolulu.com) is a website with gay and lesbian news, a list of gay bars and clubs, recommended restaurants and accommodations, plus blogs, features, shopping, classified and other info. For more gay and lesbian travel resources, visit **www.frommers.com**.

Mail At press time, domestic postage rates were 28¢ for a postcard and 44¢ for a letter. For international mail, a first-class letter of up to 1 ounce costs 75¢ to 98¢ (depending on the destination); a first-class postcard costs 98¢ (75¢ to Canada and 79¢ to Mexico). For more information, go to **www.usps.com**.

If you aren't sure what your address will be in the United States, mail can be sent to you, in your name, c/o General Delivery at the main post office of the city or region where you expect to be. The downtown **Honolulu Post Office** is at 335 Merchant St., Honolulu, HI 96813-9998. (Or call ☎ **800/275-8777** for information on the nearest post office.) The addressee must pick up mail in person and must produce proof of identity (driver's license, passport, and so on). Most post offices will hold mail for up to 1 month, and are open Monday to Friday from 8am to 6pm, and Saturday from 9am to 3pm. Always include zip codes when mailing items in the U.S.

Medical Requirements Unless you're arriving from an area known to be suffering from an epidemic (particularly cholera or yellow fever), inoculations or vaccinations are not required for entry into the United States.

Mobile Phones Just because your cellphone works at home doesn't mean it'll work everywhere on Oahu. It's a good bet that your phone will work in Honolulu and Waikiki, but take a look at your wireless company's coverage map on its website before heading out. If you need to stay in touch, consider **renting a phone** from **InTouch USA** (✆ **800/872-7626;** www.intouchglobal.com).

Money & Costs Frommer's lists exact prices in the local currency. The currency conversions quoted below were correct at press time. However, rates fluctuate, so before departing consult a currency exchange website such as **www.oanda.com/currency/converter** to check up-to-the-minute rates. You can also get help with currency conversions, tip calculations, and more from Frommer's convenient Travel Tools app for your mobile device. Go to **www.frommers.com/go/mobile** and click on the Travel Tools icon.

THE VALUE OF US$ VS. OTHER POPULAR CURRENCIES

US$	C$	£	€	A$	NZ$
1.00	1.02	0.63	0.74	0.98	1.29

Probably the only cities more expensive than Honolulu are New York City, London, and Tokyo. Honolulu is expensive—*very* expensive. Visitors are always shocked at how much things cost. Think about it: Hawaii is among the most isolated set of islands in the world. It's some 2,500 miles to the nearest continent and nearly everything is shipped in; and if it's not shipped, then it's flown at an even greater cost.

Hotel rooms in Waikiki are second in price to New York City. If you would like to stay on Waikiki Beach, you are looking at rack rates in the $350 and up range (a deal on the Internet can put you in around $250). Hotels off the beach are still expensive; expect to pay $200-plus per day. Then factor in tax (13.93%), plus (very expensive) parking of $18 to $25 a night.

It's always advisable to bring money in a variety of forms on a vacation: a mix of cash, credit cards, and traveler's checks. You should also exchange enough petty cash to cover airport incidentals, tipping, and transportation to your hotel before you leave home, or withdraw money upon arrival at an airport ATM.

The easiest and best way to get cash away from home is from an **ATM** (automated teller machine), sometimes referred to as a "cash machine," or "cashpoint." The **Cirrus** (✆ **800/424-7787;** www.mastercard.com) and **PLUS** (✆ **800/843-7587;** www.visa.com) networks span Oahu: ATMs are everywhere in Hawaii—at banks, supermarkets, Longs Drugs, and Honolulu International Airport, and in some resorts and shopping centers. Check your bank's website for exact locations.

Note: Many banks impose a fee every time you use a card at another bank's ATM, and that fee is often higher for international transactions (up to $5 or more) than for domestic ones (where they're rarely more than $2). In addition, the bank from which you withdraw cash may charge its own fee. To compare banks' ATM fees within the U.S., use **www.bankrate.com**. Visitors from outside the U.S. should also find out whether their bank assesses a 1% to 3% fee on charges incurred abroad.

Credit cards are the most widely used form of payment in the United States and include **Visa** (Barclaycard in Britain), **MasterCard** (EuroCard in Europe, Access in Britain,

Chargex in Canada), **American Express, Diners Club,** and **Discover.** They also provide a convenient record of all your expenses and offer relatively good exchange rates. You can withdraw cash advances from your credit cards at banks or ATMs, but high fees make credit card cash advances a pricey way to get cash.

It's highly recommended that you travel with at least one major credit card. You must have a credit card to rent a car, and hotels and airlines usually require a credit card imprint as a deposit against expenses.

ATM cards with major credit card backing, known as **debit cards,** are now a commonly acceptable form of payment in most stores and restaurants. Debit cards draw money directly from your checking account. Some stores enable you to receive cash back on your debit-card purchases as well. The same is true at most U.S. post offices.

WHAT THINGS COST IN HONOLULU	US$
Hamburger at Kua Aina (p. 153)	6.00
Movie ticket (adult)	10.75
Movie ticket (child)	7.50
Entry to Bishop Museum (adult)	17.95
Entry to Bishop Museum (child)	14.95
Entry to Hawaiian Water Adventure Park (adult)	42.00
Entry to Hawaiian Water Adventure Park (child)	32.00
Entry to Honolulu Zoo (adult)	12.00
Entry to Honolulu Zoo (child)	3.00
20-ounce soft drink at drug or convenience store	2.50
16-ounce apple juice	3.50
Cup of coffee	3.00
Taxi from Honolulu Airport to Waikiki	35.00
1 gallon of premium gas	4.95
Bus fare (adult)	2.50
Moderate three-course dinner without alcohol	50.00
Moderately priced double-room in Waikiki	125.00–175.00

Beware of hidden credit-card fees while traveling. Check with your credit or debit card issuer to see what fees, if any, will be charged for overseas transactions. Recent reform legislation in the U.S., for example, has curbed some exploitative lending practices. But many banks have responded by increasing fees in other areas, including fees for customers who use credit and debit cards while out of the country—even if those charges were made in U.S. dollars. Fees can amount to 3% or more of the purchase price. Check with your bank before departing to avoid any surprise charges on your statement.

No, it's not your imagination—Oahu *is* more expensive than the other Hawaiian islands. That's the result of the Hawaii State Legislature passing a bill allowing the City and County of Honolulu (which is the entire island of Oahu) to add an additional .5% tax on to the state general excise tax of 4%. Everything you buy on Oahu will have this tax, and so will your hotel bill. The funds from this additional tax are earmarked for mass transit for Oahu.

Though credit cards and debit cards are more often used, **traveler's checks** are still widely accepted in the U.S. Foreign visitors should make sure that traveler's checks are denominated in U.S. dollars; foreign-currency checks are often difficult to exchange.

You can buy traveler's checks at most banks. Most are offered in denominations of $20, $50, $100, $500, and sometimes $1,000. Generally, you'll pay a service charge ranging from 1% to 4%.

The most popular traveler's checks are offered by **American Express** (✆ 800/221-7282 for card holders—this number accepts collect calls, offers service in several foreign languages, and exempts Amex gold and platinum cardholders from the fee).

Be sure to keep a copy of the traveler's checks' serial numbers separate from your checks in the event that they are stolen or lost. You'll get a refund faster if you know the numbers.

Another option is the new **prepaid traveler's check cards,** reloadable cards that work much like debit cards but aren't linked to your checking account. The **American Express Travelers Cheque Card,** for example, requires a minimum deposit ($25), sets a maximum balance ($2,500), can be used to withdraw money from an ATM ($1.50 per transaction, not including bank fees), and can be purchased in dollars, euros, or pounds. If you lose the card, your card will be replaced, but they can't mail it out of the country.

Visa also sells a pre-paid "debit" card, locations can be found at **http://usa.visa.com/locators/travelmoney-locations.jsp**.

Newspapers & Magazines *The Honolulu Star Advertiser* is Oahu's daily newspaper, it can be found at newspaper racks all over the island. *Midweek, Pacific Business News,* and *Honolulu Weekly* are weekly papers. *Honolulu Weekly,* available free at restaurants, clubs, shops, bookstores, and newspaper racks around Oahu, is the best source for what's going on around town. It features discriminating restaurant reviews and an informed critique of the nightclub scene, plus a weekly Calendar of Events.

Passports Virtually every air traveler entering the U.S. is required to show a passport. All persons, including U.S. citizens, traveling by air between the United States and Canada, Mexico, Central and South America, the Caribbean, and Bermuda are required to present a valid passport. *Note:* U.S. and Canadian citizens entering the U. S. at land and sea ports of entry from within the western hemisphere must now also present a passport or other documents compliant with the Western Hemisphere Travel Initiative (WHTI; see **www.getyouhome.gov** for details). Children 15 and under may continue entering with only a U.S. birth certificate, or other proof of U.S. citizenship.

Residents of Australia can pick up an application from your local post office or any branch of Passports Australia, but you must schedule an interview at the passport office to present your application materials. Call the Australian Passport Information Service at ✆ 131-232, or visit the government website at www.passports.gov.au.

PLANNING YOUR TRIP TO OAHU | Newspapers & Magazines

Passport applications for **residents of Canada** are available at travel agencies throughout Canada or from the central **Passport Office,** Department of Foreign Affairs and International Trade, Ottawa, ON K1A 0G3 (✆ **800/567-6868;** www.ppt.gc.ca). *Note:* Canadian children who travel must have their own passports. However, if you hold a valid Canadian passport issued before December 11, 2001, that bears the name of your child, the passport remains valid for you and your child until it expires.

Residents of Ireland can apply for a 10-year passport at the **Passport Office,** Setanta Centre, Molesworth St., Dublin 2 (✆ **353/1-671-1633;** www.dfa.ie/home/index.aspx). Those under age 18 and over 65 must apply for a 3-year passport. You can also apply at 1A South Mall, Cork (✆ **353/21-494-4700**) or at most main post offices.

Residents of New Zealand can pick up a passport application at any New Zealand Passports Office or download it from their website. Contact the **Passports Office** at ✆ **0800/225-050** in New Zealand, or 04/474-8100; or log on to **www.passports. govt.nz**.

Residents of the United Kingdom can pick up an application for a standard 10-year passport (5-year passport for children under 16) at your nearest passport office, major post office, or travel agency; or contact the **United Kingdom Passport Service** (✆ **0300/222-0000;** www.ukpa.gov.uk).

Police Call ✆ **911** for police, fire, or ambulance.

Safety Although tourist areas are generally safe, visitors should always stay alert, even in laid-back Hawaii (and especially in Waikiki). It's wise to ask the island tourist office if you're in doubt about which neighborhoods are safe. Avoid deserted areas, especially at night. Don't go into any city park at night unless there's an event that attracts crowds—for example, the Waikiki Shell concerts in Kapiolani Park. Generally speaking, you can feel safe in areas where there are many people and open establishments.

Avoid carrying valuables with you on the street, and don't display expensive cameras or electronic equipment. Hold on to your pocketbook, and place your billfold in an inside pocket. In theaters, restaurants, and other public places, keep your possessions in sight.

Oahu has seen a series of purse-snatching incidents, in which thieves in slow-moving cars or on foot have snatched handbags from female pedestrians. The Honolulu police department advises women to carry purses on the shoulder away from the street or, better yet, to wear the strap across the chest instead of on one shoulder. Women with clutch bags should hold them close to their chest. Muggings have also been recently reported at bus stops on the North Shore, so you may want to rent a car rather than take the bus if visiting that area.

Remember also that hotels are open to the public and that in a large property, security may not be able to screen everyone entering. Always lock your room door—don't assume that once inside your hotel, you're automatically safe.

Burglaries of tourists' rental cars in hotel parking structures and at beach parking lots have become more common. Park in well-lighted and well-traveled areas, if possible. Never leave any packages or valuables visible in the car. If someone attempts to rob you or steal your car, do not try to resist the thief or carjacker—report the incident to the police department immediately. Ask your rental agency about personal safety, and get written directions or a map with the route to your destination clearly marked.

Generally, Hawaii has the same laws as the mainland United States. Nudity is illegal in Hawaii. There are *no* legal nude beaches (despite what you may have read). If you are nude on a beach (or anywhere) in Hawaii, you can be arrested.

Smoking marijuana also is illegal. Yes, there are lots of "stories" claiming that marijuana is grown in Hawaii, but the drug is illegal; if you attempt to buy it or light up, you can be arrested.

Senior Travel Discounts for seniors are available at almost all of Hawaii's major attractions and occasionally at hotels and restaurants. The Outrigger hotel chain, for instance, offers travelers ages 50 and older a 20% discount off regular published rates—and an additional 5% off for members of AARP. Always ask when making hotel reservations or buying tickets. And always carry identification with proof of your age—it can really pay off.

The U.S. National Park Service offers an **America the Beautiful—National Park and Federal Recreational Lands Pass—Senior Pass** (formerly the **Golden Age Passport**), which gives seniors 62 years or older lifetime entrance to all properties administered by the National Park Service—national parks, monuments, historic sites, recreation areas, and national wildlife refuges—for a one-time processing fee of $10. The pass must be purchased in person at any NPS facility that charges an entrance fee. Besides free entry, the America the Beautiful Senior Pass offers a 50% discount on some federal-use fees charged for such facilities as camping, swimming, parking, boat launching, and tours. For more information, go to www.nps.gov/fees_passes.htm or call the United States Geological Survey (USGS), which issues the passes, at ℂ **888/275-8747. Frommers.com** offers more information and resources on travel for seniors.

Smoking Hawaii has one of the toughest laws against smoking in the U.S. It's against the law to smoke in public buildings, including airports, shopping malls, grocery stores, retail shops, buses, movie theaters, banks, convention facilities, and all government buildings and facilities. There is no smoking in restaurants, bars, and nightclubs. Most bed-and-breakfasts prohibit smoking indoors; more and more hotels and resorts are becoming nonsmoking, even in public areas. If you want to smoke outside, you must **not** be within 20 feet of a doorway, window, or ventilation intake. (No hanging around outside a bar to smoke; you must go 20 ft. away.) Even some beaches have no-smoking policies (and on those that allow smoking, you'd better pick up your butts and not use the sand as your own private ashtray—or face stiff fines). In Hawaii, breathing fresh clean air is "in" and smoking is "out."

Taxes The United States has no **value-added tax (VAT)** or other indirect tax at the national level. Every state, county, and city may levy its own local tax on all purchases, including hotel and restaurant checks and airline tickets. These taxes will not appear on price tags. Hawaii's sales tax on Oahu is 4.17%, which will be added to every purchase. You hotel bill will have the sales tax, plus hotel-occupancy tax of 9.25%, and hoteliers are allowed by the state to tack on an additional .51% excise tax. Thus, expect taxes of about 13.93% to be added to your hotel bill.

Telephones Many convenience groceries and packaging services sell **prepaid calling cards** in denominations up to $50. Some public pay phones now accept American Express, MasterCard, and Visa. **Local calls** made from most pay phones cost 50¢. Most long-distance and international calls can be dialed directly from any phone. **To make calls within the United States and to Canada,** dial 1 followed by the area code and the seven-digit number. **For other international calls,** dial 011 followed by the country code, city code, and the number you are calling.

Calls to area codes **800, 888, 877,** and **866** are toll-free. However, calls to area codes **700** and **900** (chat lines, bulletin boards, "dating" services, and so on) can be expensive—charges of 95¢ to $3 or more per minute. Some numbers have minimum charges that can run $15 or more.

For **reversed-charge or collect calls,** and for person-to-person calls, dial the number 0 then the area code and number; an operator will come on the line, and you should specify whether you are calling collect, person-to-person, or both. If your operator-assisted call is international, ask for the overseas operator.

For **directory assistance** ("Information"), dial 411 for local numbers and national numbers in the U.S. and Canada. For dedicated long-distance information, dial 1, then the appropriate area code plus 555-1212.

Generally, hotel surcharges on long-distance and local calls are astronomical, so you're better off using your **cellphone** or a **public pay telephone.**

For information on cellphones, see p. 292.

Time The continental United States is divided into four **time zones:** Eastern Standard Time (EST), Central Standard Time (CST), Mountain Standard Time (MST), and Pacific Standard Time (PST). Alaska and Hawaii have their own zones. Hawaii is 2 hours behind Pacific Standard Time and 5 hours behind Eastern Standard Time. In other words, when it's noon in Hawaii, it's 2pm in California and 5pm in New York during Standard Time on the mainland.

Daylight saving time takes effect at 2am the second Sunday in March until 2am the first Sunday in November, except in Arizona, Hawaii, the U.S. Virgin Islands, and Puerto Rico. Daylight saving moves the clock 1 hour ahead of standard time. When daylight saving time is in effect on the mainland, Hawaii is 3 hours behind the West Coast and 6 hours behind the East Coast; when it's noon in Hawaii, it's 3pm in California and 6pm in New York.

Hawaii is east of the International Date Line, putting it on the same day as the U.S. mainland and Canada, and a day behind Australia, New Zealand, and Asia.

For help with time translations, and more, download our convenient Travel Tools app for your mobile device. Go to **www.frommers.com/go/mobile** and click on the Travel Tools icon.

Tipping Tips are a very important part of certain workers' income, and gratuities are the standard way of showing appreciation for services provided. (Tipping is certainly not compulsory if the service is poor!) In hotels, tip **bellhops** at least $1 per bag ($2–$3 per bag if you have a lot of luggage) and tip the **chamber staff** $1 to $2 per day (more if you've left a disaster area for him or her to clean up). Tip the **doorman** or **concierge** only if he or she has provided you with some specific service (for example, calling a cab for you or obtaining difficult-to-get theater tickets). Tip the **valet-parking attendant** $1 to $2 every time you get your car.

In restaurants, bars, and nightclubs, tip **service staff** 15% to 20% of the check, tip **bartenders** 10% to 15%, and tip **valet-parking attendants** $1 to $2 per vehicle.

As for other service personnel, tip **cab drivers** 15% of the fare; tip **skycaps** at airports at least $1 per bag ($2–$3 if you have a lot of luggage); and tip **hairdressers** and **barbers** 15% to 20%.

Toilets You won't find public toilets or "restrooms" on the streets in most U.S. cities but they can be found in hotel lobbies, bars, restaurants, museums, department stores, railway and bus stations, and service stations. Large hotels and fast-food restaurants are often the best bets for clean facilities. If possible, avoid the toilets at parks and beaches, which tend to be dirty; some may be unsafe. Restaurants and bars in resorts or heavily visited areas may reserve their restrooms for patrons.

Visas The U.S. State Department has a **Visa Waiver Program (VWP)** allowing citizens of the following countries to enter the United States without a visa for stays of up to 90 days: Andorra, Australia, Austria, Belgium, Brunei, Czech Republic, Denmark, Estonia, Finland, France, Germany, Greece, Hungary, Iceland, Ireland, Italy, Japan, Latvia, Liechtenstein, Lithuania, Luxembourg, Malta, Monaco, the Netherlands, New Zealand, Norway, Portugal, San Marino, Singapore, Slovakia, Slovenia, South Korea, Spain, Sweden, Switzerland, and the United Kingdom. (Note: This list was accurate at press time; for the most up-to-date list of countries in the VWP, consult http://travel.state.gov/visa.)

GETTING married IN HAWAII

Hawaii is a great place for a wedding. The islands exude romance and natural beauty, and after the ceremony, you're already on your honeymoon. And the members of your wedding party will most likely be delighted, as you've given them the perfect excuse for their own island vacation.

More than 20,000 marriages are performed annually on the islands, mostly on Oahu; nearly half are for couples from somewhere else. The booming wedding business has spawned more than 70 companies that can help you organize a long-distance event and stage an unforgettable wedding, Hawaiian-style or your style. However, you can also plan your own island wedding, even from afar, and not spend a fortune doing it.

THE PAPERWORK

The state of Hawaii has some very minimal procedures for obtaining a marriage license. The first thing you should do is contact the **Honolulu Marriage License Office,** State Department of Health Building, 1250 Punchbowl St., Honolulu, HI 96813 (✆ **808/586-4545;** www.state.hi.us/doh/records/vr_marri.html), which is open Monday through Friday from 8am to 4pm. The office no longer will mail you the brochure *Getting Married;* you can download it from the website or contact a marriage-licensing agent closest to where you'll be staying in Hawaii (also listed on the website).

Once in Hawaii, the prospective bride and groom must go together to the marriage licensing agent to get the license, which costs $60 and is good for 30 days. Both parties must be 15 years of age or older (couples 15–17 years old must have proof of age, written consent of both parents, and written approval of the judge of the family court) and not more closely related than first cousins.

Gay couples cannot marry in Hawaii. After a protracted legal battle, and much discussion in the state legislature, the Hawaii Supreme Court ruled that the state will not issue marriage licenses to same-sex couples.

PLANNING THE WEDDING

Doing It Yourself The marriage-licensing agents, who range from state employees to private individuals, are usually friendly, helpful people who can steer you to a nondenominational minister or marriage performer who's licensed by the state of Hawaii. These marriage performers are great sources

Even though a visa isn't necessary, in an effort to help U.S. officials check travelers against terror watch lists before they arrive at U.S. borders, visitors from VWP countries must register online through the Electronic System for Travel Authorization (ESTA) before boarding a plane or a boat to the U.S. Travelers must complete an electronic application providing basic personal and travel eligibility information. The Department of Homeland Security recommends filling out the form at least 3 days before traveling. Authorizations will be valid for up to 2 years or until the traveler's passport expires, whichever comes first. Currently, there is one $14 fee for the online application. Existing ESTA registrations remain valid through their expiration dates. *Note:* Any passport issued on or after October 26, 2006, by a VWP country must be an **e-Passport** for VWP travelers to be eligible to enter the U.S. without a visa. Citizens of these nations also need to present a round-trip air or cruise ticket upon arrival. E-Passports

of information for budget weddings. They usually know wonderful places to have the ceremony for free or for a nominal fee. For the names, addresses, and telephone numbers of marriage agents in the rural and suburban areas of Oahu, call ✆ **808/586-4544.**

If you don't want to use a wedding planner (see below), but you do want to make arrangements before you arrive in Hawaii, our best advice is to get a copy of the daily newspapers on the island where you want to have the wedding. People willing and qualified to conduct weddings advertise in the classifieds. They're great sources of information and know the best ceremony sites, caterers, florists, and so on. Check out the Honolulu Star Advertiser, 500 Ala Moana Blvd. #7-210, Honolulu, HI 96813 (✆ 808/529-4747; www.staradvertiser. com); and MidWeek, 45-525 Luluku Rd., Kaneohe, HI 96744 (✆ 808/235-5881; www.midweek.com).

Using a Wedding Planner Wedding planners—many of whom are marriage-licensing agents as well—can arrange everything for you, from a small, private, outdoor affair to a full-blown formal ceremony in a tropical setting. They charge anywhere from $95 to a small fortune—

it all depends on what you want. The Hawaii Visitors and Convention Bureau (✆ **800/GO-HAWAII** [464-2924] or 808/923-1811; www.gohawaii.com) can supply contact information on wedding coordinators.

If you want to get married at sea, call Capt. Ken Middleton, of **Tradewind Charters,** based in Honolulu (✆ **800/829-4899** or 808/973-0311; www.tradewindcharters.com), for a private wedding and reception on the ocean waves.

If you fantasize about being wed in an exotic setting, such as near a waterfall, on the beach, or in a garden chapel, **AAA Above Heaven's Gate** (✆ **800/800-2WED** [800-2933] or 808/259-5900; www.hawaiiweddings. com) can arrange it. The company has garnered rave reviews for their attention to detail in putting together the perfect Hawaii wedding.

Other wedding planners include: Love Hawaii (contact Rev. Toni Baran and Rev. Jerry Le Lesch at ✆ 808/235-6966; www.lovehawaii.com); Affordable Weddings of Hawaii (✆ 800/942-4554 or 808/923-4876; www.wedhawaii. com); and Aloha Wedding Planners (✆ 800/288-8309 or 808/943-2711; www.alohaweddingplanners.com).

contain computer chips capable of storing biometric information, such as the required digital photograph of the holder. If your passport doesn't have this feature, you can still travel without a visa if the valid passport was issued before October 26, 2005, and includes a machine-readable zone; or if the valid passport was issued between October 26, 2005, and October 25, 2006, and includes a digital photograph. For more information, go to **http://travel.state.gov/visa**. Canadian citizens may enter the United States without visas, but will need to show passports and proof of residence.

Citizens of all other countries must have a valid passport that expires at least 6 months later than the scheduled end of their visit to the U.S., and a tourist visa.

For information about U.S. Visas go to **http://travel.state.gov** and click on "Visas." Or go to one of the following websites:

Australian citizens can obtain up-to-date visa information from the **U.S. Embassy Canberra,** Moonah Place, Yarralumla, ACT 2600 (📞 **02/6214-5600**); or by checking the U.S. Diplomatic Mission's website at **http://canberra.usembassy.gov/visas.html**.

British subjects can obtain up-to-date visa information by calling the **U.S. Embassy Visa Information Line** (📞 **09042/450-100**) or by visiting the "Visas to the U.S." section of the American Embassy London's website at **www.usembassy.org.uk**.

Irish citizens can obtain up-to-date visa information through the **Embassy of the USA Dublin,** 42 Elgin Rd., Dublin 4, Ireland (📞 **1580/47-8472**) or by checking the "Consular Services" section of the website at **http://dublin.usembassy.gov**.

Citizens of **New Zealand** can obtain up-to-date visa information by contacting the **U.S. Embassy New Zealand,** 29 Fitzherbert Terrace, Thorndon, Wellington (📞 **0900 878 472;** http://wellington.usembassy.gov).

Visitor Information For advance information, contact the **Hawaii Visitors and Convention Bureau (HVCB),** Suite 801, Waikiki Business Plaza, 2270 Kalakaua Ave., Honolulu, HI 96815 (📞 **800/GO-HAWAII** [464-2924] or 808/923-1811; www.gohawaii.com). Among other things, the bureau publishes the helpful *Accommodations and Car Rental Guide* and supplies free brochures, maps, and *Islands of Aloha,* the official HVCB magazine.

The **Oahu Visitors Bureau,** 1001 Bishop St., Pauahi Tower, Suite 47, Honolulu, HI 96813 (📞 **800/OAHU-678** [624-8678] or 808/524-0722; www.visit-oahu.com), distributes a free 64-page visitors booklet.

A number of free publications, including *This Week* and *Guide to Oahu,* are packed with money-saving coupons offering discounts on dining, shops, and activities around the island; look for them at the airport and around town.

If you want information about working and living in Hawaii, contact the **Chamber of Commerce of Hawaii,** 1132 Bishop St., Suite 200, Honolulu, HI 96815 (📞 **808/545-4300**).

Also check out Frommer's travel app for Oahu at **www.frommers.com/go/mobile**.

Water The water is safe to drink on the island of Oahu, as well as the rest of the state.

INDEX

See also Accommodations and Restaurant indexes, below.

General Index

A

AAA Above Heaven's Gate, 299
Aaron's Dive Shop, 168
Abhasa spa, 95
Academy Shop, 254
Access Aloha Travel, 285
Accommodations, 86–121. *See also* Accommodations Index
  Ala Moana, 110
  bargaining on prices, 283–284
  best, 17–21
  booking with an agency *vs.* doing it yourself, 284
  campgrounds and wilderness cabins, 117–121
  downtown Honolulu, 110–111
  Hawaii Kai, 112
  near Honolulu International Airport, 111
  house and cottage rentals, 113–115
  Kahala, 111–112
  Kailua and Kaneohe, 113–114
  leeward Oahu (Waianae Coast), 116–117
  Manoa, 111
  nickel-and-dime charges at high-priced hotels, 105
  The North Shore, 114–116
  seasons, 86
  smoking *vs.* nonsmoking rooms, 87
  tips on, 282
  types of, 282–283
  Waikiki
    Diamond Head end, 104–110
    Ewa end, 86–88
    mid-Waikiki (makai), 91–99
    mid-Waikiki (mauka), 99–103
  Windward Coast, 113–114
Accommodations and Car Rental Guide, 300
Active vacations, suggested itinerary, 83–84
Activities desks, 61
Admissions Day, 47
Adventures for thrill-seekers, 15–16
Ae'o, 51

African tulip trees, 48
Agnes Portuguese Bake Shop, 259
Agricultural screening at Honolulu International Airport, 275
Aiea loop, 118
Air Canada, 273
Air New Zealand, 273
Air Pacific, 274
Airport shuttle, 276
Airport Waikiki Express, 276
Air travel, 273–276
Alala, 51
Alamo, 276
Ala Moana
  accommodations, 110
  brief description of, 71–72
  restaurants, 132–138
Ala Moana Beach Park, 155
Ala Moana Center, 255–256
Alaska Airlines, 273
Ala Wai Municipal Golf Course, 183
Alii Antiques of Kailua, 259
Alii Antiques of Kailua II, 259
Aliiolani Hale, 193, 221
All Nippon Airways, 273
Aloha Beach Service, 165, 171
Aloha Festivals, 47
Aloha Flea Market, 17, 208
Aloha Stadium, 190
Aloha Tower, 196
Aloha Tower Marketplace, 256
  nightlife, 264
  restaurants, 138–139
Aloha wear, 245–247
Amberjack, 54
American Airlines, 273
American Express, 273
American Express Travelers Cheque Card, 294
America the Beautiful Access Pass, 285
America the Beautiful Senior Pass, 296
Anchor house Antiques, 247
Angelfish, 52
Angel's Trumpets, 48
Anthuriums, 48
Antique Alley, 247
Antiques, 246, 247, 259
Aoki's, 260
Aquarium, Waikiki, 207–209, 227

Area code, 284
Arizona, USS, Memorial at Pearl Harbor, 205–206
Army Community Theatre, 269
Arnold Palmer Course, 185
ARTafterDark, 267
Art and architecture, 34
Art galleries, 247–248, 255, 260
Art museums
  Hawaii State Art Museum, 199
  Honolulu Academy of Arts, 199–200
Art on the Zoo Fence, 226
Asian Grocery, 249
Atlantis Submarines, 170
ATMs (automated-teller machines), 292
Attractions and sights, 193–243
  central Oahu, 237–241
  east Oahu, 228–233
  Honolulu and Waikiki, 193–228
  leeward Oahu, 237–241
  the North Shore, 241–243
  Windward Coast, 233–236
Australia
  customs regulations, 285
  embassy and consulates, 286
  passports, 294
  visas, 300
Avanti Fashion, 245, 246
Avis, 276

B

Baby Emporium, 255
Baby's Away, 287
Bailey's Antiques & Aloha Shirts, 246
Bakeries, 250–251, 259
Ballet Hawaii, 269
Bandstand, Kapiolani Park, 226
Bank of Hawaii, 211–212
Bannanas, Anna, 268
Banyan trees, 48
Banzai Beach, 162
Banzai Pipeline, 44, 242
Barefoot Bar, 264
Bargaining, 213
Barnes & Noble, 248
Barnfield's Raging Isle Sports, 261

Accommodations

Restaurants

PHOTO CREDITS

p. i: © Marco Garcia; p. 1: © Marco Garcia; p. 2, left: © Marco Garcia; p. 2, right: © Marco Garcia; p. 4, bottom: © Marco Garcia; p. 4, top: © Marco Garcia; p. 6: © Marco Garcia; p. 7: © Marco Garcia; p. 8, top: © Marco Garcia; p. 8, bottom: © Jamm Aquino; p. 9, top: © David Fleetham / Alamy; p. 9, bottom: © Marco Garcia; p. 10: © Jamm Aquino; p. 11, bottom: Courtesy Ko Olina Golf Club; p. 11, top: © Pacific Stock / SuperStock; p. 12: © Marco Garcia; p. 13, right: © Marco Garcia; p. 13, left: © Marco Garcia; p. 14, top: © Marco Garcia; p. 14, bottom: © Marco Garcia; p. 15, right: © Jamm Aquino; p. 15, left: © Marco Garcia; p. 16: © Marco Garcia; p. 17, left: © Marco Garcia; p. 17, right: © Marco Garcia; p. 18: Courtesy Halekulani Resort; p. 19: Courtesy Royal Hawaiian Hotel; p. 20, left: Courtesy JW Marriott Ihilani Resort & Spa at Ko Olina; p. 20, right: Courtesy Kahala Resort; p. 22, left: © Marco Garcia; p. 22, right: © Jamm Aquino; p. 23: © Marco Garcia; p. 25, top: © Marco Garcia; p. 25, bottom: © Marco Garcia; p. 26: Courtesy Polynesian Cultural Center; p. 29: © SuperStock; p. 30: © Marco Garcia; p. 33: © Photos 12 / Alamy; p. 35: © CSU Archives / Courtesy Everett Collection / AGE Fotostock; p. 39: © Marco Garcia; p. 41: © Marco Garcia; p. 49, left: © Marco Garcia; p. 49, right: © Marco Garcia; p. 51: © Annette Wagner; p. 67: © Marco Garcia; p. 28: © Barton Hrast / Frommers.com Community; p. 37: © ABC / Photofest; p. 53, left: © UWA / Frommers.com Community; p. 53, right: © Glenn Cummings / Frommers.com Community; p. 54: © dee2travel / Frommers.com Community; p. 69: © Marco Garcia; p. 75, top: © Marco Garcia; p. 75, bottom: © Marco Garcia; p. 76: © Marco Garcia; p. 77, top: © Marco Garcia; p. 77, bottom: © Marco Garcia; p. 79, right: © Marco Garcia; p. 79, left: © Marco Garcia; p. 80: © Jamm Aquino; p. 81, right: © Marco Garcia; p. 83: © Jamm Aquino; p. 84: Courtesy Sportfish Hawaii; p. 82: © Jamm Aquino; p. 81, left: Courtesy Honolulu Zoo; p. 78: © Marco Garcia; p. 85: Courtesy Royal Hawaiian Hotel; p. 122: © Marco Garcia; p. 154: © Jamm Aquino; p. 156, bottom: © Marco Garcia; p. 159: © Jamm Aquino; p. 160: © Marco Garcia; p. 164: © Jamm Aquino; p. 166: Courtesy Wild Side Specialty Tours; p. 169: © Marco Garcia; p. 171: © Marco Garcia; p. 172: © Marco Garcia; p. 173: © Marco Garcia; p. 174: © Marco Garcia; p. 178: © Jamm Aquino; p. 187: © Marco Garcia; p. 188: Courtesy Bike Hawaii; p. 189: © Marco Garcia; p. 190, left: © Marco Garcia; p. 190, right: © Jamm Aquino; p. 156, top: © Marco Garcia; p. 177: © Jamm Aquino; p. 180: © Ferguson / Frommers. com Community; p. 181: © Hawaii Tourism Authority / Ron Garnett; p. 184: Courtesy Turtle Bay Resort; p. 192: © Marco Garcia; p. 196: © Marco Garcia; p. 197: © Marco Garcia; p. 198: © Marco Garcia; p. 199: © Marco Garcia; p. 201: © Marco Garcia; p. 202, top: © Marco Garcia; p. 202, bottom: © Marco Garcia; p. 203: © Marco Garcia; p. 205: © Jamm Aquino; p. 206: © Marco Garcia; p. 207: © Marco Garcia; p. 212, top: © Marco Garcia; p. 212, bottom: © Marco Garcia; p. 213: © Marco Garcia; p. 214: © Marco Garcia; p. 216: © Marco Garcia; p. 219: © Marco Garcia; p. 220: © Marco Garcia; p. 222: © Marco Garcia; p. 224: © Marco Garcia; p. 226: © Marco Garcia; p. 228, left: © Marco Garcia; p. 228, right: © Marco Garcia; p. 229: © Marco Garcia; p. 232: © Jamm Aquino; p. 230: © Marco Garcia; p. 233: © Jamm Aquino; p. 235, left: © Jamm Aquino; p. 235, right: © Jamm Aquino; p. 236: © Marco Garcia; p. 237: © Marco Garcia; p. 238: © Jamm Aquino; p. 240: © Marco Garcia; p. 241: © Marco Garcia; p. 242, left: © Marco Garcia; p. 242, right: © Marco Garcia; p. 244: © Jamm Aquino; p. 249: © Marco Garcia; p. 251: © Marco Garcia; p. 253: © Marco Garcia; p. 257: © Marco Garcia; p. 261: © Marco Garcia; p. 262: Courtesy Tau Dance Theater, Photo by Darren Miller; p. 264: Courtesy Hotels & Resorts of Halekulani'; p. 267: © Marco Garcia; p. 270: © Marco Garcia; p. 272: © Jamm Aquino